GOLF MAGAZINE'S

TOP 100 COURSES
YOU CAN PLAY

GOLF MAGAZINE'S

TOP 100 COURSES
YOU CAN PLAY

BY BRIAN McCALLEN

Photographs by Jeannine and John Henebry and Others

Harry N. Abrams, Inc., Publishers

CONTENTS

Introduction and Acknowledgments

Imagine! A "100 Greatest" list that can serve as a roadmap for travelers seeking America's finest golf experiences. No Pine Valleys. No Cypress Points. No Augusta Nationals. In fact, no private clubs at all. A "Top 100" roster that is hands on, not hands off.

What a good idea. Wish I had thought of it.

In the spring of 1995, I met my fellow Senior Editors at *GOLF Magazine,* David Barrett and Mike Purkey, in the office of George Peper, Editor-in-Chief. Jim Frank, Editor, was also present. The meeting concerned an idea the Features Department—namely Barrett and Purkey—was going to present at an annual editorial powwow and golf competition known as the CEC (Coveted Editorial Cup). My colleagues' notion was to expand an annual feature I had put together, "Top 10 You Can Play" (a roundup of the year's top public-access courses), into something much bigger and more ambitious. "Top 100 You Can Play," they called it. My first impression was, I'm getting hornswoggled. All four gentlemen smiled in my direction when it came time to figure out who was going to do the work. But then, there turned out to be a silver lining these many years later: This book.

Initially, sledding for the "Top 100" was tough. A ballot containing more than 500 resort, daily-fee, municipal, and semiprivate (and therefore semipublic) courses had to be drawn up. This ballot was then mailed to dozens of USGA officials, PGA section directors, and others we'll call the gentlemen—and gentlewomen—of the trade: editors, golf industry folks, and well-traveled golf nuts whose opinion we trust. We received back more than 200 ballots, fed the returns into a computer, and established a numerical score for each course.

As with *GOLF Magazine's* "The Top 100 Courses in the U.S.," a feature first put together by Tom Doak and now captained by Gary Galyean, we did not offer evaluators a definition of "greatness" on which they should base their voting. It was left to each rater's viewpoint on which blend of difficulty, design strategy, beauty, character, condition, and ambience constitutes the ideal. We asked the panelists not to let value-for-dollar, "carts-only" policies, and other considerations influence their opinions. Grades, we stated, should be tied solely to the quality of the layout.

"Top 100 You Can Play" appeared as an eight-page special with a gatefold listing all 100 courses in the May 1996 issue of *GOLF Magazine.* Some of the courses finished predictably—Pebble Beach was number one, naturally, and Pinehurst No. 2 was second. But after that, the "Top 100" compilation was an interesting blend of established classics balanced by exciting newcomers.

For players, the news was very good: America was turning away from private clubs to embrace daily-fee facilities that offer a well-conditioned course (often by a name designer) for the price of a green fee. The "Top 100 You Can Play" story—with the accent on YOU—served notice that one of the nation's most gentrified sports was getting more public and less private every day. Indeed, nearly 90 percent of all new course openings in 1998–99 were of the public-access variety, according to the National Golf Foundation. With a daily-fee facility, there are no worries about heavy initation fees, annual dues, and monthly minimums charged by private clubs, assuming you are accepted for membership in the first place. The courses voted to this list promise only an outstanding golf experience for the price of a green fee. Nothing more, nothing less. This shift in focus signals a genuine democratization of the game in the United States, a trend the down-to-earth Scots would applaud.

With the groundwork in place and with so many fine new facilities clamoring for attention, a second edition of "Top 100 You Can Play" was published in the May 1998 issue of *GOLF Magazine.* This roster, the one I worked from to write this book, is a true meritocracy. There were 19 new courses on the roll call, 15 of them opened since 1995. The invasion of hot new courses is a tribute to the talent of their designers and an indication that developers are seeking out prime parcels of land for daily-fee course development. Whoever lamented the fact that all the good sites were taken around the time the Cold War was at its chilliest haven't poked around the nation's potato fields, horse farms, cattle ranches, sand quarries, or defunct military encampments to assess their value as potential golf course sites. Developers have. Designers, for their part, continue to push the envelope, creating their own features on land that is poor and deferring to Mother Nature on land that is good.

The results in the "pay-as-you-play" sector have been astounding. Except for Pebble Beach and a handful of imperishables, the public-access courses that have opened since the early 1990s or are currently under construction will surpass their predecessors. America's best courses, I believe, have yet to be built. The spirit of enterprise parallels the passion that golf generates within its fervent followers.

It wasn't always so. When I joined the staff of *GOLF Magazine* in 1987, one traveled to a full-service resort if one desired a pleasurable golf experience. Public-access courses, where they existed, were mostly tied to real estate developments. Public golf, in many quarters, conjured a downmarket image. Dusty, overcrowded municipal facilities came to mind.

But then something happened in the early nineties. The market's urge for fairway homes in the Sun Belt softened, but demand for better-quality courses continued to grow. Baby boomers had come of age and were ready to take up golf if they hadn't already been bitten by the golf bug. Elite private clubs were already full; new ones were few and far between. A new category emerged—the daily-fee course—to serve this new market, a market that had the money to pay for a "country-club-for-the-day experience" with no strings attached.

A fly in the ointment? Cost. Green fee rates are going up. Way up. But why should a sport like golf be any different from other forms of entertainment? Yes, green fee rates are rising, but not out of proportion to the cost of ski lift tickets, amusement park rides, and other recreation outlets. It's a given that the best is always going to cost more. There are a couple of bargains on the "Top 100" list, but with only two courses boasting a sub-$30 green fee, they're rare. On the current "Top 100" list, 12 courses are in the $31–$55 bracket, nine in the $56–$80 stratum, 12 in the $81–$100 neighborhood, and a grand total of 65 courses over the once unthinkable (except for Pebble Beach) amount of $101.

The main reasons for rising green fees are higher land costs and heftier design fees. Unless the real estate is free, as it is in state parks and on the Robert Trent Jones Golf Trail in Alabama, where land for course construction was donated by corporations, municipalities, and developers, the green fee generally reflects the price of development.

Budget-minded players can combat spiraling costs by purchasing all-inclusive golf packages where available and by visiting in shoulder season periods. Myrtle Beach in winter, for example, is a giveaway, and the weather can be mild. Admittedly, the Arizona desert in July isn't nearly as appealing as it is in January, but golf costs drop significantly in the summer. Bring a wide-brimmed hat, industrial-grade sunblock, a bottomless canteen—and arrange to play first thing in the morning.

If there is a general conclusion to be drawn from the returns, it's that our raters aren't shy about rating up tough courses. Unless a golf course offers the promise of a good tussle, our panelists aren't impressed. Thus, golf course yardages for individual holes described in the book are listed at full stretch (par is 72 unless otherwise indicated).

The name game is alive and well in the golf course design business. In fact, many traveling golfers make vacation choices based on who designed what at their favorite destination. In the same way that "designer labels" dictate fashion choices, so too have household-name designers succeeded in garnering attention (and lucrative new commissions) based on their design output and reputation.

The architect most heavily represented on the "Top 100" list is Tom Fazio, who weighs in with 16 courses. They range from his first solo effort, Wild Dunes (Links), to his latest creations, from Pinehurst (No. 8) to Primm Valley (Lakes). Other leaders in the clubhouse are Robert Trent Jones with nine courses (including three on the Alabama Trail named for him), Pete Dye with eight (including four in the top 10), Jack Nicklaus with five, and Robert Trent Jones, Jr., with five. All the top architects of the modern era are represented, as are the immortal colossi of the earlier days: Donald Ross, Alister Mackenzie, A.W. Tillinghast, C.B. Macdonald.

GOLF Magazine's Top 100 Courses You Can Play is organized by geographic region. In addition to a description of each course, I've included details on lodging, dining, sidetrips, and descriptions of other public-access courses of note in the vicinity. If a promising new course was scheduled to open at any time from late 1998 through 2000, I've previewed the course in a "New & Noteworthy" section.

It's a wonderful time to be alive if you're an ardent golfer with the wherewithal to take your game on the road and put your skills to the test around the nation. The excellence and variety of courses on the "Top 100" list are astoundingly good.

To a certain degree, the book reflects my prejudices. I like to walk when I play. If a course has an unrestricted walking or a carts-mandatory policy, it is generally noted. I also feel strongly that reminders of civilization severely detract from a game of golf. I identify the worst offenders—there are a few "Top 100" courses that have been virtually ruined, in my view, by overdevelopment—and also commend courses that fully embrace nature, noting courses that have been recognized by the Audubon Society.

As I mentioned earlier, I was able to apply some initiative to an idea that was basically handed to me by the Features Department. My first debt of gratitude goes to David Barrett, who did a lot of behind-the-scenes work to get the survey in the hands of our raters and who also processed the returns. Thanks, Dave. To George Peper and Jim Frank—a guy couldn't have better bosses.

Without Margaret L. Kaplan, Senior Vice President and Executive Editor at Harry N. Abrams, Inc., you would not be holding this book. It was she who championed its cause when she first heard the idea, she who shepherded it from conception to completion. Without her encouragement and powers of persuasion, I'd still be typing. Special thanks to Bob McKee, who swore he'd never design another golf book but came out of "retirement" to design this handsome volume. Gracias, amigo.

I used to pack my camera when I traveled and take my own pictures to illustrate my stories. No more. The talent pool is so deep now among golf course photographers, I'm more than content to let them do the heavy lifting. To the Henebrys, John Johnson, Mike Klemme, Fred Vuich, Aidan Bradley, etc., thanks for creating a colorful and impressive core around which the text can weave. Thanks as well to Abrams' Photo Editor John Crowley and his staff, who gathered the superb images that illustrate the book.

Directors of golf and public relations personnel at "Top 100" courses were extremely helpful in supplying information about their facilities. They were also kind enough to share their opinions on food and dining choices in their respective areas.

One reference book served me extremely well during the course of my research. Whenever I was in doubt about the inner workings of a "Top 100" course, I merely opened Tom Doak's "The Confidential Guide to Golf Courses" for a straight, unvarnished appraisal.

I bounced lots of ideas off friends and associates during the time this book was put together. They include Jim Finegan, Holly Geoghegan, Rees Jones, Richard Kusack, Arnold Langer, Ralph Little, Greg Midland, Reid Nelson, John Paul Newport, Hal Phillips, Dave Richards, John Thompson, Glen Waggoner, and many, many others. Thank you all for your listening ear and instructive feedback.

To my Mom, my brother and four sisters, their spouses and children, 1998 will be remembered as the year we lost a great Dad, a loving husband, and one of the most authentic public golfers who ever lived. Golf enabled my dad and me to grow closer over the years. What other sport can offer more? I hope it's warm and sunny every morning where you're playing, Dad, and I hope the grass is smooth and rich and freshly mowed. I'm sure they have no rubber mats up there like the ones at Sprain Lake.

To the women in my life—my wife Saddia, my daughters Aliyah and Jordana—please be assured I'll be more of a visible and less of a phantom presence around the house in the months to come. Without your love and support, I wouldn't have been able to complete the task.

Brian McCallen
New York City
January, 1999

Florida

Tournament Players Club at Sawgrass, Stadium Course • Sawgrass Country Club (East–West)

Grand Cypress Resort, New Course • Bay Hill Club • Emerald Dunes Golf Course

Doral Golf Resort & Spa, Blue Course • The Westin Innisbrook Resort, Copperhead Course

World Woods Golf Club, Pine Barrens • World Woods Golf Club, Rolling Oaks

Emerald Dunes Golf Course, West Palm Beach, 11th hole

Florida

Golf-wise, Florida is not, as some would have it, one big flat fairway accented by gator holes, sand traps, and palm trees. It is far more diverse than that, although for the visiting player, the fabled fountain of youth sought by Ponce de Leon may turn out to be a nonpotable water hazard at one of the nine "Top 100" courses in the state.

Jacksonville area

In Ponte Vedra Beach, an hour's drive southeast of Jacksonville International Airport, is the **Tournament Players Club at Sawgrass**, its **Stadium Course** (#7) a prototype conceived by former PGA Tour commissioner Deane Beman. His architect of choice for a target-style course that would accommodate spectactors and test the game's best players to the breaking point? Pete Dye. Which is like bringing a deranged scientist to a laboratory and daring him to throw the switch that will bring the Creature from the Lagoon to life.

In the wake of several major facelifts, the original ego buster is not the grueling test the pros once kicked and screamed about. ("They messed up a perfectly good swamp," said J.C. Snead, who called the 1980 version of the links "90 percent horse manure and 10 percent luck.") The Stadium, Florida's top-ranked course on the "Top 100" list, is still plenty tough for the average Joe. It's still the finest manufactured course ever built, but the superior challenge it poses to shotmakers tends to be put in the shade by the fiendish par-three 17th, the most diabolical hole in golf.

This little piece of poison measures a scant 132 yards from the TPC gold markers, 121 yards from the blues, and 97 yards from the white pegs. But yardage doesn't tell the story. A bulkheaded raft of green, seemingly much smaller than the one seen on TV during The Players Championship, beckons from the middle of a lake, the putting surface joined to the mainland by a raised strip of grass. The challenge it presents is not subtle. In fact, the 17th plays to every golfer's innermost fear of failure. Assuming you've successfully negotiated the vast waste bunkers, the steep hillsides of love grass, and the peek-a-boo lagoons that have gone before, here's the pint-size *Titanic* to sink your scorecard.

The white-knuckle quotient of the Stadium's 17th is directly proportional to the velocity of the wind. Even world-class pros are tested to the maximum when a strong breeze sweeps across the lake. Because there's no bailout at 17, nowhere to hide. Miss the green, and your hopes are dashed. Miss the green again, and you adjourn to a drop area to hit your fifth shot from about 50 yards. It's not an easy shot, especially if you're still trembling from the other two attempts. By the way, taking an extra club to get to the green can be just as dangerous as coming up short—there's water behind the green, too. Perhaps most distressing of all, borderline shots usually tumble into the water. Somewhere, Deane and Pete are smiling.

Whoever has the ball concession at Sawgrass won't have to worry about college tuition for his kids. According to a 1998 report in *Golf Journal,* balls that miss the 17th green are retrieved by divers once a month. They dredge up approximately 120,000 "gator pellets" a year. With roughly 40,000 rounds played annually on the Stadium, that's an average of three drowned balls per player on the 17th.

A "swallow hard and pray" hole for some, a "bleeping tricked-up piece of bleep," for others, the 17th, a Cyclopean icon, accomplishes its purpose. It also tends to overshadow the rest of the course, a textbook risk/reward design (Greg Norman calls it "cutthroat architecture") that offers an intimidating but very memorable test of golf. There's a right and a wrong place to go on every hole. Safe areas, when they're visible, are defined by a varied combination of water, sand, trees, and mounds. Strategy and course management are extremely important on the Stadium. Without formulating a game plan or playing within set limitations, amateurs might as well lie down and wait for the full nelson to be applied. Dye, a grand master of strategy, has thought everything through. Refinements over the years have softened some of the sharper edges, but with water in play at every hole, great care must be taken with each stroke. Otherwise, checkmate.

Among the layout's exceptional holes is the drive-and-pitch fourth, a short par four that calls for a dead straight drive (not necessarily with a driver) and an approach that carries a creek but avoids a

Tournament Players Club at Sawgrass, Ponte Vedra Beach, Stadium Course, 18ᵗʰ hole

Tournament Players Club at Sawgrass, Stadium Course, 17th hole

quartet of bunkers behind the shallow green. The par-five ninth, stretching to 582 yards from the tips, is a genuine three-shotter that leapfrogs a stream and then swings right to a green nestled below tall spectator mounds. At the 11th, a brilliant forking-path par five, the riskiest option is to play for the plateau green in two, its ledged surface ringed by moguls, a curved bunker, and a horseshoe collar of water. The safer choice is up the right side, with a short iron played to the minuscule green.

The Stadium's 18th, on the heels of the do-or-die 17th, asks players who may be mentally drained after matching wits with Dye for four hours or more for one last hurrah. Rated the toughest hole on the course, this onerous par four has water lurking from tee to green down the entire left side. Pulled or hooked shots are history, while heavily grassed mounds snare drives pushed to the right. The multitier green, guarded by numerous bunkers and bulkheaded to the left above a lake, is not easily reached in regulation—unless you can populate the vast bleacher-style viewing areas beside the green with an imaginary gallery and somehow produce the shot that will bring wild applause.

A few words of caution. Unless you're a low handicapper in top form, steer clear of the TPC tees at 6,857 yards. The blue tees at 6,394 yards offer more than enough golf for most, and the white markers at 5,761 yards are the only option for bogey shooters. Lastly, try to play the Stadium twice. According to *GOLF Magazine* Contributing Editor Stephen Goodwin: "The first time around is likely to be a blur, like skydiving for the first time—you're too scared to enjoy the ride. The second time you can catch your breath and appreciate the shot values in some of the holes." Even the 17th? Probably not.

NOTE: Only guests of the on-site Marriott at Sawgrass can be assured of tee times on the Stadium Course.

SIDETRIP

History buffs can drive 30 minutes south from Ponte Vedra Beach to explore St. Augustine, North America's oldest permanent settlement (1565). Plain colonial homes line narrow streets near the *Castillo de San Marcos National Monument,* a Spanish fort overlooking Matanzas Bay. The walls of the fort are roughly the same height as the spectator mounds on the Stadium Course.

Sawgrass Country Club, Ponte Vedra Beach, East Course, fourth and fifth holes

Across Highway A1A from the TPC at Sawgrass (and closer to the ocean) is the 27-hole **Sawgrass Country Club** (#98), its **East-West** combo the region's top-rated layout behind the Stadium Course.

It may be a distant memory, but the club's core 18 was the host site of the PGA Tour's Tournament Players' Championship from 1977 to 1981. Laid out by Ed Seay in 1972, it was later touched up by Gardner Dickinson, who added over 20 bunkers. This sprawling, windswept layout, with water in play on 14 of the 18 holes, posed quite a challenge to the game's best players, especially when the ocean winds howled in March, but the cream rose to the top in those years before the championship was moved to the Stadium Course. The winners were Mark Hayes, Jack Nicklaus, Lanny Wadkins, Lee Trevino, and Ray Floyd. (At the 1978 event, Nicklaus posted a winning 72-hole score of 289, 1 over par.)

The most telling story about the layout's difficulty appears in Tom Doak's *The Confidential Guide to Golf Courses,* in which he reports that one player withdrew from a long-ago tourney while his ball was still in the air, well out over a lake!

The 3,551-yard East Course, one of north Florida's hardest stretches of golf on a breezy day, calls for distance off the tee but not at the expense of accuracy. The layout has a rolling, links-style appearance—Seay moved one million cubic yards of dirt to create "movement" on the dead-flat site—but the perched, shallow greens, most of them heavily bunkered in front and fringed by heavy rough, were not designed to accept run-up shots. Only an expert can hold a downwind approach shot on a slim, fast green. Even from the forward tees, Sawgrass is a course for better players.

From a strategic standpoint, the East's best hole is the fourth, a 501-yard par five that offers the choice of bold or conservative play. A straight drive can be followed with a lay-up that carries a bayou; or an aggressive second shot can be carried all the way to the tiny putting surface. Any

LODGING

The hub of the 4,800-acre Sawgrass complex is the *Marriott at Sawgrass Resort,* reputed to be the largest convention hotel between Atlanta and Orlando. Encased in emerald glass and surrounded by lagoons, the nicely landscaped property is unabashedly commercial, but its amenities (Tour-quality practice range, handsome golf shop, expanded health club, three swimming pools, 2.5 miles of pristine beach nearby) are excellent. The resort's updated, multibedroom villas are a good bet for golfers looking for a home away from home.

The Marriott at Sawgrass Resort

Sawgrass Country Club, West Course, sixth hole

Billed as the most ambitious project ever undertaken in golf, World Golf Village (WGV) is designed to be a focal point of the game as well as a tourism destination, business center, and residential community. Partially opened in 1998, WGV, centerpiece of the 6,300-acre, $2 billion Saint Johns Development, is located off its own interchange on I-95 eight miles northwest of St. Augustine. Its main components, which have brought together all of golf's major governing organizations, include:

World Golf Hall of Fame. This 75,000-square-foot facility is one of the largest sports museums in the nation. Specifically designed to showcase the best golfers (men and women) in history, it also provides several entertaining and interactive ways to appreciate the game. Divided into the Modern Game and the Historical Game, it takes visitors through 18 holes of golf with over 70 hands-on exhibits. The "front nine" chronicles the game's history. For example, visitors can try their hand at putting on an 1880s green with a hickory-shafted putter and a gutta percha ball from the era. Visitors can also watch actual footage of Alan Shepherd's six-iron shot on the moon.

World Golf Village

The "back nine" ushers visitors into the modern era. Golfers can have their swing analyzed by state-of-the-art equipment that matches their swing to the Hall of Famer whose motion most resembles their own, and experience the sensation of attempting to sink a long putt on a tournament-slick green to clinch the "World Golf Village Open." (A leaderboard, gallery, and on-camera commentary add to the effect.)

Crystal prisms dedicated to each Hall of Fame member are illuminated by shafts of light in the Tower Shrine, the 190-foot hallmark of WGV. In addition to a list of the accomplishments that made each Hall of Famer great, an interactive data base connecting all inductees allows visitors to create their own unique narrative of the game's best players. The Hall of Fame also includes a collection of personal artifacts from each member, as well as text tributes and an audio program (in the inductees' own voices) to help illustrate the golf career and life of each member.

IMAX Theater. The only one of its kind in north Florida, the IMAX Theater at WGV is a 300-seat auditorium with an 80-foot-wide by 60-foot-high screen and an advanced sound system. The first-ever production of a large-format golf film celebrating the sport premiered in the summer of 1999.

The Slammer & The Squire. WGV's first golf course, one of three planned for the facility, opened in 1998. Named after Sam Snead and Gene Sarazen, the golf course, designed by Bobby Weed with input from the legendary Hall of Famers, skirts wetlands and a heavily wooded nature preserve on the outward nine. The back nine winds around lakes and the WGV complex. Five sets of tees ranging from 6,940 to 5,001 yards accent playability. The course can be played with a putter from the forward tees. Greens are surfaced in Floradwarf, a new strain of bermudagrass developed by the University of Florida. The Slammer & The Squire hosts the Liberty Mutual Legends of Golf, a Senior PGA Tour event.

The King & The Bear. A second course, set within a residential community four miles west of WGV, is named for co-designers Arnold Palmer and Jack Nicklaus. It is their first-ever collaboration. The layout is scheduled to open in 2000.

PGA Tour Golf Academy. Slated to open in late 1999, the academy will enable players at all skill levels to refine their games. The curriculum will include extended week-long sessions as well as one-hour lessons for visitors passing through. State-of-the-art electronic and visual teaching aids will be used.

The Shops at World Golf Village. The village features 80,000 square feet of shops, galleries, restaurants, and boutiques in four buildings. The anchor tenant, a one-of-a-kind PGA Tour Stop, offers golf equipment, apparel brand "concept shops," interactive sites, indoor-outdoor hitting bays, and museum-quality exhibits.

By the end of 2001, the World Golf Hall of Fame is expected to draw between 500,000 and 1 million visitors yearly, surpassing attendance figures at all other U.S. sports museums. Proceeds from the Hall of Fame and the other not-for-profit entities of the World Golf Foundation will be used to operate the hall, upgrade its exhibits, underwrite future expansions—and support programs that introduce golf and its positive aspects to young people who otherwise would not have the opportunity to participate in the sport.

deviation results in disaster: There's marsh left and right of the putting surface. Incoming shots that carry long end up in an alligator's den behind the green. The ocean looms into view behind the fourth green and fifth tee, the pounding surf well within earshot.

The toughest hole on the East—and an all-time Nassau nightmare—is the ninth, an S-shaped par four of 451 yards that calls for a well-placed drive and a perfect approach over a lake to a very undulating green fronted by bunkers that bleed into the water. Played into the prevailing wind, it's a par five for most.

The West Course, at 3,424 yards, is more of the same—water, wind, and sand. The par-three sixth, with its bulkheaded peninsulalike green, is a beefier if less terrifying version of the island green on the Stadium Course. A hooked tee shot, however, ends up in the drink. According to the course yardage guide: "It is better to be wise and aim for the right corner of the green than to take a risk and swim with the fish. Watch the direction of the waves so that you can adjust for the wind." Of course.

The finish on the West is strong. The 377-yard seventh calls for a double carry over water, while the sturdy par-four eighth and short par-five ninth (a gambler's delight) both have a lagoon in play up the entire left side of their fairways.

In 1984, Ed Seay returned to Sawgrass Country Club to add a third nine, the South. It is a little friendlier and a little more open than the East-West tandem, but with water in play on seven of the holes, it does not offer the promise of a carefree outing.

Drawbacks? Many of the fairways at Sawgrass serve as a greenbelt for an upscale housing development. Also, access is limited: Visitors must be registered guests at the nearby Marriott at Sawgrass Resort to gain access to a course that whiplashed the pros in its heyday.

More Golf/Sawgrass

In addition to the revered Stadium Course, the TPC at Sawgrass also has the *Valley Course,* a Pete Dye–Jerry Pate collaboration that opened in 1987 and is slightly more forgiving than the more notorious Stadium layout—although there is water in play at every single hole. *Marsh Landing,* an Ed Seay design carved from a maritime forest, is one of the prettiest, most satisfying tracks in north Florida. Marriott guests are accorded limited weekday access. It's worth the hassle to get a tee time on this gem. *Oak Bridge,* a pleasurable par-70 layout, plays tougher than the scorecard indicates from the tips at 6,345 yards. Players who've lost their shirts on the Stadium can tackle the *Sawgrass Putters Club,* an 18-hole "putt putt" track that features—gasp!—an island green on its 17th hole.

DINING

The *Augustine Grille* at the Marriott offers continental dining in a refined clubhouse atmosphere. The *100th Hole* is an informal poolside retreat ideal for lighter fare and frozen concoctions. In nearby Jacksonville Beach can be found the *First Street Grille,* arguably the best seafood restaurant in the region. Bayou shrimp, served with Cajun spice and dipping butter, has been featured in *Gourmet Magazine.* The Grille features an oceanfront deck for outdoor dining and live music on weekends. Also in Jacksonville Beach is *The Cove,* which offers alfresco dining overlooking the Intracoastal Waterway. Abaco dolphin (mahi-mahi) is the most popular entrée. *Bono's Bar-B-Q* (numerous area locations) serves the best baby back ribs in north Florida. Don't pass up the banana pudding for dessert. Atlantic Beach and Neptune Beach, sister communities located a few miles north of Ponte Vedra Beach, each have dozens of atmospheric restaurants, cafés, and nightclubs.

The Augustine Grille

Orlando

On the threshold of central Florida's entertainment kingdom, Jack Nicklaus has created a must-see attraction for amusement-weary golfers. The **New Course** (#73) at **Grand Cypress Resort**, Jack's take on the Old Course at St. Andrews, is an inspired re-creation of the ancient crumpled links. Missing is the salty tang of the North Sea, the plaintive wail of distant bagpipes, the spires of the "Auld Grey Toon" on the horizon. But then, the weather's better in Orlando.

Nicklaus borrowed liberally from the Old to create the New. So what if alligators lurk in the facsimile Swilcan Burn that snakes through the 6,773-yard links, or that the bridges and cart paths were painted to resemble weathered stone? The site, a former orange grove, is sprinkled with nearly 150 traps ranging from hidden kettles the size of city manholes to sprawling craters furnished with wooden ladders leading to their depths. Completing the legerdemain are seven double greens; low, rolling mounds covered with love grass, a subtropical version of the nettlesome whins native to Scotland; and a low white picket fence that wraps behind the home hole. With your carry bag slung across your shoulder on a brisk day, with the wind chasing the clouds across a mottled gray sky, you could be standing in the Kingdom of Fife, not the land of make-believe.

Like the attractions in nearby Disney World, the first tee on the New Course does a good job of transporting players to another realm. Beside a modest starter's shed is a closely mown section of the tee where golfers can accustom themselves to the pace of the greens, which is usually fast.

The first fairway, shared with the 18th, looks to be a mile wide, yet a tee shot pushed to the right (out-of-bounds) or an approach shot that comes up short (in the burn) is doomed. Sand traps play a prominent strategic role on the New Course, a pastiche of St. Andrews and other famous Scottish links. At the short par-five second, for example, the two

large, imposing bunkers that dominate the second shot were patterned after the "Spectacles" at Carnoustie. But the Old Course is a bottomless font of inspiration for Jack. At the par-four fifth, the penal sand pits positioned along the right side of the fairway closely resemble the Principal's Nose and Deacon Sime bunkers at St. Andrews. With its pair of cavernous bunkers defending the front of the green, the par-three seventh on the New takes its cue from the celebrated 11th on the Old, one of the game's finest one-shotters. Not content to produce a slavish imitation of the original, Jack has upped the ante with a large collection swale to the right of the green called the "Devil's Basket."

The back nine on the New Course builds in interest. The 570-yard 15th, much like the great 14th at St. Andrews, was designed to give players food for thought. Golfers must aim their drives to the fairway's upper or lower tier—a nest of pot bunkers called the Beardies and a low stone wall down the right side must be avoided at all costs—while the second shot must be played either short or over Jack's version of Hell Bunker, which sprawls across three-fourths of the fairway 100 yards from the green. Like the original, the 15th green is guarded in front by a hillock. Because the putting surface slopes from front to back, a bump-and-run approach shot is recommended. The layout's firm, fast-running fairways, uncommon in Florida, promote the ground game.

The 17th on the New is a brilliant rendition of the infamous Road Hole at St. Andrews, only here Nicklaus has wisely stretched the yardage to convert the hole to a short par five. A slight left-to-right dogleg, the tee shot must be played over a series of mounds intended to simulate old railroad sheds. The approach can be laid up short—or rifled directly to a reverse image of the real thing. Here the shelf green, oblique to the line of play, is guarded by a deep pot bunker on the right and by a pebbly road (flecked with shells) backed by a stone wall to the left. The fakery is brought to a climax at the par-four 18th, a welcome journey home on an enormously wide fairway shared with the first. A pronounced hollow, à la the Valley of Sin, indents the left front portion of the green. Avoid it, and a reasonable chance at birdie awaits.

A gentle suggestion. Caddies are available on call through the pro shop. Arrange for one. The experience of playing the New Course is enhanced immeasurably by strolling the links with a caddie. Failing a caddie, rent a pull cart or pack your own clubs. Pretend, in other words, that you're in St. Andrews.

More Golf/Grand Cypress

Jack Nicklaus's original 27-hole spread at Grand Cypress is marked by sharply ledged fairways, rows of shaggy gumdrop mounds, and tiny plateau greens perched above water or sand. The

Grand Cypress Resort, Orlando, New Course, 15th hole

Grand Cypress Resort, New Course, 17th hole

SWING FIX

Golfers seeking to elevate their games can enroll in the Grand Cypress Academy of Golf, which offers a superb practice facility, a star-filled teaching staff (Phil Rodgers, Kathy Whitworth, Fred Griffin), and a comprehensive learning experience (biomechanics, computer graphics, hands-on guidance). There's even a sports psychologist on staff to assist with the last frontier—the emotional side of the game.

Practicing at the Grand Cypress Academy of Golf

L O D G I N G

Accommodations at Grand Cypress are available in the opulent Mediterranean-style Villas located near the golf club; or in the pyramidal-shaped, 750-room Hyatt Regency, an uptempo hotel with talkative caged parrots in the atrium lobby and a giant waterfall-splashed pool that attracts kids of all ages.

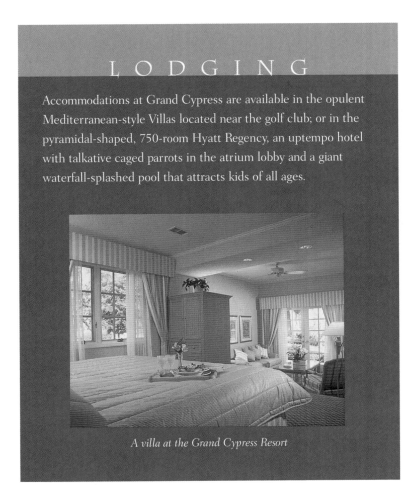

A villa at the Grand Cypress Resort

resort's North-South combo, the championship 18, is the current host of the HealthSouth Inaugural in January, the LPGA's first event of the year. The East nine is more wooded and slightly friendlier.

Orlando's **Bay Hill Club** (#21) is the winter home of Arnold Palmer, the swashbuckling, go-for-broke performer who oozed charisma, appealed to the masses, and single-handedly ushered golf into the television age. In 1965, Palmer played an exhibition match at Bay Hill, which occupies a rolling site flanked by orange groves and the Butler Chain of Lakes. Charmed by the pristine site and its beefy challenge, Palmer returned years later with a group of investors to purchase the course, a Dick Wilson—designed layout built in 1961 for a handful of Nashville businessmen who wanted a man-sized layout. Even in this Disney era, the club remains well removed from the hubbub generated by the world's family entertainment capital. This is no Tomorrowland: The club, a time warp for true enthusiasts, perpetuates Arnie's version of the good life in the Sunshine State circa 1976.

Arnie remains the guilding force behind his cherished acquisition, as well as of the Bay Hill Invitational, a springtime stop on the PGA Tour. A notorious tinkerer with golf equipment throughout his career, Palmer has also spent years refining and polishing a course that has no equal in central Florida. At press time, Palmer was listed as club president and green committee chairman. The King takes his duties seriously. Sure, the food in the Lodge and the decor in the guest rooms could be a little more con-

Grand Cypress Resort, New Course, 18th hole

temporary. But the quality of the turf and the overall golf ambience lack for nothing. First things first at Bay Hill.

With water in play at 10 holes and more than 100 well-placed bunkers dotting the layout, which stretches to 7,207 yards (par 71) from the Palmer tees, Bay Hill is not for the meek. But neither is it for those who go in for blind shots, waterfalls, and other frills. Straightforward in its presentation of challenges, gimmick-free Bay Hill has evolved into one of the nation's strongest and fairest tests of golf. According to Arnie: "You can run into any shot here that you would at the Masters or the U.S. Open." And then some.

Punctuated by evergreens, orange groves, and several man-made lakes, Bay Hill is a direct

Bay Hill Club, Orlando, eighth hole

reflection of what Palmer admires most in a championship test: Plenty of room to "let out the shaft" with the driver; boomerang-shaped doglegs that bend from right to left on hilly ground and that favor sweeping hooks; large, speedy, subtly contoured greens well defended by sand or water or both; and several risk-reward holes that invite bold, aggressive players to gamble. Pitfalls abound. Indifferent shots are punished. With its thick, wiry rough, Bay Hill makes mincemeat of wild hitters. For those who can't break 90 on their home track, Bay Hill is a tribulation. Proficient players will enjoy the championship tees at 6,638 yards, prudent bogey shooters can prevail from the men's tees at 6,220 yards, and ladies will relish the set-up at 5,235 yards. But the Palmer tees are off limits for most.

Rated among the five most enjoyed stops on the PGA Tour, Bay Hill presents a solid, no-baloney test that appeals to highly skilled players. For starters, the layout's quartet of par threes provides more resistance to scoring than those at any other Tour site. Easy to see why. From the tips, only one of the holes is listed at under 200 yards. Two of them play uphill, three are encased in sand. The 17th, nastiest of the four, calls for a long, perilous carry over water to a slippery, bi-level green. It's a killer into the wind. "Pull out your driver if you're playing from the back tees," Arnie advises.

Except for the short par-five 16th, which measures well under 500 yards from the championship tees but offers a shallow, water-fronted green for a target, there are no cream puff or "make-up" holes at Bay Hill.

DINING

At the Grand Cypress clubhouse, there's the *Black Swan*, which features continental cuisine and, for dessert, a white chocolate bread pudding with Jack Daniel's cream sauce; and *Fairways*, a fine lunch spot. Among the dining choices at the Hyatt Regency is *Hemingway's*, a festive Key West–theme restaurant; *La Coquina*, an elegant room specializing in French cuisine; the *White Horse Saloon*, a Western-style bar and grill; and *Cascade Grill*, a good place for breakfast.

Bay Hill Club, 16ᵗʰ and 17ᵗʰ holes

Each hole is scintillating in its demand for sharp play. Players are advised to make time while they can—or at least keep cool in the face of adversity. The stretch of long, testing par fours from eight through 11 is the backbone of the course, while the outstanding par-five 12th, its oblong green heavily defended by a gauntlet of bunkers, raises the bar even higher.

And then there's the murderous par-four 18th, one of the toughest finishing holes in golf. An unassuming par five until Palmer got his hands on it, the hole today, at 441 yards from the waybacks, is truly formidable: The approach shot, assuming you've bombed a long drive, must carry a pond (a.k.a. the "Devil's Bathtub") that fronts the two-tiered green. The shot must also avoid several large, cavernous bunkers cut into a hill behind the putting surface. It's the kind of hole only the Arnold Palmers of the world have the guts to attack.

Caddies at Bay Hill are snowbirds drawn from top northern clubs. Hire one. Your round will be enhanced immeasurably in their company. The

LODGING

Bay Hill Club & Lodge, treated to a $6 million overhaul in 1997, offers 58 refurbished guest rooms. They are not sumptuous by modern resort standards, but they are convenient to the putting green and the first tee. All-inclusive golf packages represent good value. There's also a fitness center and spa available to lodge guests.

practice range, given Palmer's propensity for hitting balls, is excellent. So is the Golf Academy and state-of-the-art Learning Center opened in 1998.

Bay Hill is a private club. In order to play a course designed to rock your world the old-fashioned way, you must be a guest at the Lodge. A small price to pay for the privilege of tackling Arnie's legacy.

Nightlife

Walt Disney World's Pleasure Island, where every night is New Year's Eve, features live music, comedy acts, restaurants, and cinemas. In downtown Orlando, *Church Street Station* is a popular entertainment complex (*Rosie O'Grady's, Phineas Phogg's,* etc.) in a turn-of-the-century setting. Finally, a row of lively dance clubs lines Orange Avenue around the corner from Church Street.

More Golf/Bay Hill

Don't want to go to the mat with Arnie on Bay Hill's core 18? Tee it up on the club's Charger nine, a short, sporty layout adjacent to the main track, which presents wider fairways, larger greens, and fewer bunkers. Overhauled and lengthened to 3,409 yards in 1995 by Arnold Palmer and Ed Seay, the Charger is highlighted by a mammoth double green at the first and sixth holes.

More Golf/Orlando

Incredibly, there are more than 125 golf courses within a 45-minute drive of downtown Orlando. A few highlights:

Of the six courses at *Walt Disney World*, the must-plays are *Osprey Ridge*, a Tom Fazio masterpiece with high mounds and broad fairways framed by wetlands and pine forests; and *Eagle Pines*, a low-profile Pete Dye layout marked by topsy-turvy greens. Traveling en famille? *Oak Trail*, a pleasant nine-holer, is great for kids.

At *Falcon's Fire*, a former cattle ranch on Disney's doorstep, Rees Jones moved a kingdom of earth (1.2 million cubic yards) to create rolling mounds, gentle elevation changes, and very slick greens. The watery back nine is especially memorable.

Also near Disney is *Orange County National*, home of the Phil Ritson Golf Institute, which offers golf instruction with "no blisters, no Band-Aids, no brain damage." The complex boasts two fine courses in *Panther Lake*, a splendid layout routed through oak hammocks, pines, and wetlands on rolling land with a 65-foot elevation change; and *Crooked Cat*, a shorter, tighter design that opened in 1998.

The Legacy Club at Alaqua Lakes, a semiprivate facility in Longwood, 20 miles north of town, is a superb Tom Fazio–designed layout. Opened in 1998, the 7,160-yard layout, carved from a dense subtropical wilderness, is a registered member of Audubon International's Signature Cooperative Sanctuary Program.

Southern Dunes, with its heaving fairways, clusters of bold bunkers, and striking blend of native vegetation, is designer Steve Smyers's inspired version of Australia's Royal Melbourne. The daily-fee facility is located in Haines City, 20 miles southwest of Orlando.

ACTIVITIES

The *Equestrian Center* at Grand Cypress is the first U.S. facility of its kind approved by the British Horse Society. Want to stroll through the subtropics? Visit the resort's 45-acre nature preserve,

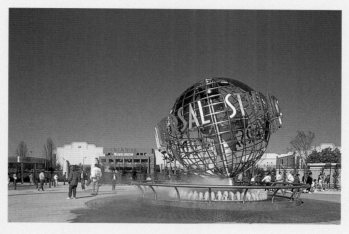

Universal Studios

The Equestrian Center

its network of raised boardwalks threaded through a cypress swamp. There's also a full-service spa, racquet club, and small lake with sailboats for rent on site. Complimentary transportation (a 10-minute ride) is available to nearby *Walt Disney World. Universal Studios, Sea World,* and other attractions are also convenient to Grand Cypress.

Church Street Station

Palm Beach area

Three miles west of West Palm Beach is **Emerald Dunes Golf Course** (#71), a trailblazing layout that signaled the arrival (and feasibility) of the high-end daily-fee golf course. Unveiled in 1990, Emerald Dunes was developed by Raymon R. Finch, Jr., the far-sighted developer of Wild Dunes outside Charleston, S.C. Five years after selling Wild Dunes, Finch approached Tom Fazio with the idea of building an upscale facility in tony Palm Beach County, home of Seminole, Pine Tree, and other strictly private clubs that are off-limits to visitors. Finch's notion was to build a top-notch course with a spacious practice facility, a lavish $2.5-million Mediterranean-style clubhouse—but no members, a relatively untested concept at the time. Indeed, Emerald Dunes was one of the first courses in the nation to offer a "country-club-for-the-day" experience. Never mind the fact that the layout, located in a corporate park less than a quarter-mile away from the Florida Turnpike, occupies the site of a featureless coral rock quarry. At Emerald Dunes, Fazio proved that he doesn't need a first-rate canvas in order to paint a memorable landscape.

Blending his signature design features into an elegant routing in which adjacent fairways are in view from every hole, Fazio wove ribbons of fairway through tall, rolling dunes manufactured with earth-moving equipment. Lagoons, marshes, swales, mounds, and bunkers (both sand and grass) also play their part in the strategic design of the 7,006-yard course, which offers five sets of tees, including two for ladies (the green markers measure 5,593 yards, the reds are 4,676 yards). Fazio also varied the grass textures to create visual contrast. The speedy, well-contoured greens, of Tifdwarf bermuda, are framed by a lusher strain of bermudagrass that is a deeper shade of green. Bahia and St. Augustine grasses inhabit the rough, offering more color contrasts. Tall palms and squat palmettos lend the course a tropical look appropriate to south Florida.

But there is one stand-out feature at Emerald Dunes that catches everyone's attention. This is the "Super Dune," a hulking molehill studded with three tees, three greens, large boulders, an assortment of bunkers, lots of bushes, even a few waterfalls. Everything except emeralds. The flattened top of the 54-foot-high "dune," one of the highest points in Palm Beach County, provides a panoramic view of 14 holes that fan out like spokes from a wheel.

In classic Fazio fashion, the golf course looks harder than it plays from the prospect of the back tees, though with water in play at 16 holes, it's no creampuff either. Cognizant of the fact that most golfers slice (especially when they're on vacation), Fazio placed most (but not all) of the hazards on the left side of the course.

Among the feature holes is the fourth, a scenic par three that plays to a green cut into the side of the "Super Dune." With its stark rock backdrop, the green site here appears transplanted from the Arizona desert. The back tee of the 11th, a short risk/reward par five with water galore on the right, is chiseled into the coral rock hill, while the marvelous 15th, a sturdy 422-yard par four, calls for a heroic carry over water to set up an approach to a green nestled in an amphitheater and ringed by bunkers.

Emerald Dunes Golf Course, West Palm Beach, fourth hole

The par-four 18th, its staggered tees nestled into the "Super Dune" near a series of cascading waterfalls, provides a fabulous finish. The tee shot, as visually pleasing as it is terrifying, must be aimed between a bunker on the left and a group of palms on the right, with a large lake in play up the entire right side. No easy task into the prevailing wind. A solid drive leaves a long second shot into a deep but narrow green guarded by sand and rock outcroppings to the right.

Golf carts at Emerald Dunes are equipped with Prolink, an advanced computerized and satellite-controlled yardage and course information system. Walkers are welcome, but most guests choose to ride to avail themselves of the local knowledge (and accurate distances) supplied by the on-board computer.

At press time, the high-season green fee at Emerald Dunes was $150. Given what players get—Fazio's fabled artistry, flawless turfgrass, a full-service clubhouse, an excellent lunch menu, basically all the ingredients of a fine private club—the fee is fair.

More Golf/Palm Beach

The Champions Club at Summerfield, a Tom Fazio–designed layout in Stuart, 25 miles north of West Palm Beach, is ingeniously routed through briny wetlands three miles from the Atlantic. This low-profile, habitat-enhancing layout has a list of resident birds (herons, kingfishers, eagles, etc.) two pages long. In typical Fazio fashion, most of the trouble borders (but does not cross) the field of play.

The Links at Polo Trace, under the same management as Emerald Dunes, is located in Delray Beach, 30 minutes south of Palm Beach. Laid out by Karl Kitten and PGA Tour player Joey Sindelar, this links-style

LODGING

Looking for luxury? Three of Palm Beach County's premier resort hotels are perennial American Automobile Association (AAA) Five Diamond award winners. They are: *The Breakers*, a grand Italian Renaissance–style resort with a sporty little course of its own; *The Ritz-Carlton*, located on seven acres of beachfront in exclusive Manalapan; and the *Four Seasons Resort Palm Beach*, home to the only Five Diamond restaurant in south Florida. Something less costly? The 280-room DoubleTree Hotel in Palm Beach Gardens, treated to a $12 million renovation in 1997, is competitively priced.

Worth Avenue

spread offers wide-open fairways framed by rolling mounds and thick rough. For value and tradition, *Delray Beach Golf Club*, a refurbished Donald Ross–designed municipal course dating to 1923, can't be beat.

Sequestered within a large equestrian center in Wellington, a suburb of Palm Beach, is *Binks Forest*, a generally uncrowded semiprivate club designed by Johnny Miller. Narrow fairways, laid through a pine tree forest, place a high premium on accuracy.

Forty-five miles north of Palm Beach is an exceptional facility well worth a detour. Billed as the "Winter Home of the PGA," the *PGA Golf Club at PGA Village* in Port St. Lucie has two exceptional layouts by Tom Fazio. The Pinehurst-style North Course, bordered by slash pines and palmetto scrub, presents wide fairways and heavily contoured greens. The bolder, grand-scale South Course sports a more tropical look, with native plantings, wetland preserves, and giant multifingered bunkers. Both layouts feature five sets of genderless tees as well as "graduated penalties," i.e., better players must contend with bigger challenges. Walkers are welcome. The club's practice facility is superb. At press time, the high-season green fee was $42 ($25 after 2 p.m.), a terrific bargain for south Florida.

Miami

Developed in the late 1950s on the fringes of the Everglades seven miles west of Miami International Airport, **Doral Golf Resort & Spa**, built on the most unpromising land imaginable, has evolved into a first-class resort—and one of the most popular stops on the PGA Tour. This south Florida mainstay boasts 99 holes of golf, but the **Blue Course** (#29), a.k.a. the "Blue Monster," is the star attraction. The monster tag conjures the wrong image—the Blue is a mature beauty unsullied by the intrusive housing so common to Sun Belt courses.

One of Florida's first manufactured layouts, the Blue Course was designed by Dick Wilson on mucky swampland studded with coral rock. Wilson, a strong proponent of strategic design, routed broad fairways

Doral Golf Resort & Spa, Miami, Blue Course, 16th hole

SWING FIX

The Jim McLean Golf School at Doral provides two-, three-, and five-day programs for all levels of golfers, with group and individual instruction available using state-of-the-art technology as well as McLean's highly successful teaching methods. (McLean is one of *GOLF Magazine*'s "Top 100 Teachers".) In addition, the facility also offers a three-day Cross Training School, a blend of fitness and instruction where students cover chipping, pitching, bunker play, and the full swing as well as flexibility and strength conditioning relating to golf.

around eight lakes and several canals of his own devising, with a legion of bunkers defining the line of play off the tee as well as the angle of approach into the large, subtly contoured greens. The course was immediately recognized as a masterpiece when it opened in 1961.

Because the wind blew strong in the inaugural PGA Tour event held on the Blue in 1962, it was dubbed the "Blue Monster" by the pros. The name stuck. And for the first five years of the tournament, the moniker was deserved: The average winning score was nine under par. But over time, the Blue Monster lost a few fangs and ceased to breathe fire. When its vaunted resistance to scoring wavered, the pros began to pillage the Blue with sub-par scores. From 1992–96, the average winning 72-hole total at the Doral–Ryder Open was nearly 18 under par. Greg Norman posted a course-record 62 in 1993. The once-feared "Blue Monster" had become a leashed puppy, at least for the game's best players.

In 1996, new management decided to bring in three-time tournament champion and local resident Raymond Floyd to put some teeth back into the Blue Monster. In conjunction with architect Ted McAnlis, Floyd, working from Dick Wilson's original plans, videos from previous tournaments and exhibitions, old aerial photos of the layout, and his own memory of how the holes once looked, set about restoring the course to what it once was. His goal was to make the course harder for the pros but easier for resort guests (a neat trick); he not only expanded and repositioned

existing bunkers, but also added 18 new ones. Finally, the Blue was put on the rack and stretched to 7,125 yards from the tips. The pros faced a monster with a full set of choppers when they arrived to play the Doral–Ryder Open in March 1997. And they screamed.

In fairness to Floyd, who fulfilled management's mandate to toughen the course, the Blue's greens were immature and the sand in the bunkers inconsistent for the tournament. The following year, due to the outcry of the pros (and the struggles of resort guests), nine of the new bunkers were

SPA

The neo-Mediterranean, 148,000-square-foot Spa at Doral, one of the nation's largest, includes 40 treatment rooms, hydrotherapy, indoor and outdoor whirlpools, hot and cold plunge pools, hydromassage, saunas, sundecks, and a full-service beauty salon. The spa's focus is "integrated wellness," a philosophy that seeks to improve and enhance body, mind, and spirit. Services range from traditional massages and physical training to hypnotherapy and dream analysis. The spa also offers a wide range of fitness, nutrition, stress relief, and beauty programs.

The Spa at Doral

Doral Golf Resort & Spa, Blue Course, 18th hole

for the remainder of the round. The fourth, a long par three, calls for a forced carry over the corner of a lake to a perched green defended by bunkers. The risk-reward eighth, a 538-yard par five with water wrapped around most of the green, is followed by the 163-yard ninth, which plays to a landscaped atoll (actually a peninsula) swept by Atlantic winds.

The Blue's back nine opens wide its toothy maw. The 10th, a king-size par five, doglegs sharply to the left around a lake. The short par-four 11th makes up in sand what it lacks in length, while the 12th, stretching to nearly 600 yards from the tips, is a par six for most snowbirds. At the uphill par-three 13th, listed at 246 yards from the gold tees, even the pros shelve long irons in favor of woods in order to reach the green.

The most significant revisions

filled in. Twenty-one others were reduced in size and depth. Also, green collars that had been shaved so that errant shots would roll away from the target were restored to three-inch rough to corral wayward approaches. The current Blue is still a beast from the tips, but the white tees at 6,281 yards give the middle handicapper with a chair and a whip at the ready a fair chance at taming it.

The Blue gets off to a reasonable start—a benign par five followed by a short, trouble-free par four. But then water and sand dominate the holes

on the Blue came at the famed par-four 18th hole, one of the great finishing holes in golf. A pair of bunkers that Floyd had built on the right side of the slim fairway to prevent players from bailing out were grassed over, although the beach bunker and palm trees installed on the left, while not in Wilson's plans, were a brilliant addition. Also, the front portion of the narrow, angled green was raised slightly to prevent approach shots from spinning off the putting surface into water, water that guards the entire left side of this potentially disastrous hole. As in Wilson's day, the right

Activities

In addition to tennis, lake fishing, bicycle rentals, jogging trails, and Camp Doral for kids, the resort opened a $7-million water feature called the Blue Lagoon in early 1999. The recreation center boasts four swimming pools, a 125-foot waterslide, lagoons, waterfalls, and a supervised children's program. Private cabanas are available for poolside massages, while open-air gazebos provide shaded lounging space.

Arthur Ashe Tennis Center at Doral

The resort's 694 updated rooms are situated in three- and four-story lodges near the main clubhouse. There are also 48 suites at The Spa at Doral featuring private whirlpools, wet bars, balconies, and video entertainment centers. The Club Lodge at Doral offers extra services and amenities, including suite accommodations, evening hors d'oeuvres, and complimentary shoeshines.

A suite at Doral

side of the 175-foot-long green, set on a gentle rise below the clubhouse, is protected by two deep traps. Lengthened by Floyd from 425 to 443 yards, the 18th, which often plays into a southeast wind, is one of the most terrifying holes the pros play all year.

The big boys, however, don't mind hard. They just want fair. In its current incarnation, Doral's "Blue Monster" is everything a tour pro (or a resort guest) could want in a round of golf. And more.

More Golf/Doral

In addition to the Blue, Doral, a smooth-running golf factory, offers the watery *Gold Course*, modernized by Raymond Floyd in 1995; the *Silver Course*, renovated by Jerry Pate in 1998 and located in the Doral Park housing complex a mile from the main resort; the *White Course*, a.k.a. the "Great White," a formerly sedate test completely transformed by Greg Norman and scheduled to open in December 1999; the *Red Course*, a short, sporty design with water in play at 14 holes; and the *Green Course*, a pleasant nine-hole par-three course. Doral also has a lighted driving range, three putting greens, and one of the nation's largest and best-stocked golf shops.

Windows, overlooking the "Blue Monster's" 18th hole, serves south Florida and Caribbean-accented dishes. *Champions* is a casual sports bar offering sandwiches, salads, and the signature Shark's Burger. *The Atrium*, located at the Spa, focuses on flavorsome, healthful foods.

Miami's Art Deco District

Off-campus, the choices are endless, notably in the revived South Beach area of Miami Beach, its hub the one-square-mile Art Deco District along Ocean Drive. South

Chefs and buffet at Doral

Beach is known for its lively streetside cafés and good people-watching. There are also pockets of fine dining in Little Havana (Cuban fare), as well as in popular nightlife districts such as Coconut Grove and Bayside downtown.

West Coast/Tampa Bay area

Towering pines and 80-foot elevation changes north of Tampa? **The Westin Innisbrook Resort**, a multicourse retreat encompassing a nature preserve in Pinellas County near the Greek sponge-diving and fishing community in Tarpon Springs, defies Florida's reputation as a pancake-flat gator hole. In fact, a blindfolded golfer airlifted to Innisbrook and unmasked at the clubhouse would be hard pressed to guess that most of the resort's golf holes occupy land hundreds of miles south of North Carolina's Sandhills.

The revitalized resort's flagship track is the **Copperhead Course** (#62), site of the annual JC Penney Classic mixed team event. Laid out by Lawrence Packard in 1972, this elegant 7,087-yard, par-71 spread (course rating 74.4, slope 140), its rolling fairways carved from stands of tall longleaf pines, has stood the test of time. Packard, an Illinois-based designer who retired to Innisbrook in 1986, was a master strategist and landscape architect who was among the first of his generation to champion an environmental approach to course design. The Copperhead, which drapes as naturally on the land as any course in Florida, is his calling card.

A proponent of double-dogleg par fives, staggered free-form teeing areas, and gently flowing bunkers marked by big capes and deep bays, Packard built a beautiful course with plenty of bite in the Copperhead.

The Westin Innisbrook Resort, Copperhead Course, Tarpon Springs, ninth hole

There are 10 water hazards on the course, but like the annual flower arrangements that brighten many of the tees, they're mostly there to delight the eye.

Testing holes of all shapes and sizes characterize the well-conditioned layout, which calls for equal amounts of power and finesse. The fifth, rated the most difficult on the course, is a formidable 576-yard par five that plays straight uphill, with trees and traps flanking both sides of the landing area. The hole then changes grade, moving downhill to a tiny green defended by high-lipped bunkers. The par-four sixth, a downhill dogleg stretching to 456 yards, asks for a tee shot to the right to neutralize the steep slope of the fairway and cut off a bit of the hairpin turn. The elevated, well-bunkered green presents a difficult target—especially from a sidehill lie. The par-three eighth, long and demanding at 235 yards, plays to a narrow, deep green pinched by sand. "Not many two's scored here," says the yardage book. Indeed.

The back nine showcases the Copperhead's signature hole, the double-dogleg par-five 14th. Two long, accurate shots must be followed by an unerring approach that avoids a small lagoon to the right and finds an undulating, oblong green protected to the left by the largest bunker at Innisbrook. Because of its speed and contour, this may be the Tampa Bay area's most treacherous green.

The finish, of championship caliber, is strong and memorable. The 16th, the Copperhead's most testing par four, is a left-to-right dogleg with water lapping at the right side of the fairway, the wide, shallow green well defended by trees and sand. The 211-yard 17th

The resort's 1,000 refurbished guest suites are contained in 28 low-rise lodges named for famous courses worldwide and sprinkled among pines throughout the 1,000-acre property. The accommodations are spacious and comfortable.

The pool at Innisbrook

plays to a heavily bunkered, bell-shaped target, and the 18th, stretching to 432 yards, proceeds uphill to a semiblind green, the putting surface divided by a prominent ridge.

Unforced and natural, with trees, sand, and rolling hills providing the challenge, the Copperhead is a perfect expression of the exceptional piece of property on which it was built. The forward tees give duffers a fighting chance, but the Copperhead, quite lethal from the black tees, was expressly designed to see if low handicappers could supply an antidote to its bite.

More Golf / Innisbrook

Innisbrook's biggest challenge is posed by the Copperhead, but the 6,999-yard *Island Course*, designed by Lawrence Packard in 1970, is an underrated track with a multiple personality, its holes spread among citrus groves, cypress swamps, and water hazards. The 12th tee on the Island, located 1.5 miles from the Gulf of Mexico, marks the highest point in Pinellas County.

The resort also offers play on *Hawk's Run* (formerly part of the 27-hole Sandpiper Course), a sporty 6,260-yard layout marked by excellent par threes and numerous water hazards; *Eagle's Watch*, its solid front nine paired with a newer, less distinguished back nine; and *Lost Oaks* (formerly Tarpon Woods), an off-property course set in a real estate development.

In a sleepy, undeveloped area 90 minutes north of Tampa is **World Woods Golf Club**, the most ambitious and in many ways the most astounding new golf complex of the 1990s. Against all odds, Interfive Corporation, a Japanese firm, hired Tom Fazio to build two full-length courses as well as a world-class practice center in the middle of nowhere. No hotels. No houses. Just golf. "Build it and they will come" is the operative cliché. It's been built, and they're coming. In droves. Because no distance is too far to drive when the golf is this good.

Pine Valley, the consensus choice for the number one course in the world, has often been imitated, never duplicated. For good reason. Heaving sand hills covered with stunted conifers are not often found in nature. But when Fazio (a Pine Valley member) explored the site's sandy wastelands with its slash pines and gnarly shrubs and 60-foot elevation changes, he saw the ideal canvas on which to fashion a public-access version of the exclusive New Jersey firebreather. On the site's flatter terrain, he also paid homage to Pinehurst No. 2, the Donald Ross masterpiece in the North Carolina Sandhills.

"We didn't start by designing golf holes," Fazio said with characteristic modesty. "We began by viewing the big picture, the land mass, the scale, the concept. Gradually the themes began to emerge, suggesting the styles of the courses. We allowed the land to tell us what to do." To this received information, Fazio added his own inimitable dash of artistry.

Like its model, **Pine Barrens** (#11) looks far more intimidating from the tees than it actually plays. There's room galore to drive the ball, but

DY's, modeled after the winning Shula's Steak House franchise, is an elegant dining room overlooking the Copperhead. The blackened prime rib and Caesar salad are superb, the wine and martini list excellent. Upstairs at the Island clubhouse is the informal *Iguana Cantina*, featuring Tex-Mex specialties. Downstairs is the Turnberry Pub, which features casual fare and framed memorabilia highlighting the famed Scottish links.

In Tarpon Springs, the top choice is Louis Pappas' *Riverside Restaurant*, a waterfront landmark specializing in fine Greek cuisine.

DY's restaurant

approach shots must be pinpointed to well-protected greens laced with bold, provocative contours, greens that are slick (especially from above the hole) but not terrifying in their speediness.

As at Pine Valley, shrubby ground and vast waste bunkers often serve as transition areas from tee to fairway and from fairway to green. And, as at Pine Valley, superior iron play is rewarded, flubbed shots punished. But with Fazio's trademark playability in place, this brilliant 6,902-yard, par-71 layout, which opened to instant acclaim in 1993, lacks the cloak-and-dagger terror of Pine Valley. There's a sense of impending doom at Pine Valley. At Pine Barrens, most first-timers can't wait to get to the next tee to see what Fazio has cooked up next. The layout, a visual smorgasbord of tufted ridges, bottle-green pines, and gaping pits of native sand, is a playable work of art.

The first hole, a straightaway par four, signals the layout's intentions. From an elevated tee, a player's attention is drawn to a large sand pit on the left side and a long sandy trench up the right side. The small, crowned green slopes away on all sides. As opening holes go, it is as pure and fair as they come.

The stakes at Pine Barrens increase significantly at the fourth, one of the finest short par fives in the nation. Only 496 yards from the back tees, this hole demonstrates that length is not necessary to fashion a heroic, risk-reward hole fraught with peril. Fazio dug deep into the site's sandy base to sculpt this hole, which presents an intimidating expanse of sand to the right and a broad landing area to the left. A finger of sand splits the fairway, offering a choice of targets. Launch your tee shot over the waste bunker—a carry of 225 yards from the tips—and the severely sloped green, perched 40 feet above the fairway, can be attempted in two. The smart play, however, is up the left side. The approach shot must avoid an array of defenses, notably a cone-shaped bunker in front of the putting surface inspired by the "Devil's Asshole," a deep pit guarding Pine Valley's

10th green. Allow your ball to trickle into the "Curse of the Barrens," as it's called, and a bogey or worse is inevitable. As much as any hole he's ever built, Fazio's creative prowess as a designer (and his penchant for the occasional penal flourish) is on full display at the fourth.

The back nine at Pine Barrens builds in drama and interest. The long par-four 12th, rated the toughest hole on the course, has a pair of alterna-

ACTIVITIES

In addition to the resort's wildlife preserve, its streams, lakes, and thickets home to cranes, herons, osprey, egret, white ibis, wood stork, and many other species, there's the $3.5 million Loch Ness pool and spa opened in 1998. Set in a three-acre park, the water playground features two waterslides, a 15-foot waterfall, a free-form adult spa that seats 36, and play areas with spontaneous pop jets and bubbling fountains ideal for children. (Camp Innisbrook, a Westin Kid's Club program, operates year-round).

In the immediate vicinity of Innisbrook is colorful *Tarpon Springs*, which offers a touch of Greek culture, from neo-Byzantine architecture and craft shops on the docks to "Spongeorama" (a museum of sponge memorabilia) and the St. Nicholas Boat Line, which provides a half-hour cruise with a demonstration by a diver.

In Tampa, 25 miles to the south, is *Busch Gardens*, a 335-acre African theme park known for its monorail "safari" and five roller coasters; and the *Florida Aquarium*, which displays nearly 4,500 specimens of fish, sea animals, and plants, many of them native to Florida. Farther south in St. Petersburg is the *Salvador Dalí Museum*, its collection of original paintings by the Spanish Surrealist second to none.

World Woods Golf Club, Brooksville, Pine Barrens, fourth hole

tive and quite different greens to play to, much like the eighth and ninth holes at Pine Valley. The left green is farther away but trouble-free; the right green, benched into a hill, is nearer at hand but sits behind a deep, U-shaped sand pit. Eight sets of tees offer plenty of options.

The 429-yard 13th, which calls for a forced carry over sandy wastelands followed by a running shot to a large green set below fairway level, qualifies as a modern classic, while players must put their thinking caps on to outfox Fazio at the option-laden par-five 14th. But it's the short par-four 15th that sticks in the memory of most pilgrims. Only 330 yards from the tips and under 300 yards from the middle tees, this exquisite gem offers a safe route to the left, or, to the right, a risky carry over a water-filled ravine fringed by sand and long grass. Beyond the trouble is a slender landing area that funnels shots to an undulating green set in a dell. Even played safely to the left, there's a good chance for birdie here.

The par-four 18th is a majestic right-to-left dogleg that calls for a blind drive over a ridge to a fairway that swings uphill to a sharply banked green

World Woods Golf Club, Pine Barrens, 18th hole

World Woods Golf Club, Rolling Oaks, third hole

well protected by sand. As at all great courses, the 18th at Pine Barrens sums up all that has gone before.

Fazio's second course at World Woods, **Rolling Oaks** (#33), was tunneled into a coastal hardwood forest and is diametrically opposed in style to Pine Barrens. If Pine Barrens is a flaming redhead, Rolling Oaks is a permed brunette. It's a miracle they're on the same site.

Patterned after classic parkland courses in the Northeast, Rolling Oaks presents a splendid sequence of holes framed by giant moss-draped live oaks, scrubbier turkey oaks, natural sinkholes, and coral rock outcrops. The heavier soil and sturdier vegetation inspired a more formal look than Pine Barrens. The layout fits its setting hand-in-glove.

Taking a page from Augusta National's nursery book, thousands of azaleas and hundreds of dogwoods were planted alongside the fairways to create an understory of color beneath the hardwoods. This grand 6,985-yard, par-72 spread is a very special place when the blooms burst forth in spring. And while the fairways at its sister facility are uniformly wide, at Rolling Oaks they're a little narrower and pinched by thick rough. The slope and course rating are slightly higher at Pine Barrens, but hitting the subtly sloped greens in regulation is no easy task on this refined layout, especially when a westerly breeze sweeps in from the Gulf of Mexico. Despite its seemingly benign appearance, Rolling Oaks generally plays two to three shots tougher for the good player than Pine Barrens. The hazards that tend to terrify the average duffer at Pine Barrens do not concern the low handicapper. The opposite is true on Rolling Oaks.

The stately, well-proportioned front nine, which swings near a gopher tortoise habitat, is highlighted by the par-three eighth, arguably the pretti-

est hole at World Woods. From an elevated perch—numerous tee boxes are terraced down the side of a hill—players must carry a flooded, rock-rimmed sinkhole and find a very deep green flanked by sand to the right and water to the left. The shot generally plays one club shorter owing to the elevation change, but the wind can play tricks with distance assessment. Aesthetically, the eighth is as attractive and harmonious as any one-shotter on Fazio's long résumé.

The front nine at Rolling Oaks is a perfect set-up for the rousing back nine, where the oaks get bigger and the drops get steeper. Among the feature holes coming in is the par-four 11th, which tumbles downhill before beckoning players to a shallow hilltop green heavily bunkered in front; the 12th, a beguiling short par four, its well-defended green framed by hickories and maples; and the 15th, a U.S. Open–style par four at 457 yards

LODGING

The top lodging facility convenient to World Woods is the *Plantation Inn & Golf Resort* in Crystal River, a 144-room Southern plantation-style property on King's Bay that offers discounts to World Woods golfers. In addition to a good dining room and nightly entertainment, the inn has a reputable 6,502-yard course of its own as well as a sporty par-34 layout, the *Lagoons Course*.

from the tips that doglegs to the left around a giant bunker before climbing uphill. The short par-five 18th, the corner of its dogleg guarded by an ancient Tarzan-worthy oak, its mighty limbs draped with Spanish moss, is especially impressive. So is the view looking back from the multitier green, the smallest on the course.

Admittedly, Rolling Oaks is not as visually arresting as Pine Barrens. Like Winged Foot and other traditional parkland venues, it does not shout its intentions. But ask the staff at World Woods which course they prefer to play, and their choice is unanimous: Rolling Oaks.

The Nation's Finest Practice Facility

It's common knowledge among the game's cognoscenti that the 36-hole complex at World Woods is world-class. But it's the practice facility at this marvelous facility on the outskirts of Brooksville near Homosassa Springs that sets the complex apart from all others.

Its centerpiece is a roughly square-shaped Practice Park fully 700 yards in diameter, with two sets of tees at each compass point. These tees are rotated every four days so that players always hit from fresh grass. More than 20 well-bunkered target greens defined by contrasting grasses are sprinkled throughout the interior of the 22-acre hitting area. Each side of the range is designed to accommodate every club in the bag. Even

World Woods Golf Club, Rolling Oaks, eighth hole

Tiger Woods could let out the shaft here and not disturb anyone. Practice bunkers (both greenside and fairway) are also available.

Beside the range is the two-acre putting course (three acres if you count the fringe), which features "every conceivable undulation you can imagine," according to Stan Cooke, director of golf. Not only can you prac-tice everything from 20-inch putts to 150-footers, you can practice them left-to-right, right-to-left, uphill, downhill, you name it. There's also an 18-hole putting course that's fun to play.

Arriving players can pay $4 for a bag of practice balls—or pay the same amount to play the three-hole Practice Course. Set in sandy waste-lands, Fazio designed these holes to emulate the look of Pine Barrens. There's a 513-yard par five that bends slightly left, a 361-yard par four that bends slightly right, and a 128-yard par three. The Practice Course offers a delightful warm-up to players who'd rather hit "game situation" shots than bang out range balls before the round. In the afternoon, serious play-ers are free to hit multiple shots from any position on the Practice Course.

The Short Course at World Woods is a charming par-29, 1,842-yard executive layout with seven par threes and two par fours. The one-shotters would fit in nicely on any of Fazio's finest designs. Popular with the golf staff, which likes to play shootouts on the minitrack in late afternoon, the Short Course at press time was $10 for walkers.

Did you underestimate the driving time to World Woods from Cin-derella's Castle in Orlando? There's a full-size range as well as two practice putting greens nestled between the first tees of the Pine Barrens and Rolling Oaks courses for late arrivals.

DINING

Not far from World Woods is *Papa Joe's,* a reliable pizza and pasta restaurant. For local color and riverside dining, head for *K.C. Crump's,* a restored fishing lodge in Homosassa, where the fresh Gulf grouper (poached with clams and bacon or baked with honey-glazed almonds and scallions in an Amaretto sauce) is highly recommended. For more casual dining on the Homosassa River, the establishment's *Ramshackle Café* serves more basic fare.

The South

The Homestead, Cascades Course • The Greenbrier, Old White Course and Greenbrier Course

Augustine Golf Club • Golden Horseshoe Golf Club, Gold Course • Royal New Kent • Stonehouse Golf Club

Pinehurst Resort & Country Club, No. 2 Course, No. 7 Course, No. 8 Course

Pine Needles Lodge & Golf Club • Pinehurst Plantation Golf Club • Linville Golf Club

Kiawah Island Golf & Tennis Resort, Ocean Course • Wild Dunes Resort, Links Course

Harbour Town Golf Links • The Dunes Golf & Beach Club

Tidewater Golf Club & Plantation • Caledonia Golf & Fish Club • White Columns Golf Club

Reynolds Plantation, Great Waters Course • The Cloister/Sea Island Golf Club (Seaside–Plantation)

Cambrian Ridge (Canyon–Sherling) • Grand National, Links Course and Lake Course

Dancing Rabbit Golf Club

_____

The Homestead, Cascades Course, 16th hole

Virginia

The North may have prevailed in the Civil War, but the South ended up with more golf courses, so who really won? The South commands a staggering 26 layouts on the "Top 100" roster, including four in the top 12 and 16 in the top 50. Based on projected developments, many more quality facilities can be expected to open in the years ahead.

The Homestead

The best mountain course in America, public or private? The legendary **Cascades Course** (#12) at **The Homestead** is the undisputed king of the hill. Located in sleepy Hot Springs, Virginia, in the foothills of the Allegheny Mountains, the Cascades draws golfers the way the town's mineral springs drew the Virginia aristocracy in the years before the Republic was founded. The Cascades is where Hot Springs homeboy Sam Snead learned the game, playing barefoot as a kid when he wasn't caddying. It was on this naturally rugged course that Snead refined his classic, syrupy swing—and learned how to play for money. Thousands of rounds on the Cascades gave the Slammer his education as a golfer. No wonder he gives it the ultimate accolade. "The Cascades," he drawls, "is the finest course

in the South. It lies out there, good-looking and inviting, just waiting to be taken—but waiting to take you if you're not extra careful."

In 1923, eight years before he transformed Shinnecock Hills on Long Island into his enduring masterpiece, designer William S. Flynn arrived at The Homestead and determined that a portion of a 1,700-acre estate in nearby Healing Springs could accommodate a golf course. After tromping through thick woods and hopscotching a rock-strewn ravine, Flynn gave his verdict: Yes, a fine course can be built—if additional land is purchased for two green sites. The land was acquired at considerable expense, and the architect known for his Irish wit and appraising eye set to work.

It was Flynn's genius to meld the strategic elements of his hole designs to the site's outstanding natural features. There's no man-made tomfoolery on the Cascades, no obvious manipulation of the landscape. The holes, free of artifice, appear shoehorned into the rolling, wooded landscape. Each is a pure, unadulterated jewel, with enough quirkiness in the par-70 routing (three par fives, two of them back-to-back, and five par threes, one of them the 18th) to give the layout character and individuality. Where Mother Nature wouldn't budge, Flynn left well enough alone. Bunkers and other flourishes, for example, were kept to an absolute minimum. But oh, those sidehill, downhill, and uphill lies! In the end, it is the ability to drive the ball straight and make solid contact from an infinite variety of uneven lies that spells triumph or disaster on the Cascades. The lightning-

Horse-drawn carriage at The Homestead, Hot Springs, Virginia

fast greens, many of them tucked among ancient oaks, provide a test of their own.

There are many select holes on this exquisite course. The 425-yard ninth, with its stunning view from a sky-high tee and its bull's-eye target pinned to a tree to guide the approach, is unforgettable. The long par-four 12th, converted from a par five to a par four in 1988, is often cited for its strategic cross bunkers and slick, well-defended green. Bobby Jones was especially fond of the 13th, a testing par four that bends gently around a stream.

But few holes anywhere can match the fifth, a 550-yard par five (576 yards from the tips) that may well be the most ornery par five in the South. First off, it plays much longer than the measured distance. Not only is flying the drive over a mammoth hill to a side-sloping fairway a major accomplishment, so is finding and holding the tiny, narrow, well-trapped green in regulation. Because of the shape of the hole, the natural tendency is to push the drive, which leaves a blind uphill, sidehill second shot out of deep rough. The course guide suggests aiming at the "far right-hand baby fir tree along the left center of the fairway." Sound advice if you drive the ball like Snead in his prime. Hook it left of the baby fir and you'll tumble into deep fairway traps. Even the most enterprising architect would never think to "build" a tilted chessboard such as this. Given its difficulty—it's the number-one handicap hole—it's probably just as well.

Some purists don't believe the round should end on a one-shotter, but the 184-yard 18th at the Cascades is a fitting climax to all that has gone before. The elevated tee here drops sharply to a lake, while the slightly raised green, canted from back to front, is cut into the side of a hill and guarded by a pair of bunkers.

The Cascades has hosted several USGA championships, including the 1988 U.S. Men's Amateur. (At the USGA's request, the layout's fairways

DINING

There is formal coat-and-tie dining at The Homestead, but golfers who don't wish to break stride from the 18th green to the supper table can enjoy *Sam Snead's Tavern*, a rustic structure built as the Bath County Bank in the 1920s and located opposite the resort. On the walls of the tavern are vintage photographs of the Slammer (with a full head of shiny black hair and without his trademark straw hat) as well as many of his contemporaries, including Ben Hogan and Byron Nelson. Dozens of Snead's trophies and mementos are also on display. Steaks, chops, and fresh rainbow trout taken from local streams are recommended.

LODGING, ETC.

You need not be a resort guest to play the Cascades, Lower Cascades, or Old Course, but lodging options in the immediate vicinity are virtually limited to *The Homestead*, formerly an exclusive summer retreat for America's social elite and these days a renovated grande dame that welcomes couples, families, spa-goers—and diehard golfers.

The list of amenities at this 521-room institution harks back to another time. There's dancing to the nightly orchestra, relaxing in one of the front porch rocking chairs, sitting by a cozy fire at teatime, exploring the library/historical museum recently added on the East Wing's ground floor, among other pastimes.

In addition to horse-drawn carriage rides (is there any finer way to tour the countryside?), The Homestead offers shooting sports, 100 miles of hiking and biking trails, canoeing, bowling (eight ten-pin lanes as well as lawn bowling), fishing for native trout (guides available), archery, horseshoes, croquet, volleyball, and numerous other activities. If you choose not to walk the Cascades Course, be sure to go for a stroll on the breathtaking Cascades Gorge Hiking Trail, which climbs 800 feet and skirts 13 waterfalls.

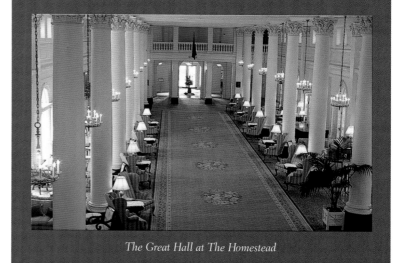

The Great Hall at The Homestead

were *widened* for that event. They're back to "normal" now.) In 1967, the U.S. Women's Open was captured at the Cascades by amateur Catherine Lacoste of Paris, France. (Her dad, tennis star René Lacoste, introduced the famous polo shirt with the crocodile insignia.) She became the first amateur, the first foreigner, and the youngest woman ever to win the event.

Site of the Men's Mid-Amateur Championship in 2000, the Cascades has been significantly upgraded since 1997. In consultation with the USGA, The Homestead has leveled, reshaped and enlarged many of the existing tee boxes, with several new forward tees added to enhance the enjoyment of higher handicappers.

The Homestead, Cascades Course, 16th hole

The Homestead, Cascades Course, 13th hole

Because the Cascades was designed to be walked, the resort introduced a caddy program in 1995 that truly enhances a player's enjoyment of this magnificent 6,610-yard layout (6,282 yards from the white tees) walled in by bear-shouldered peaks. Yes, there are some formidable climbs up the insteps of the Alleghenies on the front nine, but the incoming holes trace the valley floor and are easy walking.

More Golf / The Homestead

In addition to the Cascades, visitors can tour The Homestead's original course, its rolling fairways wrapped around the sprawling resort's stately red brick hotel. Expanded from six to 18 holes by Donald Ross in 1913 and boasting the oldest tee (1892) in continuous use in America, this museum piece was treated to a $1-million facelift by Rees Jones in 1995. Renamed the *Old Course*, the 5,796-yard layout (6,211 yards from the blue tees) has six each of par threes, fours, and fives. Pleasurable and sporty, the Old Course, with its heaving fairways, small greens, and stellar mountain

views, is the very essence of resort golf. The red tees, at 4,852 yards, promise a joyful outing to most women. Currently, the Old Course is the second-best venue at The Homestead, edging out the *Lower Cascades*, a solid if unspectacular Robert Trent Jones–designed layout marked by long tees, large greens, and a gurgling creek. The former 18th hole of the Old Course has been converted to a driving range adjacent to the resort's Golf Advantage School.

Not only has The Homestead's golf experience been greatly enhanced of late, so too has the entire resort operation. By 1998, Club Corporation of America (CCA), which rescued the ailing 15,000-acre property from its "genteel shabbiness" in 1993, had invested $30 million in the refurbishment and modernization of this National Historic Landmark, which dates to 1766. Located four hours by car south of Washington, D.C., The Homestead is the remotest great resort in America. Worth finding? Consider that Bath County has produced more than 40 golf professionals, most of whom learned their licks on the nation's most persnickety mountain track. Just ask Sam Snead.

The Greenbrier

Like a gleaming, silver-plated locomotive, **The Greenbrier** continues to ride a set of tracks untraveled by any other full-service resort in the nation, much less the world. Indeed, this legendary 6,500-acre establishment in White Sulphur Springs, West Virginia, is in a class of its own. The guest register speaks for itself: Dolley Madison, Thomas A. Edison, Judy Garland, George Burns, Margaret Thatcher, and 26 U.S. presidents. The historic memorabilia displayed in the Presidents' Cottage Museum (including the journals of Robert E. Lee) are peerless, while the vast salons and lobbies decorated by Dorothy Draper are the grandest public spaces of any resort hotel in the United States.

But it's the golf, as much as the resort's storied Old South atmosphere and fabulous amenities, that sets The Greenbrier apart. For starters, the resort's elder statesman is a man who took his first job as a professional at the resort in 1936. After a 21-year hiatus at The Homestead in Hot Springs, Virginia (the two resorts are an hour apart and are somewhat friendly competitors), the Slammer himself, Sam Snead, returned to The Greenbrier in 1993 as the resort's "golf pro emeritus" and is very much in evidence on the property, dispensing advice to awestruck patrons on the practice range and reminiscing about the number of times he shot his age or better on his beloved **Old White Course** (#97).

Sam Snead at The Greenbrier

Designed in 1913 by Charles Blair Macdonald and Seth Raynor, the course, named for the famous Old White Hotel which stood from 1858 to 1922 near the current edifice, is an enchanting, Scottish-themed test that traces the gently rolling contours of the valley floor. Stretching to 6,640 yards from the blue tees (6,353 yards from the white markers, par 70), this is a course that gives the greatest amount of pleasure to the greatest variety of players. Lined by stately hardwoods and backdropped by the Allegheny Mountains, the layout has at least three holes inspired by famous Scottish courses: the par-three eighth is a copy of the Redan at North Berwick, the tricky par-four 13th was patterned after the Alps at Prestwick, and the stout par-three 15th was modeled after the Eden on the Old Course at St. Andrews.

The heart and soul of the Old White are its glorious greens, which accept lofted approaches, low-running bump-and-run shots, and everything in between. These greens are near-textbook in size and slope and subtlety, and that is no accident. Macdonald wrote in *Scotland's Gift— Golf*: "Nothing induces more to the charm of the game than perfect putting greens. Some should be large, but the majority should be of moderate size; some flat, some hillocky, one or two at an angle, but the great majority should have natural undulations, some more and others less

The Greenbrier Hotel, White Sulphur Springs, West Virginia

undulating. It is absolutely essential that the turf should be very fine so the ball will run perfectly true." First-timers are well-advised to hire a caddy—appearances can deceive on the Old White's swift, gravity-defying greens.

In 1938, an up-and-coming golf course architect named Robert Trent Jones traveled 9,000 miles to put together his dream 18-hole golf course for *Town and Country* magazine. It included the first hole of the Old White Course. All these years later, this 425-yard par four still belongs, mainly for a setting every bit as majestic as the hotel. The spacious tee, elevated nearly 50 feet above Howard's Creek, extends back to the Casino terrace, where lunch is served, and to the resort's tennis courts, a beehive of activity.

The 394-yard 16th on the Old White, which calls for a carry over water on the drive as well as the approach, is probably the most intriguing hole on the course. But the par-three 18th, where the tee shot must carry a rock-walled stream to find a green fronted by bunkers, framed by leafy trees, and backdropped by the colorful awnings of the golf shop, offers a finish every bit as memorable as the beginning. Full of old-fashioned

SIDETRIPS/DOWN UNDER

Greenbrier County boasts no fewer than 850 caves, including Lost World and Organ Cave, but none is more fascinating than the secret Eisenhower-era underground bunker designed to house members of Congress and their staffs during nuclear attack. Decommissioned by the Federal Government in 1995, the 112,544-square-foot bunker, located 700 to 800 feet below the hotel's West Virginia Wing, is open to tours by guests. Highlights include the cafeteria, dormitories, decontamination chambers, clinic, chambers for the House and Senate, power plant, and other areas of interest. The 90-minute tour is $25 for adults, $10 for children 12 to 18. Those under 12 are not admitted.

The Greenbrier, Old White Course, first hole

virtues and strategic nuances, the Old White is a classic shotmaker's course that favors precision over power.

In 1977, the resort called in Jack Nicklaus to update the **Greenbrier Course** (#41), originally laid out in 1924 by Macdonald and Raynor, in preparation for the 1979 Ryder Cup Matches. Nicklaus eradicated the previous design, bringing forth a firebreather that yard-for-yard (it's only 6,681 yards from the tips) plays as tough as any course in the nation. Where the Old White is relatively flat, the recreated Greenbrier is a rugged mountain course, with steep inclines and dizzying drops. Best

enjoyed by accomplished players, it calls for pinpoint drives to narrow fairways, high-flying approach shots to multitiered greens, and a wily short game. With three par fives per nine, the layout has excellent variety and balance, though players receive an immediate trial by fire on the first six holes. The capper is the sixth, which stretches to 456 yards (441 yards from the white tees) and is rated the most difficult hole in West Virginia. It plays as a par five for most. Only a player with Nicklausian skills can hope to reach the tiny plateau green in two, much less get down in two putts for par.

Spa: The Homestead or The Greenbrier—Which Waters for You?

Years before the Declaration of Independence was signed, Virginia's aristocracy made its way to Bath County in the Allegheny highlands to "take the waters." In fact, Hot Springs, Virginia, is where the Founding Fathers tossed around the idea of a free republic while soaking in the colony's first hot tub.

These days, you can soak in a large ceramic tub in *The Homestead*'s refurbished spa while naturally heated, spring-fed mineral water at 104 degrees invigorates your body. Hotel guests can also take a dip in the recently updated indoor pool, which opened in 1903 and is fed by waters from the Octagon Pool.

The Warm Springs Pools are a must for those seeking a memorable soak. Here the soft, alkaline waters, as fizzy as champagne, flow at a rate of 1,200 gallons per minute, and remain within a degree or two of 96 degrees throughout the year.

Spa tub at The Greenbrier Hotel

Entrance to the Mineral Baths and Spa at The Homestead

The waters at The Greenbrier are equally storied. First discovered in 1778, White Sulphur Springs gained fame when a woman's rheumatism was "cured" within seconds of her immersion in a tree trunk filled with the sulphur water. By the 1920s, the resort's mineral baths were part of an extensive department offering packs, rubs, massages, and physical therapy. Combining early spa techniques with the latest products and equipment, The Greenbrier Spa offers private walk-in whirlpool baths, Swiss showers, Scotch spray, steam, sauna, and therapy rooms for massage and herbal body wraps. All baths use freshly drawn White Sulphur Springs sulphur water (its foul-smelling odor of rotten eggs is redeemed by its beneficial aspects) or Alvon Spring mineral water.

Amenities, etc.

With the possible exception of Gleneagles in Scotland, no resort on earth can match The Greenbrier for the excellence and amplitude of off-course activities. Among the highlights are 20 tennis courts, two heated platform tennis courts, indoor and outdoor Olympic-size pools, mountain biking, Falconry Academy, horseback riding and carriage rides, croquet, Gun Club and shooting preserve, white-water rafting trips, hiking, fitness trails, fishing, and bowling. The Greenbrier also boasts a 250-seat movie auditorium featuring a different film every night, a Gallery of Shops (everything from Orvis fly rods to homemade chocolates), and the Art Colony along Alabama Cottage Row, which features handcrafted items like petrified-wood bookends as well as original works of art. The hotel also offers a variety of cooking classes, several of them an extension of La Varenne cooking school in Burgundy, France.

Service? The lineage and dedication of the resort's 1,600-employee service staff is unmatched. There are over 40 members of the 40-Year Club at The Greenbrier, and more than 100 employees who represent the second generation to have worked here. Even when the hotel is sold out, The Greenbrier's staff far outnumbers its guests.

The Greenbrier, Greenbrier Course, second hole

LODGING

In addition to the fabulous digs at The Greenbrier (672 rooms, including 33 suites, 30 cottages, and 73 guest and estate houses), the towns of White Sulphur Springs and Lewisburg both feature a number of inexpensive motels. (You needn't be a registered guest at The Greenbrier to play either of its "Top 100" courses—tee times can be booked three days in advance on a space-available basis.) While each of The Greenbrier's eateries offers an exceptional dining experience, there are also a number of fine restaurants in the vicinity.

SIDETRIP/THE ANCIENT GAME

Want to turn back the clock and don those plus-fours your doting aunt gave you for Christmas years ago? The *Oakhurst Golf Links*, the nation's oldest organized golf club (1884), is located in a sleepy valley two miles from The Greenbrier. Revived in 1994 by property owner Lewis Keller and designer Bob Cupp, Oakhurst is a hilly nine-hole, 1,980-yard, par-34 affair that serves as a time warp for present-day golfers. Herds of sheep graze the fairways, tees are made from sand, and Keller's farmhouse doubles as the clubhouse. Most fascinating of all, the green fee of $45 includes use of four vintage hickory-shafted clubs and two gutta-percha balls manufactured by Penfolds in England especially for Oakhurst. These balls fly roughly half the distance of modern balls, while the clubs. . . well, let's just say golf was more of a sporting pastime in the old days.

Augustine Golf Club, Stafford, Virginia, first hole

More Golf/The Greenbrier

To make way for its new golf academy, the resort decided to overhaul its Lakeside Course, a charming test dating to 1910. Expanded to 18 holes by Dick Wilson in 1962, and now known as *The Meadows*, it reopened in May 1999 and features two new holes—the 14th and 15th—designed by Bob Cupp. Both hopscotch Howard's Creek, both have superb mountain views. This revised gem is the perfect third cog in a threesome of beautifully groomed courses, each with a first tee and 18th green near one of the nation's most impressive golf shops.

Moving east in the Old Dominion to the outskirts of Washington, D.C., is **Augustine Golf Club** (#94) in Stafford, a gorgeous spread that can only be described as an instant classic. Located in a quiet corner of north Virginia and named for George Washington's father, who kept a forge down the road from the club, Augustine quickly established itself as the top daily-fee course within an hour's drive of the nation's capital. The first solo effort by Rick Jacobson, who worked for six years as a design associ-

ate for Jack Nicklaus, Augustine is typical of the designs by the next generation of architects: flowing, strategic, versatile, and traditional in appearance.

Carved from a mixed forest of hardwoods and pines on rolling land dotted with 19 acres of wetlands (both grassy and submerged), Augustine gets off to a brisk start. The first hole, a 411-yard par four, plays from an elevated tee to a dual fairway split by wetlands and a clump of red maples. The slim landing pod to the left offers a worry-free route to the kidney-shaped green, while the wider landing zone to the right calls for a perilous carry over an imposing bunker to the shallowest portion of the green. It is one of the best risk-reward holes on a course that never stops asking players to assess situations and make decisions.

For most players, the only decision to be made at the stunning par-four second hole is, "Whither survival?" This 456-yard beastly beauty, Augustine's toughest hole, is also one of the most testing two-shotters in the mid-Atlantic region. The back tee, perched 100 feet above the fairway, calls for a lengthy carry over water to a semiwelcoming sliver of grass,

Augustine Golf Club, 18th hole

while the approach must again avoid water lurking to the left of a large green. This green is flanked to the right by slopes and hollows that, it must be said, were designed to feed bail-out shots back to the putting surface.

Nicklaus's design philosophy—no chicanery, all hazards and landing areas in plain view—has been carried forward by Jacobson at Augustine, which stretches to 6,810 yards and plays to a par of 71. Two of the par fives dare better players to try for the green in two, but there are consequences for misplayed shots. The back nine, like the front, is anchored by rigorous par fours, notably the 12th, a demanding right-to-left dogleg that sweeps to the crest of a ridge before dropping downhill to a waterfowl habitat. The approach is played over the marsh to a well-bunkered green benched in a hillside framed by hardwoods. It's a beauty.

Sand traps have been kept to a minimum at Augustine—there are only 41 on the course—but each is cleverly sited. The most prominent among them is the gaping pit prefacing the green at the 18th hole, a 501-yard par five that invites inveterate gamblers to go for the gusto—if they can avoid

a pair of bunkers guarding the left side of the fairway.

Set above the triple-tier green, its nooks and crannies intended for "Sunday" pin placements, is a handsome 14,000-square-foot clubhouse that offers a polished country club atmosphere to visiting golfers. The back wall of the clubhouse is mostly glass and overlooks the 18th green.

Spring, when the layout's dogwoods bloom, is the best time to head 30 miles south from the Washington Beltway to sample a course that cracked the "Top 100" four short years after opening. Walkers are welcome anytime at this superlative parkland spread.

Williamsburg

The best golf vacation in history? Rev the motor of your time machine and set the dials for Williamsburg, where George Washington, Thomas Jefferson, and other Founding Fathers came of age politically. As quickly as these upstart patriots offended the British Crown and rallied the populace, this storied corner of Tidewater Virginia near Chesapeake Bay has transformed itself into a golf getaway with genuine depth and broad-based appeal. In 1996, several area golf courses and 17 hotels joined forces to create the Williamsburg Area Golf Association. Its mission: To establish the area as the East Coast's best new golf destination.

Williamsburg's inventory of resort courses, including the Golden Horseshoe's duo, Kingsmill's three layouts, and the 54-hole complex at Ford's Colony, a semiprivate club, boast unassailable credentials. What has put the Tidewater area over the top is the recent opening of several new daily-fee courses, including two world-beaters, Stonehouse and Royal New Kent. Each vaulted into the top 25 of the "Top 100" list less than two years after opening!

Golden Horseshoe Golf Club, Williamsburg, Virginia, Gold Course, 16th hole

Golf-wise, the cornerstone of Williamsburg remains the **Golden Horseshoe Golf Club,** its **Gold Course** (#57) a Robert Trent Jones masterpiece that occupies a 125-acre arboretum of fruit trees and hardwoods spliced with draws, ravines, and ponds just beyond the south terrace of the Williamsburg Inn. Along with fabled Merion in Philadelphia, the Gold is one of the finest compact layouts ever built. Its resistance to scoring has stood the test of time: The course record of 67 was set by Jack Nicklaus four years after the course opened in 1963. (Par is 71.) Indeed, only highly skilled players tread the "Shoe" with unshakable confidence.

The Gold's quartet of par threes, each with water in play, is especially memorable. Best known is the 16th, where the tee shot is played from a leveled slot in a wooded hillside to a large, pear-shaped green that beckons from the middle of a lake. This island green is far more generous in size than the wicked little bulkheaded greens that have cropped up with alarming regularity in water hazards across the nation. It's far prettier than most, too.

The layout's remaining par threes are equally challenging and scenic. The tee at the third stands 40 feet above a long, slim green set in a lush

Gold Course, seventh hole

49

Royal New Kent, Providence Forge, Virginia, first hole

glen. A watery ditch guards the front portion of the green, with sand traps fore and aft. The front pin placement can be risky to shoot for, given the margin for error.

Take a stroll to the back tee (without your clubs) at the seventh, which is perched on a high bluff overlooking a flooded ravine. The skewed green, severely tilted from back to front and well defended by bunkers, nestles in a hillside slightly above tee level. It's a daunting target from the championship tee at 207 yards and no picnic from the blue markers at 186 yards, either. Even from the white tees at 165 yards, only a first-class shot will suffice. Small wonder the seventh is rated the most difficult of the Gold's one-shotters.

While the green at the seventh is semiblind, players need to stand on tiptoe at the par-three 12th to see a tiny shelf of a green 40 feet below on the far side of a lake. Overshoot the green, and a thick forest awaits. If this hole seems to require no more than a delicate lofted shot that carries the water but avoids the woods, a genuine test of brawn awaits at the gargantuan par-five 15th, which parallels South England Street for an unconscionable 631 yards from the tips. (The tee itself measures 135 yards!) Load up with every piece of titanium in your bag—you won't be getting home in two shots unless you arrange for Tiger Woods or John Daly to play the hole for you.

Virtually untouched since its debut, the Gold reopened to acclaim in July 1998, following a $4.5-million makeover by Rees Jones, the master's younger son, who rebuilt and in some cases enlarged and recontoured greens, reshaped bunkers, elevated a few tees, and installed a new irrigation system. Because "the tailor cut a good suit," said Jones of his father's handiwork, the routing of the Gold was left intact.

More Golf / Golden Horseshoe

The Golden Horseshoe's second venue, the *Green Course*, is a Rees Jones design opened in 1991 that fits its setting hand-in-glove. Site of the 1998 U.S. Senior Women's Amateur, the Green Course, much larger in scale than the Gold, offers a combination of ridge and valley holes. Four sets of tees provide excellent versatility, though six water holes, sweeping greens, and numerous bunkers give the Green Course plenty of muscle. There's also the nine-hole, executive-length *Spotswood Golf Course*, a miniature par-31 version of the Gold Course designed by Robert Trent Jones.

The "Top 100" course near Williamsburg most likely to rivet the attention of first-time visitors to the region is more evocative of a British seaside links than a wooded Tidewater course. Even the layout's name, **Royal New Kent** (#23), was borrowed from Kent County in England. According to developer Danny Young, when he and Mike Strantz, who served as Tom Fazio's lead designer on many key projects in the 1980s, came upon a raw, cutover site in Providence Forge 25 miles outside Williamsburg, they realized that the stark, heaving land was the ideal spot on which to fashion an epic links. With storied Irish links courses as his models, notably Royal County Down in Northern Ireland, Strantz set to work amplifying existing contours to create a topsy-turvy links for the 21st century, a grand stage on which to re-enact a semblance of the game as it's played abroad. And while the soil is heavy clay (not porous sand, as on a genuine links), the absence of tall trees at Royal New Kent invites the Tidewater breeze, a key component of links golf.

From any and every one of its five sets of tees, Royal New Kent, opened in 1996, takes on the aspects of an abandon-all-hope journey into a turfgrass Twilight Zone. Gigantic dunes planted with ground-hugging juniper and hydroseeded with a variety of fescue grasses (each a different hue and texture) frame fairways laid through scooped-out draws and ridges. Landing areas are much wider than they appear from the tees, but with only a painted rock on a shaggy hillside to aim at, it's often difficult for first-timers to gauge the challenge at hand.

Strantz pockmarked the land with 134 bunkers, many of them deep pots built in echelon to increase their dramatic effect. In size and undulation, the layout's lightning-fast greens resemble pods of breaching whales surfacing in bentgrass. Several of these enormous greens nestle behind grassy knolls only partially visible from the fairway. On the plus side, Royal New Kent is generously wide, so there's plenty of room to play the game, and the slopes of the ridges are long and flowing, so the eye is subconsciously pleased despite the turbulence of the landscape. But overall, this hurly-burly links is not a course for the faint of heart. For example, there's a *seven-foot* dip in front of the sixth green. At the second hole, a boomerang-shaped par five, failed efforts to reach the green in two or sliced approach shots plunge into a hellish wasteland far below fairway level.

Strantz may have produced a silk purse from a sow's ear, but Royal New Kent remains a scruffy landlocked brute with no ocean to provide aesthetic respite from its harsh demands. Here's the drill for playing this beast from the Invicta (Latin for "unconquerable") tees stretching to 7,291 yards, par 72. (The slope rating of 147 and course rating of 76.5 are the highest in Virginia.) First, a handicap of five or less. Next, a driver's license left in care of the pro. Why? Because you don't get it back (and therefore can't leave the premises) until you sign the scorecard. Invicta scorecards are proudly displayed in the clubhouse pub for the amusement of all.

Stonehouse Golf Club, Toano, Virginia, 11ᵗʰ hole

Attractions

Well-traveled golfers crave variety on and off the links, but only in a few places are the off-course attractions and amenities a match for the manicured turf.

The *Historic Area of Colonial Williamsburg* comprises 173 acres of gardens and public greens as well as nearly 500 reconstructed or restored buildings populated by costumed interpreters and craftspeople. Everyone from blacksmiths and wigmakers to coopers and milliners ply their trade and reenact or describe aspects of Colonial life along the cobbled streets of this living, working town. It's a very convincing time warp, perhaps the most comprehensive eighteenth-century museum in the world.

Adjacent to the restored colonial township is the *College of William and Mary*, chartered in 1693 and the second oldest college in America; Thomas Jefferson went there. Classes are still held in the Wren Building, designed by England's most famous architect, Christopher Wren.

The Governor's Palace, Colonial Williamsburg

Market Square Tavern Common Room, Colonial Williamsburg

Elsewhere, visitors can relive the nation's revolutionary past at *Yorktown Victory Center*; or board replicas of settlers' ships at *Jamestown*, where 104 men of the Virginia Company came ashore in 1607 to establish the first permanent settlement in the New World.

One of Williamsburg's most popular family attractions is *Busch Gardens*, a fanciful re-creation of "Old Europe." Consisting of eight European-style villages, Busch Gardens is a 360-acre theme park and entertainment center set with musical revues, live shows, attractions, and exhibits. For thrill-seekers, there's a roller-coaster called the Loch Ness Monster that hurtles riders through double-looping corkscrews. The newest attraction, Pirates 4-D-PLUS, combines special effects with a fourth dimension to enable patrons to feel sprays of water and gusts of wind, not to mention attacks by bats and hornets.

Summers can be sultry in Williamsburg, and on hot days visitors can shoot the rapids or catch a wave in Surfer's Bay (a giant concrete "ocean") at *Water Country USA*. A high-speed slide opened in 1998 enables guests to race each other down a hair-raising 382-foot drop.

Handicappers can drop by *Colonial Downs*, which opened in 1997 and is Virginia's first horse track. Harness racing is scheduled in the spring. The Thoroughbred season is July through November.

Unless you're a pro or aspire to be one, you're likely to total a bowling score from the Invicta tees. Especially on a day, as they say in Eire, when the "breeze is up." Forward markers at Royal New Kent give bogey shooters a fighting chance, but this gargantuan track, built to resemble an Irish links on steroids, induces vertigo in all but the stoutest competitors.

A daily-fee course with 18 signature holes? Yes, Virginia, there is one. **Stonehouse Golf Club** (#14), a mere 12 miles from Royal New Kent in Toano, is another Mike Strantz creation, but sets an entirely different stage for the game. The openness at New Kent is replaced by a more traditional frame, namely tall pines and hardwoods, their understory of dogwoods and mountain laurel splashed with color in spring. Stonehouse has defined corridors of play, and a sense of containment despite the grand scale.

Even Strantz admits that American golfers are generally more comfortable with this look. Steep-walled valleys were bellied out to create broad fairways that hopscotch deep ravines or sidle up to small ponds near beaver-gnawed trees. Gaping bunkers were gouged from ridges, while greens cling to sheer bluffs or perch precariously above spring-fed creeks. From any set of tees, golf at Stonehouse is a giddy experience.

Stonehouse was built to endure. With no weak sisters and no connective tissue, this grand-scale layout offers full-bore golf with no letup from the first tee to the 18th green. The 6,963-yard, par-71 design can be likened to a giant museum hung with 18 stunning portraits, no accident given Strantz's background as a commercial artist. Stonehouse is a testament to what a talented designer, unencumbered by tradition, can extract from a great site. It is, quite simply, one of the finest public-access courses built in the 1990s.

There is a sculptural quality to the holes at Stonehouse. Strantz, who likes to incise his bunkers deep into the sides of steep banks and ridges, says that "cutting a golf course into the land gives a more natural look than piling dirt onto existing land," the usual way of creating decorative and

Stonehouse Golf Club, 17th hole

Stonehouse Golf Club, 15th hole

strategic features. Fairways are embedded in the terrain, the enormous greens often recessed into bowl-like amphitheaters. Best of all, each hole is different from the others. Each presents an interesting problem to solve.

Strantz displays his ingenuity early in the round. At the par-four second hole, there's a choice of two tee locations. The first calls for a long carry over two gaping sand pits. The second set is more straightforward and is less perilous. The target is a turtleback green so large that there's a sprinkler head at its center. Similarly, the 399-yard fifth (all yardage quotes are from the black tees, which measure 6,551 yards) has a wishbone-shaped tee configuration. The tough tees are tucked to the right, with the easier angle of attack on the left. The short par-five seventh, a double dogleg that snakes along a well-bunkered ridgetop, brims with risk-reward options for bold and meek players alike. However, aggressive players are generally rewarded—*if* they can produce a succession of near-perfect shots.

The back nine culminates in three fascinating holes. Play it too cozy on your approach at the 346-yard 16th, and your ball slides down the giant lolling tongue appended to the front of the green, sometimes all the way down the fairway into deep, waiting bunkers. Given its scale, this tongue is almost a caricature of a false front green. The tee shot at the stunning par-three 17th is played from one hilltop to another, the 65-yard-deep green a velvet blanket of swales crowning a knoll terraced with laurel and holly.

The 431-yard 18th (453 yards from the gold tees) could decide a major championship—if the contestants would consent to play this take-no-prisoners layout four days in a row. The enormously broad fairway, wider than the length of a football field, invites one and all to take a big rip, though great care must be taken with the approach. The green here teeters on the brink of a steep ledge with bunkers fore and aft. In time, a churning 20-foot-high waterwheel will backdrop the putting surface. Beyond it is the open-air deck and the glassed back wall of the stone-faced clubhouse.

The key to good golf course architecture is bringing a piece of property to life, and Strantz has succeeded magnificently at Stonehouse and Royal New Kent. Both have taken their place among the finest daily-fee courses in the nation since their joint debut in 1996.

With a range of accommodations totaling 3,400 rooms, Williamsburg has resorts and hostelries to please all tastes. There is, however, a stand-out property often described as the most beautifully appointed small hotel in America. This is the *Williamsburg Inn*, a noble edifice of white-washed brick.

Its perfection is no accident. The Inn's creator, John D. Rockefeller, Jr., was a stickler for detail. A typical memo from Rockefeller to the building's architects in 1935 advised: "Careful brooding study of every detail of a bedroom, particularly when small, is in my experience the only way in which to get a completely satisfying result. I shall not be happy to go forward with the Williamsburg Inn until I feel that the most possible has been made of each room as regards comfort, convenience, and charm."

Present-day guests enjoy the fruits of Rockefeller's thoroughness. For example, each of the Inn's 102 individually decorated rooms has both firm and soft pillows on the beds. The morning wake-up call includes the current temperature and the day's forecast. The Inn's public rooms, scented by bayberry candles, are impressive in their simplicity of design. The openness and flow of Regency furniture is typified by the settee in the center of the lobby: its symmetrical open back invites a visitor's eye into the lobby and through it to the Inn's flagstone patio, where tall oaks and elms shade stone planters brimming with colorful flowers. Beyond the

The Regency Lounge at the Williamsburg Inn

greenswards maintained for lawn bowling and croquet lies the Golden Horseshoe's Gold Course.

On a budget? The mid-priced *Williamsburg Lodge*, also on the doorstep of the Gold Course, has Tidewater-theme public areas, folk art decor in the guest rooms, the Tazewell Club Fitness Center on site, and live piano entertainment in its lounge. All-inclusive package rates feature unlimited green fees daily, cart for 18 holes each day, dinner one night at the Lodge Dining Room, and other extras.

Other well-priced properties in town include *Williamsburg Hospitality House*, a courtyard-centered, 297-room hotel opposite William and Mary College with a concierge, outdoor pool, and Christopher's Tavern, a popular gathering spot; and the *Ramada Inn Central Williamsburg*, a family-owned inn with 160 oversize rooms.

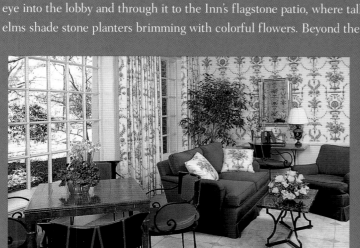

The Peacock Room at the Williamsburg Inn

More Golf/Williamsburg

Accessible TV tournament courses are generally irresistible to traveling golfers, and few offer the fun and playability of the *River Course* at *Kingsmill Golf Club*. Home site of Michelob Championship at Kingsmill, a PGA Tour event, this vintage Pete Dye layout relies on elevated greens, plunging ravines, and four sizable ponds for its challenge. The strong, scenic back nine is highlighted by the spectacular par-three 17th, which parallels the James River from tee to green.

Kingsmill's newest venue, the *Woods Course*, was one of the best resort courses to open in 1995. Presented with a rugged, pristine site free of housing, designer Tom Clark and resident touring pro Curtis Strange devised a course that looks as if it's been there 100 years. Rough is minimal—with wide fairways groomed nearly to the tree lines, this may be the most fun-to-play course in town. Among the feature holes is the par-three 12th, its double green inset with a doughnut-hole bunker, and the par-five 13th, its green guarded by a lake that doubles as the Rhine River attraction in nearby Busch Gardens.

DINING

For truly atmospheric dining, Colonial Williamsburg's historic taverns re-create supper experiences savored by 18th-century patriots. *Christiana Campbell's Tavern*, patronized by George Washington, features Chesapeake Bay regional seafood dishes. At the *King's Arms Tavern*, the oyster-stuffed filet mignon and pecan pie are extra special, while the mixed grill of wild boar sausage and quail served at *Shields Tavern* is the perfect repast for the famished golfer. *Chowning's Tavern* in Colonial Williamsburg features English pub fare (bangers and mash, shepherd's pie), a good selection of beers and ales, and festive "gambols." Visitors can learn Colonial diversions such as Goose, a gambling game (players wager roasted peanuts); enjoy backgammon and Colonial card games; or sing bawdy ballads to music played by costumed balladeers on 18th-century instruments.

Outside the Historic Area, *Backfin Seafood Restaurant*, owned by Kingsmill resident Curtis Strange's fishing buddy, is popular with locals. So is the *Trellis Café*, its co-owner the author of *Death by Chocolate Cookies*. For good cheap eats near the College of William and Mary, drop by *Paul's Deli*, which doubles as a sports bar.

With its flawless continental cuisine and exceptionally refined setting, the *Regency Room* at the Williamsburg Inn must be counted among the nation's finest resort dining rooms. Hans Schadler, the Inn's executive chef, has declined several offers to join the White House culinary staff. Small wonder seven U.S. presidents and innumerable world leaders have dined at the Inn to savor his elegant take on standard entrees from crab cakes to rack of lamb.

The other truly noteworthy dining room in town is called just that—*The Dining Room*, located at Ford's Colony. Formal and refined, The Dining Room has received the coveted Distinguished Restaurants of North America (DiRoNA) award, an AAA Five Diamond Award, as well as The Wine Spectator's "Best of Award of Excellence" yearly since 1989. (With over 1,000 selections, the wine cellar is Virginia's best and largest). The Chef's six-course Signature Dishes is the way to go if you've worked up a big appetite on the links—or won the bet for dinner.

*Continental cuisine at the Regency Room,
the Williamsburg Inn*

For top-notch, country club–style golf, there's *Ford's Colony*, which offers two well-groomed courses. The *White-Red Course* was laid out by Ellis Maples and completed by his son Dan. Holes are threaded through rolling hills and thick woodlands. The front nine is flat and watery, the back nine hillier. The challenge from any set of tees is fair, solid, and traditional. The *Blue-Gold Course* at Ford's Colony offers a good flow of holes spread out on flatter terrain than the White-Red Course, with more water in play. The smooth, slick greens, several canted from back to front, are well-bunkered. Blackheath, a third course by Maples, opened at Ford's Colony in spring, 1999.

Shopping

Follow Richmond Road (Route 60) to several outlet centers, including Williamsburg Pottery Factory in Lightfoot (a bazaar-like complex of 32 buildings with everything from fine china to dried flowers); Williamsburg Outlet Mall; and Berkeley Commons Outlet Center. Merchants Square, a shopping village adjacent to Williamsburg's Historic Area, has a charming array of small shops and boutiques specializing in pewter, brass, antiques, books, quilts, decorative accessories, and all sorts of Colonial esoterica.

North Carolina

Pinehurst

The Tar Heel State holds much in store for visiting golfers, starting with a destination synonymous with golf in America: *Pinehurst*. Five "Top 100" courses are found here, three at the **Pinehurst Resort & Country Club** (Nos. 2, 7, and 8), plus *Pine Needles* and *Pinehurst Plantation*. An additional 40, most of them public-access courses, can be found within a 26-mile radius. How did this otherwise unremarkable area of central North Carolina achieve such prominence? Pure geological serendipity.

Notwithstanding its beautiful mountains and gorgeous seashore, the state's most unusual geographic feature (at least for golfers) is a 75-mile-long, 35-mile-wide expanse of hard-packed white quartz sand that runs southwest from the state's interior. This belt of sand—the surrounding area is mostly clay—was formed eons ago, at a time when 20,000-foot peaks in the Appalachian Mountains framed the continental coastline. A tectonic shift in the ocean floor created an 800-foot-deep trench that filled with coastal sediments. When the ocean receded, the trench emerged as the now-famed Sandhills. This seismic event, coupled with the vision of a stalwart Yankee and a talented young Scotsman, gave birth to the nation's first golf destination.

escape the blizzards and chilblains occasioned by a New England winter. At a cost of $300, Tufts hired Frederick Law Olmsted, famed designer of Central Park in New York City, to plan a tidy New England-style hamlet with wide, curving lanes and white clapboard cottages set around a village green.

Horseback riding, polo, tennis, and roque (a form of croquet) were among the favorite early pastimes at Pinehurst, but golf soon began to insinuate itself. A field hand reportedly told Tufts one day that the dairy cows were being disturbed by a group of New Yorkers who were hitting small white balls with sticks. Tufts, wishing to accommodate sportsmen of all persuasions, commissioned work to begin on the No. 1 Course in 1897. Golf hit fever pitch in Pinehurst

The Putter Boy Statue, Pinehurst

Pinehurst Hotel, Pinehurst, North Carolina

When James Walker Tufts, the Boston soda fountain magnate, bought 5,500 acres of ravaged timberland in the Sandhills region in 1895, locals reckoned his purchase price of $1 per acre to be laughably high. In fact, the soil was so poor it was said to be necessary to bury a person with commercial fertilizer in order to afford some prospect of his rising on Judgment Day. Yet Tufts loved the region's mild climate and pine-scented air. He envisioned a healthful retreat for friends back home who wished to

shortly after the great English pro Harry Vardon dropped by in 1900 to play an exhibition match on the resort's rudimentary 18-hole golf course. Later the same year, Donald Ross, a Scot from Dornoch who had apprenticed under Old Tom Morris at St. Andrews, was brought to Pinehurst by Tufts from his summer club in Massachusetts to serve as professional and expand its golf facilities. It was a match made in heaven. Ross, an accomplished player with a true appreciation of proper shotmaking, set out to design a quartet of golf courses that could be enjoyed by all types of players.

Ross's best-known creation, the **No. 2 Course** (#2), was completed in 1907, though Ross tinkered and toyed with the design of the layout for most of his life. According to the late golf scribe Charles Price, who resided in Pinehurst, "Ross intended No. 2 to be something special. He was still shaping it into final form when he died in 1948, 45 years after he began and 12 after he thought it was finished." Generally regarded by the game's cognoscenti as the purest examination of golf on earth, No. 2's reputation has grown steadily. The USGA announced in 1993 that it was bringing its biggest and most prestigious event, the U.S. Open, to Pinehurst in 1999.

Pinehurst Resort & Country Club, No. 2 Course, 12th hole

Question: On what championship golf course can you spray a drive at *every single hole* and still have a chance to recover? Answer: Only one. Number Two. That is because Ross believed golf should be a pleasure, not a penance. "It is not difficult," he wrote, "to make courses impossible, but that is a betrayal of true principles. The real capacity of every great course lies in its enjoyment value; enjoyment for every class of golfer." With the possible exception of the Old Course at St. Andrews, no course is better suited to more types of players than No. 2, an ingenious layout that adds strokes in half shots (not major disasters) to increase a player's score, leaving his card in shreds but his ego intact.

On the surface, the course does nothing to terrify or unnerve the duffer. In fact, it appears tame. Fairways are unusually wide. Rough is minimal. There are no forced carries. Nearly every green is open in front. There's very little out-of-bounds. The layout's single water hazard (at the par-five 16th) rarely comes into play. It's next to impossible to incur penalty strokes, much less lose a ball.

As for the design itself, each hole unfolds on gently rolling sandhills framed by tall longleaf pines. Each hole has a natural, unforced look to it. Aesthetically, this subtle "links within a forest" is a plain Jane that tends to underwhelm at first glance. Nearly void of drama, with no island greens, pounding surf, or titillating death-or-glory shots to negotiate, No. 2 puts most novices to sleep. This is a golf course stripped of frills, its design elements reduced to the barest essentials. Still, according to Price, "There is not a hole on it that could conceivably be called a weak one, which is rare. No two are remotely alike, which is even rarer. Yet none is out of character with the others, which is almost unheard of." Straightforward almost to a fault—there is but a single dogleg in the routing, and Ross himself once said "every bunker could be removed and you'd never know it"—elusive No. 2 is utterly devoid of chicanery.

The heart of each hole on No. 2 (and the source of its enduring appeal) is an inverted saucer of a green, its undulations ranging from mild to moderate and its effective size reduced significantly by the fact that its

Pinehurst No. 2 Course, 18th hole

(a computerized device that measures green contours with lasers was used to regain Ross's original specifications), the season-ending Tour Championship was held on Pinehurst No. 2 in 1990 and 1991. The players raved about the course, setting the stage for the USGA's decision to hold the U.S. Senior Open on No. 2 in 1994, which was captured by South African shotmaker Simon Hobday. The success of that event led to Pinehurst No. 2 landing the game's ultimate challenge, the U.S. Open, for 1999.

Because golf carts must stick to the paths, it is essential that the course be walked. Indeed, there's simply no way to appreciate No. 2 while rumbling through the pines in a golf cart (there's a cadre of knowledgeable caddies at the resort). Given its current appeal to purists worldwide as well as the indelible stamp of greatness placed upon No. 2 as a U.S. Open venue, the healthy surcharge levied to play Ross's most exalted creation is justified. Just don't expect fireworks the first time around. Like the recording of a great symphony that requires repeated listenings to be fully appreciated, golfers need to play a second (or third) round on No. 2 to savor its timeless appeal.

edges are rolled off to close-cropped mounds and swales designed to test the finesse arts of chipping and pitching. According to Brad Kocher, Pinehurst's director of golf maintenance, "You have to be disciplined enough to hit shots to areas of the green where the ball will be received," he explains. "There are not many greens in this country where, if the pin is close to the edge, you have to think about whether you might putt it off the green. Some people don't like that dimension, but that's why these are some of the most unique—and challenging—greens complexes in the world."

Having slid off the green, devotees of No. 2 often elect to play recovery shots with a putter or mid-iron. The name of the game is creativity. In *Golf Has Never Failed Me,* Ross himself said, "The Pinehurst conditions offered a really exceptional opportunity. Only in a sandy soil would the drainage problem permit construction of the rolling contours and hollows natural to the Scottish seaside courses where golf was born. This contouring around a green makes possible an infinite variety in the requirements for short shots that no other form of hazard can call for." He added, "I am sure if you watch tournament play on Number Two, you will be interested to see how many times competitors whose second shots have wandered a bit will be disturbed by these innocent-appearing slopes."

Of the many testimonials accorded No. 2, perhaps Johnny Miller's is the most fitting: "I almost can't tell you how good the golf course is. It might not be the hardest golf course in the world, but for pleasure, for going out and having a pleasurable time with a smile on your face, it can't be beat. It's hard to get mad when you play here."

Much of No. 2's allure has been reclaimed of late after a fallow period in the 1970s when wrong-headed owners filled in bunkers, tore out native wiregrass, softened greens, and otherwise adulterated Ross's masterpiece. Club Corporation of America, one of the world's largest hospitality companies, acquired Pinehurst in 1984 and has since pumped well over $50 million into the resort's golf courses (new and existing), lodging facilities, and amenities. After No. 2's greens were successfully resurfaced in 1987

Pinehurst No. 7 Course, 16th hole

Pinehurst No. 8 Course, eighth hole

SWING FIX

The resort's Golf Advantage School, featuring a 5:1 student-teacher ratio, enjoys a fine reputation. Weekend and week-long programs are available. Fundamentals (grip, stance, alignment, posture, and balance) are stressed. The school combines the latest computer technology with one of the nation's most complete indoor/outdoor teaching facilities.

Even if you don't sign up for formal instruction, you need to bang out a few balls on "Maniac Hill," the nation's first practice range (1913). It was christened by Donald Ross, presumably for the legions of golfers who then as now lashed away from morning till night in quest of the magic moves to a better swing. (A mechanical sweeper clears the range of over 100,000 balls each evening.)

Pinehurst No. 2 is a tough act to follow, but to meet rising demand, the resort's current management has built two new courses and spruced up the others to satisfy the needs of its guests, many of whom are serious enthusiasts who arrive with the expectation of playing 36 holes daily.

The region's most visually stunning layout is the **No. 7 Course** (#56), a Rees Jones design opened in 1986 that offers tremendous variety along with a major-league challenge from the back tees at 7,125 yards. In fact, this multitheme layout three miles from the main resort complex is the toughest track in town (and one of the most difficult in the Carolinas) from the tips. The high ground here is hilly and wooded, while the low-lying holes skirt weedy streams and wetlands. Pronounced elevation changes give players exalted views of the task at hand, though Jones, mindful that he was working in the shadow of the master, took pains to inject his design with a fair amount of playability.

Not only is No. 7 noticeably hillier than the resort's older courses, it also changes appearance at nearly every hole. There are hints of a Scottish links in places—pot bunkers, grassy hollows, and rolling mounds are in evidence—but the dramatic elevation changes put one in mind of a mountain course. In addition to the ever-present pines, groves of poplar and dogwood frame many of the holes, providing the tranquil beauty of a parkland spread. Finally, marshes, streams, and ponds lend a coastal appearance, albeit one fraught with danger—water comes into play at eight holes.

Taking a design cue from Ross, Jones did not litter the fairways of No. 7 with an abundance of bunkers, placing the premium instead on accurate approach shots. Subtle contours on the greens require players to hit the appropriate target area in return for par, though the terrain around the greens is fairly severe. While No. 2 quietly extracts its pound of flesh throughout the round, No. 7 can spell disaster at any number of holes—especially if approach shots go astray. For example, at the seventh, a mid-length par four, players must carry their approach shots to a sloping green positioned beyond a hazard known as the "Devil's Gut"—a daunting expanse of swampland.

The plateau green at the short par-four 10th is protected by 10 pot bunkers, each a deep kettle that can run up the tally. At the double-dogleg, par-five 12th, trees and underbrush nearly enclose the perched green. The spectacular 13th, a 203-yard par three from the tips, is a penal creation that offers a taste of Pine Valley: Players must carry a natural berm and giant waste area to find the slightly elevated green. Elongated fingers of sand—"Rees' Fingers," they're called—preface the green at the par-three 16th, one of the most photographed holes at Pinehurst, while the mammoth 18th, a par five stretching to 596 yards, careens downhill to a shallow green framed by sand and flanked by water. It is a dramatic finale to a burly course that never fails to give the accomplished player a serious tussle. Then again, from the white tees at 6,165 yards, No. 7 has more bark than bite—so long as bogey shooters don't bite off more than they can chew.

To celebrate its 100th anniversary in 1996—and also to keep up with rising demand for more golf, Golf, GOLF—Pinehurst Resort hired Tom Fazio to design its Centennial Course on the grounds of its former Gun Club a mile and a half from the main complex. The site had the requisite longleaf pines and rolling sand hills, but there was more. Fazio's inspired creation also skirts an old sand pit, a manufactured dune ridge, and a pair of freshwater marshes. In places, the 7,092-yard course resembles a Low Country layout complete with maritime forest and waterfowl. From its five sets of tees, the **No. 8 Course** (#48) has as much beauty and variety as any course in the neighborhood—and enough strategic interest to keep the best of golfers alert.

Regardless of how the holes on No. 8 unfold—uphill or downhill, open or narrow, watery or dry—they lead to undulating, inverted saucer greens rolled off at their edges to closely mown swales and hollows. With their interesting shapes and angles, not to mention generous dollops of pitch and roll, these "tribute greens" are a tip of the hat to Ross, whose crowned putting surfaces on No. 2 are the essence of the course. Another Ross trick—creating optical illusions by placing bunkers 20 yards short of a green but making them *appear* greenside—has also been incorporated by

LODGING

There are numerous lodging options at the Pinehurst Resort. The renovated 233-room *Pinehurst Hotel*, where arriving players receive a gracious and cheerful welcome from the bell staff, is a short walk from the main clubhouse serving Courses No. 1 through 5. Rooms are large and comfortable. There's usually a staff pro on hand to host an informal clinic in the evenings in the lobby, one of the sport's choicest gathering spots. Roaming the halls of the hotel is also rewarding. The resort's collection of black-and-white photographs of the game's greats—here a dapper Walter Hagen, there a crew-cut Jack Nicklaus—is on prominent display. Lastly, the hotel's verandah, with its sturdy rockers, is a wonderful place to savor the day's events. Adjacent to the hotel are several four-bedroom villas, while condominium accommodations are also available.

In 1997, the resort acquired the historic *Holly Inn*, a Victorian-era hostelry noted for its curious jumble of gables, dormers, columns, and peaks. Listed on the National Register of Historic Buildings and Sites, the Inn, built by James Tufts in 1895 to resemble grand hotels he had seen as a boy on Cape Cod, is also known for its beautiful gardens, Scottish-style pub, and wraparound veranda. Following a multimillion-dollar restoration, the 86-room Inn reopened in the spring of 1999. Charming and luxurious, it is promoted as the resort's top-of-the-line product.

The Pinehurst Resort also operates a more budget-priced facility, the *Manor Inn*, a pleasant 45-room hotel with a lively watering hole, the remodeled Mulligan's Sports Bar and Grill, which features large-screen TV's, live music on weekends, signature pizzas, and locally brewed ale. There's also a world-class selection of domestic and imported beers.

Among the all-inclusive programs offered by the properties described above is the Pinehurst Putter Boy package, which features two rounds of golf daily with cart, breakfast and dinner, club storage, and range tokens. Because outside play on the resort's eight courses is limited, golfers must stay at one of the resort's properties to be assured of tee times.

Fazio in his design. And something else. The No. 8 Course is not visually intimidating and does not appear difficult on the scorecard. "You'll play it and it won't seem that hard," Fazio explained, "but when you add up your score at the end of the round, it will be difficult to fathom the total."

While No. 2 has no weak holes but no knockouts either, the No. 8 Course has five or six truly memorable golf holes. As with all Fazio layouts, the short par fours on No. 8 possess great charm and naturalness. The 370-yard seventh (only 323 yards from the white tees), offers a broad landing area and a wide but shallow green set well below fairway level. It looks like the kind of hole that can be overpowered, but finesse is required to get the ball close to the hole. And then there's the 358-yard 12th (a scant 320 yards from the white tees), which calls for a well-placed drive to the crest of a hill. The downhill approach is played to a sinuous green framed by the tawny remains of a sand quarry. Because the green

Although golf is the undisputed king at the Pinehurst Resort, there are other activities to pursue. Sailing, fishing, canoeing, and swimming are available at 200-acre Lake Pinehurst. There's an excellent 24-court tennis complex located behind the main golf shop and clubhouse. The Pinehurst Riding Club offers trail rides, hayrides, horsedrawn carriage tours, and instruction. Marksmen gravitate to the Gun Club's trap and skeet fields, where Annie Oakley, star of the Buffalo Bill Wild West Show, once instructed guests in the art of marksmanship. There's also a new fitness center at the resort. Not surprisingly, most of the exercise machines are specifically designed to stretch and strengthen golf muscles.

DINING

The Pinehurst Hotel's elegant *Carolina Dining Room* presents delightful full-course meals in the evening. (The buttermilk-battered Southern fried breast of chicken served with red-eye gravy, sweet potato mousseline, and braised spinach leaves is a signature dish.) Jackets for gentlemen (ties optional) and appropriate evening attire for ladies are required for dinner.

Every golfer should experience at least once the Brobdingnagian breakfast buffet served in the Carolina. Here is everything a golfer could possibly desire for the journey ahead: mountains of fresh fruit; four kinds of fresh-baked muffins; a variety of cereals; custom omelets (the caviar and smoked salmon combo is popular); French toast, Belgian waffles, and pancakes (accompanied by miniature bottles of Pinehurst's own maple syrup); a hot bar with bacon, sausage, hash browns, grits, corned beef hash, creamed chipped beef, biscuits with red-eye gravy, and just about anything else your heart desires. A pianist catches the mood of the day with his melodies.

The Carolina also features an express continental breakfast in the lobby from 6 a.m. to 7 a.m. for players with early tee times.

If you want to rehash the round on the doorstep of the scene, solid pub fare (steak, seafood, pasta) is available at the *Donald Ross Grill* in the golf clubhouse, which has enough memorabilia on display to double as a golf museum. The grill is also open for lunch.

runs diagonally from front left to back right, the approach shot must be delicate—and deadly accurate.

Three of the four par fives on No. 8 are untouchable by mortals from the tips, though the tempting 500-yard 17th can be reached in two shots—if you're willing to throw caution to the winds by flirting with the wetlands that creep into the right side of the fairway near the green. Overshoot the green, and you're faced with a recovery from the deepest, nastiest frog hollow on the course. Like Ross, Fazio believes the real strength of every great course lies in its enjoyment value for every class of golfer, but there's no easy way to play the daunting, uphill par-four 18th, which stretches to 447 yards. After a good drive, players are left with a long approach from a sidehill lie to a large, well-contoured green flanked by bunkers. It's the kind of hole that can unravel a good round in a hurry.

Behind the 18th green is one of the prettiest clubhouses built in the 1990s, a white-columned edifice inspired by the historic centerpiece that anchors the resort's main golf center. There's also a large, inviting practice area at No. 8. Perhaps best of all, management has seen fit to create an unsullied, contained golf experience, with only a smattering of homes on the periphery of the course. For using natural resources without depleting them in ways that support human activity, No. 8 was named an Audubon International Signature Sanctuary in 1998.

More Golf/Pinehurst

You can spend a week at the Pinehurst Resort and not play every course. But you can sure try.

No. 2 has grabbed all the headlines, but the resort's refurbishment of the *No. 1 Course* also qualifies as a success story. First opened as a nine-hole spread in 1898—"60 acres of thoroughly cleared land, well fenced in and covered with a thick growth of rye, which will be kept short by a flock of more than 100 sheep" was how the *Pinehurst Outlook* described the fledgling links—No. 1 was expanded to 18 holes the following year. The course was later formalized and reworked by Donald Ross. Through the years, the rap on No. 1 was that it was too short to interest the serious player. A renovation completed in 1998 greatly improved the layout. According to Lew Ferguson, director of golf operations, "Some of the best holes in Moore County are on that golf course. It's going to challenge good players who walk out there thinking No. 1 is a pushover."

The *No. 3 Course*, a Donald Ross design dating to 1907, is the resort's shortest and perhaps easiest course, with small, crowned greens throughout, but the integrity of the layout has been nearly ruined by intrusive fairway condos built by previous owners in the 1970s.

The *No. 4 Course*, originating in 1919 as a Donald Ross design and significantly altered over the years, was redesigned and rebuilt from scratch by Tom Fazio in 1998. The layout, billed by management as "a contemporary course in a traditional setting," is scheduled to open in fall, 1999.

The *No. 5 Course*, built by Ellis Maples in 1961 and later reworked by Robert Trent Jones, is the most watery of the Pinehurst layouts. The par-three 15th, known as the "Cathedral Hole," features a water-guarded green backdropped by tall pines and, in the spring, flowering dogwoods. It is the single prettiest hole at Pinehurst, though like No. 3, the No. 5 Course was permanently marred by an aggressive housing development in the 1970s.

Designed by George and Tom Fazio, the *No. 6 Course*, located three miles from the resort hotel, had the reputation as a brutal test that took no prisoners. Tom Fazio returned in 1990 to bring the black sheep of the Pinehurst family back into the fold, softening mounds, enlarging greens, and widening the fairways of this rugged, hilly layout. Despite its enhanced playability, the quartet of par fives on No. 6 remains very robust. The incoming nine, routed on heaving terrain, offers a memorable stretch of scenic, challenging golf.

LODGING

With 10 rustic, Swiss-style lodges serving a maximum of 142 guests (there are no local members), Pine Needles is never crowded and offers the promise of a brisk round free of delays. The resort's all-inclusive Donald Ross Package features accommodations, breakfast and dinner daily, and unlimited green fees at Pine Needles as well as its sister property, *Mid Pines Inn & Golf Club*, located directly across the street. The cooperative package,

Mid Pines Inn & Golf Club

which enables guests at either property to play both courses, represents very good value. Carts are extra, but walking is encouraged.

Mid Pines, a vintage Donald Ross design circa 1921, is virtually unchanged from the original. Hillier than most Pinehurst-area layouts, this 6,515-yard gem places a premium on accuracy. Approach shots are played from sloping fairways to crowned greens framed by sand and grassy knolls. Where Pine Needles is graceful and flowing, Mid Pines, beautifully restored by the Bell family and their partners in the mid-1990s, is more rugged and demanding owing to its tighter corridors and tinier greens. It is an exceptionally attractive course in spring, when the dogwoods bloom.

The Georgian-style hotel at Mid Pines, many of its redecorated rooms overlooking the 18th green, is quite comfortable. There are also golf villas available beside the 10th fairway. At Pine Needles, the updated cottages are more basic but entirely suitable for foursomes and eightsomes who wish to socialize at day's end in a friendly, informal setting. Also, the bar at Pine Needles is one of the best 19th holes in the sport.

Golfers at the Pine Needles Course

Renowned teacher Peggy Kirk Bell, one of the most influential women in golf and recipient of the USGA's Bobby Jones Sportsmanship Award for her contributions to the game, leads what she calls a "Golfari" for women at Pine Needles, typically in three separate sessions each spring. First begun in 1969, the resort's Golfari is now a trademarked name for four or five days of golf saturation, described by the resort as "an expedition to Pine Needles for golfers to have fun while learning to improve their golf games." These women-only sessions, led by Bell herself, are enormously popular. A typical day consists of individual instruction according to skill level in the morning, afternoon golf (alternated daily with golf instruction), and a golf or instructional movie after dinner. In the event of rain, instruction continues in special indoor facilities.

Pine Needles Lodge & Golf Club, Southern Pines, North Carolina

Pine Needles Course, third hole

Pine Needles Course, 15ᵗʰ hole

More Golf/Sandhills

Because of the sheer volume and overall excellence of its courses, Pinehurst Resort & Country Club tends to garner most of the attention directed to the Sandhills region. But it's by no means the only game in town. Four miles up the road from the village of Pinehurst is Southern Pines, a sleepy township more indicative of what the area was like in the days before graphite shafts and cut-proof balls. In other words, less commercial.

There are trendier resorts nationwide, many with spiffier accommoda-

tions and snazzier entrees on their dinner menus, but few golf resorts in the modern age function as a golf *retreat*, a hideaway where enthusiasts can take time to relax and savor the game before, during, and after the round. At the **Pine Needles Lodge & Golf Club** (#31), the clocks are stopped sometime in the mid-1950s, when Peggy Kirk Bell, one of the founding members of the LPGA Tour, and her late husband, Warren "Bullet" Bell, built their alpine-flavored hostlery on the doorstep of a picture-perfect resort layout.

Pine Needles Course, 14th hole

Pine Needles Course, 16th hole

In addition to horsedrawn carriage tours of the charming village of Pinehurst, a driving tour of the region's Thoroughbred horse farms and fox hunting country can be arranged. Twenty minutes north of Pinehurst is *Cameron*, its well-preserved buildings dating from 1875 through the early 1920s and housing antique shops that carry everything from fine English furniture to antique glassware. Stop for lunch at Miss Belle's Tea Room or the Dewberry Deli, where dewberry cobbler is the dessert of choice. In nearby *Seagrove* more than 80 potteries can be found. (European potters first settled in the Moore County area adjacent to Seagrove more than 200 years ago because clay is plentiful. These folks know how to throw a pot. Many allow visitors to watch them at work.) Three miles from Pinehurst is *Midland Crafter's Gallery*, a charming shopping complex filled with one-of-a-kind pieces by North Carolina artisans as well as jewelry, paintings, toys, and ornaments. Like to walk? Go for a stroll along the beautifully laid-out paths at *Weymouth Woods*; or explore the horticultural gardens designed and maintained by *Sandhills Community College*. Rainy day? Visit the *Tufts Archives* in the *Given Memorial Library* in the village to catch a glimpse of what life was like in the early years of Pinehurst.

Of the hundreds of courses laid out by Donald Ross (including seven in the Pinehurst area alone), the prolific designer pointed to Pine Needles, completed in 1927, as his personal favorite. It was the course he most enjoyed playing in later years when Pinehurst No. 2 was beyond his abilities. Easy to see why. Endowed with near-perfect terrain, Ross conjured a rolling, tree-lined layout with generous fairway undulations as well as a good mix of crowned greens, strategic bunkering, even a few blind shots. Untouched except for agronomic improvements and the rearrangement of a few holes when new lodges were built in the 1950s, Pine Needles received the national exposure it richly deserved when it hosted the 1996 U.S. Women's Open. Defending champion Annika Sorenstam's eight-under-par total of 272 provided a six-stroke margin of victory over runner-up Kris Tschetter. Despite the ideal weather and flawless playing conditions, they were the only two players in the field to better par during the championship, a tribute to the enduring quality of the layout. So popular was Pine Needles as an Open venue, the USGA returns the most prestigious event in women's golf to this classic Ross course in 2001.

What makes this very pleasant but seemingly innocuous layout so good? There are, after all, a scant 42 bunkers and three relatively tame water hazards in the routing. The back tees stretch to a modest 6,708 yards (par is 71). None of the par fives exceeds 500 yards from the tips. Fairway corridors are generously wide. But like so many Ross courses, the "Needles" calls for inspired play around the slick, inverted saucer greens, greens that year-in, year-out are groomed to perfection. Miss a green, and you're asked to manufacture the cleverest chip, most delicate pitch, or greatest flop shot you've ever hit to get close to the hole. Otherwise, it's another bogey.

Play commences with a straightforward par five that parallels the extensive practice area before confronting players with the toughest hole on the course, the 451-yard second. Here the drive must be essayed to a plateau, while the approach must find and hold a well-bunkered green set below the fairway. The 134-yard third, one of the sweetest par threes in the South, plays from an elevated tee over a small lake to a deep, kidney-shaped green staked out by five bunkers. Towering pines and an understory of dogwoods backdrop the green, which slopes sharply from back to front. Par is a major accomplishment if you miss the green—or leave your tee shot above the pin.

The other par threes at Pine Needles are every bit as impressive as the third. At the sturdy fifth, 207 yards from the gold tees, the tee shot must carry a deep chasm to reach the plateau green. The gorgeous 13th plays 189 yards downhill to a slippery green embraced by elongated bunkers, while the 177-yard 16th parades golfers through a broad avenue of pines to a good-size putting surface. The 18th is a great finishing hole, perhaps the best in the region. This 426-yard par four (400 yards from the white tees) calls for a blind drive over the crest of a hill, followed by a long downhill approach shot (often from a hanging lie) to a well-guarded green nestled below the resort complex.

Pinehurst Plantation Golf Club, Pinehurst, North Carolina, 18th hole

Midway between Pinehurst and Southern Pines is the sleeper course of the Sandhills, **Pinehurst Plantation Golf Club** (#92). An Arnold Palmer–Ed Seay design opened in 1993, this semiprivate club offers an appealing blend of traditional and modern design styles. A real estate venture where lots are sold to prospective members, the club welcomes outside play on a limited basis.

The layout's strong suit is its versatility. Based on the tees selected, Pinehurst Plantation can be a bear or a lamb. From the Palmer tees at 7,135 yards, this is one of the longest and strongest tests of golf in town, if not the entire state. However, multiple sets of forward tees offer a good variety of manageable challenges. Of all the "Top 100" courses in Pinehurst, the Plantation's Club tees at 6,011 yards promise one of the milder and more agreeable tests of golf to the higher handicapper.

Routed on generously rolling terrain, with five water features in play, the course comes alive on the back nine. The quartet of finishing holes showcases the layout's distinctive risk-reward scenarios. The 15th is a short par five that dares players to flirt with the water and sand to the left of the green, while the 16th, a par four stretching to 400 yards, has water in play on both the drive and the approach. The 17th is a long par three with a tilted, well-bunkered green for a target, while the 18th is a true championship par four of 445 yards from the Palmer tees (and a sporty two-shotter from the Club tees at 365 yards). The hole angles to the right and calls for a carry over water to a giant hourglass-shaped green it shares with the ninth hole.

Golf packages featuring Pinehurst Plantation are available through several area hotels, including the 12-room *Magnolia Inn*, the second oldest (1895) building in Pinehurst and a delightful family-run hostelry noted for its fine cuisine (the rack of lamb is outstanding). The *Pine Crest Inn*, a legendary establishment (see below), also features Pinehurst Plantation in its golf packages.

The venerable Pine Crest Inn, built in 1913 and owned by Donald Ross for 27 years until his death in 1948 (there's a portrait of the Scotsman behind the front desk), is one of the coziest places to hang your hat in all of golfdom. Not that it's fancy. It's not. In fact, the floorboards creak and the carpets are faded, but the orange juice is fresh, the mattresses are firm, and the kitchen is good. (The Inn's chef, Carl Jackson, has been perfecting his classic Southern dishes for over *60 years*. The braised pork chops and

Lobby area at the Pine Crest Inn

The Crystal Room at the Pine Crest Inn

roast duckling served in the Crystal Room are recommended). Best of all, there is room enough on the front porch to demonstrate a proper takeaway to interested onlookers. On cool nights, the Pine Crest offers "lobby chipping" to a covered plywood platform with a hole cut in its center at night. It's an amusing post-round diversion.

Even if you don't stay at the Pine Crest, as Jack Nicklaus did in the days he played in the North and South Amateur held on Pinehurst No. 2, no visit to Pinehurst is complete without a visit to the Inn's bar, Mr. B's Lounge. The watering hole of choice for locals and in-the-know pilgrims, this is *the* place to talk golf in Pinehurst. A resident pianist performs in the lobby most nights and knows every great sing-along tune ever written (and then some). As a place to have a few laughs, harmonize (on or off key), and even pick up a few swing tips, the homey Pine Crest Inn is in a class of its own.

North Carolina Mountains

As a backdrop for the game, the Great Smoky Mountains in western North Carolina rival any in the nation. A branch of the Appalachians, the Smokies are not only the oldest mountains in America, they are among the most dramatic, their hulking, rounded peaks usually veiled in blue "smoke" (a mixture of water vapor and plant-secreted oils). This lovely, rugged area, anchored by Great Smoky Mountains National Park, the nation's most-visited national park, is bisected by the Blue Ridge Parkway, which winds 469 miles through the southern Appalachians and passes through all five counties in the North Carolina High Country. It is, by popular consent, one of the most scenic roads in America. It will remain

so, too. A "ridge law" passed by the state legislature in 1983 forbids the disruption of the famous skyline by man-made developments.

Donald Ross, the ubiquitous Scotsman, laid out several of the region's finest courses, including **Linville Golf Club** (#25), a masterpiece routed in the shadow of Grandfather Mountain. Ross's participation, while limited, was more than sufficient. He led a team of surveyors into deep woods and rhododendron thickets for only two days of work, later supplying the plans for the course from his office in Pinehurst. When the holes were routed, they fit the topography hand-in-glove.

With its slick elevated greens, tight twisting fairways, and meandering Grandmother's Creek in play at 10 holes, this 6,286-yard charmer (the

Linville Golf Club, Linville, North Carolina, eleventh hole

LODGING

Linville is a private club that welcomes guests of the adjoining *Eseeola Lodge*, a bark-clad 29-room inn listed in the National Register of Historic Places. Each guest room offers a little mountain history along with hand-made quilts and authentic antiques. Like the golf course, the lodge fits in perfectly with its surroundings. Breakfast and dinner are included in the room tariff, a terrific value considering the quality of the meals. The blueberry pancakes and hearty omelets are irresistible at breakfast, while the well-paced five-course meals served at dinner (coats and ties required) are superb.

In addition to golf at Linville, Eseeola Lodge guests can hike, bike, and sightsee throughout the High Country. There's also excellent trout fishing in area streams. Antiques and native crafts are available in nearby shops. Nightlife is virtually nonexistent: it's an "early to bed, early to rise" kind of place designed for pure relaxation.

Golf packages are offered during the week in the spring and fall. (Summer lodgings are booked long in advance.) May and June bring a riot of dogwood, apple, and volleyball-size rhododendron blossoms. Autumn's blaze of fall foliage is breathtaking.

Eseeola Lodge, Linville, North Carolina

In Asheville, the 250-room, 100,000-acre *Biltmore Estate*, completed in 1895, remains the nation's largest private residence and is open for tours. It took 1,000 men five years to complete the mammoth project. Priceless antiques and works of art collected by the Vanderbilt family are on display. The grounds, landscaped by Frederick Law Olmsted, include 75 acres of formal gardens as well as extensive vineyards. With the exception of San Simeon, the Hearst castle in California, there is nothing to rival Biltmore in America. It is truly a sight to behold, especially in spring, when the flowers are in bloom.

Like the auditory thrill of falling water? South of Asheville is *Transylvania County* ("trans" for across, "sylvania" for the woods), where you can glory in the discovery of more than 250 cataracts. There's Looking Glass Falls, Slippery Witch Falls, Horsepasture Falls, Turtleback Falls, Whitewater Falls, Rainbow Falls, and, most especially, *Sliding Rock*, where thrillseekers can suit up and ride down a 150-foot natural water slide. (About 11,000 gallons of 50- to 60-degree water flow over this mammoth rock every minute). Several of the waterfalls can be reached by traveling North Carolina's Forest Heritage National Scenic Byway, a 79-mile stretch that loops through the Pisgah National Forest in Transylvania and Harwood counties. Portions of the byway, dedicated in 1989, wind through old settlement roads and logging towns. Also, pack a pair of sturdy hiking shoes—there are nearly 500 winding miles of scenic trails to enjoy in the region, many of them skirting rivers and streams.

"Long Course" measures 6,780 yards) offers a firm, fair, and aesthetically pleasing test. In the words of *GOLF Magazine* correspondent Lee Pace, "For older golfers, Linville is a time capsule. For younger ones, it's a history lesson." The immortal Bobby Jones was so enamored of the course that he often made the long overland journey from Atlanta to play Linville. (A number of Augusta National members repair to Linville each summer to seek respite from the searing heat in the lowlands.)

Routed on the floor and etched into the sidewalls of a mountain valley at 3,800 feet, Linville presents shotmakers with an endless variety of uphill, downhill, and sidehill lies. The canted terrain, ranging from subtle to severe, literally keeps golfers off balance from start to finish. As for Linville's tiny greens, they're domed, interwoven with subtle contours, and as fast as greased lightning. As on all Ross courses, there is plenty of room to drive the ball at Linville. Problems arise when approach shots go astray, leaving delicate pitches and chips to the slippery, crested greens.

Except for the charming cottages in view on the first and second holes, players are free from the reminders of civilization until they glimpse the stately Tudor facade of Linville's clubhouse from the 18th fairway. Along the way are a brace of memorable golf holes crafted by Nature and refined by Ross. At the head of the class is the par-four third, which calls for a carry over water on the drive and a second carry over a creek to an elevated green that repels all but the truest shots. The collection of one-shotters at Linville is exceptional, while the view from the lofty tee at the par-four 11th—a broad, beckoning fairway crossed by a brook in the far distance—is postcard material.

Golf carts are mandatory at Linville, but with several cart paths tunneled through dense thickets of foliage, the course is a joy to ride.

New & Noteworthy/North Carolina

Mike Strantz, who works very selectively, has authored a pair of courses in North Carolina well worth finding. About 20 miles north of Pinehurst in Sanford, Strantz has built a housing-free layout called *Tobacco Road*, its holes routed among sandy hills covered with scrubby pines. There's a 70-foot elevation change on site. Strantz called Tobacco Road, which opened late in 1998, "the best project I've ever worked on."

In Ashborough, south of Greensboro, is *Tot Hill Farm*, where Strantz had giant rocks, natural waterfalls, and a dizzying 250-foot elevation change at his disposal. The family-owned facility, which has limited housing in the hills above the course, will be unveiled in 2000.

Blue Ridge Parkway, North Carolina

South Carolina

The Low Country

Low Country native Pat Conroy, author of *The Prince of Tides,* has this to say about his homeland: "The island country where I grew up was a fertile, semitropical archipelago that gradually softened up the ocean for the grand surprise of the continent that followed." Because of their geographical uniqueness, the "Top 100" courses occupying this aqueous terrain are very special.

Kiawah Island, a barrier reef island 21 miles south of Charleston, was already a well-established Low Country destination before the arrival of the 1991 Ryder Cup Matches. However, the gut-wrenching drama of the "War by the Shore," as the event came to be known, ensured that Kiawah will forever be associated with the rousing, tearful U.S. victory—and with a course that brought many of the contestants to their knees. Designated the Ryder Cup venue before ground was broken, the **Ocean Course** (#10) at **Kiawah Island Golf & Tennis Resort** fully justifies the PGA of America's confidence in Pete Dye's ability to conjure a masterful, memorable test from a 2½-mile stretch of scrub-covered dunes and salt marsh.

Kiawah Island Golf & Tennis Resort, South Carolina, Ocean Course, 17th green

Kiawah Island, Ocean Course, fifth hole

"No one in America has ever had a site to compare with this one," Dye said before moving to Kiawah to supervise construction of his newfangled links. Dye made the most of his opportunity, and he did it his way.

Unlike genuine British links courses that weave through protective dunes and trace the natural contours of the surrounding terrain, Dye bull-dozed more than a million cubic yards of sand and muck to elevate the layout's tees, fairways, and greens well above sea level, thereby exposing the holes to the wind. The gargantuan layout is propped on top of facsimile dunes manufactured from fill, their contours, according to *GOLF Magazine* contributing editor Tom Doak, designed so that "drainage water generated by the course could be recycled into a central pond, protecting the surrounding marshes from contamination." Dye is the first to admit that he created everything on site, including 22 acres of new wetlands. "If people want to call this course artificial, they are absolutely right. It is completely artificial." In the designer's defense, Ryder Cup member Ray Floyd said before the 1991 matches, "The greatest tribute to Pete is that the whole course looks like it's been there for years. I think it's as fine a golf course as you could ever want. It just flows. Even though it was done with a bulldozer, it's a course that looks like it was done by nature." Call it the most convincing piece of legerdemain in the South. Call it also the leviathan of the Low Country.

Exceptionally well-balanced, the layout's figure-eight routing has the same par configuration on both nines. Ten holes (the closing five on both the outward and inward halves) parallel the shore and are within earshot of the pounding surf. There's an ocean view from the other eight holes as well. Best of all, there are no condos or homes to intrude upon the golf-at-the-beach experience. Because of the sensitive nature of the site (and the lack of terra firma surrounding it), there never will be a housing subdivision at the Ocean Course.

SIDETRIPS

Kiawah and Wild Dunes are both convenient to historic *Charleston*, a well-preserved colonial port city. A sightseeing walk or horse-drawn carriage tour of the city's Historic District (antebellum Georgian mansions graced by wraparound piazzas, ornamental ironwork, and formal gardens) is a must. Civil War buffs should make a beeline for *Fort Sumter National Monument*, a man-made island in the city harbor where the first shots of the Civil War were fired on April 12, 1861. The restored fort, open for free tours, houses a museum. Interested in an "eerie journey into Charles Towne's haunted past"? The city's ghastly cast of pirates, murderers, and restless spirits are the focus of nocturnal *Ghost Walk* tours that depart from the courtyard of The Mills House Hotel Monday through Saturday at 5 p.m.

Horsedrawn carriage in Charleston's Historic District

LODGING

In addition to one- to five-bedroom villas and private homes contained in two resort villages on the island, the big news at Kiawah is the luxurious 310-room hotel complex scheduled to open in 1999. Interior decor was inspired by design found in the British West Indies, while guest rooms have marble bathrooms and French doors opening onto large balconies. The 65-foot-high ceiling in the lobby offers a spectacular ocean view. This low-key island resort finally has lodgings to match the exceptional quality of its golf courses.

Kiawah Island Golf & Tennis Resort, 14th hole

Mindful of the incessant coastal winds, Dye created plenty of room to drive the ball on the Ocean Course—fairways are up to 60 yards wide. The approach shot, however, must be spot on. Or else. The crowned, pulpit greens, several of them projected well above fairway level, will repel all but the truest shots. Dye left most of the greens open in front, so that low-running shots can be played into them, though it should be noted that the thick-bladed grass on the Ocean Course is a very distant cousin to the fine-bladed fescues that thrive in Britain and encourage the ball to scurry along the ground. Offline approach shots, which are the only kind average players tend to hit in the wind, generally find trouble on this fearsome links. What's trouble? Sea oats and beach grass, loose sand and tidal muck. On the plus side, there are no bunkers per se on the Ocean Course. All sand is contained in "waste areas," where the club may be grounded.

The front nine tiptoes through a marsh, while the back nine traverses an artificially raised sand bank. Among the most visually striking holes is the par-five second, which skirts wetlands and a smattering of wind-twisted oaks. The drive must carry over the marsh (the fairway is far more commodious than it appears, a sleight-of-hand trick), while the approach shot must clear boggy ground to reach an inverted saucer of a green that falls away on all sides.

Another standout is the 14th, a dramatic one-shotter with a spectacular view of the ocean behind the green. Swirling winds ensure the hole never plays the same way twice. Dye himself noted that five strong par fours (4, 6, 9, 12, and 18) are balanced by five relatively short par fours (1, 3, 10, 13, and 15). The par threes are splendid (although other adjectives have been applied to the 17th, which calls for a forced carry over water), while the par fives are exceedingly well-defended.

While intended to give good players more golf course than they can chew, Dye claims that "in no way has the design of the Ocean Course been meant to test only the pros." He added: "If handicap players stick to a yardage they can handle, they will enjoy playing here." But not every day. On a windy day, which is just about every day on Kiawah Island, the regular tees at 6,031 yards will suffice for most players, according to 1991 Ryder Cup captain Dave Stockton, who greatly admires the course. Even sunny optimists with low handicaps usually come undone from the championship tees at 6,552 yards. The current back tees are listed at 7,296 yards, but no one plays them. No one can. That's because the Ocean Course isn't just another test of golf. It's Turfgrass in Chains.

In the wake of the Ryder Cup, Dye's dunescape has become the Holy Grail for a certain kind of player bristling for a chance to slay the dragon. Needless to say, the dragon is usually full of fire at day's end, while most players end up dazed and wind-burned.

The entire back wall of the Ocean Course clubhouse is glass, affording players who arrive for breakfast or lunch a spectacular view of the links and the ocean. In addition, the practice facility, in view of the sea, is exceptional. Walkers are welcome at the Ocean Course.

Much like the fastest roller coaster at an amusement park, there's a surcharge to play the Ocean Course.

More Golf / Kiawah

Kiawah's other courses are uniformly excellent and, after a windblown tour of the Ocean Course, refreshingly normal. For starters, there's *Turtle Point*, a low-profile, understated layout by Jack Nicklaus that winds through a maritime forest for 13 holes, then brings players to the brink of the sea at holes 14, 15, and 16 before turning inland at the finish.

Osprey Point, a gorgeous Tom Fazio–designed track built around impounded lakes, lagoons, and brackish marshland, brings water into play at 15 holes, but it's not overly penal from the regular tees. The 6,678-yard layout is anchored by a gorgeous clubhouse.

Cougar Point, formerly Marsh Point, was the weak link in the resort's line-up of layouts until it was completely reworked by the Gary Player Design Group and reopened in 1996. It is now in demand by aces and duffers alike.

On Johns Island at Kiawah's doorstep, is *Oak Point*, an appealing track added to the resort's roster in 1997. Nestled between marshlands and a live oak forest, this Clyde Johnston–designed course features a scenic finish along the Kiawah River, where bald eagles are known to nest.

Wild Dunes

In the late 1970s, developer Raymon R. Finch, Jr., who had acquired a 1,600-acre parcel of land on the tip of Isle of Palms a few causeways east of Charleston, called Tom Fazio with an offer. "Tom, a thousand dollars says I've got the best site made available for a golf course in the last 30 years," Finch told Fazio, who at the time was working under the tutelage

of his uncle, George Fazio. After flying in the 34-year-old designer, Finch, a persuasive mover and shaker who had once run for Governor of South Carolina, took young Tom on a tour of the site's mile-long, 50-foot-high dune ridge, which was created by a prehistoric hurricane. They also passed by gentler oceanside dunes and low thickets of vegetation surrounding tidal inlets and salt marsh. The story goes that after the tour, Fazio wrote Finch a check for $1,000—and signed on to build the course that would launch his solo career.

The **Links Course** (#32), as it's now known, opened to immediate acclaim in 1980. Unlike most other courses occupying flat, featureless terrain in the Carolina Low Country, the Links had a generous change of elevation as well as the kinds of natural hillocks and swales common to links courses in Britain. Fazio's inaugural effort was not only a tactician's delight where finesse and accuracy (not mindless power) were required to score, it was never the same layout twice because of the wind.

All was peace and prosperity at Wild Dunes until a fateful day in September 1989, when Hurricane Hugo laid waste the resort. Not only were the two oceanside holes on the Links—17 and 18—rent asunder by the terrible storm, but the marina, most resort structures, 80 golf carts, $100,000 worth of pro shop inventory, and 1,200 trees were demolished. Wild Dunes simply was no more.

But, like the reconstruction of the South following the Civil War, the resort slowly rebuilt itself. With Fazio providing (gratis) architectural direction, the two ocean holes, both severely damaged, were rebuilt and actually improved. At the par-four 17th, the sand heaped up on shore by the storm was used to shape mounds down the left side of the hole (they were kept low enough to give players a good view of the ocean). At the colossal par-five 18th, the hole length was shortened from 540 yards to 501 yards from the blue tees to tempt go-for-broke gamblers to try for the green in two. The boomerang-shaped hole, which skirts the seashore, was felicitously altered by the storm: The beach is now in play in the elbow of the dogleg.

Fortunately, the ancient live oak that stands sentinel along the right side of the 14th fairway survived the wrath of the storm (it figured prominently in Edgar Allan Poe's short story "The Gold Bug"), but many more oaks and pines were torn from the ground or utterly denuded of their vegetation by the hurricane. Still, many of these trees had begun to encroach

LODGING

Accommodations at Wild Dunes include rooms and suites, one- to three-bedroom villas, and four- to six-bedroom homes, all with a variety of ocean, golf, tennis court, lagoon, and marsh views. In addition, the resort opened The Boardwalk Inn, a 93-room seaside hotel, in late 1997. Inspired by old Charleston architecture, the five-story inn is accented by wicker rocking chairs on its broad veranda. Al fresco dining is available in The Grill.

on play, and Hugo served to open up several holes that had become claustrophobic. The Links, at 6,772 yards from the blue tees (6,131 yards from the whites), is today breezier and better-conditioned than the original edition, with more room for recovery shots.

The only fly in the ointment at this reclaimed treasure is the chock-ablock development flanking many of the fairways. The frame of housing around the Links infringes upon the beautiful landscape it contains.

Players who can telescope their vision to some of the best golf holes Fazio ever designed will fully enjoy the magnificent challenge posed by the Links. This is especially true if you choose to walk. Two years after initiating a "walk-anytime" policy on the Links in 1994, Wild Dunes followed up with a caddy program. The caddies, most of them area college students available on weekends, are well-versed in the nuances of the Links.

More Golf / Wild Dunes

Another consequence of Hurricane Hugo's stormy match with Wild Dunes was the complete remaking of the Fazio-designed *Harbor Course*, which was transformed from a long, schizophrenic layout with great disparity between the front and back nines into an appealing 6,446-yard, par-70 layout (5,900 yards from the white tees) with *six* par threes in the routing. A target-style design with water and/or marsh in play on 17 holes, the Harbor Course gives shotmakers all they can handle on a windy day. With nine holes routed alongside the Intracoastal Waterway and two holes (16 and 17) that play from one island to another across Morgan Creek, the Harbor Course is both scenic and challenging.

More Golf / Charleston

In addition to the fine courses at Kiawah and Wild Dunes, several excellent daily-fee courses can be found north of Charleston. *Charleston National*, conceived as an ultra-private club, resurfaced as a top daily-fee course after its destruction by Hurricane Hugo. Seven miles of cart paths and numerous bridges link the five islands on which the breezy links,

DINING

A culinary capital, Charleston has dozens of distinctive restaurants. *Vickery's* has "Cajun popcorn" (crawfish tails), thick pork chops on mashed potatoes, and indoor-outdoor seating. *Slightly North of Broad*, a self-described "Maverick Southern Kitchen," is renowned for its chunky jambalaya. *82 Queen*, occupying a refurbished carriage house and two restored 18th-century townhouses between King and Meeting streets, has seven dining rooms adjoined by an open-air courtyard. Locals and visitors alike go for eclectic Low Country cuisine with wines to match. At *Carolina's*, black, white, and peach bistro decor as well as late-night "appeteasers" such as crawfish and *tasso* (spiced ham) draw diners, while *Magnolias*, occupying an 1823 warehouse, turns out superb Low Country fare, including shrimp and sausage over grits. *Saracen*, located in what was once the Farmers and Exchange Bank of 1853, is also recommended. If you won the bet for dinner, Charleston's top choices for fine dining include *Anson* (try the cashew-crusted grouper with champagne sauce), *Restaurant Million*, and the *Peninsula Grill* in the historic Planters Inn. Something more basic? *Southend Brewery & Smokehouse* has hand-crafted beers, oven-baked pizza, and live entertainment. *Sticky Fingers* (three locations) has unbelievable ribs and pork barbecue. *Wild Wing Cafe* has chicken wings in 21 flavors.

Uplifted by your day on the links? The downtown market area adjacent to Meeting and King streets comes alive after dark with cafés, bars, and clubs.

Wild Dunes Resort, Isle of Palms, South Carolina, Links Course, tenth hole

OFF THE COURSE

The resort maintains a full-service marina located on the Intra-coastal Waterway, offers 2.5 miles of white sandy beaches, and operates a complimentary family recreation program in summer (day-long supervised kids camp, beach and pool activities, etc.) regarded as one of the best in the country. Wild Dunes also conducts two- and three-day Junior Golf Schools for players ages 8–18 in the summer. If tennis is also your game, you'll like Wild Dunes. The property's Tennis Center, with 17 Har-Tru courts, is ranked among the top 50 tennis resorts in the United States by *Tennis* magazine.

bounded by marshes and the Intracoastal Waterway, is routed. Rees Jones, the course designer, noted that while the hurricane destroyed the frame of the layout, the holes survived. *Dunes West*, a semi-private course built on the site of an antebellum plantation, has huge greens, nice marsh views, and a tidal creek in play on its closing holes. *Coosaw Creek* features a gently rolling course by Arthur Hills cut from wetlands and a maritime forest where accuracy is the first order of business. *Crowfield Golf & Country Club*, a bold, burly layout with mounded fairways and large rolling greens, is one of the region's longest courses at 7,001 yards from the tips. *Legend Oaks Plantation* is a traditional, rolling test carved from tall pines, cypress swamp and giant live oaks draped with Spanish moss. Arguably the prettiest course north of Charleston, Legend Oaks sports a devilish semi-island green at par-three 17th.

Wild Dunes Resort, Links Course, 17th hole

Hilton Head Island

At the southern tip of Hilton Head Island, within Sea Pines Resort, Pete Dye and design consultant Jack Nicklaus set to work in the late 1960s to carve a shotmaker's course from moss-draped oaks and towering pines. They wanted to test a player's accuracy, mettle, and ability to think a situation through before pulling the trigger. Railroad ties, cypress planks, and sawn-off telephone poles were used to fortify bunkers and define lagoons on this prototype links. These soon became Dye's trademarks.

Immediately recognizable by the 90-foot-high, candy cane–striped lighthouse rising behind the 18th green, **Harbour Town Golf Links** (#9) is a seminal layout that changed the direction of golf course architecture in America. Previously, long courses punctuated by big greens emphasized the power game. Harbour Town was the antithesis of that style. With the blessing of visionary developer Charles Fraser, Dye and Nicklaus conjured a quirky, low-profile layout hemmed in by lagoons, salt

79

Yacht Basin at Hilton Head, South Carolina

marshes, and trees. Lots of trees. If you aren't exceedingly accurate, you can expect to spend a good portion of the round maneuvering under, over, and around the boughs and limbs of magnolias, pines, and oaks. Unless, of course, you carry a chainsaw as a 15th club.

Opened just in time to host the inaugural Heritage (now MCI) Classic in 1969, captured in exciting fashion by Arnold Palmer, the links has won rave reviews ever since. (*Sports Illustrated* magazine called it "nothing short of a work of art" shortly after its debut).

Harbour Town is an exceptionally well-balanced golf course. There are four long par fours (including the fearsome 18th, which measures 458 yards from the *white* tees) requiring long approaches to tightly guarded greens. The ninth and 13th are petite par fours that demand pinpoint accuracy off the tee. The first pair of par fives can be reached with two perfect shots, but the burly 15th, one of the nation's finest strategic par fives, is a true three-shotter. The highest praise is reserved for Harbour Town's quartet of par threes, each a watery terror from the white markers. Not one offers the slightest margin for error, yet all are fair.

Harbour Town's built-to-grade, fairway-level greens, patterned after those of a seaside links, range in size from small to tiny. Long putts are rare. Says Dye, "Something that makes a golfer chip with finesse is a lot more interesting to him than a 95-foot putt." These wafer-like greens, the tamest Dye ever built, are also rather flat. Getting to them without suffering a severe case of claustrophobia is the order of the day.

Some words of advice from Cary Corbitt, Harbour Town's long-time director of golf: "Unless you carry a handicap of five or better, stick to the white tees at 6,119 yards." From the Heritage tees at 6,916 yards, Harbour Town is a demanding test of pinpoint accuracy and uncommon finesse that calls for every shot in the bag—and then some. (The red tees, placed by Alice Dye, Pete's wife, measure 5,019 yards and are readily manageable by most women.)

Regardless of handicap, first-timers should study the yardage book carefully to see which side of the fairway sets up the best angle of attack on each par four and five. Despite a recent tree-pruning program, it's perfectly possible to hit the fairway and be faced with a semiobstructed approach shot at Harbour Town.

Power hitters who tend to stray are in for a long day on this tree-lined links, because any ball that isn't hit to the proper spot will find trouble. There simply is no way to conquer Harbour Town by swinging from the heels. In fact, no championship course in America defuses the power game faster than this seemingly innocuous lowland links. Harbour Town is

For those seeking a discounted rate at Harbour Town, *Sea Pines Resort* offers over 550 one- to four-bedroom villas with kitchens, living and dining areas, and balconies or patios. A partnership between the Low Country Golf Course Owners Association and the Hilton Head Island Visitor & Convention Bureau has led to the all-inclusive packaging of golf vacations. Accommodations in the program range from top resort hotels (Westin, Hyatt Regency, Hilton) to mid-priced properties. Budget motels are also available on the island. Villa rentals enable families—or foursomes—to stretch out in spacious home-style comfort. For golfers, spring and fall are the best times to visit—summers can be hot and sticky. The winter months are value-priced and appeal to golfers who don't mind playing in a sweater (the average daily high in February is 62 degrees). Sea Pines and other resorts on Hilton Head "transition" (aerate greens and fairways) in June, a month to be avoided.

Penthouse at Sea Pines Resort

a placement course, pure and simple. At hole after hole, the ball must be safely threaded down a narrow corridor and a crisp iron shot played to a waferlike green. Leave the driver in the bag (or, better, in the trunk of your car) if you're wild off the tee.

The 17th and 18th holes at Harbour Town deserve a closer look. Both are exceptionally challenging, and at both players can hear the distant sounds of boat horns and whistles in Calibogue (pronounced, appropriately, Cal-i-BOGEY) Sound. The 17th, one of the most beguiling par threes in the game, measures only 161 yards from the white tees, but what a nerveless shot must be played to reach the green! The wind, invariably, is in the player's face, and the tee shot must carry water for most of its journey and hold a kidney-shaped green fronted by a sinuous, 90-yard-long bunker planked with wood that forms a line of demarcation

between success and failure. From the tips at 192 yards, the 17th green looks no bigger than a doily.

In the original land plan for Harbour Town, the 18th hole returned to the clubhouse, away from the water. Dye and Nicklaus campaigned successfully for a finishing hole that would proceed directly along the marshy shore of Calibogue Sound. The result was Harbour Town's spectacular 18th, a lengthy, windswept par four that plays as a par four-and-a-half for all but the best of players. Both the drive and approach shot must carry tidal marshes and oyster-shell deposits that border the entire left side of the hole. There is out-of-bounds up the right side near a row of condos, though the fairway, liberated from the confines of the maritime forest encasing the previous holes, is wider than most in the driving area. The problem comes with the second shot. The bold line to the pin travels across the marsh and over a long, fearsome sand pit that bellies up to the front of the green. Shots pulled to the left plug in the marsh. There is bailout room to the right of the putting surface, but subtle mounding usually confounds the best-laid plans to get up-and-down for par. Bogey is not a bad score on this, the finale of a truly memorable course.

Off Course Activities/ Hilton Head

While no longer the pristine subtropical getaway it was in the 1960s, Hilton Head remains a tastefully developed destination, with no garish towers to crowd the island's beautiful beaches. A boot-shaped barrier reef island off the South Carolina coast, it's an hour's drive from Savannah, Georgia.

Want to relax and unwind? Take a leisurely stroll, rent a balloon-tire bike, or fly a kite on one of the island's firm-packed ocean beaches. Beachcomb for sand dollars, conch shells, and driftwood. Explorers can rent a canoe or kayak at Fish Creek Landing and paddle through nine miles of picturesque lagoons. Want to master a new sport? The island's protected waters are a good place to learn how to windsurf or sail. Tennis, anyone? The island sports more than 300 clay, grass, and artificial-surface courts. Fishing? Hilton Head's waters are among the most productive on the East Coast. Narrated dolphin watch cruises are available on *Cheers*, a 47-foot sailboat anchored at Harbour Town.

Back on land, Lawton Stables organizes horseback tours of the pristine 605-acre Sea Pines Forest Preserve. Sea Pines Eco-Tours also offers guided wagon and walking tours of the preserve. Nature lovers can visit Newhall Audubon Preserve and Whooping Crane Pond Conservancy—or join one of the informative beach walks conducted by Coastal Discovery—The Museum on Hilton Head Island.

Harbour Town Golf Links, Hilton Head, South Carolina, seventh hole

Harbour Town Golf Links, 18th hole

While Harbour Town is the course that put Hilton Head on the map as a golf destination, it was by no means the island's first course. That distinction belongs to the *Ocean Course* at *Sea Pines Plantation*, a George Cobb design dating to 1960. In 1994, the resort brought in Mark McCumber to direct a $3-million makeover of a frumpy spinster teetering on the brink of obsolescence, and today the Ocean Course can hold its own with any public-access course on the island. Only the routing and most of the fairway corridors remain from the original. Everything else has been transformed. At the signature par-three 15th, the tee was elevated and the green lowered, affording players a better view of the Atlantic. McCumber also rebuilt the Sea Pines practice facility, which serves the Ocean as well as the Sea Marsh courses. (The *Sea Marsh Course*, a delightful resort spread, was remodeled in 1990 by Clyde Johnston.)

In addition to the three courses at Sea Pines Plantation, there are a trio of courses at *Palmetto Dunes Resort*, two at *Palmetto Hall Plantation* (including the *Arthur Hills Course*, next to Harbour Town the best resort course on the island), three at *Port Royal Golf Club*, 27 holes at *Shipyard Golf Club*, and several other top daily-fee facilities on Hilton Head. In addition, a number of excellent public-access facilities have cropped up on the mainland near the entrance to the island.

DINING

With over 160 restaurants, Hilton Head offers a good array of dining choices. For down-home Southern cooking, *Abe's Native Shrimp House* is the place to go. Schedule a morning round in order to enjoy a tasty, casual lunch at *Captain's Seafood*, which doubles as a retail fish market.

For fancier dining, there are proven mainstays (*Charlie's L'Etoile Verte* offers continental cuisine in a flower-decked room), reliable standbys (*The Gaslight* prepares superb French cuisine in a candlelit room), promising newcomers (*Primo* serves eclectic and contemporary Italian dishes, with the accent on seafood), and more informal choices, including *Hilton Head Brewing Company*, the *Old Fort Pub* (oyster pie, chicken-fried steak, plus a nice setting beside Skull Creek), and *Le Bistro*, a popular spot in the Pineland Mall shopping center with a Mediterrean-themed menu. *Reilley's*, a welcoming Irish establishment, serves up basic pub fare—and lots of local hospitality. Dyed-in-the-wool players should drop by the *British Open Pub*, which combines the best aspects of a Scottish tavern with the attributes of a Low Country watering hole.

GOLF SIDETRIPS

If you're willing to travel a short distance from Hilton Head for a special golf experience, there are two options worth exploring.

In the charming, historic town of Beaufort, 45 minutes north of Hilton Head, there is *Callawassie Island Club*, a private residential development built around a 27-hole facility designed by Tom Fazio. Players must bring a letter of referral from their home pro to gain access to Callawassie. It's well worth the effort. The club's Palmetto, Dogwood, and Magnolia nines skirt salt marshes separating the Chechessee and Colleton rivers, with undulating fairways carved from a dense maritime forest of palmettos and magnolias. Mounds, swales, and encroaching trees provide plenty of challenge. After the round, have a look at some of the eye-popping antebellum homes in Beaufort's Historic Landmark District. These fabulous mansions, many fully restored, range in style from Greek Revival to Gothic. Movies including *The Big Chill*, *Forrest Gump*, and *The Great Santini* have been filmed in Beaufort.

Across Calibogue Sound from the Sea Pines Resort is the *Daufuskie Island Club & Resort*, a formerly private enclave now owned by the same company that operates Pinehurst and The Homestead. Accessible via a relaxing 30-minute ferry ride, the resort offers 52 rooms in the Melrose Inn, many with ocean views; 37 two- and four-bedroom cottages; and two fine courses, each with its own driving range and practice putting green. *Bloody Point*, a Tom Weiskopf–Jay Morrish creation, is a traditional, parkland-style test framed by tidal marshes and ancient live oaks. *Melrose*, a Jack Nicklaus design, boasts three oceanfront finishing holes that rank among the most dramatic and exciting in the Low Country. Both courses at Daufuskie welcome walkers.

Myrtle Beach

Since the 1950s, the self-proclaimed "Golf Capital of the World" has flourished as a raffish seaside town of amusement parks, pinball arcades, and giant beachwear emporiums, a place where mom-and-pop motels share space with saltwater taffy stands, fried seafood joints, and miniature golf courses marked by concrete dinosaurs and ersatz shipwrecks. This is honky-tonk Americana at its best and most unapologetic. Its redeeming virtue, then and now, is the "Grand Strand," a 60-mile stretch of firm-packed ocean beach ideal for strolling, jogging, and beachcombing. Readily accessible by car or air from major population centers in the Northeast and Midwest, Myrtle Beach was proud to be known as the reddest of golf's red light districts.

Myrtle is still Myrtle, but there's been a sea change of late. The old gal has cleaned up her act. Also, the clientele has changed. Yes, workers hailing from industrial cities in the Rust Belt still pile into cars and drive all night to make their morning tee times, but word has leaked to players with the means to play anywhere they choose that Myrtle boasts more topnotch public courses (and the promise of more fun) than any other destination in America.

With the opening of the Tournament Players Club at Myrtle Beach in 1999, this multifaceted destination achieved the unthinkable century mark of 100 golf courses (95 of them public-access). Around these courses are found nearly 60,000 accommodation units (budget motels to plush condos), over 1,800 restaurants, nonstop nightlife, tons of shopping and, best of all, genuine Southern hospitality. The consistently warm welcome is perhaps the destination's greatest asset.

Myrtle Beach doesn't get the credit it deserves for pioneering the concept of the golf package. In 1967, six hotels and three golf courses decided to promote the area by offering an all-inclusive vacation program that featured accommodations, green fees, and full breakfast, a novel concept at the time. Then as now, rates were adjusted to reflect seasonal desirability. The golf package formula linking lodging entities and golf courses for mutual benefit has been copied by every major domestic and international golf destination.

While no longer the bargain basement destination it was in the days when it flourished as a "Redneck Riviera," Myrtle Beach still represents good value. At no time of year, for example, do green fees and room rates peak simultaneously. In summer, the most popular season for family vacations, accommodations are at a premium but golf costs are low. In spring and fall, the most desirable seasons for golf, green fees are at their highest but hotel room rates are moderate. Seeking the all-time deal of deals? Myrtle Beach is a virtual giveaway in the winter months, when lodging tariffs and green fees both bottom out. From mid-December through the end of January, it was still possible in 1998 to purchase an all-inclusive seven-night package (with seven rounds of nonsurcharge golf and motel accommodations) for under $250! Myrtle, by the way, generally enjoys mild winters, with temperatures in the high 50s and low 60s.

For many seasoned traveling golfers well-acquainted with the vintage designs of Robert Trent Jones, his finest creation is **The Dunes Golf & Beach Club** (#36) in Myrtle Beach. Routed by Jones on a former turkey-hunting grounds in 1948, the Dunes functions as a semiprivate club that permits access to guests of six select Myrtle Beach hotels. It is well worth making the necessary lodging arrangements to play the Dunes, which despite the town's addition of many new facilities remains the undisputed King of the Beach.

Jones, given free rein at a time when Myrtle Beach had only one other course to its name, built a roomy, big-time layout that usually takes dead aim at carefree holidaymakers. The Dunes is a serious course that pumps the competitive juices of serious players. In addition to its elegant, classic appearance—rolling fairways, sculptured bunkers, superb green sites—the Dunes presents a supreme challenge, sea breeze or no breeze, thanks

Aerial view of The Dunes Golf & Beach Club, Myrtle Beach, South Carolina, 13ᵗʰ hole

The Dunes Golf & Beach Club, ninth hole

to its elevated greens. To separate duffers from champions, Jones perched the greens at 15 of the 18 holes atop pedestal knolls five feet or more above fairway level. He also carved bunkers into the face of these pedestals, further complicating the issue of getting the ball on the green. Dribbled ground balls and worm-burners finish miserably in these deep sand pits.

Touched up by Jones in 1977 and treated to an agronomic facelift in 1992, the Dunes, host site of the Senior PGA Tour Championship from 1994 to 1998, is today a sprightly dowager with a full set of teeth. The one-time club trophy says it all: A foot-long silver alligator with a golf ball lodged in its jaws.

There's not a single creampuff hole among the 18. Seemingly benign holes are anything but, and most of the par fours, even from the middle tees, call for long, straight drives followed by accurate approach shots. The front nine concludes with a gorgeous par three, called "Dunes," that offers a fine view of the Atlantic from the green. But this hole also confronts players with strong prevailing sea winds, winds that invariably complicate club selection.

With water or marsh in play at half the holes on the back nine, the Dunes picks up steam through the round. The short par-four 11th, redesigned to accommodate a bi-level peninsula green set above a brackish swash to the right of the original (and where Jones had always wanted it), has been lauded by Lee Trevino as one of the finest par fours he has ever played.

A salt marsh must be negotiated at the par-three 12th, but the green provides a sizable target and will yield to a nerveless, well-played shot. In fact, many a golfer has survived the first 12 holes only to be undone by the famed and feared par-five 13th, rightly known as "Waterloo." Stretching to 590 yards from the tips, the 13th is a boomerang-shaped hole that bends

110 degrees around Singleton Lake. After driving out of a chute of pines and willows to a landing area that bottlenecks as it nears the water, golfers must then decide how much of the lake to bite off in order to reach the fairway on the far side of the water. The 150-yard marker is a good target—if you stay with the shot and don't peek to see the result. Slice, and you're destined for dampness.

While the 13th is the Grand Strand's most famous hole, the 18th at The Dunes is arguably the finest finishing hole in town. Called "Little Gator," this lengthy par four, originally intended by Jones to be a par five, calls for a perfect drive to a rising fairway that narrows and doglegs slightly to the right in the landing zone. The full-blooded approach must carry a lake fronting a slick two-tiered green flanked by three bunkers. Par here is a very good score.

Tidewater Golf Club & Plantation (#39), opened in 1989, occupies a magnificent site in North Myrtle Beach. Four of the holes on this stellar track are stretched along forested bluffs overlooking Cherry Grove Inlet. They offer exceptional views of the bright green marsh and the deep blue Atlantic. The remainder of the Tidewater layout runs inland through a dense forest of pines and hardwoods, swinging near the Intracoastal Waterway at the conclusion of both nines.

A stately course that drapes onto the land quite naturally, Tidewater was the brainchild of Ken Tomlinson, a tax attorney turned golf course designer who used fabled Merion and Pine Valley as his models during construction. With Hale Irwin serving as player consultant, the result was a grand, refined spread that would fully utilize the natural features of the site.

Tomlinson struck a perfect balance between beauty and utility at Tidewater by eschewing the manufacture of decorative mounds (he calls them "warts") and by steering clear of sharply defined target areas: "The player is not spoon-fed and forced to aim tee shots to the preferred fairway positions. Desirably, the player will have the mental discipline, skill, and daring to execute tee shots to the most logical fairway positions suiting his or her own shotmaking abilities."

Placement and strategy, not mindless hitting, are called for at Tidewater. So is an appreciation of a classic, unassuming design style that masks a deceptively demanding course from the back tees. The smooth bentgrass greens—among the best in Myrtle Beach—are "located, sized, shaped, and contoured to reward approach shots from a specific position in each fairway," noted Tomlinson, who left very little to chance at his pet project. Best of all, five sets of tees (7,078 to 4,615 yards, including a thoughtful set for seniors at 5,097 yards) give players at all ability levels a chance to return a par or two.

The first hole, a straightaway par five, signals Tomlinson's intentions. The fairway is invitingly wide, but large-scale, multifingered bunkers located well beyond the driving area (but well short of the green) hint at things to come. The most pleasant and immediate surprise comes at the par-three third, which departs the tall trees for a windswept bluff set above the tidal marsh. At 157 yards from the tips, Tidewater's tiny terror is living proof that a golf hole does not have to be long to be challenging. Not only does the marsh protect the entire left side of the hole, but the

Tidewater Golf Club & Plantation, North Myrtle Beach, South Carolina, fourth hole

Tidewater Golf Club & Plantation, 12th hole

triple-tiered green is defended by deep bunkers. The par-four fourth, the most visually stunning hole at Tidewater, sweeps around the marshy inlet on rolling land elevated well above a sickle-shaped bunker that runs the length of the fairway and prevents hooked shots from disappearing into the gook.

While the front nine offers a few birdie opportunities, Tidewater's longer back nine tightens the screws. The game is on at the par-three 12th, which stretches to 198 yards from the black tees and calls for a bold tee shot over a corner of the inlet to a large, bulkheaded green. The tee, set well above the target, is usually swept by sea breezes. The grand par-five 13th, perhaps the best strategic hole on the course, serves up distracting ocean views from a rolling fairway hugged by a salt marsh down the entire right side of the fairway. With its subtle contours, the enormous green at the 13th is very testing to the best of putters.

Tomlinson, who said he "wanted to design a course that could host the U.S. Open," concludes the round with a hole built to crown champions.

DINING

With over 1,800 restaurants in town, you will not go hungry in Myrtle Beach. Most hotels include a hearty breakfast in the golf package rate.

In addition to hundreds of fast-food outlets offering burgers, pizza, and tacos, cafeterias offer good food at great prices. *K & W Cafeteria* and *Morrison's* are two of the best.

No visit to Myrtle Beach is complete without dinner one night at *The Old Pro's Table*, a steak house that doubles as a golf museum. Rare and valuable golf collectibles, including feathery balls from the 1820s, wooden-shafted clubs used by early Scottish champions, and sepia prints of Bobby Jones, Walter Hagen, and all the greats decorate every corner of the restaurant. Opt for the aged prime rib served with horseradish sauce.

Another long-time favorite is the *Sea Captain's House*, which features a nice oceanfront location in a converted beach house. The seafood preparations here are excellent. Another reputable seafood restaurant is *Marker 350* in North Myrtle Beach, where the blackened tuna over angel hair pasta is superb, as is the selection of wines. Marker 350's Conch Room Lounge overlooks the Intracoastal Waterway and marina basin.

For those unconcerned about the effects of cholesterol, *Calabash,* located across the state line in North Carolina, is the unofficial fried seafood capital of the South.

New York Prime, patterned after famous steakhouses in the Big Apple, is a cigar-friendly restaurant with a bustling, friendly atmosphere—and serious steaks. A popular newcomer to Myrtle Beach is *Collector's Café*, which not only serves excellent Mediterranean cuisine and homemade desserts, but also offers fine art for sale ($25–$5,000), much of it locally produced.

In the sleepy fishing port of Murrells Inlet at the south end of the beach is *Bovine's*, where many of the entrées are cooked in a wood-burning oven. A little farther south in Pawleys Island is *Frank's Restaurant & Bar*, which might well be the finest dining spot on the Grand Strand. Special praise is reserved for the cornmeal and black pepper encrusted grouper with crab, corn, and roasted red pepper cream, a truly exceptional dish. The wine list and homemade desserts are also excellent. Behind the dining room, which occupies a former grocery store, is *Out Back at Frank's*, a casual al fresco eatery with a covered patio, large brick fireplace, and tall heat lamps to warm patrons on cool nights. Also in Pawleys Island is *Tyler's Cove*, which serves Creole-style Low Country cuisine (shrimp and grits, crabcakes) in a cozy room where the ceiling beams are fashioned from old ships' timbers.

Tidewater Golf Club & Plantation, 18th hole

Oak trees leading to the clubhouse at Caledonia Golf & Fish Club, Pawleys Island, South Carolina

Nightlife

The Skee-Ball arcades are still around, as are the old-time thrill rides at Pavilion Amusement Park, but Myrtle Beach broadened its appeal significantly in 1996 with the opening of *Broadway at The Beach*, a $250-million entertainment complex with nearly 100 shops, restaurants, and nightclubs. It is currently the state's top tourist attraction. The *All Star Café*, which Tiger Woods co-owns with several other sports superstars including Joe Montana, Shaquille O'Neal, and Ken Griffey Jr., is very popular with sports fans who stay glued to the huge video wall that highlights every sporting event currently being broadcast as well as 30 video monitors replaying the greatest moments in sports history. The café's Tiger Woods Clubhouse, with Tiger's memorabilia on display, is a must for Eldrick's fans, as is Tiger's favorite entrée—a cheeseburger. *Ripley's Sea Aquarium*, a giant IMAX Discovery Theater, a 16-screen cineplex, and Celebrity Square, a pulsating nightclub district, round out the list of Broadway's attractions.

Broadway at the Beach

The *House of Blues* in North Myrtle Beach at Barefoot Landing is renowned for its 2,000-seat music hall, which offers a broad range of musical acts and performers, with the accent on Chicago and Mississippi Delta blues headliners. The restaurant decor is reminiscent of a Mississippi Delta home (lots of folk and "outsider" art), with a menu to match: jambalaya, fried catfish bites, bread pudding, etc. It's worth rearranging your weekend tee times to attend the fabulous Gospel Brunch on Sundays, at which guests can enjoy a true Southern buffet to the accompaniment of a spirited, soulful gospel choir.

Country-and-western music is very popular in Myrtle Beach. There's the *Carolina Opry* and *Alabama Theater*, both of which offer top-name entertainment. If you own more than one pair of cowboy boots, head for the *Dixie Stampede* (built by Dolly Parton's Dollywood Productions), where a four-course meal is served during a horse-and-dance show.

Mass market entertainment outlets not your thing? There are plenty of restaurants and watering holes with local flair. The *Player's Club* and *Corbin's*, both with big-screen TVs, are Myrtle's two top sports bars. Gentlemen's clubs are very popular in Myrtle Beach, their clientele predominantly golfers. *Thee Doll House* is a well-run, always fun topless club.

If you've got the energy to dance after 36 holes of golf, the dance step of choice is the "Shag," a sort-of jitterbug shuffle that is done to the accompaniment of "beach music" (old soul classics) played by DJs at numerous clubs in town, including the *Beach Music Café* at Broadway's Celebrity Square. The Shagger Hall of Fame is located in *Celebrations*, where T-shirts and other items celebrating this popular dance are available.

Caledonia Golf & Fish Club, 13th hole

This lengthy, oak-lined par four doglegs gently to the left, away from the marshes lining the Intracoastal Waterway. The landing area is generous, but the approach shot must avoid the marsh in front and to the right of the green. Only great shots will come to rest on the putting surface of one of the purest two-shotters in all of Myrtle Beach.

A magnificent multilevel clubhouse overlooking the ninth and 18th greens as well as the Intracoastal Waterway anchors this modern classic.

Caledonia Golf & Fish Club (#85) occupies the site of a colonial rice plantation along the Waccamaw River that until recently was a hunting and fishing retreat for a local group of good ole boys. The old fishing shed, with its brick fireplace used for oyster roasts and barbecues, still stands next to the club's antebellum-style clubhouse. As sportsmen, the owners wanted to build a course preserving as much of the land's natural beauty as possible. As southerners, they wanted to create an atmosphere of

SIGHTSEEING

Brookgreen Gardens, the world's largest outdoor display of American sculpture, is a National Historic Landmark. Located near Murrells Inlet, it features an outstanding collection of more than 500 American figurative sculptures, with works by artists like Gutzon Borglum, Daniel Chester French, Frederick Remington, Gaston Lachaise, Paul Manship, Augustus Saint-Gaudens, Carl Milles, and by Anna Hyatt Huntington, who founded the gardens with her husband in 1931. In addition to the exquisite sculpture gardens, visitors can stroll through themed horticultural gardens (Herb, Folk Remedy, and Economic, the last planted with regional cash crops such as rice, indigo, tobacco, and cotton), a Carnivorous Plant Bog, and the Cypress Bird Sanctuary, where visitors can view ibises, herons, and egrets from a raised boardwalk. Nature cruises aboard a 48-foot pontoon boat explore tidal creeks and abandoned ricefields on the Waccamaw River. Across from Brookgreen's entrance is Huntington Beach State Park, a 2,500-acre preserve of sandy beaches and salt marshes. The Huntingtons' unusual beach house, a squat brick edifice patterned after watchtowers built by the Moors along the Spanish coast, is open for viewing. Brookgreen and its environs is the perfect antidote to the hurly-burly of Myrtle Beach.

A sculpture at Brookgreen Gardens

Caledonia Golf & Fish Club, 11th hole

warmth and hospitality that each golfer could take home with him. The compact layout, occupying a scant 125 acres, was the first solo effort of Mike Strantz, a former Tom Fazio protégé who successfully grafted gently rolling fairways, large undulating greens, and sweeping flashed-face bunkers to a classic Old South palette of marshy rice fields, towering pines, and giant moss-draped oaks. Caledonia artfully blends links, Low Country, and parkland styles into one cohesive whole. Memorable from start to finish, with each hole distinctively different one from the other, Caledonia offers the most delightful test of golf in Myrtle Beach. There are longer courses in town, and tougher courses too, but none can match the beauty and charm of Caledonia.

Sporty from the Wood Duck tees at 5,710 yards (decoys are used for tee markers), enjoyable for middle handicappers from the Mallard markers at 6,121 yards, and a scintillating test for experts from the Pintail tees at 6,526 yards, this par-70 layout has exceptional pace and variety, with three par fives (two of them back-to-back) and five par threes on the card. Each of the one-shotters is exceptional. The ninth proves that backbreaking distance is not required to fashion a great hole. All of 118 yards from the back tees and flanking the oak-lined entryway, this tiny terror demands a nerveless carry over a sandy wasteland to a shallow green backdropped by a wall of thick-waisted oaks seemingly transplanted from *Gone With the Wind*. Only a perfect wedge shot will do.

At the 11th, 153 yards from the middle tees, a serpentine creek fronts a long, lolling green that appears far smaller from the elevated tee than it actually is. Strantz then turns up the knobs with five par fours in a row (holes 12–16), each measuring 400 yards or more from the tips. At two of the holes (13 and 14), a huge oak dictates strategy off the tee for the better player. The par-three 17th, which again calls for a forced carry over a sandy wasteland to a raised green guarded in front by a pot bunker with an appended tongue, is followed by a glorious finale. Caledonia's par-four 18th plays opposite a limitless expanse of old rice fields, its fairway doglegging around the arm of a creek. Directly behind the green on the far side of the water is the clubhouse and its wrap-around porch set with rockers. It is an ideal post-round gathering spot.

During peak season, complimentary helpings of steaming hot fish chowder are served to players as they make their way from the ninth green to the 10th tee. The chowder is especially welcome on a cool day. Caledonia, by the way, is still a Fish Club. Drop by on a Thursday from November to April, and those good ole boys may even invite you to their fish fry, which is usually accompanied by homemade slaw and the kind of grits only a professional Southerner can make.

New & Noteworthy in Myrtle Beach

Across the street from his first solo design at Caledonia, Strantz was given the opportunity to create his own version of a target-style test on the site of a 17th-century indigo plantation. Called *True Blue*, the layout, opened in 1997, is woven through low brushy vegetation and pristine woodlands.

Much like Pine Valley, the exclusive top-ranked course New Jersey's pine barrens True Blue has several island-like fairways and greens surrounded by large expanses of scrub and sand. A rugged shotmaker's course, it already ranked among the best tests of golf in town.

The *Tournament Players Club of Myrtle Beach*, a joint venture between the PGA Tour and Myrtle Beach Golf Holiday, was designed by Tom Fazio with PGA Tour pro Lanny Wadkins serving as player consultant. The region's 100th course to open is not only the permanent home of the Senior Tour Championship, it has bolstered the region's high-end daily fee sector and enabled Myrtle Beach to reach new audiences by virtue of the TPC imprimatur. The layout, unveiled in early 1999 and located at the south end of the Grand Strand near Socastee, is a player's course blessedly free of the conspicuous spectator mounds found at most TPC courses.

More Golf, Golf, Golf

With the greatest assemblage of public-access courses on earth (no other destination is remotely close), the Grand Strand has tremendous depth. You could play every day for three months, never drive more than an hour, and never play the same hole twice! There's quality, too. In addition to the Dunes, Tidewater, and Caledonia, dozens of other courses are wholeheartedly recommended. Newer courses, it should be noted, are generally more expensive than the older ones, though in the great Myrtle Beach tradition, it is possible to play agreeable, well-kept courses from one end of the Grand Strand to the other without paying a surcharge.

Highway 501, a hotbed of new growth directly inland from the beach, is chockablock with golf developments. Can't make it to Scotland anytime soon? Check out the three courses at *The Legends*, a sprawling 54-hole complex south of the highway. On a treeless plot of land ripe for a humdrum layout, *GOLF Magazine* contributing editor Tom Doak tapped his encyclopedic knowledge of British linksland courses to create the *Heathland*, its broad, windswept fairways pitted with pot bunkers and its rolling dunes tufted with tall grasses. The *Moorland*, a P.B. Dye creation, is just as stark but far sterner, while the *Parkland*, a watery, tree-lined, and heavily bunkered affair, was inspired by early American courses designed by Alister Mackenzie and George C. Thomas, Jr. The Scottish Villas at The Legends are a popular lodging option.

Another Highway 501 mainstay and the single largest complex in town is *Wild Wing Plantation*, a sprawling retreat with four excellent layouts (the imaginatively contoured *Avocet Course* by Larry Nelson and Jeff Brauer is especially noteworthy). The facility also offers accommodations at Aviary Village, a superb practice facility and, for those bent on improvement, the Wild Wing School of Golf, one of eight golf academies in town.

Also located off the highway is *Belle Terre* ("Beautiful Earth"), its traditional-style Championship Course a large-scale layout built by Rees Jones around lakes, wetlands, and pine groves. In addition to the main track, Belle Terre, opened in 1995, also features the Rees Jones Par 58 Course, a delightful 3,201-yard executive layout (14 par threes and four par fours) intended to "provide real golf for people in a hurry." With its reasonable green fee, walker-friendly policy, and 2½-hour completion time, this shortie has become very popular.

Just as themed restaurants have captured the public's imagination, so too have themed courses joined the superheated competition for the visiting golfer's green fee in Myrtle Beach. *Man o' War*, opened in 1996, is a Dan Maples design built around a mile-long, multifingered lake north of Highway 501. Not only does Man o' War have back-to-back island greens at 14 and 15, the par-four ninth features an island fairway. Forget the ball retriever—bring a mask and snorkel. After the round, players can repair to Man o' War's fish camp–style, net-draped clubhouse built on pilings in the middle of a lake.

Dirt scooped to create water features at Man o' War was used by Maples to fashion a sister course, *The Wizard*, currently the epitome of entertainment architecture in Myrtle Beach. While Man o' War appears to have more water than grass in play, the Wizard offers an intriguing landscape of hills, peaks, and berms, all of them stabilized with hundreds of different species of plants. The signature hole is the par-four 18th, which has an island fairway *and* an island green set below an imposing clubhouse of stucco and stone designed to resemble an ancient Irish castle.

Located in Calabash, North Carolina, an hour's drive from Myrtle Beach (but still part of the Grand Strand circuit) is *Marsh Harbour*, the first course in the region (1980) to be built into low-lying marshland. Carved from a maritime forest, with excellent marsh and water views from its elevated tees and greens, the links, one of Dan Maples's first solo designs, rewards precise shotmaking. The spectacular par-five 17th, set on raised fingers of land above the salt marsh and spartina grass, is truly memorable.

The runaway success of Marsh Harbour led to the creation of *Oyster Bay* in nearby Sunset Beach. Another Dan Maples creation, it has water in play at 15 holes. Well-placed tee shots and unerring approaches are required to score here, though the longer par fours have broad fairways and large greens. Often overshadowed by newer, snazzier layouts, the *Surf Club* is a time-honored test marked by numerous doglegs hinged on cypress swamps. The collection of par threes on this George Cobb classic is especially strong. A $1-million facelift directed by John Lafoy (a Cobb protégé) greatly enhanced the appeal of this popular layout, as did a conversion to bentgrass putting surfaces in 1992. Always in top shape, the Surf Club, anchored by a gorgeous clubhouse, is well-liked by canny shotmakers.

Dating to 1927, *Pine Lakes International*, a.k.a. "The Granddaddy," is the oldest course in town. A pleasant test marked by tree-lined fairways and small greens, Pine Lakes is renowned for the white-glove treatment offered by its kilted staff and for the refreshing mimosa (or Low Country clam chowder) served at the seventh hole. This venerable layout was built by Robert White, the first president of the PGA of America. White reportedly had a little help with the course design from an old friend (and fellow Scotsman), Donald Ross.

Georgia

What Tom Fazio, Mother Nature and Fuji Development Georgia achieved at **White Columns Golf Club** (#27), located 25 miles north of downtown Atlanta is nothing less than a public-access version of Augusta National, home of the The Masters and Holy Grail of inland layouts. Carved from a broad expanse of rolling hills, towering pines, lakes, and meandering streams, this superlative daily-fee facility can hold its own with any private club in the nation by virtue of its design integrity and attention to detail.

Opened in 1994 to reprise The Golf Club of Georgia, Fuji's nationally ranked private club, which is also located in Alpharetta, the fairways and tees at White Columns were sodded, a costly process rarely done even at the most exclusive facilities. Fuji selected the advanced strain of bent-

SIDETRIP

Twelve miles east of Atlanta is 3,200-acre *Stone Mountain Park*, which surrounds an exposed-granite mountain. Chiseled into the north face of the granite peak is the biggest sculpture in the world. If you're a Civil War buff, here's your chance to see Confederate heroes Jefferson Davis, Robert E. Lee, and Stonewall Jackson, each on horseback, on an unmatched scale. (A cable car will carry you 825 feet up the mountain for a closer look at the Mt. Rushmore of the South.) There's also a pair of fine courses within the park, including 18 holes (divided between two designs) by Robert Trent Jones.

Confederate Monument at Stone Mountain Park, Georgia

grass, "Crenshaw bent," to blanket the greens. The result? An instant classic with a level of maturity normally seen in a 20-year-old facility. Not only is White Columns the best course money can buy, it is a showcase for what the leading designer of his generation can produce when let loose on a tremendous piece of property with no strings attached.

Admittedly biased, head pro Scott Mahr describes White Columns as "probably the fairest golf course in America, because you can mishit the ball a little and still have a chance to recover." Fairway corridors are wide, forced carries are rare (except from the gold tees at 7,053 yards) and the superb greens are quite large. White Columns is not heavily bunkered, but the sand traps Fazio did install are of the flashed-face variety and quite penal.

On a course with "about nine signature holes," according to Mahr, it's difficult to single out the consummate challenges presented by this flawless parkland spread. Suffice it to say that the quartet of par threes is smashing, while the par fives (two reachable, two out of reach for most mortals) are highlighted by the brawny 13th, which plays to a slightly inclined, tree-lined fairway framed by the same lofty pines that make Augusta National a revered cathedral of golf. A well-positioned lay-up leaves a short iron shot to a large hilltop green ringed by bunkers and backdropped by a lake that wraps behind the green at the par-three eighth. A five here is worth savoring.

More Golf/Atlanta

Looking for an eminently "good track" convenient to Stone Mountain Park? *Cherokee Run* in nearby Conyers is that and more. Designed by Arnold Palmer and Ed Seay, the layout, opened in 1995, lies within Georgia International Horse Park.

White Columns Golf Club, Alpharetta, Georgia, 17th hole

94

White Columns Golf Club, ninth hole

White Columns Golf Club, eighth hole

More choices in the Atlanta area? Head north of the city to sample *Cobblestone* in Acworth, *St. Marlo* in Duluth, and *Towne Lake Hills* in Woodstock. For a deluxe resort experience, *Chateau Elan* is a 3,100-acre property in Braselton, 30 minutes north of Atlanta, that lends a sophisticated European touch to the agricultural setting. In addition to an inspired copy of a 16th-century French chateau that houses a wine-making operation, there's an art gallery, open-air café, and Lé Clos, where the six-course meals are sublime. Golf is pursued on the resort's original Chateau Course, each of its holes named for a different grape; at The Legends, a private club (accessible to guests) that hosts the Sarazen World Open Championship; and at the Woodlands, a sterling design opened in 1996 that is marked by tree-lined fairways, large greens, and 70-foot elevation changes. There's also a nine-hole par-three course (à la Augusta National) that's ideal for walkers. A superb practice facility, European-style spa, 200-stall equestrian center, and a welcoming inn round out the amenities at this upscale vineyard devoted to the good life.

Heading 75 miles east from Atlanta toward Augusta, there is **Reynolds Plantation** in Greensboro, a thriving 5,200-acre residential and resort community where Jack Nicklaus created a playable, aesthetically pleasing course. Opened to rave reviews in 1992, nine holes at **Great Waters** (#28) flank the shores of Lake Oconee, at 19,000 acres one of the largest man-made lakes in the South. The layout's front nine runs inland through

Reynolds Plantation, Great Waters, Eatonton, Georgia, 18th hole

rolling hills cloaked in pines, while the back nine circulates players from one lake cove to the next. The distance between greens and tees is minimal—Great Waters, its name derived from the English translation of the Creek Indian word, "oconee," is very walkable. And while the challenge from the tips at 7,048 yards is pure Nicklaus, staggered sets of forward tees give everyone a chance to enjoy one of the more user-friendly courses Jack has built.

The routing, arguably Jack's best, brings players to the brink of the lake at the ninth, a mid-length par four where the tee shot cascades to an open, descending fairway. Players must then cross one of the lake's fingers to reach a green guarded in front and to the right by water. It is a preview of things to come: The back nine at Great Waters, with a portion of each hole tracing the lakeshore, and with six greens flush against the water, is perhaps the finest peninsula-and-cove golf experience in America. Why? Because there's just enough terra firma to offer strategic options and more than enough water to keep things interesting, especially when a breeze stirs off the lake.

Among the more intriguing holes on this dazzling stretch is the petite par-four 11th, which Nicklaus actually shortened during the design phase

to tempt big hitters to try for the green with their drives. A 200-foot-wide peninsula green attached to the fairway by a narrow spit provides a generous target, but with water down the entire left side, an aggressively hooked drive is doomed to a watery grave. The 14th and 17th holes are both bewitching par threes that require bold shots over the lake, while the

DINING

Meals are something special at The Cloister. A full breakfast is served in the main dining room, while lunch can be taken at the golf club or the Beach Club, which offers the likes of cornbread-dusted crabcakes as well as shrimp and oyster Po Boys. Dinner at the main hotel is a gala six-course meal accompanied by live music. Coats and ties are required for men and young men over 12. Dancing is available nightly (except Sundays) during cocktails and after dinner, while black tie is encouraged (but optional) on Wednesday and Saturday nights. Genteel traditions such as teatime are still observed, and homemade cookies and milk are set out in the lobby for guests at night. It's that kind of place.

Two important notes. Reservations at The Cloister require a deposit. Also, the resort does not accept credit cards. Accounts are settled with cash, traveler's checks or personal checks.

Dining at The Cloister Restaurant, St. Simons Island, Georgia

par-five 18th calls for a fair amount of planning in return for par. Once again, an inlet of the lake must be negotiated to reach a rock-rimmed green protected to the rear by a deep bunker that is designed to foil those who overclub in an attempt to take the water out of play. This brand of conservatism (or cowardice) is rewarded with a downhill bunker shot to a putting surface that slopes to Lake Oconee.

A 14,000-square-foot clubhouse graced by verandas overlooking the ninth and 18th greens, the lake, and a large practice putting green was opened in 1998. This much-admired layout served as an early round host site for the Andersen Consulting World Championship of Golf in the mid-1990s. Given its inherent drama and strategic makeup, Great Waters was lauded by competitors as an ideal match-play golf course.

More Golf/Reynolds Plantation

The community's *Plantation Course*, opened in 1988, was designed as a member's course that everyone could enjoy. Laid out by Bob Cupp in collaboration with former U.S. Open champions Fuzzy Zoeller and Hubert Green, this 6,656-yard, par-71 course (6,017 yards, par 72 from the white tees) has wide fairways, minimal rough, and a scant 14 bunkers. Many of the holes play downhill, with elevated tees providing nice views of Lake Oconee and the surrounding countryside. The smooth bentgrass greens are mildly defended by grassy hollows, but overall the Plantation was built for pleasure. From the white tees, the weekend player will hit a few greens in regulation and perhaps make a birdie or two. How many newer resort courses can promise as much?

Residents and guests alike are still buzzing over the opening in 1997 of the community's third course, *Reynolds National*, a stellar Tom Fazio design that may one day give Great Waters a run for its money. This 7,015-

yard layout lacks the extensive lakefront exposure of its sister course (only two holes on The National, as it's known, border Lake Oconee), but all of Fazio's trademark playability and artistry have been lavished on a majestic site. As with all Fazio layouts, the whole is greater than the sum of its parts, though there are more than a few standout holes on The National. At the par-five sixth, the two-tiered green is guarded on three sides by water, with only a narrow ramp left open in front to accept low, running shots for those who eschew (consciously or otherwise) an airborne approach.

The National's stirring par-four 18th offers a classic risk-reward scenario: The tee shot is straightaway, but the fairway eventually bends sharply to the right around a small pond, calling for a second shot over water to reach the green in regulation. Want to limber up before teeing off? Reynolds National features a superb 10-acre practice facility.

Moving farther east and south are the Golden Isles, a chain of barrier islands stretching along the Georgia coast an hour's drive from Savannah and accessible via a string of causeways east of Brunswick. Here is found

Activities

The resort's Beach Club Spa offers therapeutic treatments, fitness classes (including morning beach walks), and spa cuisine. There's skeet at the Gun Club, riding stables, waterways fishing, boat cruises, nature tours, windsurfing, sea kayaking, bicycling, and shopping excursions. The setting, undeniably romantic, attracts honeymooners and couples celebrating anniversaries or special occasions.

The Cloister/Sea Island Golf Club, St. Simons Island, Georgia, Plantation Course, seventh hole

LODGING

Only registered guests of *The Cloister* can play Sea Island, which simplifies the lodging choice. All-inclusive golf packages (three-night minimum stay) that include three full meals daily are available. Play is usually unlimited.

Rooms range upward in size from the smaller, traditional accommodations in the original hotel designed in 1928 by Addison Mizner, who worked in the Spanish-Mediterranean style (red-tiled roofs) with a Georgia twist (peach stucco walls). Now, as then, antebellum oaks and luxuriant gardens grace the grounds. The resort has greatly expanded over the years, with nearly 300 rooms currently available. Newer additions, including Harrington House near the beach, are lighter, airier, and reflect architectural stylings more typical of the Caribbean.

Aerial view of St. Simons Island coastline

the **Sea Island Golf Club (Seaside-Plantation, #87),** a superlative facility linked to *The Cloister,* a languorous getaway that remains one of the nation's most exclusive resorts. George and Barbara Bush honeymooned at The Cloister in 1945 and returned for their 50th wedding anniversary. Before his election as President, Dwight D. Eisenhower learned to play golf at Sea Island. Gerald Ford, an enthusiastic golfer, has visited often. In this staunch Republican environment, Jimmy Carter, a native Georgian, has managed to squeeze in a few fishing trips. Small wonder that many of the Fortune 500's top executives maintain homes on Sea Island and drop by The Cloister for dinner after testing their skills at the 36-hole Sea Island Golf Club, which, oddly enough, is located on neighboring St. Simons Island. (The resort complex at The Cloister occupies Sea Island, a five-mile-long sandy strip of pristine beaches and Old South vegetation.)

The Cloister/Sea Island Golf Club, Seaside Course, seventh hole

The impressive Avenue of Oaks heralds the entrance to the Sea Island Golf Club, which occupies the former site of the Retreat Plantation, renowned as a producer of long-staple Sea Island cotton in the late 1700s. It was on these former plantation grounds that Walter Travis laid out the resort's first nine in 1927, routing fairways over old cotton fields hemmed in by marshland, lagoons, and a dense maritime forest of palmettos, pines, and oaks. The Plantation nine, as it is known, was reworked two years later by the English design duo of H.S. Colt and C.H. Alison, who removed many of the "chocolate drop" mounds Travis had created to emulate the seaside hillocks common at British links courses. In the early 1990s, makeover maestro Rees Jones was brought in to install a new drainage system at the chronically marshy Plantation nine—and also to nudge the holes gently into the modern era. This he accomplished with his usual creative flair and sensitivity to traditional design. Bunkers were repositioned, pedestal greens recontoured and new tees created to add length.

Among the feature holes on this gorgeous tree-lined nine is the par-four second, called "Shady Nook," where players must negotiate deep bunkers and looming oaks to find and hold the elevated green with their approach shots. The third, a long par three called "Bald Eagle," is balanced by the short par-three seventh, known as "Noah's Ark," which calls for a wee pitch over a boot-shaped lagoon to a well-defended green. It's a relatively simple shot—except when the wind is in your face.

After refashioning the Plantation nine, Colt and Alison set to work devising the Seaside nine, which not only contains Sea Island's best

stretch of golf, but is one of the finest nine-holers in the nation. Constructed over filled marshland, with several holes drawing near St. Simons Sound, it is the closest approximation of a British links to be found anywhere in the South. Small raised greens, gaping pits of sand, and fickle sea breezes defend par commendably. So does the ever-present marsh and its tributaries.

Sea Island's core 18 was supplemented in 1960 by Dick Wilson, who built the *Retreat* nine, often described as a woodsier version of the Seaside nine. Marked by big bunkers, giant greens, and a pair of lakes very much in play at four holes, the Retreat, like the Plantation, was completely overhauled by Rees Jones, reopening to acclaim in late 1998. According to Scott Davenport, Sea Island's director of golf, the Retreat and Plantation nines will eventually be paired to create the Parkland Course. The club's fourth nine, Marshside, a short, tight, Joe Lee creation that meanders through a brackish marsh laced with tidal inlets, will one day be recast in the image of the Seaside nine and grafted to it to create the Seaside Course.

Sea Island attracts a corps of professional caddies, each intimately acquainted with the four nines and each readily recognizable in his white coveralls. Walking is the way to go: Greens and tees are close together, while each of the nines is relatively flat. Walkers who wish to carry their own bags can do so after 4 p.m. Lastly, the club offers complimentary green fees to juniors (under 19) who are staying with their families at The Cloister.

The Trail

Alabama's Robert Trent Jones Golf Trail Redefines Public Golf

The best and biggest public golf story of the 1990s can be summed up in two words: The Trail. The Trail, for players living a sheltered existence, refers to Alabama's extraordinary Robert Trent Jones Golf Trail. Imagine: four 54-hole facilities and three 36-hole complexes stretching from the Gulf of Mexico to the foothills of the Appalachians, all served by handsome clubhouses, each with an affordable green fee, and all designed by living legend Robert Trent Jones on prime land donated to the state by municipalities, corporations, and developers. Completed in 1994, the Trail signaled a defining moment in the evolution of public golf in America. Never before had a state undertaken a golf construction project of this magnitude for the public good. Taken together, the facilities offer nothing less than an epic journey through a gorgeous state that touristically has always lived in the shadow of its neighbors to the south and east—Florida and Georgia. For the unattached player accustomed to the short end of the stick, the Trail is an answered prayer. Its fascinating genesis is worth detailing.

The year was 1990, and the speaker was Dr. David Bronner, CEO of Retirement Systems of Alabama, whose idea it was to use state pension funds to build a chain of public courses after he learned that the main reason people visit Alabama was to drive through it. His idea was BIG—apply $120 million from a $13-billion superfund to construct 18 layouts. (Though some state residents were appalled at the outlay of cash, the development monies spent to build the Trail represented about 45 days' worth of interest on the fund's principal.)

The network of courses, all located within 15 minutes of an interstate highway and each within a two-hour drive of the next, were intended to divert golfers bound for Florida and elsewhere. The idea was to bolster tourism, spur growth, and attract retirees, though the layouts were hardly intended for slow-swinging geriatrics. At full strength, the Trail's layouts are bar none the strongest collection of public-access courses in the nation.

It took more than big money, free land, and a mild climate to get the Trail off the ground. It also took a team comprised of a visionary gambler

Robert Trent Jones, Roger Rulewich, and Bobby Vaughan at The Trail

(Dr. Bronner), a tireless enabler (Bobby Vaughan), and the world's best-known designer (Robert Trent Jones). Vaughan, a former director of golf at Tanglewood Park in Clemmons, N.C., and the man hand-picked by Dr. Bronner to head up SunBelt Golf Corp., the Trail's parent company, can be accurately described as a "type AA" personality. He worked directly with Roger Rulewich, formerly Jones' chief design associate, in creating the golf courses. According to Vaughan, "Rulewich is the best router of golf courses in the world. He has the ability to extract maximum value from a given site." Rulewich, however, tends to favor blind shots and semiobscured pedestal greens in the design of his holes, elements generally abhorrent to better players. Vaughan, like most golf pros, wants to see the target clearly when he's planning a shot. The push-pull collaboration between Rulewich and Vaughan resulted in the creation of 18 outstanding golf courses with strategic options for all types of players.

Given their overall excellence, the average green fees at a Trail facility are a bargain. But then, the Trail's ringleaders wanted championship-caliber courses that would be technology-proof well into the next century. "Torture the men and pamper the ladies" is Vaughan's motto. Like Jones, he firmly believes that technological advances in golf equipment are stacking the deck too high in favor of the player these days. Multiple tee boxes (up to *11* on some holes) will prevent Trail sites from becoming outmoded, while giving the average duffer a fair chance of success. The purple tees at each course are guaranteed to scare the daylights out of anyone with a number in his handicap. *Behind* the purple tees on several key holes are what the directors of golf refer to as the "marketing" tees—the *way-waybacks* that will prevent the big boomers of the future from making mincemeat of the Trail's courses. As it stands, there isn't a pro alive who could tour the entire Trail and return an even-par score from the tournament tees.

Despite their amazing topographical variety, the Trail's uniformity provides the comfort of recognition. The clubhouses at the 54-hole layouts, each a large brick edifice with a wraparound verandah, are stamped from the same mold. Inside, each has exposed beam ceilings, a large cut-stone fireplace, green leather chairs and sofas, and rich tartan carpeting. The

DINING

Five miles south of Cambrian Ridge is *The Smokehouse*, a down-home restaurant and country store where the smoked meats, camp stew, and ham biscuits served with grits and redeye gravy are a must. Very fattening desserts (the coconut cream pie is devastating) are also available. The establishment's secret recipe barbecue sauce makes an excellent gift—if you can resist using it all yourself.

The Robert Trent Jones Golf Trail, Cambrian Ridge, Alabama, Canyon nine, ninth hole

pro shops, spacious and airy, are stocked with top-of-the-line merchandise. Only the golf memorabilia on display in the lounge and the menu selections in the grill vary from site to site. No beat-up metal lockers and scuffed linoleum floors in the locker rooms, either. Louvered wooden lockers (there's a modest daily fee for their rental), spotless showers, and clean carpeting deviate sharply from the ramshackle facilities at most public courses. Clubhouses at the 36-hole facilities, also uniform, are smaller and more intimate. The green-and-white signage is the same at each site, and Bronner prevailed upon the highway department to put up nearly 90 Trail signs on interstates throughout Alabama so that golfers are properly guided to their destinations.

There is uniformity on the golf side, too. Each of the 54-hole complexes has an out-and-back 18-hole course; an 18-holer with returning nines; and an 18-hole Short Course of par threes that is far beyond the norm of the typical pitch 'n putt layout. In fact, many of the one-shotters on these courses, their large, multitiered greens framed by water, sand, or trees, are the equal of the par threes on the main tracks. "The Short Courses are not a secondary product, just a *different* product," commented one director of golf. As a place to settle a few wagers at day's end or merely to sharpen your short game, they're unparalleled.

The Trail's 36-hole facilities have three returning nines, each with a distinct personality, as well as a nine-hole Short Course.

More uniformity: There's a green-and-white-striped 150-yard stake in the center of the fairway at each par four and par five. It is most welcome.

This point of reference is all any average golfer needs to size up a shot—marked sprinkler heads tend to glue a golfer's nose to the ground and hinder the pace of play.

There's a sign on the first tee of each course that sets the tone for the Trail. It reads: "For your enjoyment the following tees are recommended:

> Purple (Tournament) 5 and under
> Orange (Championship) 6–12
> White (Regular) 13–19
> Teal (Forward) 20 and over

The departure from the traditional red, white, and blue color scheme for tee markers enables a rank beginner or senior male golfer to play from the forward tees without feeling he's on the ladies' tee. Tee markers on the Trail are pegged to ability level, not gender. The secret to enjoying the Trail is to choose the color tee markers best suited to your skill level.

There's something else posted on the first tee, something that evokes the true spirit of the game. It's called Suggested Rules of Play, and reads as follows: "Play the ball as it lies. Play the course as you find it. Play fair. A four hour round is expected." It amounts to a golfer's credo.

The Trail, which recorded over 400,000 rounds in 1997, has had a $1 billion economic impact (hotels, restaurants, etc.) since its opening. In a state where tourism is now the top industry, the Trail is Alabama's number one tourist attraction.

Head north to Montgomery, the first capital of the Confederate States of America, to see the Civil Rights Memorial, where excerpts from Dr. Martin Luther King, Jr.'s "I Have a Dream" speech are inscribed on a black granite wall. With its well-preserved antebellum homes and pioneer log cabins, the city's *Old Alabama Town* is worth exploring. Also, Montgomery's renowned *Alabama Shakespeare Festival* stages the Bard's dramas and comedies as well as other productions on two stages (October through July). Farther afield, in Tuscaloosa—home of the University of Alabama—is the visitor center of *Mercedes-Benz*, the firm's only passenger vehicle assembly facility in North America. Factory tours are available.

Forty miles south of Montgomery is Greenville, the "Camellia City," a sleepy little town where the Courtyard Café serves a peanut-butter-and-jelly sandwich (on white bread) for under $1 and where the mayor holds office in a shoe store. Hank Williams grew up nearby Georgiana. This, after all, is the Heart of Dixie. It is also home to **Cambrian Ridge (Canyon-Sherling, #40),** the sweetheart of the Trail.

A 36-hole complex with the severest elevation changes on the Trail, Cambrian Ridge is best experienced by degrees. The first swats should be taken on the *Loblolly* nine, which presents the kindest, gentlest golf holes at the facility. Here, gently rolling fairways, cathedral-like pines, and water-fronted greens conjure a serene, Augusta National ambience. However, the 70-yard-long, tri-level green at the par-three fourth is far more radical than anything confronting the pros in the Masters. Loblolly is the facility's most walkable nine, which makes it a favorite of locals.

First-time visitors to Cambrian Ridge often experience vertigo on the *Canyon* nine, the opening stanza of the core 18 voted to the "Top 100" list. For example, the drop from tee to fairway at the first hole, a 501-yard (!) par four, is over 200 feet from the purple tees. (Imagine driving the ball from atop a 20-story building.) This hole kicks off a thrilling stretch of target-style, roller-coaster golf carved from former hunting grounds (deer blinds remain nailed to the larger hardwoods) where accuracy is everything. Hog-backed fairways bisected by meandering creeks call for precision drives (but not always with a driver) in order to set up pinpoint approach shots to severely contoured greens. With its steep drops, crowned fairways, and dipsy-doodle greens, the Canyon offers a style of golf otherwise unavailable in the Deep South.

And then there's the *Sherling* nine, which may well offer the best and most beautiful stretch of golf on the entire Trail. The first hole, a par five, runs along the top of Cambrian Ridge, an ancient geologic feature that partitions the course and from which elevated tees have been carved. Drama takes center stage at the par-four third, where players tee from a wooded bluff directly to Sherling Lake, the city's reservoir. The drop from tee to fairway is a dizzying 200 feet; the hilltop green site is equally spec-

tacular. At the fifth, another par four stretching to 428 yards from the tips, players must decide how much of the lake to bite off with their drives. Will it be the ideal target line, or the safe route? This is a classic Cape hole that asks players to weigh the risk-reward element of the tee shot carefully. The sixth, director of golf Kenny Szuch's favorite hole, is a pure, bunkerless par four with a creek down its right side and a green backed into a forest of tall pines and dogwoods. The eighth, a titanic 636-yard par five with a heavily bunkered fairway and a semi-island green, should remain a three-shotter well into the next century. Sherling's testing par-four ninth marches straight uphill past a deep ravine strewn with ochre-colored boulders to a lolling tongue of a double green shared with the ninth on the Canyon nine. Above this green is a tidy clubhouse set atop the highest point in Butler County, its veranda serving up expansive 35-mile views of Dixie forestland. Settle into a rocking chair with a refreshing beverage on this porch sited above the treetops, and you'll understand the local sentiment that there can be few finer places in the South to rehash the day's events than here.

Cambrian Ridge was expected to be the Trail's sleeper site, but word of mouth quickly turned the facility into one of the "must-plays." Which is just fine with Szuch, who moved to Greenville from Miami and hasn't stopped smiling since the charming Short Course, tucked between ridge and lake, opened in 1995. Players who tour the Short Course in early morning or late afternoon will likely see wild turkeys and white-tailed deer during the round.

A few miles from Auburn University and only 90 minutes by car from Atlanta is **Grand National,** the Trail's superstar. Nestled in pine forests along the shores of 600-acre Lake Saugahatchee (32 of the 54 holes are draped along its capes and coves), this extraordinary facility lives up to its advance billing and exalted name. Even the directors of golf at the other Trail sites, while fiercely proud of their facilities, concur that Grand National is, overall, the best complex on the Trail. Trent Jones, who has gazed upon some promising terrain in his long career, pronounced the setting for Grand National the "best natural location for a golf course" he had ever seen.

LODGING

In addition to a Holiday Inn in Greenville, there's also *Pine Flat Plantation*, a cozy bed-and-breakfast with five spacious guest rooms located in Forest Home, west of Cambrian Ridge. The columned front porch of the plantation house, built in 1825 and one of the area's best-preserved homes, has old-time rockers and swings overlooking gardens of camellias, azaleas, and lilies. Pine Flat serves the finest country breakfast in the county. Horseback riding and hay rides are available on the premises.

They're usually loath to admit it, but golfers are suckers for aesthetics. Enthusiasts will admit to enjoying elevated tees—aaah, that hang time—and they like to see water. Beautiful trees are a bonus. Grand National has all three elements in abundance. It also presents a fair but rigorous challenge from each set of tees. However, first-timers planning to take the full measure of either the *Links* or *Lake* courses would be well-advised to regrip their ball retriever prior to arrival. Grand National can be a soggy experience for the uninitiated.

The cornerstone of the complex is the **Links Course** (#51), which sizes up as a collection of finishing holes. It is without a single weakness and, from the tips at 7,311 yards, can hold its own with the most rigorous public golf courses in the nation. Were it stuck for a site at the eleventh hour, the USGA could host any of its top events here, including the U.S. Open. It would simply be a question of persuading the contestants to pull up their socks and play it.

Relentless from start to finish, the backbone of the Links is its prodigious par fours, several of which cartwheel around the lake's weedy coves. Following the lakeside par-three third, the game is on at the fourth, a sturdy par four that bends from right to left around the shore of the lake. As is true throughout the course, the green here is backed into a marshy area, further reducing the margin for error. The fifth and seventh holes are both lengthy, left-to-right doglegs that play uphill and call for extra club on the approach shot. A finger of the lake sticks into the fairway at the short par-four eighth, necessitating a lay-up off the tee, while the 13th, 418 yards from the tips, invites players to carry or lay up short of a pair of bunkers in the center of the fairway. The approach must carry water to reach a tricky green. Each of the holes thereafter is somehow stronger and more terrifying than the one preceding it.

Robert Trent Jones Golf Trail, Grand National, Links Course, third hole

Even if you've somehow managed to survive the first 17 holes on the Links, the par-four 18th (471 yards from the tips) is designed to undo all the good that might have gone before. Knowing full well that most golfers are mentally fatigued from the tireless demands of the course at this point in the round, Jones nevertheless insists that players uncork a flawless drive over water and then launch a laserlike approach over a corner of the lake to reach a pedestal green shored up by large, rough-cut boulders. The 18th is a fortress of a golf hole that demands two absolutely perfect shots—and a steady hand with the putter. Bogey is a good score for most.

The **Lake Course** (#59), with 12 holes hugging the shore, is every bit as scenic as the Links but is perhaps two or three shots friendlier. Because it's less grueling and more manageable than the Links—fairways more open, approaches less demanding—it is generally preferred by a broader range of enthusiasts. It is, however, no walk in the park. When players in the Nike Tour Championship took on the full measure of the Lake in 1997, the average 18-hole score for the field over four days was 73.75 (par is 72).

The layout, hillier in places than the Links, gives players a chance to warm up on the opening six holes before kicking into gear at the rugged par-five seventh, where the grayish-blue lake comes into play around the green. Wind dictates the shot at the beautiful par-three eighth, where the lake yokes two-thirds of the green, while the ninth and 10th holes are both tremendous uphill par fours. The 12th, a risk-reward par five with water in play down the entire left side à la Pebble Beach, would be the signature hole on the Lake if it weren't for the exquisite par-three 15th hole, which may be the single prettiest hole on the Trail. It's certainly the most photographed. Players must carry their tee shots over a watery expanse and land their ball on a slender natural isthmus that juts into the lake. Ranging from 230 yards from the purple markers to 93 yards from the teal tees, the Lake's 15th is one of the finest natural one-shotters in the nation.

Both the Lake and Links courses feature smooth bentgrass greens syringed by a "wilt patrol" on hot summer days. The full-size layouts command most of the attention, but the facility's Short Course is a thing of beauty: Half its holes are flanked or fronted by water. Bring a ball retriever and a healthy sense of humor if you decide to play it from the tips.

The rear veranda of Grand National's clubhouse, with its wet bar and outdoor grill overlooking Lake Saugahatchee, is one of the best 19th holes anywhere. As a place to tally up your score at the end of the day (you may need an adding machine after tackling the Links Course), it is peerless.

Ease of access has added to Grand National's popularity. And, by the way, the change from Eastern to Central time passing from Georgia to Alabama adds an hour to a golfer's day.)

If it weren't so great, Grand National could be accused of being immodestly named. But with two "Top 100" courses on site, plus a superlative Short Course as a bonus, it *is* that great.

Robert Trent Jones Golf Trail, Grand National, Lake Course, 15th hole

Robert Trent Jones Golf Trail, Grand National, Lake Course, 16th hole

The Full Trail

Interested in blazing the entire Trail? Here are thumbnail sketches of the other facilities on the Robert Trent Jones Golf Trail.

Magnolia Grove, Mobile. While much of Alabama's coastal area is flat, the 54-hole complex at Magnolia Grove on the outskirts of Mobile occupies hilly terrain, with holes carved from a thick maritime forest of hardwoods, pines, and flowering shrubs bisected by creeks and streams. The Falls Course, stretching to 7,240 yards from tips, features elevated, liberally contoured greens framed by enormous cloverleaf bunkers. Holes eight through 15 are called "Amen Avenue" because of their difficulty. The Falls is named for the stair-stepped waterfall that cascades across the 10th fairway and leads to a heavily contoured green that falls *eight feet* from back to front! The Crossings Course, only slightly less difficult than the Falls, doubles across railroad tracks. Strategic options abound on this surprisingly hilly layout. The final two holes—the intimidating par-three 17th and long, uphill par-four 18th, a.k.a. "The Terminator"—provide one of the toughest finishes on the Trail. The facility's Short Course has several classy one-shotters that call for forced carries over wetlands. Mobile, a port city on the coast of Mexico, is known for its spicy Creole-style seafood—the Original Oyster House and King Neptune's are among the top choices.

Highland Oaks, Dothan. Located in the southeast corner of the state outside Dothan, the "Peanut Capital of the World," this 36-hole complex features the most traditional, classically designed holes on the Trail. Also the longest. The watery, wide-open Highlands nine stretches to an ungodly 3,892 yards from the purple tees. The rolling Marshwood nine, carved from mossy hardwoods, is anchored by the infamous sixth, a par five of overnight journey proportions stretching to *701 yards* from the tips. It's the Trail's longest hole and a fine, strategic three-shotter from the forward tees. The Magnolia nine proceeds from low-lying wetlands to higher ground dotted with magnificent magnolias. Nettlesome rough can bury wayward players on all three nines. The Short Course, with its demanding bunker placements and water in play at three holes, is testing. The bermudagrass greens at Highland Oaks are superb. Like to fish? Nearby Lake Eufala is one of the nation's top spots for largemouth bass.

Oxmoor Valley, Birmingham. Situated at the southern terminus of the Appalachian Mountains, this 54-hole facility was built on former mining land owned by U.S. Steel. The Ridge Course, the Trail's first layout to open, is a dramatic track with 150-foot elevation changes. Tree-lined, roller-coaster fairways lead to "buried elephant" greens, with several forced carries over ravines required. The flatter, more conventional Valley Course treads more lightly on the average duffer's ego, though the layout's uphill par-four 18th, listed at 414 from the tips (it plays at least 475 yards) has been dubbed "The Assassin." Oxmoor Valley's Short Course splits the difference between the Ridge and the Valley. All three courses feature smooth bentgrass greens. The clubhouse, sited atop Little Shades Mountain, is a popular gathering spot.

Silver Lakes, Calhoun County. For golfers with advanced skills who feel they've arrived as players, the 36-hole Silver Lakes facility serves up three of the toughest nines in the nation, appropriately named Mindbender, Heartbreaker, and Backbreaker. Set on rolling terrain beside Talladega National Forest, each nine is anchored by long par fours and fives that lead to skytop greens perched 30 to 40 feet above fairway level. Because all the trouble is in front, the best strategy at Silver Lakes is to try to overshoot the green. And eat your Wheaties. The Mindbender can be outfoxed, but the Heartbreaker, which stretches to 3,828 yards from the tips, offers the golfing equivalent of cardiac arrest. Backbreaker is nearly as wrenching, but its fine views of Appalachian foothills are fair compensation. The Short Course, with water in play at seven holes and a 12-foot waterfall beside the sixth green, is the Trail's toughest collection of one-shotters. Worked up an appetite? The Top o' The River in nearby Gadsden features a Riverboat Special (half-pound catfish filet with all the trimmings) for under $10.

Hampton Cove, Huntsville. This 54-hole complex at the northern end of the Trail occupies a bowl-shaped valley in the Appalachian foothills. The Highlands Course, routed on hilly terrain, is only average by Trail standards, though there's a decent mix of holes and nice mountain views. The River Course is the only Trent Jones layout in the world without a single sand trap. Driving zones are roomy, though accurate approaches and clever pitches must be played to score. The enormous 250-year-old black oak behind the 18th green is the best tree on the Trail. The nearly treeless Short Course, also located within the flood plain, has water in play at more than half the holes. Because of its northern location, Hampton Cove is best enjoyed from April to mid-November. Huntsville's top attraction is the U.S. Space and Rocket Center, which offers tours of NASA labs as well as hands-on exhibits.

The New Trail

A work in progress, the Trail cut the ribbon in 1999 on a new facility in Prattville, on the outskirts of Montgomery, the state capital. SunBelt Golf brought Jones, at 91, out of retirement and reunited him with Rulewich to develop a 54-hole facility on a superb 1,500-acre site near I-65. The large tract of privately held and city-owned land, as well as a parcel of federal property, was made available to the design team, who were free to conjure three full-size layouts stretching from a prominent escarpment to a river basin. The 54-hole complex has the potential to become the jewel in the Trail's crown. There are sharp elevation changes (like Cambrian Ridge) and a large, beautiful lake (like Grand National). The plantation-style clubhouse will look directly from a ridgetop across a lake to the Montgomery skyline.

The facility's upper course is a treeless, Scottish-style design routed on former cotton fields atop a 350-foot-high ridge, while the middle course tumbles down from the side of the ridge from the first tee, circulating golfers around the shores of 250-acre Cooters Lake. The lower course also has dramatic elevation changes, with several island greens accenting the design.

Because the preexisting Trail sites have a reputation for difficulty, the Prattville courses were designed to be a little more "user-friendly." Each is tough as nails from the tips, but greens overall have milder undulations than those at the other sites, while forested borderlines have been cleared so that golfers can find stray shots and attempt a recovery.

THE DEAL

Three-, five-, and seven-day Trail Passes entitling holders to unlimited green fees at any facility (tee times for initial and secondary rounds can be made 45 days in advance) simplify the planning of a trip. A Trail Sampler entitles pass holders to one green fee per course at each complex. In addition, golf packages with motels, inns, and bed-and-breakfasts have been negotiated by the Trail. Depending upon the package purchased, players can devise a southern or northern itinerary that covers three or four sites. All are within five to 15 miles of interstate highways, and each is within two hours of the next. (A minimum of 10 days is required to play the entire Trail.) No two facilities resemble each other—all are topographically diverse.

Golfers can play the Short Course following a full round for just the price of a golf cart. Walkers are welcome at all times. Nine-hole rates, twilight rates (after 4 p.m.), and early bird specials (7 a.m. to 9 a.m. on full-length courses) are also available, as is a 15 percent discount on green fees and merchandise to AAA members.

Mississippi

Casino gambling aboard giant riverboats lashed to the shore has sparked resort hotel and golf course growth along the Mississippi Gulf Coast, but the state's top-rated public-access course is a bit upcountry from the Gulf.

East of the famous Natchez Trace Parkway, on 352 acres of tribal land belonging to the Mississippi Band of Choctaw Indians, Tom Fazio and Jerry Pate have joined forces to develop the state's greatest asset since Elvis came of age in nearby Tupelo. Far removed from the dead-flat Delta, the land in central Mississippi is marked by ridges and streams and red clay hills dotted with sturdy oaks and tall pines. Entirely sodded with bermudagrass (only the greens were sprigged), the superbly conditioned **Dancing Rabbit Golf Club** (#63) is a brilliant 7,128-yard layout named for the tribe's final treaty with the U.S. government.

Granted total freedom to develop the finest course possible on a site of his own choosing, Fazio created a refined, parkland-style spread marked by 13 elevated tees and numerous raised greens. Nearly five miles of spring-fed creeks crisscross the fairways and dictate play at half the holes. No expense was spared by the tribe to create a first-class venue—an underground air ventilation system protects the delicate bentgrass greens in hot, humid summer weather.

It's difficult to single out feature holes on this seamless, flawless 18 that opened to instant acclaim in 1997. The quartet of one-shotters, three of which plunge sharply downhill, are exceptional. The eighth hole, rated the toughest on the course and stretching to 465 yards from the tips, is one of the finest natural par fours in the nation. The driving area is generously wide, but the approach must be rifled into a chute of trees, the green tucked deep in the woods and well-defended by bunkers. The ninth and 18th holes, both testing par fours graced by strategic water features,

are memorable Nassau nightmares that can make or break a match.

A pure golf experience unsullied by real estate, Dancing Rabbit is anchored by a clubhouse described by the tribe as "the house your grandmother should have lived in." It's a three-story, plantation-style brick structure with high ceilings and two wrap-around verandas overlooking rolling, wooded hills. Designed for purists, walkers are welcome and caddies available at the club. There's also a 15-acre driving range with seven targets, two putting greens, and a chipping green.

New & Noteworthy

Jerry Pate, who calls Dancing Rabbit Mississippi's answer to Augusta National (in common with Augusta, it does have towering pines, azaleas and dogwoods, dramatic elevation changes, and superbly manicured turfgrass), feels that Dancing Rabbit's second venue, opened in spring, 1999, is even more spectacular than the original. A rugged, challenging test with 100-foot elevation changes, it picks up where the first layout left off. As on their first effort, very little dirt was moved to make way for the holes. Fazio is a master at coaxing dramatic, playable holes from existing topography. Pate, a former U.S. Open champion with several design credits of his own, has "strategized" both courses from the perspective of the accomplished golfer.

One difference from the original course, in addition to the fact that the second layout sprawls across 450 acres, is the zoysia grass used to carpet the fairways. Zoysia tends to perch the ball, giving players a consistently perfect lie every time.

LODGING

Clubhouse at Dancing Rabbit Golf Club, Philadelphia, Mississippi

The casino at The Silver Star Resort & Casino

You must be a guest of *Silver Star Resort & Casino* to play Dancing Rabbit. Want to overnight on the doorstep of the courses? The second floor of the golf clubhouse boasts eight upscale bedrooms with king-size beds and French doors leading to the veranda. Given their luxury and attention to detail, they are priced well below market value ($125–$150 at press time).

SIDETRIPS

The *Natchez Trace Parkway*, part of the National Park System, is a modern, beautifully landscaped two-lane road, free of billboards, that closely follows the route of the original "trace," a 450-mile Indian trail stretching from Tennessee to Natchez, Mississippi.

One of the key stops along the way is *Tupelo*, the largest city in north Mississippi, where Elvis Presley was born in a modest shotgun house built by his father for $180. The house, restored to the way it was when the Presleys lived in it, is surrounded by *Elvis Presley Park* (the gift shop carries Elvis souvenirs). Want more Elvis? The *Tupelo Museum* features additional Presley memorabilia.

Sixty miles north of Philadelphia is *Columbus*, where fans of elaborate antebellum homes can view some of the finest examples of their kind in the South. There's *Waverley* (1852), a National Historic Landmark outside Columbus renowned for its octagonal atrium and twin spiral staircases; *Rosedale* (1856), an Italianate masterpiece; and *White Arches* (1857), another beautifully detailed plantation mansion. The Welcome Center in Columbus is playwright Tennessee Williams's boyhood home.

New & Noteworthy

Grand Pines. The region's gold-plated poker chip. A Jack Nicklaus Signature course opened in spring, 1999, this fabulous track located midway between the Grand Casino Gulfport and Grand Casino Biloxi has the finest natural features of any course in the area. Bounded by white sand beaches along the Little Biloxi and Big Biloxi rivers, Grand Pines is a multitheme design that skirts a cypress swamp, surmounts a huge ridge, and plays beneath a canopy of 60-foot-high magnolia trees. Towering pines up to 120 feet in height frame several holes, while oxbow bends in the two rivers must be carried from the championship tees at several holes. Grand Pines is a "destination" course worth a detour.

Dancing Rabbit Golf Club, ninth hole

The Northeast

Bethpage State Park, Black Course • Nemacolin Woodlands Resort

Mystic Rock Golf Course • New Seabury Country Club, Blue Course

Taconic Golf Club • Sugarloaf Golf Club

Sugarloaf Golf Club, Carrabassett Valley, Maine, 11th hole

New York

There are only a handful of "Top 100" courses in the original colonies, but what's there is historic or hair-raising or downright appealing, despite the relatively short season.

An hour's drive east of New York City on Long Island is **Bethpage State Park**, a 90-hole golf factory where everything mirrors the size and scale of Gotham itself. The parking lot would play as a par 10 were it surfaced with grass, the supermarket-size pro shop could host an equipment trade show, and the bar at the 91st hole is nearly as long and busy as the nearby Long Island Expressway. None of these items, however, exceeds the measure of the infamous **Black Course** (#4), site of the 2002 U.S. Open.

A.W. Tillinghast, best known for his work at Winged Foot, Baltusrol, and Quaker Ridge, to name three storied New York area clubs, used work relief crews totaling 1,800 men in the early 1930s to revise an existing layout (the former Lenox Hills Country Club, now the Green Course); and to sculpt three new layouts from the spine of central Long Island's hills and hardwoods. (A fifth course was added in 1958.) The Black, opened in 1936 and acknowledged to be Tillinghast's final creation, is the flagship of the facility, itself the nation's largest public golf complex. A strategic tour de force clearly intended to separate the men from the boys, the Black is brute testimony to "Tillie the Terror's" design wizardry and farsightedness, given recent advances in equipment.

Perhaps prompted by a feature that appeared in *GOLF Magazine* in June 1993, in which it was gently suggested that Bethpage Black could host the U.S. Open in place of Baltusrol that month "were it not for the caravan of golf nuts who queue up daily to cross swords with one of the greatest layouts in the nation," the USGA sent a posse to Bethpage shortly before the U.S. Open was held at Shinnecock Hills on eastern Long Island in 1995. Notwithstanding its threadbare condition, the raters were duly impressed by the design and rigor of the Black. It was also fortunate that David Fay, executive director of the USGA, had long fostered the notion of bringing the national championship to a true public course. (Pebble Beach and Pinehurst No. 2 are, after all, high-priced resort spreads. The green fee on the Black is $25 weekdays, $30 weekends.)

It also helped that Fay, who grew up in the New York area, saw the Black Course as an enduring symbol of public golf in America, a beloved-by-the-masses venue designed by the same man who laid out many of the courses favored by the USGA for its championships. Fay also noted that over 60 percent of the USGA's member clubs are public facilities—the exclusive private clubs that traditionally host the association's top events are in a minority.

On the downside, the Black had endured 50,000 rounds of golf a year, decade after decade, with minimal upkeep. The course had deteriorated badly. On the plus side, no misguided greens chairman or club president (Bethpage has neither) had seen fit to deface the layout or alter its design.

Bethpage State Park, Farmingdale, New York, Black Course, fifth hole

It was a tarnished original, a battered masterpiece, but not beyond repair. It took a $2.7 million commitment by the USGA, the donated services of "U.S. Open Doctor" Rees Jones, and a state government eager to attract the national championship to one of its parks for Bethpage Black to get the major refurbishment it sorely needed. But what work needed to be done!

According to Jones, who took on the Black as his sixth restoration project in preparation for a U.S. Open, trees had sprouted in bunkers, tees were beaten to dust, greens were worn to the nub. Working from a 1938 aerial photo of the course (original plans were not available), Jones returned the layout to its original scheme, with a few inspired embellishments of his own that he felt completed the work Tillinghast never finished. The 11-month facelift, which began in July 1997, included the reconstruction of all existing tee boxes as well as the addition of new ones designed to benefit duffers and experts alike. Irrigation lines were dug and sprinkler heads installed at tees and greens. Bunkers that had been abandoned over time were reestablished and brought back into play. In particular, greenside bunkers that had shrunk away from their original positions and ceased to serve a purpose were moved closer to the putting surfaces, their faces flashed up in the Tillinghast style. (The construction crew was taken on a field trip to Winged Foot to see how Tillinghast bunkers should look.) After the bunkers were reshaped, 8,500 tons of sand was trucked in from Pennsylvania to fill them.

The layout's greens, which are relatively flat and average a scant 3,200 square feet, were agronomically improved but were otherwise left alone, although Jones expanded the putting surfaces at three of the par threes (holes 3, 8, and 17) as well as the 15th. Conversely, he reduced the size and changed the shape of the 18th green, creating a small, crescent-shaped putting surface undercut by gaping pits of sand. Most of the holes were lengthened without difficulty, a side benefit of working within the confines of a public park with no real estate boundaries to worry about.

From the blue tees, which only pros and scratch players attempt, the par-71 Black Course stretches to 7,295 yards. With a course rating of 76.6 and a slope of 148, it is by far the toughest course in the New York area. Even from the white tees at 6,789 yards, the Black presents a very formidable test. (For the 2002 U.S. Open, the Black Course will play as a par-70, 7,055-yard layout, with the par-five seventh converted to a 479-yard par four for the event.)

After touring the proposed site for the Black, Tillinghast was quoted in the April 1934, issue of *Golf Illustrated*: "The terrain presents infinite variety. Never quite flat but gently undulating, it grades to impressive ruggedness." Does it ever! With only basic earthmoving equipment at his disposal, Tillinghast let the rise and fall of the land dictate the plan of the course and the shape of the holes. Many of the pedestal greens, for example, occupy knolls or natural plateaus. Others are pushed-up, soil-based surfaces with very mild contours.

The bunkers are something else. Before the makeover, the layout's horrifying maws looked as if they were gouged from the earth by a steam shovel run amok. Today they are larger, more stylized, and very imposing, their capes and bays clearly defined, as if a blurry photograph had been brought into sharp focus. Happily, the loose rocks are gone, as are footprints that had not been raked since the 1950s.

A hole-by-hole review of the Black might be as burdensome as playing the course from the blue tees on a windy day. (Ironically, Tillinghast, the man who coined the word "birdie," provided very few birdie opportunities on his swan song.)

First off, the Black is probably the grandest of the nation's public-access parkland tests. Second, the Black has as fine a collection of par fours as any course in America, public or private. If not the finest, then certainly the toughest. (From the *white tees,* seven of the par fours exceed 420 yards in length.) Last, the Black is not just a beast. It's also a beauty. Most of the holes are framed by stout, thick-waisted oaks rising to 40 feet, with other hardwoods, pines, and thickets of native scrub (including poison ivy) present as well. Each hole is memorable and distinctive in its own way. Played cautiously, the modest but straight hitter with a good short game can manage bogeys most of the way. Those attempting pars will have their work cut out for them, for Tillinghast emptied his arsenal on the Black. Jones, for his part, identified and brought to light every nuance.

The Black begins with a 421-yard par four (all yardage quotes are from the white markers) that plays from an elevated tee over an expanse of rough to a fairway that swings to the right around a grouping of trees. The target is tightly guarded by deep greenside bunkers, a recurring theme. After crossing Round Swamp Road, a local thoroughfare, players are confronted by a short par four where a drive of 220 yards or so must be positioned in a narrow fairway laid into a valley. Only the top of the flagstick is visible from the green, which nestles atop a hill to the left. Prefacing the green is a sandy wasteland of appalling proportions. One Bethpage golfer stationed in London during World War II wrote after the blitz: "I've seen no bomb craters that I've studied as anxiously as I have the bunker guarding number two of the Black Course."

At the par-three third, Jones pushed the tee back 30 yards and repositioned it, creating a more difficult angle of attack to a skewed green pro-

DINING

Following a major restoration and expansion of the clubhouse, Bethpage now offers meals that are a match for its courses. *Carlyle on the Green,* which opened in 1999, offers excellent buffet dining for hungry golfers. According to park superintendent David Catalano, the restaurant offers "good meals without extraordinary expense." When the weather is clement, golfers can enjoy their meals on a slate patio shaded by leafy trees and umbrellas. There's also an air-conditioned bar and lounge in the clubhouse.

Bethpage State Park, Black Course, 12th hole

tected by a gaping pit of sand. When players finish putting, they can look through an opening in the trees to one of the grandest sights in American golf—the rising fairway of the fourth hole and its crest, the distant "glacier bunker."

A "short" par five of 486 yards (522 yards from the tips), the fourth is defined by a series of large sand pits up the left side and by a majestic filigreed bunker cut into a huge embankment that crosses the fairway. Jones completely retooled this colossal hazard, which makes the biggest traps on normal courses look puny by comparison. While pros can fly this bunker at will, average players must decide whether to lay up short of it or attempt to carry its imposing wall of flashed sand, depending on their drives. A steep drop into an old scrub-filled quarry awaits over the tiny, well-defended green. All but the longest-hitting pros will play the fourth as a three-shotter in the Open.

Even when it was dilapidated, the Black's fifth hole was recognized as a world-class par four. A classic risk-reward hole, arguably the best two-shotter on Tillinghast's résumé, the hole asks for a mammoth drive over broken ground and an elongated waste bunker that runs diagonally opposite the right side of the fairway. Take the bunker out of play by hitting safely to the left, and this subtle double-dogleg hole is turned into a par five. Beckoning from a plateau at the far end of the fairway is a semiblind, saucerlike green ringed by sand and long grass. At over 450 yards, even the pros may take notice of this one.

At the par-three eighth, which calls for a sharply downhill tee shot over a pond (it's the only water hole on the Black), Jones lengthened the tee by 25 yards and also stretched the green fore and aft. When the pin is cut back right, Open contestants will be forced to hit a high fade about 220 yards to get close to the hole. If the pin is set up front, the shaved bank

above the pond may encourage timid efforts to roll back into the water.

At the 10th and 11th holes, each a very testing par four, Jones rediscovered and enhanced long-lost bunkers cut into a ridge dividing the two holes. Fescues were planted to further delineate the two fairways. The par-four 12th, another world-beater that will stretch to an ungodly 496 yards in the Open (it's merely 432 yards from the white tees), calls for a heroic drive over a rampart embedded with cavernous bunkers. The hole swings left and rewards a high draw that carries 250 yards or more. The safe route to the right turns the hole into a par five. Adding to the difficulty is the wind, which usually is in a player's face on the 12th.

The 15th is yet another of the Black's infamous par fours. Called the "corral hole" for the split-rail fence that swings down the right side of the fairway (there were horse stables nearby many years ago), the 15th plays uphill to a green tucked deep in the woods 60 feet above fairway level. To reach it, a ghastly chasm of sand must be carried or somehow avoided. Jones not only extended the green to the right, bringing the trap further into play, he reintroduced a long-lost false front to the green. The putting surface, canted from back to front, is treacherously contoured.

At the 16th, a par four listed at 457 yards from the whites, Jones improved the angle of attack by shifting the pulpit tee to the right. Also, the trough crossing the fairway—an insidious ditch that snared the average player's drive—was filled in and grassed over. The green, oblique to the line of play, is bigger than it looks but does not present an easy target.

Except for the fact that it lacks the Pacific Ocean lapping greenside, the Black's par-three 17th is every bit as impressive as the 17th at Pebble Beach. The green on this 195-yarder is encased in a Sahara-like sea of sand, the yawning traps swept up to the brink of a shallow figure-eight-shaped green. For the average campaigner, par here is a minor miracle.

By the time players climb the hill to mount the tee of the par-four 18th, there's almost a sense of relief at the sight of the rambling Colonial-style clubhouse in the distance. Jones completely redesigned the 18th hole, previously the Black's weakest link. The tee was pushed 40 yards

Bethpage State Park, Black Course, 17th hole

back into a chute of trees, while the bunkers pinching the landing area were reworked into a fanciful array of inkblots and cloverleafs. Pretty, but punishing. The well-defended hilltop green, reduced in size by nearly half, is set in a natural amphitheater that will give spectators plenty of room to watch the world's best players attempt to win what Jones has dubbed the "People's Open."

Best of all, the Black Course will reopen to the public five days after the conclusion of the Open. The State of New York has pledged to the USGA that in the two to three years after the event, green fees will be raised only in line with the overall rate of inflation.

Because of various calamities over the years, a sign printed in big red letters is posted behind the first tee. It reads: "WARNING: THE BLACK COURSE IS AN EXTREMELY DIFFICULT GOLF COURSE WHICH IS RECOMMENDED ONLY FOR HIGHLY SKILLED GOLFERS." But the Black is not a charmless brute. It has strategic value. Now more than ever, given its improved condition, players who exercise sound course management can navigate their way around trouble at nearly every hole.

Who plays the Black? Oh, a few out-of-towners find their way to Bethpage. Even members of area clubs occasionally jump through the hoops required to get a tee time. But most of the Black's devotees are incorrigible (and fit) New Yorkers who carry or pull their bags (no golf carts are permitted on the Black) and who fully appreciate the fact that the green fee charged by this U.S. Open–quality course is the most golf for the money in America. Closed on Mondays for maintenance, the Black Course is open from mid-April to Thanksgiving, weather permitting.

In 1989, when the Black hosted the Met Open, a prestigious regional event captured in the past by the likes of Walter Hagen, Gene Sarazen, and Byron Nelson, the contestants raved about the course, warts and all. George Zahringer III, a seasoned amateur who lost in a play-off for the title that year and who has played every course of note in the area, called the Black "the best layout I ever saw, public or private. There is a uniqueness to every hole, and it's gorgeous. You could certainly play any national event here, without question." As it happens, THE national event will be played here, and the locals are beside themselves with pride and joy. A

1995 survey of 2,400 golfers at Bethpage revealed that 90 percent supported the idea of bringing the U.S. Open to the Black Course. In addition, nearly 70 percent said they would be interested in working as volunteers for the event.

Think the top players in the world will have their way with "Tillie the Terror's" retrofitted masterpiece, a course that come June of 2002 will have narrow fairways, rock-hard greens, and shin-high rough? As a typical Bethpage golfer might say, "FUGGEDABOUDIT!"

SIDETRIPS

In addition to golf, Bethpage State Park has trails for hiking and biking as well as bridle paths for horseback riding. Playgrounds, picnic areas, and tennis courts are also available. From mid-May through mid-October, polo matches are held twice weekly in the park. *Old Westbury Gardens,* located nearby, is a must destination for flower lovers. An hour's drive from Farmingdale is *Jones Beach State Park* and *Robert Moses State Park* (on Fire Island). Both offer wide, sandy stretches of superb ocean beach.

Old Westbury Gardens

Manhattan skyline

Times Square at night

And then, of course, there is New York City, accessible from Long Island by car or train. Only out-of-towners call it the Big Apple, but any way you slice it, New York City offers more cultural diversity and round-the-clock excitement than any other city in America. Maybe the world. From ethnic neighborhoods (Chinatown, Little Italy) to venerable attractions (Statue of Liberty, Empire State Building, Rockefeller Center), from the western hemisphere's largest art museum (Metropolitan Museum of Art) to the bright lights of Broadway and the sylvan meadows of Central Park, New York, New York has it all—and more.

More Golf/Bethpage

"Were the other three courses at Bethpage as severe as the Black," Tillinghast once wrote, "the place would not enjoy the great popularity it has known since it was opened to the public. If they had to play under such punishing conditions week in and week out, they'd probably chuck their clubs into the lake and take to pitching horseshoes." Thankfully, there are options.

The *Red Course* at Bethpage, were it treated to the kind of T.L.C. lavished on the Black in preparation for the Open, would instantly jump onto the "Top 100" list. Like the Black, the Red is a grand-scale parkland test, its key feature a succession of long par fours that dogleg sharply in the landing area. The *Blue Course,* like the Red a Tillinghast design opened in 1935, is a fine, well-balanced layout with several testing holes on the front nine. It is, however, much less daunting overall than the Black or Red. Several of its holes were incorporated in the design of the *Yellow Course,* an Alfred Tull layout opened in 1958 and considered the least difficult of the facility's five courses. The sleeper at Bethpage is the *Green Course,* a Devereux Emmet layout circa 1924, later touched up by Tillinghast. This 6,267-yard layout occupies a beautiful, rolling site and has a great variety of holes. The Green, like the Black, is reserved for walkers only. The Blue, Yellow, and Green courses are open year-round, weather permitting.

Pennsylvania

When lumber baron Joe Hardy went shopping for an architect to dynamite a course from the dome of a mountain in the Laurel Highlands 65 miles southeast of Pittsburgh, there was only one choice: Pete Dye. Three years in the making, Dye's $18-million **Mystic Rock Golf Course** (#96), the marquee track at the **Nemacolin Woodlands Resort**, is a tour de force punctuated by giant boulders strewn in the rough, Sahara-like bunkers pinching the fairways, and some of the most wickedly undulating greens imaginable. From the tips at 6,832 yards, Mystic Rock's slope rating of 146 exceeds that of Oakmont, Pittsburgh's seven-time U.S. Open site. This is a course that produces the kind of nervous chuckles only Pete Dye can elicit.

Among the layout's more distinctive holes, which from the back tees call for numerous forced carries over scrub-choked ravines, rock-rimmed ponds, and fields of overgrown fescues, is the 496-yard eighth, where players must avoid an acre of sand up the left side and land their approach shots on the layout's smallest green. On the 10th, a long par four, staggered tee boxes are perched atop a narrow dam. The ribbonlike fairway is hemmed in by water and a steep, wooded slope. At the 173-yard 12th, one of four superb one-shotters, the target is 12,000 square feet of bentgrass turmoil prefaced by a rock-walled pond, while at the par-five 16th, golfers tee off from the summit of a man-made "volcano" (built from a pile of rocks) and proceed to a peninsula green edged into a lake beside a waterfall. For good measure, the green is flanked by deep bunkers. Dye used

LODGING, ETC.

A former 1,200-acre game preserve, *Nemacolin Woodlands Resort* in Farmington has been transformed by the Hardy family into a full-service resort. Accommodations are available in the Tudor-style Lodge (rooms range in style from Elizabethan to Art Deco); Château LaFayette, a re-creation of the Ritz in Paris; and two-bedroom condos.

Falling Brook Miniature Golf Course

The Tea Room

In addition to a world-class spa (20,000 square feet of polished marble with treatments to match), the resort offers a 48-stall equestrian center, regulation croquet court, private trout stream, giant free-standing saltwater aquarium, larger-than-Olympic-size pool, simulated turn-of-the-century shopping arcade, interactive video games, a house of meditation, and several lounges, including the Cigar Bar, The Tavern (outfitted with four antique billiard tables), and the Hitchin' Post, a roadhouse-style bar with a mechanical bull. The property's eclectic $30-mil-

The Golf Academy

lion art collection has everything from Tiffany lamps and Calder mobiles to four oversize volumes of James J. Audubon's *Birds of America*. There are also touches of whimsy: Among the more than 100 outdoor sculptures, the life-like cast bronze fisherman, gardener, and jogger can catch the unwary by surprise.

DINING

Fine dining is available in Château LaFayette's signature dining room, *Lautrec,* a stylish bistro with a wood-burning oven and rotisserie as well as a 10,000-bottle wine collection; and the *Golden Trout* at the Inn, a showcase of contemporary American cuisine (the pecan-crusted rainbow trout is superb). For more casual meals at the resort, there's *The Tavern* (pub fare) and *Caddy Shack* (good burgers). Down the road from Nemacolin Woodlands in Chalkhill is the *Stone House,* an early 19th-century inn offering a varied menu of beef, seafood, and pasta dishes.

every trick in the bag—and then some—to manufacture a resort course unlike any in the East.

Given the unyielding nature of the site, it was a complicated engineering feat merely to devise a routing and extract golf holes from the land. (An Ice Age glacier ground to a halt in this corner of Fayette County, depositing massive amounts of rock.) Some of the rock was cut into slabs and used to trim tees and greens; much more was left scattered beside the fairways. After four lakes were dug, excavated material was used to create features—or merely cover the granite mantle. Visually striking, with fine views of rounded peaks from the topmost holes, the designer confined his signature railroad ties to a single green and a few stairways.

Dye gives players of lesser attainment a better-than-even chance of matching their handicaps from the white tees at 6,300 yards or, better yet, the gold tees at 5,860 yards. (As always, Alice Dye, Pete's wife, sensibly placed the red tees well forward of most trouble. They measure 4,800

yards.) Select the correct set of tees, and your ricochet shots off the rocks will be kept to a minimum. Doom and gloom gathers mainly over the heads of bogey shooters who insist on tackling the blue tees.

More Golf / Nemacolin Woodlands

Woodlands Links, the resort's original course, is an engaging, agreeable parkland spread marked by tree-lined fairways, occasional blind tee shots, craggy rock outcrops, and a pond or two. It is overshadowed by Mystic Rock, but with its string of challenging, memorable holes on the back nine, it's well worth a tour. The outdoor dining deck at *The Gazebo* beside the golf shop serves up a three-state view (Pennsylvania, Maryland, and West Virginia).

Nemacolin Woodlands Resort, Farmington, Pennsylvania, Mystic Rock Golf Course, second, 16th, and 17th holes

Massachusetts

Cape Cod

Cape Cod, a two-hour drive south of Boston, is a 70-mile-long flexed arm of land extending into the Atlantic. It was put on the national vacation map in the early 1960s by John F. Kennedy, who used the family compound in Hyannisport as a summer retreat. During that era, farsighted developers built **New Seabury Country Club**, a 2,000-acre resort on the southwest shore of the upper Cape near Mashpee, its gray-shingled townhouses and cottages set back from Nantucket Sound. William Mitchell, one of the most underrated architects of his time, was given free rein to sculpt two courses at the fledgling development. The **Blue Course** (#83), opened in 1964, remains one of Mitchell's finest creations.

Stretching to a ponderous 7,200 yards from the gold tees (6,909 yards from the blue markers and 6,508 yards from the white tees), this Jekyll-and-Hyde layout, touched up by Rees Jones in 1987, opens with a spacious par five that proceeds directly to the sea. The par-four second traces the shore of a sandy beach, the crushed-shell cart path skirting overgrown dunes down the entire left side of the fairway. Eight miles across the sound are the forested bluffs of Martha's Vineyard.

Like the best holes in Britain, the second on the Blue requires golfers to cope with swirling breezes on their tee shots—and avoid well-placed sand pits defending the firm, fast green. The par-four third, rated the toughest hole on the course, also parallels the shore. Here, however, the demands are heightened by a slimmer fairway and a smaller, more tightly bunkered green. The par-three fourth, fully 230 yards from the tips, flanks a tidal marsh that indents the fairway near the green, while the par-five fifth bends to the left around a brackish inlet, its tall reeds crowding the shore. The course thereafter departs the flattish linksland for rolling, wooded terrain where players are shielded from the breeze—but where the greens match the swells and swales of the fairways. This is good golf, very challenging in fact, though less spectacular than the opening holes along the shore.

Happily, the Blue Course tacks back to the sound at the 16th tee for a rousing finale. Indeed, the Blue's trio of concluding par fours provides as strong a finish as any course on the Cape, especially from the back tees. The holes are inland in character, though the sea is in view from the 17th green and 18th tee. The Players Club, an upstairs lounge with an outdoor

New Seabury Country Club, New Seabury, Massachusetts, Blue Course, second hole

DINING

At New Seabury Country Club, the *Popponesset Inn* is an excellent waterside restaurant specializing in traditional New England seafood (broiled scrod, lobster pie, etc.). In addition to trendy fusion cuisine, the featured appetizer at *The Regatta* in Falmouth, located at the harbor entrance, is a lobster martini: chunks of chilled lobster and shrimp served in a martini glass with Stolichnya vodka sauce, marinated olives, and a lemon garnish. *The Regatta* in Cotuit, a sister restaurant occupying an 18th-century Federal mansion, hangs its hat on Cotuit oysters, reputed (along with Wellfleets) to be the Cape's finest. Seeking the perfect baked stuffed lobster? Try *The Black Cat* in Hyannis. Nightlife? Hyannis has several nightclubs and bars featuring live rock and jazz. Serious foodies can journey to *Chillingsworth* in Brewster, a 1689 house furnished with antiques that serves the finest (and most expensive) French haute cuisine on the Cape.

SIDETRIPS

At the elbow of the Cape is Woods Hole, an international center for marine research. Visit the *National Marine Fisheries Aquarium,* browse the craft shops on Water Street.

Provincetown Harbor

Sand dunes in Provincetown

Beachcombers can scour Old Silver Beach on Buzzards Bay, one of the prettiest strands on the upper Cape. Cyclists can pedal Shining Sea Trail, which skirts the southwest coast. Farther east, travelers can stroll Main Street in Hyannis (bric-a-brac shops); drop by the *John F. Kennedy Memorial Museum;* or drive to nearby Barnstable Harbor to join a *Hyannis Whale Watcher Cruise.* Willing to depart Cape Cod for a great day trip? Board the ferry in Woods Hole for Martha's Vineyard, one of the most enchanting islands in the Atlantic. Visiting players can check out *Farm Neck,* a semiprivate club in Oak Bluffs.

deck, serves up a stirring view of the links, the sea, and the Vineyard. It's as fine a place as any in the East to rehash the round.

Note: Cape Cod is only "a land where the blue begins and the frets of life end" in spring and fall. The Cape is thronged with tourists in July and August. For golfers, autumn is the best time to visit. Not only is the air clear and crisp, the water—"the unwearied and illimitable ocean," according to Thoreau—is still warm. (The arm of the Cape deflects the warm Gulf Stream current.) Best of all, the region's courses are in peak condition in the fall. They're also uncrowded. Many, like the Blue, permit walking in the shoulder seasons.

New Seabury Country Club, Blue Course, first, seventh, and eighth holes

LODGING

New Seabury Country Club is a self-contained resort with a private three-mile beach and clusters of one- and two-bedroom villas fronting Nantucket Bay. Golf packages are available.

More Golf/Cape Cod

Overshadowed by the Blue Course, the *Green Course* at New Seabury is a fine test in its own right. A petite 5,939-yard, par-70 layout by William Mitchell, the Green has nice ocean views, small, slick greens, and a stirring collection of par fours.

Elsewhere on the upper Cape, there's *Cape Cod Country Club* in North Falmouth, a classic spread dating to 1929, with heaving fairways and elevated greens. Also in North Falmouth, barely a mile from the sea, is *Ballymeade,* a semiprivate club featuring an exceptionally hilly course swept by capricious winds.

In the middle of the Cape can be found *Olde Barnstable Fairgrounds,* a pleasant test with good amenities (fine clubhouse, nice practice facility); *Bayberry Hills,* a heavily wooded, 7,172-yard layout in West Yarmouth ranked among the Cape's longest and most challenging courses; *Dennis Pines,* its narrow fairways hemmed in by tall conifers; *Hyannis Golf Club* at Iyanough Hills, a rolling, wooded test known for its smooth, fast greens; *Captains Golf Course* in Brewster, a flat, tree-lined test with holes named for salty dogs (sea captains); and *Cranberry Valley,* a well-run facility in Harwich carved from marshes and cranberry bogs.

New Seabury Country Club, ninth hole

The Berkshires

Taconic Golf Club (#61), a historic, jewel-like layout walled in by the Berkshires in the northwest corner of Masssachusetts, is the home course of Williams College. With eager students, visiting alumni, college staff, and local members all champing at the bit to play this dreamy mountain track, outside tee times can be scarce. (Selected weekdays in spring and fall as well as campus-clearing school holidays offer your best opportunity.) Worth the trouble? Most emphatically, yes. Few courses anywhere can match Taconic for scenery, charm, and character.

Taconic got its start in 1896, when three farmers armed with tomato cans (used for cups) laid out a rudimentary course. Nine holes were in play until 1927, when Wayne Stiles of Stiles & Van Kleek, a Boston firm, was brought in to expand and refine the course. The designer found his Camelot at Taconic, molding holes to the existing terrain and taking full advantage of the abrupt elevation changes and glorious mountain setting. The course, like Williamstown itself, is set in a bowl, with tall, curved ridges dominating views from the topmost holes. On a clear day, the Green Mountains of Vermont can be viewed to the north.

Seemingly innocuous on the card—the championship markers are listed at 6,640 yards (par 71), with the tournament course 400 yards shorter

SIDETRIPS

Rainy day? Williams College has a wealth of indoor culture. The *Sterling and Francine Clark Art Institute* is renowned for its 19th-century American art and French Impressionist paintings, including more than 30 by Renoir. The *Williams College Museum of Art,* representing a broad range of periods and cultures, houses one of the nation's finest college art collections. The *Williamstown Theatre Festival* stages plays (classic and contemporary) from late June to August.

Hot summer day? There's public swimming in Williamstown at Margaret Lindlay Park as well as the mineral waters of Sand Springs. Hiking, cycling, and horeseback riding are also popular activities.

More performing arts? Jacob's Pillow in Becket is the nation's oldest dance festival, while Tanglewood, near Lenox, is the summer home of the Boston Symphony Orchestra.

Taconic Golf Club, Williamstown, Massachusetts, eighth hole

Taconic Golf Club, 16th hole

and the white tees stretching to 6,002 yards—Taconic is anything but easy, this despite the fact that the longest of its three par fives, the 18th, is a scant 510 yards from the tips. The front nine, short and picturesque, is where good players hope to score, but driving areas are tight and nearly every approach is narrowed by clumps of birches, grassy hollows, and cavernous bunkers. Many of the greens are elevated above fairway level, further complicating the issue. When the sloping, tilted greens are rolling fast, an approach shot placed above the pin is in jeopardy. Taconic, then, is a shotmaker's course. Have a complaint about the cant of the greens or the preponderance of sidehill lies? There's a suggestion box fixed atop a pole in a small stream at the fourth hole. The front nine finishes in fine style at the par-three ninth, which plunges downhill to an undulating green nearly encased in sand and set in a hollow below the clubhouse.

The back nine, comprising many of the holes completed by Stiles, proceeds to higher ground, with lofty mountain backdrops for many of the tee shots. One of the best risk-reward scenarios on the course is posed at the par-four 12th. The closer players hew to the "wolf pit," a scrub-filled

DINING

A short downhill stroll from the golf course is *Water Street Grill*, which serves excellent pub fare in its casual Tavern (large mahogany bar, indoor waterfall). Also in Williamstown, *Mezze Bistro & Bar*, overlooking the Green River, is a stylish culinary hotspot. For fine French cuisine, there's *Le Jardin*, a Williamstown fixture. In New Ashford, south of Williamstown, is *The Mill on the Floss*, a cozy, comfortable spot with a well-varied menu. Rising late? *Miss Adams Diner*, prefabricated in a diner factory and opened in 1949, serves breakfast all day.

ravine to the left, the better the angle to the well-bunkered plateau green. Play safely to the right, and a semiblind uphill approach awaits.

An engraved rock behind the tee at the par-three 14th commemorates a hole in one made by Jack Nicklaus during the 1956 U.S. Junior Amateur Championship (Jack, 16 at the time, was eliminated in the semifinals). It's a feat worth attempting to duplicate, although the hole plays tougher than it looks from 173 yards. One of the USGA's cherished New England venues, Taconic hosted the U.S. Senior Amateur Championship in 1996 to mark its centennial.

A place for teenagers and granddads? Hardly. The final holes at Taconic were designed for the varsity. Both the 15th and 16th are long par fours that invite players to have a rip off the tee but are unkind to offline shots, while the 17th, the strongest one-shotter on the course, calls for a tee shot of 221 yards from the back tees. The 18th, a straightaway par five, admittedly is a birdie hole for better players. But then, Taconic is first and foremost a match-play golf course.

It is also a club that adheres to tradition. The sign outside the golf shop reads: "No Preferred Lies—We Play Golf Here." There also is a firm expectation that a round at Taconic should not exceed four hours. Lastly, only the home club of a distinguished liberal arts college would print a Latin inscription from Ovid on its scorecard: "medio tutissimus ibis," which translates loosely as "you will go more safely down the middle." When the ancients exhort you to hit the ball straight, it's worth bending an ear.

The lovely blue-shuttered white clubhouse, nicely landscaped with flowers, displays team pictures of the Williams College golf team dating back to the era of hickory-shafted clubs, high-collared shirts, and handlebar mustaches. If a scenic test interwoven with plenty of Yankee quirki-

Taconic Golf Club, 12th hole

LODGING

Ten minutes from Taconic Golf Club is *Field Farm Guest House,* a 296-acre country estate with good views of 3,491-foot Mt. Greylock, the state's highest peak. The main house, built in 1948 in the American Modern style, features five large, spacious bedrooms, each with private bath. Rates include breakfast. Original art hangs on the walls and outdoor sculptures decorate the gardens at this one-of-a-kind bed-and-breakfast.

ness is what you're after, Taconic is the place. The best time to visit the Berkshires is early October, when the forested peaks are ablaze with the colors of autumn.

More Golf/Williamstown

A few miles south of town is *Waubeeka Golf Links,* a sporty 6,394-yard layout with a good mix of hilly and flat holes. The setting and mountain views are lovely.

Maine

Maine, bigger than all the other New England states combined, yields plump blueberries, celebrated lobsters—and the finest wilderness golf experience in America. Rustic and remote, **Sugarloaf Golf Club** (#20) in Maine's western mountains is a place apart, a majestic layout that shares the marquee with Sugarloaf/USA, the best ski area in the East.

The brainchild of Peter Webber, a local mover and shaker who invited his ski buddy, Robert Trent Jones, Jr., to have a go at a pristine parcel of woodlands cleaved by the Carrabbasset River, Sugarloaf has risen in stature each year since its opening in 1985. Ironically, Webber and his partner, Larry Warren, had originally planned to build the course at the resort's ski touring center. Jones, however, wanted to see the site from the air. When he found out the land around the river at the base of the mountain was available, his creative juices began to flow. Pushed by Webber— an architect, after all, is only as good as the person he works for—Jones produced a world-class course that put central Maine on the golf map,

this despite harsh, snowy winters that foreshorten the season and a far-away location. (Sugarloaf is two-and-a-half hours from Bangor or Portland, nearly double that from Boston.)

Each hole at Sugarloaf was carved from a thick forest of white birches and pines, creating a compartment for each fairway. "Designers," says Jones, "view heavily treed areas as major obstacles, and players should take all appropriate measures to avoid the woods." Which is like telling visitors to avoid plowing into one of the moose that freely wander the resort's access roads. Accuracy, not gorilla length, is the name of the game at Sugarloaf. No recovery is possible from the woods. They are jail, no key. Sugarloaf has a 74.4 course rating and 151 slope from the black tees at 6,910 yards (par is 72). Single-digit handicappers will enjoy the blue tees at 6,451 yards, while duffers are advised to stick to the white markers at 5,946 yards. The forward tees (for ladies and seniors) measure 5,376 yards. A genuine BLOB (Bring Lots of Balls) course, Sugarloaf is one of the few

Sugarloaf Golf Club, 10th hole

layouts in the nation where spray hitters should carry a compass. And unless you can tear bark from a tree with your teeth, take a cart. Only mountain men attempt to hike the hills of this prodigious course.

The front nine, with its sweeping doglegs and epic views of hump-backed peaks in the Bigelow Range, is replete with doglegs that call for shrewdly positioned tee shots. For example, the second and fourth holes are both double-dogleg, Z-shaped par fives that call for chesslike strategy in return for par. The ability to hit the ball high is also essential: At the fifth, sixth, and ninth holes, the approach shot must be flown nearly straight uphill to reach the green.

As good as they are, these holes are a mere warm-up for the stunning back nine. The 10th, a short par four with a 110-foot drop from the tee to a serpentine fairway pinched by flashed-face bunkers, kicks off a six-hole sequence along the Carrabbasset River nicknamed the "String of Pearls" by Jones. For beauty, challenge, memorability, and any other criteria you can think of, this may be the best stretch of mountain golf in America. The 11th, a 216-yard par three, plunges nearly 130 feet to a two-tier green flanked by the foaming river and a long, deep trap designed to save players from a fate worse than sand. The entire length of the massive par-five 12th parallels the river, its current interrupted by huge glacial erratics and its banks strewn with smooth white stones. The 401-yard 13th traces a bend in the river, with a hidden pot bunker defending the green's entry, while the par-four 14th, damaged by Hurricane Bob in 1991 and since rebuilt by Jones, doglegs left to a green that beckons from the far side of

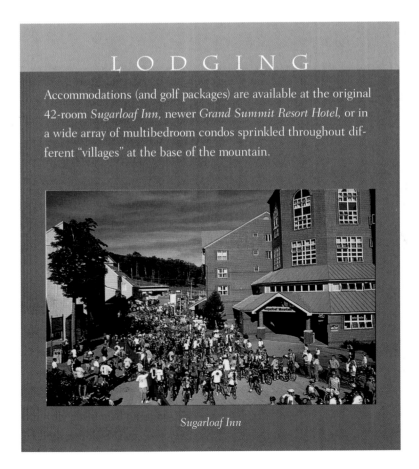

LODGING

Accommodations (and golf packages) are available at the original 42-room *Sugarloaf Inn*, newer *Grand Summit Resort Hotel*, or in a wide array of multibedroom condos sprinkled throughout different "villages" at the base of the mountain.

Sugarloaf Inn

DINING

D'Ellies, at the base of Sugarloaf Mountain, offers hefty sandwiches on fresh-baked bread (including a superb lobster roll), as well as homemade soups, chowders, and chili. At the Sugarloaf Inn, the *Seasons Restaurant* has a well-varied menu, excellent salads. In Village West at the base of the lifts is *Gepetto's*, a large greenhouse overlooking the slopes offering pasta, steak, and Cajun specialties. For fine dining farther afield, there's the *Herbert Hotel* in Kingfield (candlelit room, good wine list) and *The Porter House Restaurant* in Eustis, which occupies a 1908 farmhouse (roast duckling is recommended). The fare at *Theo's Microbrewery & Pub* along the resort's access road is basic, but the ales produced by the Sugarloaf Brewing Company (including the robust "String of Pearls" porter) are superb.

the river. The approach shot is strictly a do-or-die affair, a fact not lost on the river's hard-headed brook trout.

By the time tee shots are launched to the semi-island green at par-three 15th, most players have been hypnotized by the layout's scenery or anesthetized by its charm. By the time the bi-level green at the sharply uphill par-four 18th is surmounted, the (high) numbers don't matter anymore. Even local powderhounds admit that getting around this Bunyanesque golf course with dignity intact is more difficult than mastering Sugarloaf's black diamond ski trails. The reason? Even if you've managed to survive the front nine, the "String of Pearls" tends to unravel a good round in the making.

More Golf/Sugarloaf

An hour's drive from Sugarloaf is *Mingo Springs*, a lovely, well-established course at 2,000 feet above sea level in the Rangeley Lakes region. There are also sporty nine-holers in the region, including *Lakewood* and *Wilson Lake*.

New & Noteworthy

Belgrade Lakes, opened in 1998 and located an hour's drive south of Sugarloaf, is Englishman Clive Clark's first design effort in America. Giant boulders unearthed during construction were used to frame several of the fairways and greens. The topmost holes overlook Great Pond and Long Pond. Looking ahead, both Sugarloaf and Sunday River, a popular ski area near Bethel, plan to open new courses by Robert Trent Jones, Jr., in 2001.

Maine lighthouse

SIDETRIPS

Though renowned for its skiing, Sugarloaf, which borders the largest tract of wilderness east of the Rockies, has a good range of fair-weather activities. There are guided nature walks and hiking (the 100-mile view from 4,237-foot Mt. Sugarloaf is worth the climb); mountain biking (more than 50 miles of trails and 1,400 feet of elevation in the Longfellow Mountains); whitewater rafting on the Kennebec River;

Fishing at Sugarloaf

Mountain bikers on Mt. Sugarloaf

and excellent lake and stream fishing. Want to see Bullwinkle in the flesh? Hop aboard the *Champagne Moose Express,* a guided Saturday night tour that departs from the Sugarloaf Inn and visits likely gathering places for the area's shy vegetarians.

In nearby Kingfield, a charming New England town, the *Stanley Museum* houses two Stanley Steamer cars (Yankee ingenuity at its best) and memorabilia left by the twin Stanley brothers. Fifty miles north of Sugarloaf lies Quebec's scenic Lake Megantic region. The Maine coast, notably Boothbay Harbor, is two hours east.

The Midwest

Boyne Highlands, The Heather Course • Bay Harbor Golf Club

Treetops Sylvan Resort, Tom Fazio Premier Course • Treetops Sylvan Resort, Rick Smith

Signature Course • High Pointe Golf Club • Lakewood Shores Resort, Gailes Course •

The Wilds Golf Club • Grand View Lodge, The Pines • Fowler's Mill Golf Course (Lake–River)

Eagle Ridge Inn & Resort, The General • Cog Hill Golf & Country Club, No. 4 Course

Cantigny Golf & Tennis (Woodside–Lakeside) • Kemper Lakes Golf Course

University Ridge Course • Blackwolf Run Golf Club, River Course

Blackwolf Run Golf Club, Meadow Valleys Course

The Wilds Golf Club, Prior Lakes, Minnesota, 14th hole

Michigan

It's been called the "Hilton Head of the Heartland" and the "Golf Mecca of the Midwest," but northern Michigan is both—and more. Its self-conjured title is "America's Summer Golf Capital," but even that moniker does little to capture the excitement of the many new and established resort and daily-fee courses sprinkled in the valleys of the glacier-carved, sand-based hills between Traverse City and Gaylord. Six courses in northern Michigan are fixtures on *GOLF Magazine*'s "Top 100 You Can Play" list, a surfeit of riches for a region that until recently was known mainly for its cherry orchards, fudge stores, and taxidermists.

The area, by the way, does not touch the Arctic Circle. It's no more than a four-hour drive (or a short flight) from Detroit. The season is May through October, and the summer climate, tempered by cool breezes off Lake Michigan, is ideal for golf. Also, extended daylight in these northern latitudes allows play until 10 p.m. in the summer months. Many a golfer has looked up from his final putt to see the aurora borealis throbbing on the northern horizon.

It's a well-kept secret, but the state of Michigan led the nation in new course openings throughout much of the 1990s. According to the National Golf Foundation, Michigan had 906 courses as of 1998. Only Florida and California have more. Over 750 of these venues are public-access (no state has more), with 90 percent of the 103 facilities under construction at press time slated to be public tracks. The reason for the growth? Golf is lucrative. An economic impact study commissioned by a state tourism commission in 1997 found that golfers in Michigan spend nearly $1 billion annually.

Vying to become the Pinehurst of the Midwest, **Boyne Highlands**, in the fashionable lakeside community of Harbor Springs, was promoting 144 holes of golf at three different locations in 1998, with more golf to follow. The catalyst for growth at this popular ski resort and the region's first exceptional public-access course, **The Heather** (#90) is a Robert Trent Jones–designed layout opened in 1968. Courses with more bells and whistles have been built since, but none have aged as gracefully as this elegant test built at a time when Jones was at the height of his artistry.

Occupying a heavily wooded, gently rolling site at the base of the ski mountain, The Heather is that rare breed of course capable of giving the scratch player a headache without overwhelming the novice. It is also an instant reminder to design mavens of just how good Jones was in his heyday. There is plenty of room to drive the ball on the Heather, but strategically deployed cloverleaf bunkers coupled with large, undulating greens (up to 10,000 square feet in size) do a very good job of defending par.

On most Trent Jones courses, broad, sweeping fairways emulate the effect of a retreating glacier on the land. Jones had a big assist from Mother Nature at Boyne Highlands—the terrain, with its glacier-shaped ridges and hollows, was perfectly suited for the game. After devising an ideal routing, Jones carved fairways through a thick stand of pines, cedars, maples, and tamaracks, wrapping holes around bogs, ponds, and swamps dotted with cedar stumps.

With water in play on eight of the first nine holes, players must arrive ready to do battle on The Heather. Each of the three opening holes is a relatively short and manageable par four that doglegs left to right, but the game is on at the par-three fourth, where players must fly a reed-fringed pond to reach the green. The fifth is a stirring introduction to The Heather's brilliant array of par fives. Only 511 yards from the tips, this classic risk-reward hole cartwheels to the left around a cattail-rimmed pond, daring better players to go for the green in two. Played conservatively, it can be conquered. The Heather's ninth is a tremendous par five that bends to the left around a weedy pond, proceeding to a hilltop green underslung by three gaping pits of sand and backdropped by the resort's original Bavarian-style pro shop. Play too safely to the right, away from the hazard, and a grove of trees will block your progress.

Seamlessly woven together, The Heather's back nine is as good if not better than the front. The 11th, a short, cleverly plotted par five, plays to a kidney-shaped green guarded by a fortresslike array of traps, notably a pair of flashed-face, high-lipped bunkers in front that hide the bottom half

Boyne Highlands, Harbor Springs, Michigan, The Heather Course, fifth hole

Boyne Highlands, The Heather Course, fourth hole

of the pin. The 15th, yet another par five measuring well under 500 yards from the forward tees, plays to a green that tapers away from the fairway, with deep bunkers at the rear to catch the unwary.

The long par-four 18th is The Heather's most controversial hole. Jones had wanted to route the hole through a glacier-cut valley to the left. Resort owner Everett Kirchner, a man accustomed to getting what he wanted, pushed Jones to create a hair-raising hole with a large, man-made pond in front of the green. Kirchner got what he wanted, although the in-your-face 18th is out of character with the other 17 holes on the course.

On the plus side, management can arrange for caddies if players call ahead. For riders, a Yardmark GPS (Global Positioning System, a computer display unit mounted on the golf cart) automatically informs golfers of yardages, from the length of their drives to the distance required to clear a hazard.

Beautifully conditioned, the fairways clearly defined and the greens smooth and true, the Heather is the course most preferred by the resort's long-time guests and members.

Boyne Highlands Resort

Bay Harbor Golf Club, Petoskey, Michigan, Quarry nine, 17ᵗʰ hole

Few courses anywhere have had the advance fanfare of **Bay Harbor Golf Club** (#8), a 27-hole residential, marina, and equestrian development along Little Traverse Bay near the resort town of Petoskey. Because nearly two and a half miles of shoreline along Little Traverse Bay was dedicated to golf holes, Bay Harbor, the blue chip in the bulging portfolio of Boyne USA Resorts, has been touted (mostly by Michigan golf writers) as the "Pebble Beach of the Midwest." Despite the hype, the golf course has exceeded all expectations. Though only partially opened in 1997, Bay Harbor leapfrogged the competition and catapulted into the eighth spot on the "Top 100" list in its first year of eligibility, an extraordinary achievement for a new facility.

Bay Harbor is the proverbial silk purse created from a sow's ear. Five holes occupy the site of an old limestone quarry and cement factory, an industrial eyesore blighted with piles of arsenic-laced kiln dust and a pair of giant smokestacks. Notwithstanding the gorgeous lake views available from high bluffs at the east end of the property, the site's interior acreage looked like hell with the fires burned out. But not to Arthur Hills, the Ohio-based architect who was tapped to transform an environmental Hades into golf heaven.

"Early on, it looked like we knocked down a six-story building, but I knew it was going to be beautiful when we were done," Hills stated. "The views of Lake Michigan were awesome." Assisted by design associate Bryan Yoder and Stephen Kircher, general manager of Boyne USA's Michigan operations and chairman of Bay Harbor, the three set to work routing holes on the most varied landscape imaginable. Bay Harbor not only has the longest coastline of any course in America, the holes occupy clifftop, sand dune, rock quarry, and woodland settings. Taken all together, it may be the nation's most diverse layout.

The opening holes on the Links nine, the first portion of the course to open, set the stage for the game. Propped up on bluffs 160 feet above an arm of Lake Michigan, an inland sea of oceanlike scale, the par-four first hole proceeds directly to the edge of the cliff and hits players with an aesthetic jolt akin to lightning. The third, a short par four, tumbles downhill to a slim green fronted by a deep sand pit, with a view beyond of the development's deep-water harbor. The fourth hole is a downhill par three stretching to 178 yards, with a well-defended bi-level green teetering above the water and backdropped by one of the multimillion dollar homes in the neighborhood. The Links turns inland at the fifth, where a scrub-covered sand dune must be carried to reach a fairway that doglegs sharply to the right. The crowned green spills off to a deep, cone-shaped bunker that the developers claim is natural. However, it just so happens to be the same size and dimensions as the famed "Devil's Asshole" bunker defending the green on the 10th hole at Pine Valley.

Even if you've chosen to play the forward tees (and unless you're a low handicapper, you're cautioned by the starter to do so), follow the wooden walkway to the back tee at the par-four sixth hole. From here, a broad, sandy wasteland must be carried to reach a fairway walled in to the right by a dune ridge.

Hills maintains that the seventh hole on the Links, a 500-yard par five, "is perhaps the best hole I've ever designed." It certainly has everything a golfer could want: drama, beauty, and a myriad array of strategic options. Here, comparisons to the great sixth hole at Pebble Beach, the nation's definitive headlands par five, are justified. The semiblind tee shot on the seventh is played to a fairway that swings gently right to the brink of a cliff, the full expanse of the lake flooding the horizon. Farther along it drifts to the left and climbs a steep hill to a plateau green undercut by a deep, penal bunker. There are dozens of ways to play this hole, although when the breeze is blowing strong off the lake, low, boring shots that knife through the wind are the only way to go.

The eighth, a long downhill par three, is followed by a testing par five that measures only 518 yards from the tips, but which plays hide-and-seek with the wetlands. Players are returned to the clubhouse, there to commence the second half of the journey.

There are few experiences in the realm of resort or daily-fee golf to compare with Bay Harbor's Quarry nine. Shale was once mined in the 600-yard-wide quarry, but industrial activity had long ago ceased by the time Hills arrived, and nature had begun to reclaim the ravaged site. Pools of water collected in hollowed-out depressions, and wetlands cropped up below the gorge's dull gray rock slopes. After huge piles of toxic kiln dust were sealed with a thick layer of rubble and topsoil and

SIDETRIPS

Explore Harbor Springs, a lovely lakeside town and the former retreat of Al Capone and his Purple Gang. Nice shops, fashionable cafés, impressive lakeside homes. Petoskey is known for its historic Gaslight District and numerous specialty shops. Gift shops carry jewelry made from "Petoskey stones"—unique hexagonal-patterned petrified coral found along the shore.

Farther afield is *Sleeping Bear Dunes National Lakeshore,* where visitors can explore massive coastal dunes, hike marked trails, or take the 7.1-mile Pierce Stocking Scenic Drive, which offers fine views of the dunes, lake, and Manitou Islands.

reshaped, Hills set about devising holes to provide a counterpoint to the Links nine. Where the clifftop holes on the Links are open and flowing, the key holes on the Quarry nine are contained, their surroundings austere, even ominous in places.

The showstopper is the third, an ingenious par five of 561 yards where the developers wisely tabled $2 million in prime condo frontage in order to build an unforgettable three-shotter. Fraught with exciting risk-reward scenarios, the third skirts the rim of the quarry on the right, with sandy dunes and strategically placed bunkers up the left side. The payoff shot is played to a slick hilltop green defended in front by a deep pot bunker.

Below to the right is broken ground and an overview of upcoming holes routed through the worn-out pit. Ugly never looked more picturesque than it does here.

The Quarry's fifth, a short par five stretching to 495 yards, calls for a nerveless carry from an elevated tee over a corner of the quarry to a sloping fairway that bends gently to the left. The green, fronted by a pond, is encased within an amphitheater of sheer rock walls from which a waterfall trickles. Reachable in two? Only by the boldest of players.

At the sixth, a short par four, Phil Mickelson failed to drive the green in his match against Tom Lehman in a "Shell's Wonderful World of Golf" episode staged at Bay Harbor in 1998. Perhaps the quarry walls played havoc with Mickelson's depth perception, a common post-round comment by first-timers. The 406-yard seventh calls for a heroic drive over a wooded defile that somehow must avoid a bunker placed smack in the middle of the fairway. The fairway then proceeds downhill along an escarpment to a slim, angled green set high above the lake. Players depart the quarry at the eighth, a mid-length, downhill par three that plays to a moated, rock-rimmed green, while the par-four ninth, the grand finale, tumbles sharply downhill to a lakeside green. The outdoor patio of the 12,000-square-foot stucco-and-stone clubhouse looms high above the green.

Bay Harbor Golf Club, Links nine, first hole

Bay Harbor is the kind of course most players can't wait to play again, regardless of score. Not that many will ever catch up to it, even on a calm day. Why? The layout is brilliantly strategized. Driving zones are wide, though well-placed bunkers snare errant shots. The greens, among the largest and most imaginative Hills has ever built, are firm, fast, and generously contoured, with lots of spilloffs to close-mown chipping areas to give players a fair chance at recovery.

The Preserve nine at Bay Harbor, opened in 1998, was completed shortly after Hills returned from an extended tour of Ireland's links. Which may account for its heaving fairways, peek-a-boo blind shots, and cavernous bunkers. Woven through a thick stand of maples, pines, and birch trees on high ground set back from the lake, the Preserve provides a fine test of golf, especially from the black tees at 3,378 yards. But it's the Links and Quarry nines that have separated Bay Harbor from the pack in northern Michigan and given the facility its national stature and well-deserved limelight.

Guests of Boyne USA properties now receive preferred pricing at Bay Harbor, as do residents of The Inn at Bay Harbor, a six-story waterfront inn inspired by San Diego's Hotel del Coronado that was scheduled to open in spring, 1999. However, once the club's membership ranks swell, Bay Harbor will become a private club. Traveling golfers have until 2004 or 2005 to experience a golf course unlike any other.

More Golf/Boyne USA Resorts

Across the street from Bay Harbor is *Crooked Tree,* an appealing layout marked by undulating greens and spectacular views of Little Traverse Bay.

In addition to The Heather at Boyne Highlands, there's the *Donald Ross Memorial,* a tribute course inspired by the Scottish master's finest designs. The layout, spread across a rolling, wooded site, features faithful replications of Ross-designed holes from Pinehurst No. 2, Oakland Hills, Seminole, Inverness, and other timeless classics.

The Moor, a solid test cast in the Jones mold and the resort's longest course at 7,127 yards, has numerous doglegs hinged on traps or bent around lakes and wetlands. Bring your sand wedge and a ball retriever.

LODGING, ETC.

Boyne Highlands, with accommodations for over 1,400 guests, offers everything from rooms and suites to well-appointed condos and townhouses. (*Boyne Mountain* can accommodate an additional 700 guests.) Top accommodations are found at *The Inn at Bay Harbor.*

Boyne's "Super Five Golf Weeks," a five-night, value-laden package available from mid-May through mid-September, offers avid golfers the opportunity to play 36 holes per day, unlimited instruction with video analysis, breakfast and dinner daily, cocktail parties, and other perks.

The Inn at Bay Harbor

Nine holes of the *Arthur Hills* course at Boyne Highlands debuted in 1997, with the second nine scheduled to open in 2000. A large-scale layout, the Hills course, comparable to the Preserve nine at Bay Harbor, meanders invitingly through pines, oaks, and blueberry bogs, with broad fairways, huge greens, and sculptured target bunkers that serve as directional aids.

The practice facility at Boyne Highlands, modeled after the state-of-the-art range at Muirfield Village, is exceptional. Just getting started? There's a delightful par-three executive course at the resort.

At Boyne Mountain, a sister property, there's the *Alpine,* a charming, scenic, and well-maintained test; and the *Monument,* a bruising mountain course with sharp elevation changes and an island green at the 18th.

From a mom 'n pop ski facility with a few bunny slopes has emerged **Treetops Sylvan Resort,** a major golf complex near Gaylord with a diverse array of layouts. The resort's original 18 was designed by Robert Trent Jones, and his course was a success, but the back-to-back opening in the early 1990s of top-notch courses by Tom Fazio and swing guru Rick Smith really set this four-season retreat on a pinnacle of its own.

Tucked in the scenic Pigeon River valley four miles from the main

Treetops Sylvan Resort, Gaylord, Michigan, Tom Fazio Premier Course, first hole

19th Hole

With more than 300 domestic and imported brands of bottled beer (from Anchor Steam to Wild Boar) as well as 10 varieties on tap, the resort's Top of the Hill Club sports bar is one of the best-stocked 19th holes in the nation. In addition to the wide-ranging collection of beers, fresh-baked pizzas are available. So are dart boards and pool tables.

complex at Treetops North is the **Tom Fazio Premier** (#80), a user-friendly course threaded through rolling woodlands that relies on elevated tees, concave fairways, and a fine collection of short par fours for its appeal.

With the accent on visual drama and playability, Fazio fashioned a gorgeous layout framed by second-growth hardwoods and dense vegetation. The majority of the fairways tumble downhill into troughs framed by heavily wooded ridges, their bowl-shaped landing areas designed to corral errant drives. The wind off Lake Michigan funnels through these amplified valleys, adding excitement to the shotmaking requirements. Swales and bunkers defend the slick, bentgrass greens, several of them among the boldest Fazio has ever built. Though the short par fours (notably the 15th, its two-tier green canted nine feet from front to back) are among the best Fazio has ever designed, there are no "signature" holes per se on this 6,832-yard layout, which opened in 1992.

"If you take five foursomes, let them play the course, and then take a poll on their favorite holes, I wouldn't be surprised if you got 18 different opinions," Fazio said. "There are so many dramatic holes with so many different settings."

Not one to traffic in superlatives, the designer had the last word on a project he nearly sidestepped: "I really couldn't pick my best course, but I've designed about 10 courses—and I include Treetops in that list—that if you wrote down their names and had to pick one out of a hat, I'd base my whole reputation on the one selected."

Treetops Sylvan Resort, Tom Fazio Premier Course, seventh hole

Treetops Sylvan Resort, Rick Smith Signature Course, 14th hole

The Tom Fazio Premier is probably the resort's best-liked and most-requested course, but not until the debut of the **Rick Smith Signature** (#89), a 6,653-yard, par-70 layout designed by the resort's multitalented director of golf, did Treetops spread its wings and take flight. Opened in 1993, the Smith course is a large-scale design spread across 300 acres that fully embraces the north woods.

Smith claims that when it came time to build the course, he was given "a compass and a map" by resort owner Harry Melling. Smith wore out a four-wheel-drive vehicle, lost 15 pounds hiking the site's hills and valleys, and sketched 13 different routings before arriving at the best sequence of holes. The extensive field work, Smith explains, was necessary "to see what the land forms felt like and looked like. I had to focus beyond what was on the [topographic] map and visualize each hole in my mind." The result: a fun and wonderfully varied layout with panoramic views and excellent playability throughout.

The layout is Smith's first full-fledged design. It features five sets of tees (from 6,653 yards to 4,604 yards); 135 bunkers (most are decorative); and enormous green complexes (up to 12,000 square feet) designed to test short-game creativity and prowess. The par threes, each with a different look and each facing a different direction, are exceptional. Two of them, the fourth and the Pine Valleyesque 11th, were hand-cleared to preserve the bracken fern and scrub pine that preface the greens. So lightly does the course tiptoe around the land that it was certified as a Cooperative Sanctuary by Audubon International shortly after it opened.

In the name of research, Smith visited classic spreads at home and abroad before breaking ground for the layout. Garden City Golf Club, an exclusive men's club on Long Island, New York, known for its subtle, flowing lines and broad fairways framed by sculpted bunkers and tall fescues, made a strong impression. In fact, the par-four third hole on the Smith

LODGING

Treetops Sylvan Resort offers standard rooms, deluxe suites, two- and three-bedroom condos in six slopeside chalets, as well as four-bedroom resort homes. A variety of all-inclusive golf packages are available.

SIDETRIPS

Guided wilderness tours that combine driving and light hiking are available through Treetops Sylvan Resort. (Northeast Michigan is home to the only elk herd east of the Mississippi. Bring binoculars.) There's also world-class fly fishing in the area, notably on the AuSable, Black, Manistee, Pigeon, and Sturgeon rivers. (Ernest Hemingway, who spent his boyhood summers at the family cottage on nearby Walloon Lake, set several of his short stories, notably the "Nick Adams" sagas, amid the woods and streams of northern Michigan.) More excitement? Paddle a canoe down the upper Sturgeon River.

Course is a brawny version of Garden City. From the elevated tee, a 60-yard-wide fairway angled gently to the right beckons below, with a small pond to the right and large, decorative bunkers framing the entire left side of the hole. For challenge and beauty, it's as good a two-shotter as a golfer could hope to play, especially from the championship tees at 467 yards.

More Golf / Gaylord Area

The *Robert Trent Jones Masterpiece*, the original track at Treetops Sylvan Resort is a brutal 7,060-yard affair by Robert Trent Jones characterized by ponderous uphill holes and giant, rolling greens. Threetops, a delightful 1,182-yard, par-three course designed by Rick Smith, is known for its dramatic vertical drops from tee to green. There's also a two-acre practice putting green at Treetops North. Generously contoured, it's a paean to the famous "Himalayas" putting green at St. Andrews in Scotland. Finally, there's the Tradition, another Smith design, opened in 1998, that was originally intended for walkers only (carts are now permitted).

Gaylord, its Main Street architecture reminiscent of a Swiss Alpine village, is the gateway to several fine resort and daily-fee courses. *Garland*, a full-service facility, has four owner-developed courses. *Hidden Valley* offers The Lake, The Loon, and The Classic. *Beaver Creek* has The Natural. There's also *Fox Run*, *Black Bear*, and *Elk Ridge*, the last-named known for its pig-shaped bunker on the 10th hole.

Wilderness Valley boasts the region's sleeper, the *Black Forest Course*, a rugged 7,044-yard, par-73 layout by Tom Doak marked by small, sloping greens and sensational bunkering.

Located 10 miles outside Traverse City, **High Pointe Golf Club** (#74), opened in 1989, was *GOLF Magazine* Contributing Editor Tom Doak's first solo design effort. Doak, who has an encyclopedic knowledge of golf courses (he has seen or played more than 800 layouts in Ireland and Great Britain), built a naturalistic course that takes full advantage of the 240-acre site's exceptional (for golf) terrain. Indeed, High Pointe is a throwback to the days when a designer allowed existing contours to dictate the shape of the holes. "My goal," Doak says, "was to design holes that give maximum advantage to imaginative shotmaking—the principal difference I found between the British courses I grew to love and the current era of American design." Doak believes most modern designers tend to flatten out all borderline slopes in the interest of "fairness," but in doing so "allow the well-equipped modern golfer to approach every hole the same." At High Pointe, golfers must consider steep greenside slopes and other worst-case scenarios before pulling the trigger. Course management is the key to scoring.

To promote the ground game, namely the bump-and-run shots as they're played on seaside links courses, Doak left most of the greens open in front and planted the fairways in fescue grass to provide a firm yet playable surface. The greens, originally planted in fescue grass, have since been converted to bentgrass, although Doak's heavily contoured, multitier putting surfaces weren't built with modern green speeds in mind. When these greens, some of them resembling giant potato chips, are running fast, they present putting challenges not even Doak, who doesn't mind getting under the skin of better players, could have imagined.

High Pointe Golf Club, Williamsburg, Michigan, 14th hole

Pond at the High Pointe Golf Club, 18th hole

Occupying the site of an old cherry orchard and unencumbered by real estate, High Pointe has several faithful reproductions of renowned Scottish holes. The par-three fourth, which requires a carry over a shallow depression to a sizable green guarded front and back by large, engulfing bunkers, is an artful copy of North Berwick's famous Redan hole. The mountainous 10th, which can play as a par four or par five, was inspired by the Alps hole at Prestwick. There's excellent diversity throughout. The front nine wanders across open, rolling fields, while the back nine leads into hillier, more forested terrain where hidden valleys choked with ferns, wild sumac, and scrub pines put one in mind of a British heathland course. When the east wind blows off Grand Traverse Bay, High Pointe's exposed holes can play tough.

Despite its conditioning, which can be spotty, High Pointe succeeds as a public course, especially with a green fee far below that of the area's high-priced resort spreads. Like an ambitious first novel, High Pointe has its ups and downs, but is well worth investigating for those who wish to experience a golf course that reflects the character of the land, not an artificial version of it.

More Golf/Traverse City

Want to flex your golf muscles? Try wrestling *The Bear,* the Jack Nicklaus–designed behemoth at *Grand Traverse Resort.* With its terraced fairways, tiny greens, and water in play at 10 holes from the tips at 7,065 yards (slope 149, course rating 75.8), The Bear is a bruiser. Far friendlier is the resort's second venue, *Spruce Run,* a pleasant, playable spread lined with conifers.

Heading north to Bellaire near Torch Lake, named one of the 10 most beautiful lakes in the world by *National Geographic Magazine,* is *Shanty Creek,* a full-service resort with three fine courses. There's *The Legend,* an outstanding Arnold Palmer–Ed Seay design that offers a scenic roller-coaster ride through the woods. (The par-five first hole, for example, drops 175 feet from tee to green.) There's also *Schuss Mountain,* a well-

conditioned layout known for its very slick greens; and *Shanty Creek,* a short (6,276 yards), roomy test woven through hills and valleys.

EXTRA-SPECIAL: *Belvedere Golf Club,* a storied club in Charlevoix that has played host to the Michigan Amateur on 38 occasions and was Tom Watson's summer playground as a boy, opened its doors to the public in the mid-1990s. A classic, serene, and walkable parkland spread laid out in 1927 by William Watson, who had a hand in the design of the famed Lake Course at the Olympic Club in San Francisco, Belvedere is a traditionalist's delight. (Tee times from noon to 2 p.m. are reserved for members.)

New & Noteworthy/Northern Michigan

Three standout courses were scheduled to open in 1999 in this golf-rich corner of the state. They are:

Cedar River. Shanty Creek's fourth course, a Tom Weiskopf–designed layout, is a classic 6,955-yard spread free of frills. Carved from a second-growth forest, several of the holes skirt the Cedar River. Others are shoehorned into a glacially formed valley. The layout is subtle and understated.

Northern Knight. The third layout at Grand Traverse Resort, designed by Gary Player, features plenty of flexibility (up to six sets of tees on some holes) as well as playability (landing areas are generous). The front nine occupies lowland terrain dotted with ponds and wetlands. The back climbs to higher, more rolling and wooded terrain, with views of East Grand Traverse Bay.

Arcadia Bluffs. Located 50 miles southwest of Traverse City, this Rick Smith–designed course, built on a 245-acre site tilted to Lake Michigan, has a lake view from every hole, fields of overgrown fescues dividing the fairways, and dramatic sod-wall bunkering throughout. Unusually, there are five par threes and five par fives in the routing.

While the northwest corner of Michigan has been busy turning itself into a Myrtle Beach of the north woods, the state's northeastern extremity, the "Sunrise Side," has several good to exceptional layouts set back from Lake

SIDETRIPS

If angling appeals, your chances of landing a Big One are good—fishing in Lake Huron and its tributaries is excellent. Trout, salmon, and walleye charters are available. Nature lovers can look for soaring bald eagles from overlooks along M-65 in Huron National Forest. Or travel the River Road Scenic Byway above the Au Sable River. Shopping? *O'Connor's Pendleton Shop* in Tawas City has everything from crystal vases and birdfeeders to a complete line of Lady Pendleton shirts. Sweet tooth? Drop by *Sherni's Candies* near Whittemore, which carries an enormous variety of homemade chocolates and candy.

Lakewood Shores Resort offers standard and deluxe hotel rooms as well as one- and two-bedroom Jacuzzi Suites. All-inclusive two-for-one packages (two golfers for the price of one) are available in spring and fall and represent excellent value.

Huron. The scene here is woodsier, homier—and far less crowded (and costly) than the higher-profile tracks to the west.

If you can't get to the Auld Sod anytime soon and want a taste of a Scottish-style links every bit as potent and peaty and bracing as a single malt whiskey, there's a fine domestic alternative. Three hours north of Detroit, in the quiet lakeside town of Oscoda, is the **Lakewood Shores Resort**, its **Gailes Course** (#42) a splendid pastiche of several famous Scottish links.

On a flat stretch of treeless farmland, Bob Cupp and Kevin Aldridge, the resort owner's 26-year-old son, engaged in major earthworks to conjure rippled fairways, grassy swales, rugged mounds, and giant putting surfaces, including a pair of enormous double greens. Working from Cupp's routing, Aldridge commandeered a bulldozer and did most of the shaping on his own. According to Craig Peters, the resort's general manager and head pro, "Kevin and his father spent three weeks in Scotland walking all the famous courses—St. Andrews, Carnoustie, Royal Troon. The Gailes isn't a copy of any of them, but it's a copy of the look of them, right down to all the details," including small rectangular tees and round brick buildings (with pointed roofs) for the starter's shed and rest station. "If you've watched the British Open on television," Peters said, "you'll have an idea of what it's like."

The course, its name inspired by Western Gailes, a storied links along Scotland's Ayrshire coast, is pockmarked with 139 bunkers, most of them deep pots revetted with layers of sod. Several are hidden from view. A few are inconveniently located in the center of the fairway, but whoever said golf was meant to be fair? Brisk winds off nearby Lake Huron routinely sweep the Gailes and add mightily to the challenge, which attains major proportions from the back tees at 6,954 yards (slope 75.0, course rating 138). It must be assumed these ratings were established on a calm day. When The Gailes is savaged by boisterous winds, it closely resembles Carnoustie, Scotland's most fearsome links. There is, however, admirable playa-

bility from the multiple sets of forward tees. You can match your handicap on the Gailes by selecting the correct set of markers, driving the ball straight—and getting a few breaks along the way.

The fairways, planted with a blend of bentgrass and fescue grasses and replete with humps and hollows, are close cropped, inviting bump-and-run shots. Except for the airborne approach required at the third hole, where a burn (creek) purls in front of the green, a ground-hugging, worm-burning shot can be played to every green. At which point the real fun starts. The greens on the Gailes, as on the Old Course at St. Andrews, are gigantic, averaging well over 8,000 square feet. Extremely swift, there's scarcely a flat spot on any of them. If you've always wanted to know what it's like to make a full arm swing with your putter, hit away from the pin at the gargantuan green on the 18th hole, a putting surface that covers more than half an acre and measures 57 yards from front to back!

More authenticity: The tee at the seventh hole, a continuation of the sixth green, captures the flavor of the game's original rules, which decreed that players tee off within a club length of the previous hole. Small wooden boxes filled with sand are found on the tees of the par threes. In the old days, sand was provided so players could make sand tees from which to hit. Today, sand mixed with fertilizer and seed is used to fill the divots on the tee. Cart paths, while virtually nonexistent in Scotland, were at least left unpaved on the Gailes. Walking the out-and-back layout is not only encouraged, it's advisable—you'll risk seasickness riding the topsy-turvy fairways in a golf cart.

The length of the holes, the width of the fairways, and the size of the greens are all well varied, a tribute to Cupp's artistry and attention to detail. And there are surprises in store: Overshoot the 11th green (a vast surface shared with the 14th), and you'll find your ball in the bottom of a pit with a 10-foot-high sod wall staring you in the face. Mishit your

Lakewood Shores Resort, Oscoda, Michigan, Gailes Course, 14th hole

Lakewood Shores Resort, Gailes Course, 15th hole

approach to the 14th, and it may end up in the Mole Hole, a nasty bunker the size of a hot tub. Only deeper. The seemingly innocuous par-four 15th has five bunkers in the landing area, each invisible from the tee, plus a tiny blind green tucked below a swale. The par-four 17th hole, called Bunker Hill, has—you guessed it—17 bunkers indenting the landscape. All are well worth avoiding.

There are replicas of famous holes—the first at St. Andrews, the famed "Postage Stamp" hole from Royal Troon—but the Gailes, opened in 1992, stands on its own as an inspired salutation to the game's birth-

place. Facsimile links-style courses are all the rage these days, but no public-access course in America captures the look, feel, playing conditions, and climate of a Scottish links better than the Gailes. Just be sure to bring a windbreaker and a sense of humor.

More Golf/Sunrise Side

The original resort course at Lakewood Shores, now called the *Serradella Course,* is a pleasant country club–style test with well-groomed fairways and greens. It was the region's best track until the Gailes opened. There's also *The Wee Links,* a pleasant pitch 'n putt course.

White Pine National, a fine public course in Spruce near Hubbard Lake, was sculpted from mature pines and hardwoods in 1994. The 6,883-yard layout has broad fairways, excellent greens, clever bunkering, and no water in play. Walkers are welcome.

Farther afield is *The Rock at Drummond Island,* a fascinating course built by Domino's Pizza magnate Tom Monaghan on Drummond Island. This sprawling layout is a remote beauty blasted from limestone. Each hole occupies its own wooded compartment, with lots of wildlife (including bear) alongside the fairways. To reach it, drive to the Upper Peninsula and take a short ferry ride from DeTour Village.

DINING

Dining is casual on the Sunrise Side. *The Pack House* in Oscoda has a good, well-varied menu. In Tawas City, *Pier 23* features seafood fettucini Alfredo and crab-stuffed walleye. *The Bear Track Inn,* near Au Gres, boasts an 80-item salad bar and an excellent seafood buffet on Friday nights.

Minnesota

Minnesota, the "Land of 10,000 Lakes," not only has more boats per capita than any other state in the nation, it claims more shoreline than California, Florida, and Hawaii combined. But it's the golf statistic that's most telling: Roughly 23 percent of Minnesota's residents are golfers, giving it one of the highest participation rates in the nation. The layouts are a match for the fevered interest in the game, with many more first-rate designs on the way.

Twenty-five miles south of Minneapolis is a magnificent layout that set the golf-happy Gopher State on its ear when it opened in 1995. One of the final collaborations between Tom Weiskopf and Jay Morrish, **The Wilds Golf Club** (#68), was fashioned from an upper Midwest palette of wetlands, hardwoods, and numerous ponds, with a grove of Ponderosa pines and 150-foot elevation changes thrown in for good measure.

The integrity of the golf course took precedence over the development of the real estate at The Wilds. When developer Dick Burtness purchased three Prior Lake farms and named them The Wilds, land planners told him he could squeeze 1,500 homes onto the 635-acre parcel due south of the Minnesota River. Instead, Burtness told Weiskopf: "Find me the best 18 holes of golf on this site." Lots for 274 single-family homes and 200 townhouses—one-third the number originally projected—were selected only after the golf course was laid out.

Stretching to 7,025 yards from the Weiskopf tees, which carry a slope of 140 and a course rating of 74.7 (second highest in the state behind Hazeltine, a U.S. Open site), The Wilds is tough as nails from the tips, although multiple sets of tees (including forward tees at 5,095 yards rated for both men and women) as well as generously wide fairways enable everyone to enjoy the course. Flanked by Mystic Lake and a 40-acre marsh studded with stumps, The Wilds has water in play at nearly half the holes. But it's the gracefully contoured bunkers, each cleverly sited and filled with the same sparkling white sand from Ohio that is used at Augusta National, home of The Masters, that provide the strategic fulcrum.

The developer's goal was to produce a course that could host the U.S. Open. Morrish, for his part, said The Wilds reminds him of Shinnecock Hills on Long Island. "It has that kind of feeling," he said. "It flows, it rolls." Among the more distinctive holes, and there are many on this majestic spread, is the fourth, a (potentially) driveable short par four where players drive over a lake to a broad landing area framed by a series of deep bunkers on the far side of the fairway. A mighty oak braided with copper wire to protect it from a chance encounter with lightning guards the left side of the tricorn-shaped green.

The fifth, the longest par four on the course at 478 yards, is a brute that plays uphill into the prevailing wind, but the sixth hole, Weiskopf's personal favorite, is an intriguing par four with a double fairway that offers multiple options. The right side offers an easier tee shot but a more difficult approach, with only the top of the flagstick in view from the fair-

The Wilds Golf Club, Prior Lakes, Minnesota, 16ᵗʰ hole

way. The landing area to the left side is narrower and calls for a longer and more accurate tee shot, but it rewards players with a better angle to the green—and a clear view of the flagstick. A straight tee ball spells doom at the sixth—deep bunkers and tall trees crowd the center of the split fairway.

According to Weiskopf, the par-five eighth "exemplifies the personality of The Wilds—wetlands, hardwood trees, and terrain change." The sinuous fairway describes a subtle double-dogleg, weaving from one fairway bunker to the next before plunging downhill to a green guarded by a giant sand trap to the right and wetlands dotted with spectral trees to the left. It's a beauty.

Each of the par threes on The Wilds plays to a different point on the compass. At the lengthy 11th, angled to the southwest, gusty winds off Mystic Lake can make club selection difficult from the elevated tee. The oblique green, pinched by large, flowing bunkers, is nearly 50 yards deep from front to back. The 16th, yet another of the design team's intriguing short par fours, has for its target the largest, most undulating green on the course—and a frightful pit of sand beside it to defend against routine birdies. There's also water beyond the putting surface to penalize Bunyanesque drives. After a grueling par five that climbs 120 feet from tee to flag, players are rewarded by the sight of the gleaming Minneapolis skyline looking north from the lofty 18th tee. A spectacular par four stretching to 444 yards, this classic two-shotter, bent to the right around a pond, calls for a bold drive over a directional bunker followed by a prudent approach to a green designed to receive a run-up shot. Given its length, challenge, and beauty, it is the kind of hole that could decide a major championship.

After the round, players can repair to the club's superb practice facility or relax in one of the largest and most stylish clubhouses in the Midwest. The Wilds Pub features excellent casual meals by day and fine dining at night with the twinkling lights of the Twin Cities in the distance.

SIDETRIP/THE MEGAMALL

The mall to end all malls is the *Mall of America* in Bloomington, the largest enclosed retail and family entertainment complex in the world (it's as big as 88 football fields!). In addition to more than 500 shops and stores, including Macy's and Bloomingdale's, there's a large amusement park, Camp Snoopy, beneath the central dome.

More Golf/Twin Cities

Opened in 1997, the *Chaska Town Course* in the western suburbs of Minneapolis, an Arthur Hills design overlooking the Minnesota River valley and Lake Bavaria, is an exceptional municipal facility spread across 280 acres. The holes, most with alternate routes and different angles of play, ramble through oak forests, rolling farmland, and marshy wetlands. Walkers are welcome. At press time, the weekday green fee was under $40.

In 1995, designers Bob Cupp and John Fought converted a forested, pond-dotted plot in Maple Grove, 20 minutes northwest of Minneapolis, into *Rush Creek*, a superb daily-fee course that hosts an LPGA event. The site's terrain was so varied—open prairie, pockets of hardwoods, cattailed marshes, floating bogs, generous elevation changes—that little dirt was moved, least of all the spongy earth in the bogs. The showstopper is the par-five 18th, a majestic right-to-left dogleg with water up the entire left side, à la Pebble Beach. There's also an excellent golf academy and indoor practice facility at Rush Creek.

Edinburgh USA, a well-established public track in Brooklyn Park, 12 miles north of Minneapolis near the Mississippi River, occupies rolling woodlands, with cavernous bunkers and numerous water hazards lurking alongside the fairways. Designed by Robert Trent Jones, Jr., on land donated privately to the town, the 6,701-yard layout, site of the 1992 USGA Public Links Championship, is exceptionally well conditioned. The signature hole is the par-four 17th, which features an island fairway and a peninsula green.

A little farther north in Coon Rapids is *Bunker Hills,* a well-conditioned 27-hole layout located within a 1,400-acre park. Site of a Senior PGA Tour event, Bunker Hills offers a good variety of holes cut through pine forests and sand dunes left behind by retreating glaciers. There's also a nine-hole executive course at the facility.

Real golf got you down? Go virtual at *The Bunker,* an indoor facility in the western suburb of Minnetonka that offers 13 big-screen golf course simulators. Enthusiasts can play lifelike "rounds" on Pebble Beach, Pinehurst No. 2, and other famous courses.

New & Noteworthy

In Hudson, Wisconsin, 20 miles east of the Twin Cities is *Troy Burne,* a daily-fee course with limited housing opening in May 1999. The course, stretched across 500 acres of a former dairy farm, was designed by Michael Hurdzan and Dana Fry with input from Tom Lehman. Native fescue grasses and groupings of trees frame the holes, most of which have large greens. Lehman, who is fond of Shinnecock Hills, emulates the look and strategic elements of the famous links on eastern Long Island at Troy Burne.

In Minnesota's Brainerd Lakes region, 140 miles northwest of the Twin Cities, is **Grand View Lodge**, a venerable 900-acre north woods retreat dating to 1919. Its impressive cedar-log lodge is listed on the National Register of Historic Places. Until 1990, fun at this family-oriented getaway in Nisswa was confined to fishing, swimming, or boating in Gull Lake; strolling wooded paths lined with thousands of annuals and flowering shrubs; and bunting the ball around the modest nine-hole Garden Course. The opening of **The Pines** (#86), a splendid 27-hole spread anchored by a gorgeous clubhouse, gave Grand View Lodge instant recognition as a full-fledged golf resort.

The layout, designed by native son Joel Goldstrand, a former PGA Tour player, is carved from a thick stand of birches and pines. (It took

Grand View Lodge, The Pines, Nisswa, Minnesota, Lakes nine, seventh hole

Grand View Lodge, The Pines, Woods nine, ninth hole

three years to log the trees to create compartments for each hole, although specimen trees were left to guard the corners of doglegs and even a few green entrances.) The clever routing makes good use of the gently rolling terrain and natural water features, including small ponds, Roy Lake, and several marshy areas. In addition to the spellbinding, Augusta-like beauty of tree-enclosed fairways occasionally patrolled by bald eagles, The Pines offers large, subtly contoured, and very swift bentgrass greens. Thoughtful, accurate shotmaking is rewarded here, but carefree duffers can have plenty of fun from the forward tees, too.

The feature hole on the *Lakes* nine is the seventh, a 152-yard par three that calls for a carry over a pond to a green flanked by water to the left and a pair of bunkers to the right. Railroad ties landscaped into a hill to the right will ricochet a stray tee shot onto the green—or into trouble.

LODGING

Prior Lake is located near Bloomington, the state's third largest city. Convenient accommodations can be found at the *Radisson South*. More choices are available in the Twin Cities.

The par-three ninth on the Lakes offers a pair of targets connected by an umbilical cord of bentgrass. The green closer to the tee is guarded by sand traps, while the more distant green, larger and less well defended, is trickier to putt.

The *Woods* nine is marked by testing par fours, notably the second, a 433-yarder that bends to the right through a forest and leads to a kidney-shaped green sloped from back to front and protected by a pair of bunkers. The ninth, a strong par five stretching to 541 yards, is a classic of its kind, a right-to-left dogleg calling for a draw off the tee. Backdropped by the clubhouse, the large, undulating green can be reached in two—if you're able to avoid the traps fore and aft as well as water that protects all but the front of the green.

The *Marsh* nine at The Pines, routed on lower-lying ground than the Lakes and Woods, has four holes banked around wetlands. At the third, a mid-length par four, the driving area is amply wide, but the approach must find and hold a green fronted by a small pond and squeezed to the left by the marsh. At the fourth, a short par four, a portion of the swamp must be carried to reach the tree-lined fairway, while the wide, shallow green is well protected by two bunkers in front and a large trap behind the green.

In addition to a superb practice area, players can enjoy patio dining at Freddy's Grille at the clubhouse following the round. As on most Minnesota courses, walking is encouraged on The Pines.

Grand View Lodge, The Pines, Marsh nine, third hole

More Golf / Brainerd Lakes

Of the 25 or so courses in the Brainerd Lakes area, a few are especially recommended.

Seven miles from Grand View Lodge is a sister facility, *The Preserve*, which opened for play in 1996. Similar in character to The Pines, The Preserve, laid out by Dan Helbling and Mike Morley on 240 acres of rolling woodlands, has 14 elevated tees and 40 acres of wetlands. The 6,601-yard layout was the region's first to offer bentgrass tees, greens, and fairways. The Preserve's clubhouse offers a fine view of the course.

The main track at *Madden's on Gull Lake*, a 63-hole resort in Brainerd, is *The Classic*, an outstanding 7,109-yard layout debuted in 1997. Designed by Scott Hoffmann, Madden's long-time superintendent, the course winds up and down hills, skirts wetlands, lakes, and streams, and disappears at times into a thick forest. Some of the greens are multitiered, others are more subtle. Bright white sand fills the flashed-faced bunkers. A big-time test from the tips, The Classic accents playability from the multiple sets of forward tees.

The region's other layouts of note include *The Lakes* at *Ruttger's Bay Lake Lodge,* a solid resort course by Joel Goldstrand with numerous water features and a par-three 18th hole that plays across Bass Lake; *Whitefish Golf Club,* a scenic, mature gem in Pequot Lakes that calls for accuracy; *Irish Hills,* a superb public track north of Brainerd routed around the Whitefish Chain of Lakes; and *Pine River,* a charming nine-holer cut through tall Norway pines.

Grand View Lodge clubhouse

DINING

In addition to fine dining at Grand View Lodge and good casual dining in the area's many family-owned resorts, the Brainerd Lakes region has a good range of choices. Hungry? *Black Bear Lodge & Saloon* in Baxter has an all-you-can-eat Prime Rib Loft. *Bar Harbor Supper Club* in Lake Shore is known for its charbroiled steaks. *The Quarterdeck,* on the west side of Gull Lake in Nisswa, offers lakeside dining, good BBQ ribs. Walleye, renowned as the most delectable of freshwater fishes, is a specialty throughout the region, notably at *Iven's on the Bay* in Brainerd. Want to eat pizza and watch a game on TV? Check out *Mario's Sports Bar.* For a refreshing iced coffee drink or Italian soda, drop by *Coco Moon* in Brainerd.

New & Noteworthy

Vying to become a Midwest golf mecca, the Brainerd Lakes area has several high-profile projects in the hopper.

At *Cragun's Resort* in Brainerd, a unique 36-hole facility designed by Robert Trent Jones, Jr., opens in summer 1999. Developed by resort owners Dutch and Irma Cragun, the property features gently rolling hills, expansive marshland, open prairie, and an 80-acre lake. As many as 11 tee boxes provide maximum flexibility. In addition to a championship-class 27-hole spread with three distinctive nines (plus room for a fourth), Cragun's offers a reversible nine-hole, par-three course that circles around the practice facility. The course, with par threes ranging from 80 to 225 yards,

SIDETRIPS

With 465 lakes within a 30-mile radius, fishing is extremely popular in the Brainerd Lakes area. Guide and launch services are available. For kids of all ages, *Paul Bunyan Amusement Center* in Brainerd has 30 rides and attractions (including helicopter rides over the lakes), not to mention a giant animated statue of the legendary logging character. Brainerd is where the *Paul Bunyan Trail* begins its 100-mile journey northward to Bemidji, with 50 miles of paved paths available for biking. Two state forests—Crow Wing and Pillsbury—offer hiking trails, as does the 500-acre *Northland Arboretum.* For one-of-a-kind items, explore the 30 antique shops scattered throughout the area. Lastly, Las Vegas–style gaming is found at the *Grand Casino Mille Lacs.*

can be played clockwise or counterclockwise, depending upon the direction of play posted for the day.

Deacon's Lodge at Pelican Lake is a sterling 7,017-yard daily-fee facility named for Arnold Palmer's father. The Palmer Course Design Company was given free rein on an exceptional 499-acre site marked by three large lakes, high bluffs, numerous wetlands, and thick stands of birch and pine. To create authentic waste bunkers, the site's five-inch layer of black topsoil was peeled back in places to expose a sand base that's 170 feet deep. Holes, especially the two short par fives, brim with strategic options, but Deacon's Lodge doesn't play as tough as it looks from the forward tees. There's also an 18-acre practice facility framed by towering Norway pines.

LODGING

Accommodations at Grand View Lodge range from charming historic suites in the lodge to townhouses and cottages. Many of the lakeside cottages feature decks, kitchenettes, and fireplaces that can be lit on cool nights. The resort, an ideal family getaway, offers a wide range of supervised programs for children.

Grand View Lodge

Ohio

Fowler's Mill Golf Course (Lake–River #77), is a prime example of early Pete Dye at his best. Opened in 1972 and one of the Ohio native's first 10 designs, this 27-hole layout traces the gentle rise and fall of the land. In fact, the core 18 at Fowler's Mill presents a subtle, craftily plotted course long on strategic options and short on the crash-and-burn holes Dye later built from one end of the Sun Belt to the other.

On rolling, wooded terrain bisected by a river, Dye routed holes that give pleasure from the forward tees and pause for thought from the tips at 7,002 yards. For example, on the signature fourth hole, both the tee shot and second shot must clear a 55-acre lake, its shores bulkheaded with Dye's signature railroad ties. Great blue herons fish the shallows and bald eagles occasionally glide overhead. According to John Sobecki, the facili-

ty's general manager: "The fourth has been voted the toughest hole in the state by the *Cleveland Plain Dealer.*"

The Chagrin River splits the fairways of the ninth and 12th holes, each a shortish par four that challenges players to go left or right—but not straight. In classic Pete Dye style, golfers who elect to play the tougher shot off the tee are rewarded by a less taxing approach shot. Conversely, those who take the easy way out with their drives face a very challenging shot from an awkward angle. This is Dye, who loves to get inside a golfer's head, at his finest.

Even seemingly innocent holes can be deadly. The 11th is a short par four apparently free of trouble—until players reach the green, which is tilted radically from left to right and may be responsible for more three putts than any other green in Ohio.

As on most Pete Dye golf courses, the par fives at Fowler's Mill are exceptional. There's an out-of-reach par five, the 588-yard eighth, but Dye invites players to a chess game on the 18th, a right-to-left dogleg stretching to 550 yards that is reachable by an accomplished long hitter who can

SIDETRIPS

Twenty-five miles south of Fowler's Mill in Aurora are two major attractions. There's *Geauga Lake,* a theme park and water park with over 100 rides and attractions, including the Serial Thriller, a suspended looping roller coaster; and *Sea World,* where kids of all ages can get splashed by Shamu and Namu, the killer whales.

If you grew up with rock 'n roll and want to relive the soundtrack of your life, backtrack to Cleveland to the *Rock and Roll Hall of Fame and Museum.* There's everything from Elvis memorabilia to original film footage of the Beatles.

Clubhouse at Fowler's Mill Golf Course, Chesterland, Ohio

Fowler's Mill Golf Course, 12th hole

More Golf/Outside Cleveland

North of Fowler's Mill near Lake Erie is *Quail Hollow Resort,* a 36-hole facility. The feature track is the *Weiskopf–Morrish Course,* a modern classic debuted in 1996 and carved from rolling, wooded countryside. The design duo dusted off motifs from the past, from bunkers that play havoc with depth perception to false front greens. Wide fairways wend through a thick stand of hardwoods, with numerous lakes, creeks, and wetlands in play. This brilliant 6,872-yard, par-71 layout exemplifies Weiskopf's design philosophy: "Each hole must create risk and challenge, and every hole should reward a well planned and executed golf shot."

The Weiskopf–Morrish Course is routed around the perimeter of Quail Hollow's *Devlin–Von Hagge Course,* site of the Nike Tour's Cleveland Open and a strong test in its own right.

In the Cleveland suburb of Highland Heights, 20 minutes from downtown, is *StoneWater Golf Club,* a superb public-access course designed by Michael Hurdzan and Dana Fry and opened in 1996. Water comes into play on 16 holes, while 22 bridges carry players across the course. Caddies are available.

For a trip back in time, check out *Manikiki Golf Club,* a storied Donald Ross design (1929) in Willoughby 18 miles east of Cleveland. This former PGA Tour site, with its crowned greens and classic Ross touches, is a must for traditionalists.

avoid a series of bunkers guarding the left side. According to Sobecki, "At Fowler's Mill, you'll use every club in your bag—and your brain." If it isn't turned to toast early on by Dye's shenanigans.

The Lake–River combination (formerly the Blue–White nines) form the championship 18, but Dye also built the Maple (formerly the Red) nine across the street from the main complex. Shorter and narrower than the core 18, with smaller targets and fewer water hazards, the Maple is a superb placement course of 2,989 yards. Always well conditioned, the Maple is the perfect choice for a quick and pleasurable nine—if you can keep your tee ball on the short grass.

In 1998, Fowler's Mill opened a $1.4 million clubhouse that resembles a wealthy settler's farmhouse. Set on a plateau and commanding a fine view of the course, the clubhouse, inspired by whitewood frame farmhouses in the area and compatible with a 150-year-old dairy barn at the entrance to the course, has a full-service pro shop, grill room with vaulted ceiling and exposed beams, and a covered porch that runs along the entire back side of the building. Interiors are decorated in an Early American style, with dark wood trim and wainscoting. It's the perfect place to relax after matching wits with the wiliest designer alive.

DINING

In addition to the *Bass Lake Taverne* at the Bass Lake Inn, where fine suppers are served beside brickwork fireplaces or on a spacious outdoor patio, there's *Annie's Slovenian Restaurant* in Chesterland, which features Slovenian-Austrian-Hungarian cuisine, from Chicken Paprikash to Segadin Goulash. For a taste of the Amish Country, head east to Middlefield, where the *Dutch Family Restaurant* and *Mary Yoder's Amish Kitchen* serve home-cooked, family-style meals.

Illinois

On a topsy-turvy site in northwest Illinois, at the **Eagle Ridge Inn & Resort**, designer Roger Packard teamed with two-time U.S. Open champion Andy North to fashion a momentous layout within the rugged 6,800-acre Galena Territory. Named for Ulysses S. Grant, who lived in Galena before the Civil War, **The General** (#95), opened in 1997, was a tough nut to crack. The swell-and-swale property required the blasting of 140,000 cubic yards of solid rock to uncover steeper drops than are normally found at most Midwestern ski areas.

According to Packard, "the topography of The General is the most dramatic I've ever worked on. Andy and I both agreed . . . that the best thing we could do from a design standpoint was to work with Mother Nature and incorporate our course into her overall pattern." Players, he added,

DINING

After the round, players can savor a fine meal overlooking Lake Galena in the resort's elegant *Woodlands Restaurant*; try their hand at darts or billiards in *Shooters Bar & Grill*; or enjoy a frozen confection in *Scoops*, an old-fashioned ice cream parlor. In Galena, there are *Café Italia*, a charming trattoria featured in the movie "Field of Dreams," and the *DeSoto House Hotel*, an 1855 mansion that served as Grant's presidential headquarters and which today offers good steaks.

Eagle Ridge Inn & Resort, The General, Galena, Illinois, 11th hole

Eagle Ridge Inn & Resort, The General, 18th hole

Among the more memorable holes is the third, a mid-length par three that plays from an elevated tee to a raised green defended in front and to the left by a horseshoe-shaped pond. The tee shot is strictly a hit-or-miss affair. The eighth is a 372-yard par four that doglegs to the right around a ravine and climbs to a green that sits in a bowl blasted from rock, the jagged limestone walls nearly encasing the putting surface. The "quarry hole," it's called.

With its wild elevation changes, the back nine of The General is a call to arms. At the 11th, a 163-yard par three, golfers play from a series of tees sited on rock outcrops over a cavern to a green benched into a hill and defended in front by deep, grassy hollows. Tall hardwoods frame this picture-perfect one-shotter.

If one hole on The General marches to its own beat, it's the gravity-defying 14th, a short 357-yard par four that drops a staggering 180 feet to the fairway from a hang glider's ledge. From the topmost tee, players can take in a tristate view (Illinois, Iowa, Wisconsin) of rolling hills that stretch west to the Mississippi River. The landing area is generously sized, while a lone bunker defends the green to the right. The 14th is not only drop-dead beautiful, it offers all players a very reasonable chance at par.

What goes down must come up, and up players must come at the final two holes. The perilous par-four 17th calls for a nerveless carry over a deep gully followed by an uphill approach that avoids strategically placed rocks and finds a green tucked

can use the layout's landscape to their advantage. "The terrain, trees, creeks, and even shadows show how the holes play, and where to hit for best results."

Needless to say, better straight than crooked on The General, especially from the 4-Star tees at 6,820 yards. The front nine, traditional in appearance, proceeds into valleys, over hills, and around water features.

in the woods. The home hole, a mammoth par five, calls for an accurate tee shot over a ravine to a split-level fairway. High road or low, only the best players can reach the 18th green in two.

The General is served by a 10,000-square-foot clubhouse set atop a ridge with a glass facade for a back wall. The views through the building to the layout's rolling hills and valleys are outstanding.

SIDETRIPS

Galena, known as The Town That Time Forgot, is a living time capsule of winding streets filled with antique emporiums, museums, and specialty shops located a few miles west of the resort near the Mississippi River. Over 85 percent of the town's buildings, built in a variety of architectural styles between 1836 and the Civil War (a time when Galena was a lead-mining center), are listed on the National Historic Register.

Galena's main street

More Golf/Eagle Ridge

The resort's formidable North and South courses, each routed among rolling hills, limestone bluffs, and specimen oaks, offer exceptional golf. While much of the area off the fairways on The General was left natural, the North and South courses are manicured to the tree lines, offering polished, country club–style golf. The sporty par-34, 2,648-yard East Course at Eagle Ridge is great for beginners. It also gives middle handicappers a chance to break 40.

Chicago

Chicago, the "Second City," takes a back seat to no burgh when it comes to daily-fee golf, boasting more public golf holes than any other metropolis in America. In addition to the three "Top 100" courses voted to the list, dozens of well-kept, public-access venues beckon from leafy suburbs to the north, south, and west of the Windy City. Not only is the welcome warm at these facilities, walkers are always welcome at Chicago's public courses.

The king of Chicagoland's parkland spreads is the **Cog Hill Golf & Country Club** and its **No. 4 Course** (#16), the impregnable foundation of a stellar 72-hole public complex in Lemont, 30 miles southwest of the city. Site of the Motorola Western Open, a prestigious PGA Tour event, from 1991–99, Cog Hill No. 4, a.k.a. "Dubsdread," is twice as difficult as the other three courses on site. That is by design. In the early 1960s, golf pro/developer Joe Jemsek, the Chicago area's patron saint of public golf, hired Dick Wilson to build two courses and revise a pair of preexisting layouts at Cog Hill. Mostly, he wanted a tournament-class venue, something on the order of Medinah, one of Chicago's top-ranked private clubs. And he got it. Opened in 1964, its holes strung from ridge to ridge or cut diagonally across sidehills on the rolling, wooded terrain, No. 4 was the Midwest's first true championship-caliber public course.

Dubsdread is solid, honest, straightforward. All hazards are plainly visible. There is no hint of chicanery or caprice. However, each and every hole is fiercely defended by sand. Lots of it. In fact, there is no better or

Cog Hill Golf & Country Club, Lemont, Illinois, No. 4 Course, sixth hole

Opposite: Eagle Ridge Inn & Resort, The General, eighth hole

more heavily bunkered public course in America than Cog Hill No. 4, a fact not lost on accomplished players who try to tiptoe around the track without getting a single grain of sand in their shoes. With nearly 120 bunkers dotting the layout, each poised to bury a mistake, it's easier said than done, especially from the tips at 6,940 yards.

To have any hope of success on this Sahara of the Midway, golfers must tack their way from one safe landing area to the next—and play the par threes well. Dubsdread's quartet of one-shotters, among the finest in the nation, range from 170 to 226 yards and call for accurate, well-placed tee shots. Or else. Like many older public courses, the undulating, medium-quick greens have their own logic. Conservative (not bold) putting is favored.

Of all the holes on No. 4, Jemsek's personal favorite is the sixth, a long par three that plays downhill to a two-tiered green sloped from back to front and embraced by five large, deep bunkers defined by Wilson's signature capes and bays. A par here is to be cherished.

Dubsdread's final holes were designed to separate the wheat from the chaff. The par-four 16th plays from a pulpit tee to a fairway banked like a racetrack around a brush- and water-filled ravine. Spreading oaks guard the right side. The difficult approach is played from a sidehill lie, the ball above one's feet, to a deep, elevated green. The par-four 17th is a left-to-right dogleg that calls for a well-positioned drive and an accurate second shot, while both the fairway and green on the 18th, a tremendous two-shotter stretching to 449 yards, slope toward a pond on the left. It is by far the toughest hole on a course that well deserves its nickname.

Cog Hill Golf & Country Club, No. 4 Course, 18th hole

Tweaked and upgraded in the mid-1990s to accommodate the prestigious PGA Tour event as well as the 1997 U.S. Amateur Championship—bunkers were reshaped, greens recontoured, and dense brush cleared from under trees lining the fairways—Dubsdread is today a wrinkle-free, thoroughly traditional test of golf. Nothing is concealed—except the challenge.

A final note: Caddies are available by calling 48 hours in advance. Cog Hill's No. 4 Course is quite hilly for a Chicagoland layout, especially the back nine. A caddy will enhance your round (and save your legs).

Cog Hill's practice area and learning center are first-rate. The staff

Cantigny Golf & Tennis, Wheaton, Illinois, Lakeside Course, ninth hole

Cantigny Golf & Tennis, Woodside Course, second hole

goes out of its way to make arriving golfers feel welcome and special. (Jemsek, who worked his way up from caddie to course owner, is committed to doing everything he can to create a private club aura for the daily-fee golfer.) Lastly, the milk shakes served in the clubhouse are as rich and thick as Dubsdread is long and testing.

Aside from the championship track, Cog Hill's most popular venue is the No. 2 Course, a short (only 6,268 yards from the tips), attractive design set on fairly rugged terrain, with steep drops from tee to fairway. No. 1, a bit of a plain Jane, is a breeze for experts, mildly challenging for novices. No. 3, marked by broad, rolling fairways framed by tall trees, boasts an excellent collection of par fives.

In the suburb of Wheaton, 30 miles west of Chicago, is **Cantigny (Woodside–Lakeside #66)**, a 27-hole spread situated on the former estate of Colonel Robert McCormick, longtime editor and publisher of the *Chicago Tribune*. Cantigny (pronounced Canteeny) is owned and operated by a well-endowed foundation instructed by McCormick's will to create an outlet that would provide a source of recreation and welfare for the public. Among the nation's classiest and best-run public-access facilities, Cantigny takes its name from the French village where the U.S. Army staged its first offensive battle in World War I. (McCormick served as an artillery battalion commander in the First Division which fought in that battle. A military museum on site immerses visitors in the sights and sounds of conflicts from World War I to Vietnam.)

The golf course, perfectly groomed, was carved from former soybean fields and a forest of hardwoods by Roger Packard, son of long-time architect E. Lawrence Packard. Packard's talent for blending superior visual characteristics with playability and easy maintenance, coupled with his roots in the region—he was born in Chicago and maintains offices there—made him a logical candidate for the job. He took on the Cantigny commission, which he called a "dream job for a great client," shortly after remodeling the No. 3 Course at Medinah Country Club outside Chicago in preparation for the 1988 U.S. Senior Open. (The No. 3 Course also hosted the 1990 U.S. Open.)

Working on prime acreage marked by beautiful stands of 200-year-old oaks and giant hickory trees, Packard conjured a brilliant test full of intrigue and nuance, with over 70 bunkers and a dozen lakes to keep things interesting. Many of the features were designed to provide subliminal enjoyment. For example, the opening holes on the Woodside nine, which proceed from the impressive clubhouse, are formal in appearance, the raised rectangular tees faced with flagstone walls. As the course moves away from civilization, the holes begin to reflect the countrified setting: free-form tees, tall fescue grasses waving in the wind, wooded areas left in their natural state. As the incoming Lakeside nine swings around the main pond and begins to head home, the holes once again assume a more formal appearance.

Kemper Lakes Golf Course, Long Grove, Illinois, 11th hole

The most controversial hole at Cantigny—and the one Packard spent the most time building—is the par-five second. It enjoys a love-hate relationship with Cantigny's regulars. Stretching to 539 yards, the hole's strategic linchpin is a recirculating stream that comes into play early and often. The tee shot is played to a rising fairway guarded to the right by the brook. The second shot must be aimed to a peninsulalike landing area nearly encircled by the stream, while the approach must again carry water to find and hold a small green defended to the left by a lone bunker. Birdies and even eagles are possible here, but so too are double and triple bogeys, the price for gambling efforts gone astray. Packard's defense: "The better the golfer you are, the smarter we ask you to be, and the straighter we want you to hit it."

In addition to the sixth, a classic par four of 446 yards that rewards a long, accurate drive, the other standout hole on Woodside is the eighth, a stellar 165-yard par three that plays over a pond to a large, semi-island green it shares with the sixth hole on the Hillside nine.

The Lakeside nine, which provides the most resistance to par of Cantigny's three nines, puts water in play at five holes. The par-four ninth hole (typically played as the 18th by those following the Woodside–Lakeside routing) must rank as one of the best closing holes in Chicagoland, especially since the hole was lengthened by 40 yards in 1998. The tee shot on

this right-to-left dogleg is played to a slim fairway framed by Swan Lake on the right and by trees and more water on the left. The 18th's sizable green is defended by bunkers fore and aft and by water everywhere but in front of the green. The hole's extra distance, created by pushing the tee back, has greatly enhanced the challenge for better players. From the back tees, it will handcuff all but champions.

Cantigny's Hillside nine, with fewer water holes, is slightly less taxing than the Woodside-Lakeside combo. As on the main 18, the small to medium-size greens on Hillside are interwoven with baffling contours.

The 27-hole spread, which looks mature beyond its years, is as well-conditioned as a private club, with tens of thousands of flowers planted each year to brighten the premises. From the tree-lined entryway to the extra-friendly staff, Cantigny is first-class all the way.

Cantigny Youth Links

Debuted in 1998, this nine-hole course, designed by Roger Packard and Andy North specifically for young players, is served by its own clubhouse and has its own set of rules. According to James Sutherland, Cantigny's executive director, "When school is not in session, the only ones who can make a tee time are children ages six to 15." Children may bring adults to the Cantigny Youth Links as their guests. "We wanted to encourage family play, but we didn't want the overdoting 'Little League parent' syndrome here," Sutherland explained. Holes range in length from 55 to 200 yards, but no par is listed on the scorecard. It's up to kids to determine their own scoring standards without relation to a predetermined number. Greens and tees are big, providing maximum flexibility on the 20-acre site. At press time, the green fee for kids was $7—about the price of a movie.

In the leafy suburb of Long Grove, 35 miles northwest of downtown Chicago, is **Kemper Lakes** (#84), a golf course worth skipping by those afflicted with aquaphobia. Even those who claim not to mind water on a golf course might consider selecting an aqualung as the 15th club in their bags. Because Kemper Lakes, as the name implies, is a big swimming pool spliced with fairways and greens.

Designed by Ken Killian and Dick Nugent in 1979, Kemper Lakes was developed by the Kemper Insurance Company, its glass-and-steel corporate headquarters bordering a portion of the course. *GOLF Magazine* contributing editor Tom Doak, in his "Confidential Guide to Golf Courses," dismissed Kemper Lakes as "the corporate approach to giving the public-course golfer what he wants: fast greens, high-dollar maintenance, lots of water hazards, and a premium price." But that judgment is perhaps a bit harsh for a course that has been a fabulous success both as a public-access venue and a tournament site. Kemper Lakes, after all, hosted the 1989 PGA Championship won by Payne Stewart. It also staged the 1992 U.S. Women's Amateur, and at press time was a regular stop on the Senior PGA Tour. Tested by champions, Kemper Lakes has evolved into one of Chicagoland's must-play tracks, a thrilling match-play course where no lead is safe and where anything can happen—especially if players are not averse to attempting heroic shots over wide expanses of water.

Kemper Lakes Golf Course, 18th hole

From the back tees, Kemper Lakes stretches to 7,217 yards (140 slope, 75.7 course rating), but very few players tackle the course at full stretch. The blue tees (6,680 yards) and white markers (6,265 yards) present more than enough challenge for most campaigners. Not that Kemper Lakes tries to deliver the knockout punch right away. The first few holes were designed to get players off to a good start. Two short par fours are followed by a reasonable (but watery) par three with a peninsula green for a target. The bell sounds at the fourth, a sickle-shaped par-five that swings to the right around a lake, while the king-size 557-yard par-five seventh, with water down the entire left side, usually has hookers on the ropes by the conclusion of the hole.

The ninth, a long par four that plays uphill to a well-bunkered green, is rated the number-one handicap hole, though with no water in play, many others could be placed ahead of it in difficulty. The 11th, for example, is a brilliant par five that bends to the right and asks players to avoid giant oaks that encroach upon both sides of the landing area. The approach must carry a creek that gurgles in front of a tree-framed green. Burly oaks appear again at the short par-four 12th, but this and the three holes that follow are breather holes compared to the finale.

The 16th, at 469 yards the longest par four at Kemper Lakes, asks players to land their drives safely on a fairway flanked by a lake on the right and a pair of large traps to the left. The scenario is repeated on the approach: water right, sand left. The par-three 17th calls for a forced carry over water to a bulkheaded green that beckons from the middle of a lake, while the 18th has probably ruined more rounds than the Great Fire of Chicago did buildings. This grueling par four, which doglegs sharply from right to left, demands water crossings on both the drive and second shot. In the 1989 PGA Championship, Greg Norman drove straight to the green from the tee on this 433-yard hole. A tree has since been planted to discourage such efforts.

Home of a David Leadbetter Golf Academy, Kemper Lakes boasts a superb clubhouse with a nicely appointed pro shop as well as a full-service grill room, restaurant, and bar. Sea World in Softspikes? Maybe. A snail-like pace of play? Yes, numerous forced carries over water do slow up play, with five-hour rounds not uncommon. This drawback aside, the golf course earns its stripes as one of the Midwest's best-conditioned and most challenging layouts—especially for those who can block out the blue and focus on the green.

More Golf/Chicago

Inner-city golf? It's available in Chicago. Two blocks from bustling Michigan Avenue and 60 feet below street level is the *MetroGolf Illinois Center,* a nine-hole, par-three course by Perry Dye dubbed "the ultimate urban golf experience." Walled in by skyscrapers, this verdant downtown playground, built on a former railroad yard, offers holes ranging from 83 to 145 yards. The ninth calls for a trusty shot over a lake to a semi-island green. There's also a 92-station driving range at this one-of-a-kind facility.

Occupying a pair of former toxic landfills encircling Lake Calumet on the industrial South Side of town is the 36-hole *Harborside International Golf Center.* Both the Port and Starboard courses, designed by Dick Nugent and opened in 1995–96, are marvels of environmental engineering. Treeless and windswept, the fairways are defined by rolling fescue-covered mounds and deep pot bunkers. Both courses are evocative of a British seaside links, notwithstanding the grain elevators and smokestacks on the horizon. Harborside's 58-acre practice facility and learning center are exceptional. So are the views of Lake Michigan and the downtown skyline.

In the city's northern suburbs is *Pine Meadow* in Mundelein, a 7,141-yard test set within an arboretum owned by the Catholic Archdiocese of Chicago. Leased by Joe Jemsek in 1985 and completely remodeled, Pine Meadow is one of Chicagoland's best-run and most beautiful courses. Another good choice north of Chicago, especially for traditionalists, is *Glencoe Golf Club,* a vintage 1921 layout that skirts the city's Botanic Garden.

Heading west, there's *Prairie Landing,* a Robert Trent Jones, Jr.–designed layout located beside DuPage Airport. This prairie-style links is marked by prominent fescue-covered mounds, several rock-fringed lakes—and 130 bunkers. Because a steady breeze of 20 knots sweeps the course, fairways were built wide and greens were left open in front to encourage bump-and-run approach shots.

In Chicago's southern suburbs is *George W. Dunne National* in Oak Forest, a Ken Killian–Dick Nugent spread considered the jewel in the Cook County Forest Preserve crown. Laid out over nearly 300 acres of rolling, wooded terrain, "the National," known for its giant greens, steep-walled bunkers, and numerous lakes, is one of the best-conditioned municipal courses in the nation. At press time, the weekday green fee was $30.

There are many, many other excellent daily-fee courses in and around Chicago. Pick up a copy of *Chicagoland Golf* at any pro shop in the area for a complete directory.

New & Noteworthy/Chicago

North of Chicago in Libertyville is *ThunderHawk,* the Lake County Forest Preserves' latest golf course. Designed by Robert Trent Jones, Jr., the layout, with a blend of mature woodlands, pristine wetlands, and native prairie, opened in spring 1999. Multiple tees, roomy fairways, and large greens will challenge players at all ability levels. Accepted into Audubon International's Signature program, ThunderHawk, free of commercial development, is poised to become one of Chicagoland's finest public-access layouts.

A few miles away in Zion is *Shepherd's Crook,* a compact layout by Keith Foster with dramatic features (punchbowl greens, heroic bunkers) inspired by classic Chicago clubs from the 1920s and earlier.

Other promising newcomers include *Prairie Bluff,* a Roger Packard–Andy North design in the city's southwest suburb of Lockport; and *Mistwood* in nearby Romeoville, a Ray Hearn design that encompasses an abandoned quarry and a 65-acre lake.

Wisconsin

The University of Wisconsin in Madison is the quintessential Big Ten school, but until an off-campus golf course, **University Ridge** (#99), opened in 1991, its list of extracurricular activities was incomplete. For those weary of homework of any kind, this stellar track offers a pleasing form of higher education in a beautiful outdoor classroom.

Located in Verona, eight miles southwest of Madison, the golf course is positioned atop a terminal moraine marking the northernmost reach of glacial movement during the last Ice Age. Home to the school's men's and women's golf teams and also open to the public, it occupies 225 acres of rolling hills, sprawling meadows, and dense woodlands.

University Ridge, designed by Robert Trent Jones, Jr., offers exceptional pace and variety on a heaving site with 180 feet of elevation change (it hosted the 1998 NCAA Women's Championship). The front nine flows through former cornfields and waving grasslands, with a wooded ravine, a pair of ponds, and a patch of marshland in play. The back nine, equally undulating, disappears into a deep forest of oak, maple, and cherry trees before reemerging at the 16th hole.

While manageable for most from the multiple sets of forward tees, University Ridge calls for an advanced degree in golf smarts from the tips at 6,888 yards. Jones, ever the strategist, laid out a beguiling chess game on the surpisingly hilly site, the topmost holes offering fine views of the state capital to the east and rolling plains to the west. There is room enough to drive the ball on most holes, and bail-out areas are generous, but Jones clustered 70 percent of the layout's sand bunkers and bluegrass hollows around the putting surfaces. Green sizes, it should be noted, are well matched to the length and prevailing difficulty of each hole, giving the layout its ideal proportions.

The game is on at the par-four first hole, where the open spaces of the links-style front nine are in full view from the elevated tee. At the par-three fifth, players can take aim at an old silo that rises beyond a green

University of Wisconsin, Verona, Wisconsin, University Ridge Course, ninth hole

University of Wisconsin, University Ridge, 12th hole

University of Wisconsin, Camp Randall Stadium

guarded by a ravine and five bunkers, while the par-four 10th kicks off a six-hole, Hansel-and-Gretel-type journey through thick woods. Jones leaves a trail of clues directing players where to go, but only well-executed shots will keep players out of the jaws of trouble. The picturesque par-three 12th drops nearly 50 feet to a well-bunkered green encased in trees—players must guard against overclubbing here—but it's the par-five 16th hole that has emerged as the signature hole at University Ridge.

While not especially long from the gold tees at 533 yards, the 16th

Madison's west side has a number of budget motels and mid-priced hotels. Literary-minded travelers can book into the *Canterbury Inn,* which occupies a 1924 building on State Street. Each of the Inn's six rooms is named for a pilgrim in Chaucer's poem.

A well-run facility, golfers on arrival at University Ridge are greeted by a friendly, knicker-clad staff. The green fee includes a sleeve of logoed golf balls. Walkers are welcome, though only the fit need apply. University Ridge has an excellent practice facility and, as of 1999, an expanded clubhouse that offers good casual dining.

Kohler

A few epochs ago, a pair of retreating glaciers not only sculpted rivers and stacked up hills an hour's drive north of Milwaukee, they smeared a thick layer of till over the Wisconsin bedrock. From this rich alluvial soil sprang hardwoods, conifers—and the current generation of Kohlers, who run the well-known plumbing fixtures company and who transformed a former dormitory built to house immigrant employees into a superlative resort hotel, **The American Club**.

Pete Dye, himself a Midwesterner, was enticed to visit the region by the head of the clan, Herb Kohler, who in the mid-1980s decided to build a golf course in a river valley he had roamed as a child. A better match could not have been made than the one forged between Kohler, an avid

offers a double fairway routed on either side of a wooded hollow. Playing to the right side shortens the hole but requires a near-perfect drive. Aiming to the left offers a safer option, but this route asks players to hit an approach shot to a green guarded by a large, spreading tree and 14 bunkers. The 17th is a knee-knocker of a par three where tee shots must clear a pond that separates tee from green, while the uphill par-four 18th, with grassy hollows and rolling farmland on the left and a thick copse of trees to the right, is a perfect summation of the layout's open-and-wooded, dual personality.

The clubhouse at Blackwolf Run Golf Club, Kohler, Wisconsin, The American Club

Blackwolf Run Golf Club, Meadow Valleys Course, 14th hole

golfer with the vision and deep pockets to create a world-class facility, and Dye, a creative iconoclast who rolled up his sleeves to build a pair of Big Impact layouts.

The first 18 holes at **Blackwolf Run Golf Club** opened in 1988. A third nine was added a year later, with a fourth nine completed in 1990. Wisconsin's amiable dairyland reputation has never been the same.

With subtle refinements made along the way to enhance the landscape or amplify the challenge—Dye is forever tinkering—Blackwolf Run's two courses, **River** (#3) and **Meadow Valleys** (#34), feature Mother Nature and Pete Dye at their respective best. Dye's trademarks—giant grassy mounds, split-level fairways, vast waste bunkers, kettle-like pot bunkers, perched greens defended by huge swales—are beautifully melded to the site's glacially formed ridges, hollows, and elongated troughs. Both layouts are contained within a 500-acre nature preserve, with no reminders of civilization to intrude on the wilderness experience.

With only Pebble Beach (1919) and Pinehurst No. 2 (1907) ranked ahead of it on the "Top 100" list, the River Course must be considered the nation's finest public-access course of modern times. With its target-style landing areas, harrowing bunkers, outrageously contoured greens, and flowing water or river banks in play on 14 holes, it is by turns the most dramatic and intimidating course in the Midwest. Maybe the world. Dye emptied his bag of tricks to delight and confound players, throwing the proverbial kitchen sink (a Kohler model, of course) into the Sheboygan River when he was done. The pristine river, filled with trout and salmon, meanders through the property for seven miles, offering scenic relief from the exalted challenges.

Dye provided four sets of tees on the River ranging from 6,991 yards down to 5,115 yards. (The course rating is 74.9 and the slope is 151 from the tips.) It is of paramount importance that visiting players choose a set of markers that best suit their game. Otherwise, it's five hours of anguish, a dozen lost balls, a deflated ego. Play from an inappropriate set of tees, and you may even be left for dead. (There is precedent. The great Winnebago chief, Black Wolf, scalped his enemies and stole their ponies one dark and stormy night in the early 1800s.)

Blackwolf Run Golf Club, River Course, 13th hole

Of the resort's eight restaurants, the finest, occupying The American Club's former laundry room, is *The Immigrant,* its six connected rooms each decorated to honor the ethnic mix of early settlers. Fine wines are matched to superb regional dishes, including pecan-crusted lake trout with citrus segments and brandy butter sauce. For more casual dining, the *Horse & Plow* serves hearty soups, sandwiches, and salads in a casual tavernlike atmosphere, with over 75 varieties of domestic and imported beers available.

The Wisconsin Room

The original segment of the River Course (holes one through four, 14 through 18) bookends the newest nine opened in 1990. The setting, with wooded glades framing nearly every hole on the rolling terrain and the river's meandering path defining the perimeter of the course, showcase some of the best and most intriguing golf holes Dye has ever built.

Take the very first hole, a formidable par five called "Snake." Because the Sheboygan River flows down the entire left side, golfers may sensibly wish to favor the right side. That would be a mistake. There's trouble, mostly shaggy, fescue-covered mounds, in that area. Though well-guarded by the river, the hole is actually more open on the left than a first glance might indicate. Even before he's had a chance to get started, the innocent-minded resort player guarding against a splash landing on his opening tee shot is foiled.

"Gotcha," the long par-four third, may be the most difficult hole at the entire 36-hole complex, this without a drop of water. From an elevated tee, players must avoid trees, a chasm, and elaborate fairway bunkers up

Blackwolf Run Golf Club, Meadows Course, 12th hole

the right side. The elongated, pulpit green slopes to the right to an extended bunker that eats into the green.

Among the more scenic holes is the par-four fifth, "Made in Heaven," where golfers drive from a bluff 50 feet above the river to a fairway guarded to the right by a long sand pit. The green, with a pronounced slope to the right, is perched 30 feet above the fairway and is protected in front by a hellish sand pit. Because the greenside terrain falls off sharply to the right, the prudent shot is played well left.

The next three holes unfold beautifully, each asking for a well-placed tee shot to a specific landing area followed by a thoughtful approach. It's golf by the book, although the short par-five eighth, "Hell's Gate," has a split fairway that offers strategic options and asks for good decisions in return for par. Players will know immediately if their reach exceeds their grasp. Nobody hands out double bogeys faster than Pete Dye.

The front nine reaches a climax at the ninth, "Cathedral Spires," a short par four that Dye claims may be the best hole he's ever built. Why? The hole, only 337 yards from the tips, offers a choice of three fairways! Golfers must play a shell game with the designer to determine the proper strategy by choosing a path that suits their ability level and comfort zone. The left route is safest, though players must guard against rolling into a pot bunker. Hit down the middle, and a stand of 90-foot-high cottonwoods may block your path. Big hitters—the "high and mighty," Dye calls them—can fly their go-for-broke tee shots over a bend in the river in an attempt to reach the wide, shallow green. Except in a fun match, it's a very risky play. This pivotal hole can produce anything from a tap-in birdie to an irksome triple-bogey.

For better or worse, the River's back nine is more of the same. The sickle-shaped, par-five 11th is a deceptively alluring three-shotter that

traces a sweeping curve in the Sheboygan, while the par-four 12th, "Long Lagoon," is rated the second-toughest hole on the course. After a forced carry over water and sand to a plateau fairway, the approach must be placed safely to the left away from the river, which swings along the right side of the green. At 465 yards from the black tees, even the pros squirm on this one.

The par-three 13th, "Tall Timber," is one of the more controversial holes at Blackwolf Run. A stand of 60-foot-high willows nearly blocks the entrance to the green, forcing better golfers on the blue or black tees to hit a high fade over the trees—or play a bold draw that starts out over the river and turns to the left toward an enormous, pear-shaped green over 50 yards deep from front to back. This sprawling green can spell a four-club difference, depending on pin placement.

At the short par-four 15th, the downhill approach to a partially hidden green is played over an appalling pit of sand. The putting surface, interwoven with subtle undulations, is one of the most difficult on the course to read.

"Dyehard," the par-four 18th, was described by the designer himself as "a severely long finishing hole" (it stretches to 421 yards from the white tees, 440 yards from the blues, 469 yards from the black tees). The broad, raised fairway sweeps to the left around a grassy trench planked with railroad ties that is filled with river water for major events. The 23,000-square-foot double green, shared with the 18th on Meadow Valleys, is set in a natural amphitheater below a rustic clubhouse built from lodgepole pine logs. Par here is a fabulous score for most.

The Meadow Valleys Course at Blackwolf Run, rated three to five shots easier than the River, is nevertheless an outstanding layout in its own right. The River grabs the limelight based on its extended river frontage, but hole for hole, Meadow Valleys is every bit as good. When the 1998 U.S. Women's Open was played at Blackwolf Run, equal parts of each course were used to create a hybrid. Meadow Valleys is the course Dye prefers to play with his two sons when they're in town.

The front nine, set on gently rolling terrain in the southeastern watershed of the Sheboygan River, ambles across open meadows pockmarked with bunkers and framed by wildflowers and tall prairie grasses. The openness can be deceiving. Four lakes, swirling winds, and a brace of lengthy par fours make this nine play tough.

The back nine at Meadow Valleys, part of the original layout, shows the region's glacial influence, with narrower holes set near sculpted ridges and high bluffs. Deep ravines cross or border several of the fairways, with sharp elevation changes and water in play on six holes. There are one-of-a-kind touches: A pair of old flatbed railroad cars serve as bridges across Weeden's Creek, while chipmunks with plaid markings (are they Scottish?) occasionally dart across a cart path. From the white tees at 6,169 yards, Meadow Valleys is manageable by the average golfer who exercises caution and restraint. The blue tees at 6,735 yards and the tips at 7,142 yards are something else again.

The long par-five fifth, its double fairway pierced by a large incisor-like tooth of sand, is one of the finest holes at Blackwolf Run. Called "Gamble," the hole dares better golfers to play dangerously down the right side,

For golfers and naturalists alike, the best place to relax in Kohler is River Wildlife, a 500-acre wilderness preserve where guests can enjoy hunting, fishing, hiking, horseback riding—and country gourmet dining in a secluded log cabin in the woods. Sports Core, the resort's 85,000-square-foot fitness center and racquet club, offers salon and spa services. The Kohler Design Center is a showcase of Kohler Co. products, with more than 25 designer baths and kitchens displaying the latest Kohler products. In addition to the Water Deck, an impressive display of whirlpool baths, the center's highlight is Kohler's "Great Wall of China" (mostly commodes and tubs). Half-day factory tours are also available. The Shops at Woodlake Kohler, an eclectic collection of boutiques, galleries, and markets, offer everything from Armani sunglasses to fresh-from-the-garden zucchini. A gardening shop carries the seeds of every plant and flower used to landscape the resort.

The Kohler Design Center

left and water to the right. From the tips at 462 yards, it's an assassin.

The back nine of Meadow Valleys builds in drama and excitement. The 12th, "Ledge Walk," is a long, demanding par four that kicks off the layout's own version of Amen Corner. A ravine played as a lateral hazard gobbles pulled or hooked approach shots, while the bunkerless green, a plateau that falls away to grassy hollows, presents a difficult target.

The par-four 13th is a short right-to-left dogleg that calls for a blind tee shot drive over a hill (not necessarily with a driver) followed by a full pitch uphill to the flattest green on the course. Anything to the right of this pedestal green, unless snared by a long skinny trap, is history.

The 14th, a magnificent par four outlined by meandering Weeden's Creek and the Sheboygan River, plays 40 feet downhill to a peninsula green of modest size guarded by water on three sides. Of the par-three 15th, Dye said, "There is probably no hole like it anywhere else in the world." Just as well. The tee shot—196 yards from the blue tees, 227 yards from the tips—is played over a shallow ravine tangled with vegetation to a monster-size green replete with four-foot swales in the center. This bentgrass roller-coaster can give shaky putters a permanent case of the yips.

The par-four 18th at Meadow Valleys, "Salmon Trap," furnishes a spectacular finish. A long, accurate drive is required to set up the approach, which calls for a forced carry over the river to a giant double green shared with the 18th of the River. According to Dye, "If you're not in good position, you're going to save a lot of shots by laying up short of the river. Good luck. The folks on the verandah will be cheering for you."

After the round, players can relax in the rough-timbered clubhouse set on a hill overlooking the Sheboygan River and the 18th holes of both courses. Inside are vaulted ceilings, a huge fieldstone fireplace, and a display of Indian artifacts unearthed during course construction. Outside is a dining terrace with a panoramic view of the river valley. The hearty sandwiches and delicious entrée salads go a long way toward restoring players sapped by the relentless challenge of these two courses.

Whistling Straits: The Emerald Isle Drifts to Wisconsin

"I should say this with some degree of modesty, but in my lifetime I've never seen anything like this. Anyplace. Period." That is 72-year-old Pete Dye's preamble to a golf course that could well be his crowning achievement as a designer. Opened in July 1998, on a 560-acre site in the village of Haven nine miles east of Kohler, Whistling Straits may come to be known as the greatest piece of legerdemain in the history of golf course architecture.

Herb Kohler gave Dye carte blanche to build a course for walkers only that would capture the experience of playing a seaside links in Ireland or Scotland. While Blackwolf Run was a wonderful site blessed with fantastic natural features created by glacial run-off and deposits, the parcel in Haven, a former military camp, was dead-flat and had little to recommend it—except for the glorious two-mile sweep of Lake Michigan shoreline.

leaving a blind second shot over two hillside bunkers to a green guarded in front by a menacing pot bunker. "Now play your cards," reads the original course guide, which also outlines a smart, conservative way to play the hole.

The sixth, "Serpentine," is a long par four that reverses direction, angling right-to-left off the tee and then left-to-right toward the green. According to Dye, "Here is a hole where you might as well look for bogey." It is indeed a par squelcher. The ninth is equally demanding, another sturdy par four. Here the drive must clear a long trench of sand, while the approach must find and hold a sloping green protected by bunkers to the

Whistling Straits, Haven, Wisconsin, Straits Course, seventh hole

And so Dye, for whom earthmoving is second nature, attacked the site with an army of bulldozers, displacing nearly three million cubic yards of muck and clay to fashion 80-foot-high "dunes" reminiscent of those found at Ballybunion in Ireland, Cruden Bay in Scotland, Royal St. George's in England. He later brought in nearly 800,000 cubic yards of sand to flash the tops of these manufactured dunes to give them a naturalistic appearance. Equally impressive are the narrow, sandy paths leading through coarsely grassed broken ground stretching between tee and fairway. This land was created to resemble the rippled and scrubby terrain created by years of wave action and found on genuine links courses. A small flock of Scottish Black Face sheep grazes the course.

Drawing upon a lifetime of design experience as well as numerous field trips he and Kohler made to Ireland and the U.K., Dye routed 14 holes in nearly uninterrupted sequence within a stone's throw of the lake. Eight holes (including all four par threes) hug the shoreline. The holes proceed from just above beach level to restored 40-foot-high bluffs to Dye's colossal hills and berms that serve up panoramic views of the watery horizon. The course stretches to 7,645 yards from the championship tees, though five tee placements give the course exceptional flexibility for players at all ability levels. The prevailing wind in summer is from the south-

west, but inversions on the lake produce swirling winds that constantly change direction, complicating club selection. Given the conditions, Dye built very large greens. These greens were planted in bentgrass, but the fairways, many of them 50 yards wide, were sown with a blend of three fescues to create a hard, fast-running surface. The deep pot bunkers are vintage Pete Dye and look very much at home on the treeless moonscape.

Site of the 1999 PGA of America Club Professional Championship, a national title event, this lakeside tour de force has been dubbed the Straits Course, the first of two Pete Dye courses on site. In late 2000, the Creeks Course, a manicured, parkland-style spread crisscrossed by four streams, will make its debut behind the towering artificial dunes of the Straits.

To the artfully contrived fakery of the Straits has been added an Irish manor-style clubhouse with whitewashed stone exterior walls, slate shingles, and masonry fireplaces. Inside are hand-hewn timbers, cathedral ceilings, and a 64-seat restaurant offering "American fare with Irish flair." The second-floor bar/lounge, with its soaring windows, commands views of the ninth and 18th greens as well as Lake Michigan, which is often flecked with whitecaps. As a stage set, Whistling Straits, from the contingent of Irish caddies to the Traditional Bangers and Mash served in the clubhouse, is very convincing. Only the shamrocks and leprechauns are missing.

The Southwest

Troon North Golf Club, Monument Course • Troon North Golf Club, Pinnacle Course

Grayhawk Golf Club, Talon Course • Grayhawk Golf Club, Raptor Course

Legend Trail Golf Club • The Boulders, South Course • The Boulders, North Course

The Raven Golf Club at Sabino Springs • The Lodge at Ventana Canyon, Mountain Course

Karsten Creek Golf Club • La Cantera Golf Club • Horseshoe Bay Resort, Ram Rock

Barton Creek Resort & Country Club, Fazio Course • University of New Mexico,

Championship Course • Piñon Hills Golf Course • Primm Valley Golf Club, Lakes Course

Edgewood Tahoe Golf Course

Troon North Golf Course, Scottsdale, Arizona, Monument Course, 16th hole

Arizona

Valley of the Sun

Phoenix, the nation's sixth-largest city and second-fastest-growing metropolis (behind Las Vegas), is a Sun Belt boom town nonpareil. According to the National Golf Foundation, Maricopa County, which includes the greater Phoenix–Scottsdale area, has built more golf courses since 1992 than any other county in the nation. Many are topnotch—four of the region's seven courses on the "Top 100" list have opened since that year. Credit enterprising developers, a (hopefully) bottomless aquifer, and surging demand by snowbirds and residents alike for the area's runaway growth of high-end daily-fee facilities.

Because of limits imposed on irrigated turfgrass, accuracy is everything on newer desert layouts. Golfers must play their tee shots not to broad, welcoming lawns but to narrow landing pods hemmed in by decomposed granite and thorny vegetation. Tom Weiskopf, a designer who works wonders in the desert, believes 82 acres of improved turf (the present quota) is plenty of grass for golf. It's all in the allocation. Modified parkland-style layouts that accentuate playability—roomier fairways, more accessible greens—are currently in vogue. The trick, for an architect, is to give players the appearance of narrowness, the sensation of impending doom, but actually have more grass in play than is readily visible.

Hackers, take heart. You have a good chance of matching your handicap in the desert *if* you select the right set of tees for your ability level and *if* you play the desert as a lateral hazard. Should your ball depart the fairway, drop another within two club lengths of where it last crossed the grass line, penalty of one stroke, and move on. No thrashing around in the cactus, please.

Troon North Golf Club in Scottsdale (named for Royal Troon in Scotland), is the undisputed king of what *GOLF Magazine* Editor-in-Chief George Peper calls the "kitty litter" courses. Etched in the foothills of the McDowell Mountains off East Dynamite Boulevard, it is the 36-hole complex by which all other desert facilities are judged.

Troon North's original layout, the **Monument Course** (#6), established itself as the ultimate desert arena the day it opened in 1990. A Tom Weiskopf–Jay Morrish collaboration, it is the top-ranked cactus course on the "Top 100" list. Formal in appearance, with all hazards in plain view, the Monument's holes appear draped on the land, with natural contours intact throughout. Pains were taken to keep things in place: The corner of the dogleg at the par-five third hinges on a giant wind-carved monolith that dictates play off the tee, while the par-four fourth hole was rerouted to preserve a 600-year-old saguaro.

The demands of this stunning target-style design are offset by large, subtly contoured greens and shallow bunkers. These bunkers give the average duffer (who would rather corner a rattler than play from sand) a decent chance to escape from trouble. Also, players aren't required to hit a delicate flop shot from the side of a mound if they miss the green: Chipping areas are gently sloped and very fair.

There are, however, consequences for the wayward at Troon North. In fact, spray hitters should wear a pair of leather chaps to avoid finishing the round in shreds. Depart the fairway at Troon North, and you enter a hellish landscape that can damage both ego and apparel. The rough here is *really* rough. And it won't be the rattlesnakes or the Gila monsters that get you—it'll be the chainfruit or "jumping" cholla, which has a habit of embedding its hook-shaped barbs into roving golfers. But overall, the Monument is friendly to first-timers honest enough to select a set of tee markers to suit their ability. The copper tees, at 5,901 yards, are rated both for pro ladies and senior gentlemen. They also are ideal for higher handicappers. The jade tees, at 5,050 yards, are manageable by most ladies.

Despite its elegant, refined appearance, the Monument is a horned toad of a course from the tips (course rating 73.3, slope 147). From the back tees, at 7,028 yards, experts must weigh the relative advantages of distance and accuracy at every turn. Much like Pinehurst No. 2, there's something to unravel the better player (and comfort the novice) at each and every hole on the course.

One of the signatures of a Weiskopf-Morrish course is a driveable (by better players) par four. On the Monument, it's the sixth, called Gamble, which plays a scant 306 yards from the tips and is usually downwind. The path to the green is fraught with danger, however. There's not only a pair of bunkers in the center of the fairway 60 yards

Troon North Golf Course, Pinnacle Course, 18th hole

short of the green, there's a bunker directly in front of the green to snare less-than-perfect shots.

The par-four 10th was built to honor the ingenuity of Alister Mackenzie, the great Scottish designer. Once the drive is laid up short of a scalloped bunker and rock-strewn arroyo, the approach must carry uphill to a triple-tier green backdropped by boulders. The green has a false front, a ruse borrowed from Mackenzie's bag of tricks. Hit a high-flying shot with lots of backspin on the front of the green, and it will likely roll back off the putting surface to the mild perdition of a grassy swale. For drama, challenge, and beauty, this may be the finest two-shotter in Scottsdale.

Regardless of the tees you've chosen, have a gander from the rock-encased black markers at the 14th hole, a grand par five stretching to 604 yards that bends to the right and calls for three well-planned shots to reach the small, skewed green in regulation. Drink in the view from the elevated tee of endless desert and looming mountains before plotting your own path at the 14th: It is perhaps the best of the Monument's colossal par fives.

The par-four 18th, a sweeping right-to-left dogleg, is a modern classic. With deciduous trees in place of the mesquite and cacti, it could serve as the finishing hole at any of the finest clubs in the Northeast or Midwest. The Monument's 18th may appear benign, but the hole has plenty of length (444 yards from the black tees) and usually plays into a slight breeze. A pair of bunkers to the right directs traffic to the left, while the approach must find a large green flanked by a pair of shallow traps. These traps, which look as if the turf was peeled back to reveal a layer of sand, fit well the profile of the desert. By the way, the back right-hand portion of the 18th green vanishes behind a large rock outcropping and becomes the practice putting green. It's a unique finale to the finest daily-fee course in the desert.

Troon North's second venue, the **Pinnacle Course** (#30), is a solo design by Tom Weiskopf that debuted in 1996. Same cactus-and-rock landscape as the Monument, same 50-mile views of hulking buttes and serrated peaks, but the similarities end there. Occupying higher, more rugged terrain than the Monument, the Pinnacle is bolder and more beguiling than its predecessor, with bigger rocks and steeper drops in the routing. To a site brimming with raw natural ingredients, Weiskopf added double the number of bunkers as well as bigger greens than the original. The bunkers, many of them multifingered and quite deep, are strategic, directional—and very compelling. Weiskopf deploys bunkers the way a baker uses buttercream, to add flair and delight the eye.

But all is not as it seems. The bunker at the par-four first hole appears to be greenside, but is in fact 30 yards short of the putting surface. Surprise, surprise. With less visual certainty of what lies ahead (semiblind situations unnerve many players), the Pinnacle has a will-o'-the-wisp quality designed to capture a golfer's imagination. Also his loyalty, once he's played it often enough to reveal its quirks and hidden elements. The Monument Course is straightforward, the task clearly stated at every turn. On the Pinnacle, which plays three to four strokes harder from the back tees (7,044 yards) than the original, "the fairways look like Band-Aids," according to the pro shop staff.

Weiskopf, who resides in nearby Paradise Valley, allowed the site to dictate the flow of the course and the shape of the holes. A scant 120,000 cubic yards of dirt was moved to make way for the layout, a pittance by modern standards. "The Pinnacle is a remnant of an old-time golf course, with the tees and greens on hills and the fairways in valleys," Weiskopf explained.

Much like Pebble Beach, the Pinnacle opens gently before building momentum. The par-37 front nine, which climbs higher and has longer views than the back, is a birdie-bogey affair. There are opportunities to score as well as opportunities to crash and burn. The par-35 back nine, set lower in the valley, lacks the aesthetic charge of the front but is packed with one superlative golf hole after another. A round of golf on the Pinnacle is a giddy whirlwind of great scenery followed by major challenges.

Among the feature holes is the sixth, Canyon Pass, a driveable par four with a lolling tongue of a green tucked behind a hill. Overshoot the green, which tapers away from the fairway, and you're lost among the cattle skulls and old wagon wheels. Boot Hill North, it's called. There's a charming tribute hole, the short par-four ninth (named St. Andrews), its green rolled off in front to a venial Valley of Sin, but thereafter the holes get tough. Very tough. The 405-yard 10th, called Bobcat Hill for the family of lynx that regularly observed Weiskopf and his design team during construction, calls for a forced approach over a two-lane-wide arroyo to a pedestal green. The par-five 13th, Dos Caminos (Two Roads), offers a pair of routes (both promising) to the putting surface. The most memorable par three on either course at Troon North? The Pinnacle's spectacular 16th, which plays to a green laid into a hollow above a deep, menacing bunker. The view of the McDowell Mountains from the tee is commanding.

The best is saved for last. The par-four 18th, aimed directly at the topmost columns of Pinnacle Peak, rates as one of the most vivid finishing holes anywhere. The sight of scalloped, flash-faced bunkers banked along the right side of the fairway and nosing into the landing zone will delight classicists—if they can find the fairway. Even players who lay up short of trouble are faced with an approach shot to an elevated green (the smallest on the course) protected by a rock garden and two gaping pits of sand. Most players would rather sleep naked in the desert than be faced with the prospect of making par here to win a match.

On very few courses are the shot values a match for the aesthetics. The Pinnacle, like the Monument, is among the elite. Secure inexpensive lodgings, skip a few dinners if you must—the extravagant green fee charged to play either course is worth it.

A final note: Caddies are available upon request at Troon North. The Monument is a pleasure to walk. The Pinnacle is more of a hike, especially on the front nine, which climbs more than 300 feet in the first six holes.

Mindful that first impressions count, the literature disseminated to the media by **Grayhawk Golf Club** prior to the facility's debut in 1994 was eye-catching to the point of immodesty. Its first layout, the **Talon Course** (#47), was specifically designed, according to the club's scribes, "to grip the imagination of its players and tear them from the realm of an ordinary golf experience." A tall order by anyone's measurement. But the Talon

Grayhawk Golf Club, Scottsdale, Arizona, Talon Course, 11th hole

made an immediate impact in the Valley of the Sun, presenting a sharp-edged layout that looks like a fantasy golf calendar airbrushed with outlandish holes.

Routed by David Graham and Gary Panks in the raw desert north of Scottsdale, this unusual target-style links winds around box canyons, drainage canals, and sandy arroyos. Given free rein by Grayhawk's developers, the design team set about creating a silk purse from a sow's ear. More than 40,000 native plants and trees were used to landscape the 6,973-yard, par-72 course. A massive manufactured drainage channel (up to 70 yards wide and 10 feet deep) comes into play at five holes, while tall,

steep ridges were built to encase several holes on the front nine to mitigate the visual impact of a group of pylons that cross the course.

With only 73 acres of irrigated turf, the Talon presents players with some of the slimmest fairways in Scottsdale. Many of the traps are nasty "bogles" (deep, penal pot bunkers), while several of the greens are so severely contoured that they look as if they were overcooked in the desert's own microwave.

The Talon's signature holes are not without gimmicks. At the par-three 11th, a swinging bridge must be crossed to reach the back tee, which is perched on an island in the middle of a deep box canyon. Once the crossing is made, players must carry their tee shots to a green fronted by a massive eight-foot-deep, timber-lined sand bunker. At the short par-three 17th, called Devil's Drink, golfers play from a bulkheaded tee that juts into a lake to a bulkheaded island green. At the par-five 18th hole, a five-level waterfall behind the green provides the window dressing. The Talon has succeeded magnificently in the ultracompetitive Scottsdale market despite its apparent frivolities. How? Why?

First, the welcome. Few clubs, private or public, go to Grayhawk's lengths to make visitors feel like a million bucks. Each golfer is assigned a country club–style locker on arrival. The guest service staff at Grayhawk was the first in Scottsdale to wear radio-microphone headsets and treat each player as if he's about to embark on a special mission, something on the order of a space launch. There's a basket of fruit and bottles of chilled spring water on the first tee, a concept borrowed from the PGA Tour. The complimentary ball markers, divot tools, yardage books, and range balls are par for the course, but Grayhawk also presents players with a special-edition golf book at the completion of their rounds. The first year it was *Golf in the Kingdom*, Michael Murphy's mystical classic. Other titles have included *The Legend of Bagger Vance* and *Final Rounds*.

LODGING

Opening in Fall 1999, the *Four Seasons Resort Scottsdale*, located adjacent to Troon North, transforms the 36-hole complex into a bona fide golf resort. Designed to blend into the surrounding desert, the low-rise property has 181 rooms and suites arranged in one- and two-story casitas. Patio doors open to balconies or landscaped terraces that offer desert and mountain views. Suites include private plunge pools and outdoor showers. There also are a full-service spa, three restaurants, and a nine-hole practice putting course. Guests receive preferred tee times on both the Monument and Pinnacle courses as well as full guest privileges at the dazzling Troon North clubhouse, its floor-to-ceiling smoked-glass windows angled to the fairways of the Monument Course.

BURNED OUT?

If you're really toasted, there's only one way to go—down the river. Rent an inner tube at Salt River Recreation in Mesa, east of Phoenix, for a leisurely float down the Salt River. It's a great stress-reliever.

Hot-air ballooning is also very popular in the Valley. Rides are smooth and offer a slow-flying bird's perspective of the desert floor. Unicorn Balloon Company in Scottsdale has top-quality balloons and certified pilots.

Would-be cowboys should proceed directly to Rio Verde Ranch Riding Stable, which offers rides across the Verde River into Tonto National Forest.

Hiking? Squaw Peak Park is the most popular hiking spot in Phoenix. The relatively easy 1.2-mile route to the summit is worth the climb for the spectacular view below of the Valley of the Sun.

For years, Jeep tours have been a popular way to tour the desert. Now there's another way—in a Hummer, the all-terrain military vehicle with the wide wheel base. Desert Storm Hummer Tours operates a four-hour trip into the high Sonoran Desert near Four Peaks.

Lastly, gold panning expeditions turn up enough dust and nuggets to keep amateur prospectors enthused.

And then there's the club's personality cult. Del Cochran, the likable Captain of the Club, is a pied piper who early on signed Phil Mickelson and Howard Twitty as Grayhawk's PGA Tour representatives. He's also retained the services of Michael Pock, one the region's top superintendents, and brought in TV golf personality Gary McCord and respected instructor Peter Kostis to form the Kostis–McCord Learning Center. Grayhawk's biggest coup was landing the finals of the Andersen Consulting World Championship of Golf, an international match-play event that paid $1 million to the winner. The semifinals and finals were held on the Talon in 1995–96 before moving to the **Raptor Course** (#49) in 1997, the final year of the event. Raptor? Oh, yes. Cochran and company somehow enticed Tom Fazio to have a look at a second parcel of slightly more promising land adjacent to the Talon Course. Fazio has designed better courses on more interesting sites, but at Grayhawk he rendered a classic test on a merely average desert canvas.

"Good players, those who really understand the game, recognize its challenges and dangers right off the bat," Cochran explains. "There's a dozen ways to play nearly every hole, and it makes you think your way through the game."

Before ground was broken, Fazio said of the Raptor: "The course will have a strong visual impact but will be more playable than it looks. For instance, there will be virtually no hazards perpendicular to the tees, making for few, if any, forced carries. Landing areas will be generous. There will be an overall theme, but it will be very diverse. We want to keep players anticipating what's next."

What nature failed to provide, Fazio created to look as if the Creator himself had fashioned the rolling landforms. In tune with the 1990s emphasis on strategic designs, Fazio supplied extra-wide fairways, large-scale (but not penal) bunkering, and a wide array of green shapes and sizes. The layout doesn't impose strategy, but rather presents options for players to develop their own strategy.

There are many, many fine holes on the Raptor. Among the standouts is the par-three eighth, called Aces & Eights, which features a semihidden green as well as a stellar view of the McDowell Mountains. Like all great holes, a story goes with it. According to Western lore, Wild Bill Hickok was shot in the back during a poker game. Clutched in his fist, he held two pair—aces and eights. Ever since, this has been known as the Deadman's Hand. There isn't the same sense of foreboding here, though the bunkers in front can easily bury your chances of making par.

At the 390-yard 10th, a creek gurgles from left to right in front of the green and then flows along the right side of the fairway to a large lake near the tee. It is one of several strong par fours that give the back nine its teeth—or claws, depending on the tees chosen. Par, by the way, is 72 from the three sets of forward tees, 71 from the Raptor tees. The water-bound, downhill 18th, which plays as a short par five from the forward

Grayhawk Golf Club, Talon Course, 17ᵗʰ hole

markers, is a killer 494-yard par four from the tips. Called Big Sky, it serves up a fine view of the Phoenix skyline. And while the Raptor lacks the huge boulders and elevation changes found at Troon North, thousands of mature trees and cacti were preserved during construction, with additional desert shrubbery planted alongside the fairways. Finally, the Raptor's greens are replete with subtle breaks. Locals claim they're the hardest greens to read in the Valley.

"Lifestyle" takes over after the round. Grayhawk's two courses are served by a circular lodge-style clubhouse constructed from juniper wood and sandstone that was designed to blend into its desert surroundings. The pro shop, called the Grayhawk Golf Shop & Trading Company, is one of the nation's finest, offering many items not normally associated with a golf retail operation, including pocket knives and exotic watches.

For dining, the menu in the Quill Creek Café is best described as "upscale cowboy," while Phil's Grill (named for Mickelson) has glove-leather couches, a big-screen TV, and a working fireplace to warm players on cool days.

Quill Creek Café at the Grayhawk Golf Club

Near Stagecoach Pass Road, in the foothills of the Continental Mountains 30 miles northeast of Phoenix, is **Legend Trail Golf Club** (#88), northernmost of the region's top daily-fee courses.

This is a golf facility with an appropriate sense of place. There's a Conestoga wagon wheel out by the first tee, while painted horseshoes mark the tees (players can "saddle up" for the Long Trail, Legend Trail or Short Trail). The territorial-style clubhouse houses a fine collection of Southwestern art, much of it taken from Legend Trail founder Al Mengert's collection.

The golf course, surrounded by state land and the centerpiece of a 792-home community, was designed in 1995 by Rees Jones, the youngest son of Robert Trent Jones. Legend Trail is proof positive that the apple doesn't fall far from the tree. The layout, stretching to 6,820 yards, resembles nothing less than Jones the Elder's traditional, strategic designs from his fertile mid-1960s period. Jones pushed the limits of his turf-

Legend Trail Golf Club, Carefree, Arizona, 14th hole

grass allocation to create a parkland-style layout with broad, welcoming fairways, a far cry from the narrow landing pods found at most desert courses. The fairways, framed by rolling mounds, lead to subtle, low-profile greens. Close-cropped ramps preface many of them, inviting bump-and-run shots. There are a handful of forced carries to be played over dry washes, and bold players attempting to eagle the shorter par fives (none exceeds 535 yards) must produce heroic shots in order to succeed, but overall this gimmick-free layout was designed for a pleasurable outing. Water only comes into play at a single hole (the 490-yard par-five seventh), while the sizable greens are gently (not radically) sloped, with no hidden bunkers to trap the unwary. Take away the desert backdrop, and Legend Trail could easily pass for a temperate zone layout. You won't lose a dozen balls and shoot a million here, but neither will you blaze the Long Trail tees at 6,820 yards without a few adventures along the way.

This is especially true on Legend Trail's back nine, which plays two to three strokes harder than the front. Routed on hilly, rock-studded terrain that coyotes, javelinas, and bobcats call home, the back nine signals its intentions at holes 10, 11, and 13, each a sturdy par four that calls for a well-placed drive and an accurate approach. The 14th, called Navajo Tapestry, is a short, charming two-shotter with a sandy wash fronting a well-trapped green, while the back-to-back par fives, 16 and 17, call for sound shotmaking in return for par.

Like most of the newer high-end daily-fee facilities in the Valley of the Sun, Legend Trail, managed by the same folks who keep Troon North in fine fettle, is always in top condition. Want to improve your swing tech-

nique? The facility is home to the Jim McLean Golf Academy and its 2,300-square-foot "video superstation."

Legend Trail was developed by longtime Oakland Hills Director of Golf Al Mengert, who wanted a traditional (i.e., country club–style) operation where players could walk (tees and greens are close together), soak up the desert scenery, and relax afterward in a pleasant setting. The clubhouse is well worth exploring. The Anasazi-style petroglyphs on the fireplace chimney are particularly well rendered, while one of the more rustic tabletops in the grill room was formerly a Mexican jailhouse door. In late afternoon, when the shadows fall, the views from the clubhouse patio of Pinnacle

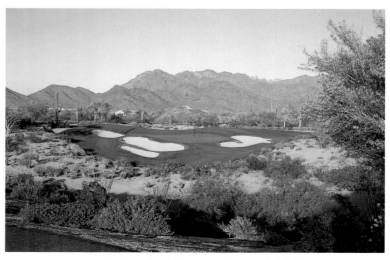

Grayhawk Golf Club, Raptor Course, eighth hole

Peak, Goldie's Butte, and the foothills of Tonto National Forest are the very stuff of the Wild West.

So world renowned is the resort experience at **The Boulders,** the desert hideaway in Carefree, 20 miles northeast of Phoenix, that its pair of well-groomed courses are sometimes overlooked. Ironically, The Boulders never set out to be recognized as a blue-chip golf resort. According to the resort's executives, golf was originally intended to be just another amenity for its pampered guests, another recreation option on a long list of creature comforts. All that changed when *GOLF Magazine* draped a Gold Medal around the neck of The Boulders in 1988 as one of the top golf resorts in the nation. Discriminating enthusiasts began arriving shortly after, and the rest, as they say in the cowboy saloons in nearby Cave Creek, is hist'ry.

The most distinctive course feature at The Boulders? Why, the giant tawny granite boulders spewed from a crack in the earth 12 million years ago.

Into this stark environment entered Jay Morrish, who was beginning to venture out on his own in the mid-1980s after working as the lead designer for Jack Nicklaus on several key projects. Here was the place to craft golf holes that would bring players face-to-face with the high Sonoran Desert, holes that would seem every bit as much at home in the desert as the adobe casitas that mimic the shape and color of the boulders.

Don't be deceived, as many have been, by the scorecard yardage at The Boulders. The par-72 **South Course** (#53) is only 6,589 yards from the blue tees, but its slope (140) and course rating (72.0) tell the story. With the desert flanking both sides of every hole, slicers and hookers will spend quite a bit of time reloading here. Accuracy, not distance, is everything at The Boulders. Indeed, the canny strategist can bankroll the wayward boomer every day of the week here. Drive with the club you hit straightest—or take your chances attempting a recovery among the centipedes and sidewinders.

The first four holes, routed through a rock-strewn desertscape at the north end of the property, are among Morrish's new conceptions. (Golf at The Boulders has evolved in stages. Morrish completely revamped a preexisting 18-hole course in 1984. He added a third nine in 1986, returning to

build a final nine in 1991, giving the resort 36 holes of textbook desert golf.)

The South's par-four first hole is visually arresting. Stretching to 421 yards from the tips, the elevated tee points directly to Chimney Rock and Black Mountain in the distance. The fairway, guarded on both sides by deep washes, tumbles downhill and eventually leads to a rocky arroyo that holds water. Beyond it is a well-bunkered green backdropped by a six-story-high wall of granite. What an opener!

The stretch of holes five through eight on the South, a holdover from Morrish's original Boulders nine, is truly memorable. The fifth, a short par five measuring a scant 529 yards from the tips, presents players with an interesting array of options. The drive can be played as a lay-up short of a dry creek bed that cuts diagonally across the fairway. Unless, of course, you can carry your tee shot more than 230 yards on a straight line to a sliver of fairway nestled between the creek bed and the desert up the left side. This route, fraught with danger, nevertheless cuts the distance of the hole by 50 or 60 yards and puts the green in range for a long, accurate second shot—and a putt for eagle. The prudent play, after the lay-up, is a long iron or fairway wood followed by a wedge or nine-iron to an undulating green staked out by bunkers and backdropped by a mammoth jumble of sorrel-colored rocks. The green, like many others on the course, is interwoven with subtle undulations. The pro shop staff will advise first-timers that all putts break toward Phoenix, which is generally true—except when it isn't.

Regardless of handicap, hike up to the back tee at the sixth, a short par four that bends to the right around the resort's main lodge. The tiny sky-box tee is perched atop a pile of rocks 40 feet above the fairway, and players must produce a high-flying tee shot that carries the resort's entrance road to find the fairway. It's fun. The setting of the par-three seventh, its rear tee set atop a 30-foot-high platform shadowed by a huge balancing rock, is truly inspired. The target is a green embraced by sand, with a giant multiarmed saguaro sprouting from the front right bunker. This cactus has taken its share of hits over the years. At the eighth, a lengthy par four rated the toughest hole on the course, a spiral staircase leads round the side of a tall boulder to a tee that fits the rock as snugly as a flat-top crewcut. The hole itself calls for a long, straight drive followed by an unerring approach that must carry a dry wash that snakes in front of the perched green.

The seamless back nine, which presents one exquisite challenge after another, with each hole set apart from the other, features a pair of enticing back-to-back par threes (15 and 16) and concludes with a short, dangerous par five, its greenside pond reshaped in 1993 to create a more dramatic (and potentially watery) finish.

While it lacks the aesthetic charge delivered by the South, the par-71 **North Course** (#91) at The Boulders is a solid test in its own right. Fashioned from the original Saguaro and Lakes nines, the North, laid through dry washes and virgin desert, has slightly wider fairways and somewhat less development along its corridors than the South. Well balanced, with a good variety of holes, it is the preferred venue of local members.

Stretching to 6,739 yards from the tips, the North wastes no time in getting down to business. The first hole, a short par five measuring well

NIGHTLIFE

Toolie's Country Saloon and Dance Hall, modeled after an 1890s saloon and annually voted the nation's best country-and-western nightclub, is a must if you travel with cowboy boots. The revitalized *Arizona Center* in downtown Phoenix has a number of fascinating bars and nightclubs, with everything from dueling piano players who duke it out at baby grands to a sports bar with five big screens and 53 TVs. *Jackson Street Grill* stages live music on weekends in a restored 1908 brick warehouse behind America West Arena, home of the NBA's Phoenix Suns.

SIDETRIPS

The $47-million *Arizona Science Center*, opened in 1997, showcases Arizona talent and achievements in science through 350 hands-on exhibits, activities, and presentations. In downtown Phoenix, the *Heard Museum* maintains one of the nation's foremost collections of traditional and contemporary Native American arts and artifacts. The 420-piece kachina doll collection is exceptional, as are the Hohokam, Zuni, Hopi, and Navajo weavings. *Taliesin West*, Frank Lloyd Wright's studio and school in Scottsdale, is a complex of low-lying stone buildings that reflect Wright's concept of "organic" architecture. This National Historic Landmark is a must for architecture buffs.

Didn't see enough cactus during your round? Take a walking tour of the *Desert Botanical Garden* in Scottsdale. Founded in 1937, the 13-acre complex in Papago Park displays more than half of the world's cactus species (over 1,000 varieties) and is the ultimate showcase of plant life from the planet's arid regions.

Want to take a journey back in time? *Montezuma Castle*, a 90-minute drive north from Phoenix, is a well-preserved remnant of a vanished people. This spectacular five-story Indian dwelling, built more than six centuries ago in the alcove of a towering limestone cliff, provides a detailed look at the area's early human occupation.

Farther up the road is Sedona, its Wild West landscape the backdrop for more than 80 movies. Surrounded by towering cliffs at the foot of Oak Creek Canyon, Sedona's red-rock buttes and bottle-green pines reach to a perpetually deep blue sky. The village of Tlaquepaque has fine art galleries and eclectic shops that sell Indian crafts.

Castle Rock, Sedona, Arizona

WOMEN TO THE FORE

The fairer sex has everything to look forward to at *The Boulders*, which launched its "Women to the Fore" program in 1996 to help women learn the game and to ease the intimidation new-comers often feel on the golf course. The program ensures all women golfers—novice and experienced alike—equal access to tee times, plenty of personalized attention, and a pro shop stocked with appealing golf apparel. The resort is also sensitive to the specific needs of women executives who want to use golf (as men have for years) as a business networking tool.

At The Boulders, "Women to the Fore" works like this: When a reservationist determines that a novice woman golfer has booked a reservation, a letter of welcome is sent that includes tips on what she needs to know or to bring for golf at the resort. Upon arrival, women are provided with high-quality rental equipment as well as lessons (there are two lady teaching pros on staff whose sole mission is to demystify the game and ingrain the fundamentals). Women are also given the option to play short course loops (four holes) and take 30-minute "refresher" courses at no charge twice a week. In addition to playing lessons and unlimited use of the practice facilities, the program includes a 50-minute spa treatment.

under 500 yards from the blue tees, can pop your bubble before you've drawn your first breath. For normal players, the drive must be laid up short of an arroyo, while the approach shot must be hit with dartboard accuracy to a narrow plateau, with the payoff shot played to a pulpit green defended by three deep bunkers. Only precise, well-planned shots are rewarded here.

The toughest hole on the course, and arguably the toughest hole at The Boulders, is the third, a boomerang-shaped par five stretching to 548 yards. After flying the desert directly in front of the tee, a blind second shot must be played uphill to a fairway that bottlenecks as it climbs to a creek that crosses in front of the sloping green. Par here is to be treasured.

With its added length, the North's back nine favors the big hitter but penalizes players who go for broke and fail. Without giant boulders and tall saguaros to frame them, the holes on the incoming nine are perhaps less stirring than the others, though they do not lack for challenge. The 10th, for example, is a long, uphill par four with a phalanx of grass bunkers defending the green; the 11th is another long par four, this one requiring an accurate tee shot to the right side of a boulder that protrudes from the middle of the fairway; and the 13th, a daunting two-shotter, calls for a second shot over a wide, scrub-filled barranca. There's a brief respite at the par-three 14th, where a timber-lined pond must be carried from all tees (including the ladies tee at 80 yards) to reach the large, welcoming green. It's one of the prettiest par threes in the Phoenix area.

The Boulders, Carefree, Arizona, North Course, 18th hole

The Boulders, South Course, first hole

SUMMER SIZZLERS

Room rates and green fees throughout greater Phoenix tend to be high from November through April, but you get what you pay for when you're chasing the sun in peak season. Hotels and courses alike slash prices in summer, when the mercury routinely soars to 100 degrees or more. If you want to play the finest collection of desert courses on earth at a fraction of the peak season price, book a package from mid-May through mid-September; stick to layouts at the northern end of the valley, where elevations are higher and the temperatures a little cooler; play as early or as late in the day as possible; drink lots of water; and be sure to wear a wide-brimmed hat and use double-digit sun block.

The North and South courses at The Boulders are rotated daily between members and resort guests. Outside tee times are very limited in high season. As for conditioning, firm, slick greens and fast-running fairways are the order of the day. One final perk: Daytime temperatures at The Boulders are generally 10 degrees cooler than in Phoenix.

There are fine touches on both courses. For example, sandy areas around the tee boxes are raked daily. Also, the color of the cart paths was designed to blend into the desert. What was left out at The Boulders (showy annuals) and what was discreetly put in (desert species from other arid parts of the world) shines through.

After the round, players can cool off at the Boulders Club restaurant, its shaded terrace affording views of the Sonoran foothills and the golf course. Served here are grilled Southwestern entrées—and the best club sandwich in America.

The Boulders, South Course, seventh hole

The Boulders, South Course, fifth hole

The accommodations and amenities at *The Boulders* are more than a match for its superb courses. From the outside, the resort's 160 casitas mimic the shapes and colors of the site's massive granite boulders. Inside, guest rooms are accented by hand-hewn, wood-beamed ceilings (with fans), wood-burning fireplaces, large dressing and bathroom areas, Indian artifacts, earth-tone furnishings, and private deck or patio. (Two- and three-bedroom houses are also available.)

Since becoming a member of Grand Bay Hotels and Resorts in 1998, The Boulders has announced plans to build a state-of-the-art Golden Door Spa, which will open in 2000.

The Boulders offers five distinctly different restaurants, ranging from the casual Palo Verde, which serves delectable Southwestern cuisine, to the formal Latilla, from whose hand-sculpted booths there are views of softly lit boulders creased by a waterfall that draw the desert night indoors.

The list of off-campus activities readily arranged by the resort's concierge—llama treks, hot-air ballooning, biplane flights, desert jeep tours—is the stuff of memorable vacations.

Casita interior at The Boulders

Main Lodge at The Boulders

The Valley of the Sun is home to many of the nation's finest resorts, though golfers seeking less expensive lodgings also have some options. The best deals are offered by smaller, all-suite properties that include area courses in their golf programs.

Resort Suites of Scottsdale, specifically designed to cater to visiting golfers, was updated in 1998. The condo hotel, which books more than 40,000 rounds on area courses per year (including many of the "Top 100" layouts), offers large rooms with full kitchens priced about the same as a standard hotel room.

More Golf/Valley of the Sun

Traveling golfers love to play TV tournament courses. One of the few capable of challenging the pros without overwhelming the duffer is the *TPC of Scottsdale (Stadium Course)*, an agreeable Tom Weiskopf–Jay Morrish layout built to host the Phoenix Open, a PGA Tour event. Players will encounter two "driveable" par fours and good risk-reward par fives on the well-conditioned course, which is located beside the Scottsdale Princess.

Tired of steering the ball around the desert's narrow, target-style courses? *The Wigwam* in Litchfield Park, 20 miles west of Phoenix, has three traditional layouts in a parklike setting. The top track is the *Gold Course*, a vintage Robert Trent Jones design from his fertile mid-1960s period. This 7,021-yard layout is marked by date palms, eight ponds, long runway-style tees, and nearly 100 bunkers. The Wigwam's *Blue Course*, a Trent Jones redesign of a 1930 layout, is a near-perfect 6,130-yard resort spread with superb greens. The roomy *Red Course*, formerly the West Course, is built around five lakes. Caddies are available on all three courses.

Want to tee it up with the locals? *Papago Municipal Golf Course*, former site of the U.S. Public Links Championship, is a gently rolling, tree-lined muni with an excellent variety of holes. At press time, the high-season green fee at this popular facility topped out at $28.

A traditional Midwestern-style layout in south Phoenix? *The Raven at South Mountain* is that and more. Designers David Graham and Gary Panks moved 800,000 cubic yards of dirt and planted nearly 7,000 mature pines to create rolling, tree-lined fairways, with nearly 50,000 bales of Georgia pine needles distributed in nonturf areas to lend a down-home look. It is possible to duff every single tee shot and not lose a ball here, although accomplished players will have all they can handle from the tournament tees at 7,078 yards. Convenient to the airport, the Raven is a good choice for those who wish to squeeze in one more round before flying home.

In Fountain Hills, east of Scottsdale, are two noteworthy venues. *Sun-Ridge Canyon*, nestled within a steep-walled canyon that plummets 300 feet from start to finish, is an entertaining test with several ego-building downhill holes on the outward nine—but an equal number of ego-deflating uphill holes on the incoming nine. Across the street from SunRidge Canyon, but in a wholly different setting, is *Eagle Mountain*. Laid out by Scott Miller, creator of *Coeur d' Alene* in Idaho, this 6,755-yard, par-71 course sports wall-to-wall turfgrass and features expansive 50-mile views of distant peaks.

Farther afield in Mesa, 40 minutes east of Phoenix, is *Las Sendas*, a notorious gunslinger routed by Robert Trent Jones, Jr., through mountain foothills dotted with rock formations. Fairways serve up fantastic views of the Phoenix skyline, Papago Buttes, and tall saguaros. The subtly sloped bentgrass greens are extremely well defended. Bring your straight ball and a six-shooter to get to them.

DINING

At the high end, *Marquesa* at the Scottsdale Princess serves traditional Catalan and Basque dishes (tapas, paella) in gorgeous soft-hued rooms hung with portraits of Spanish nobility. *RoxSand* features transcontinental "fusion" cuisine, with a seemingly disparate variety of influences (the house specialty is air-dried duck with buckwheat crepes, pistachio-onion marmalade, and three sauces). *Christopher's and The Bistro* are sister restaurants with two distinct choices: There's fine French dining with service and setting to match in the namesake; less expensive but equally wonderful fare in The Bistro. At The Phoenician, the region's most opulent resort, *Windows on the Green* offers definitive (and creative) Southwestern cuisine in a beautiful ground-floor setting. The tortilla soup is terrific. Beef lovers flock to *Ruth's Chris Steak House* (two locations). *Avanti* (two locations) offers reliable Italian cuisine (homemade pastas, definitive saltimbocca), while *Sam's Café* serves distinctive Southwestern cuisine at its Arizona Center and Biltmore Fashion Park locations.

One of the more eclectic Mexican restaurants in town is *Such Is Life*, which features dishes from various regions of Mexico. The chicken mole and adobo pork dishes here are authentic, as are the margaritas. If you can stand the heat of lip-searing salsas, *Los Dos Molinos*, occupying the former garage of Hollywood cowboy Tom Mix, is a popular cantina specializing in New Mexico–style cooking. The ribs and chimichangas are exceptional, the green chili enchiladas incendiary. Dinner for two with beer (which you'll need to put out the fire) runs about $35 for two.

El Pedregal Festival Marketplace

Scottsdale, as every golf widow knows, is famous for its fine and varied shopping. For Native American jewelry and crafts, downtown Scottsdale's *5th Avenue* is the place to go. More centralized shopping? Here's a sampling of the area's top plazas, malls, and outlet centers.

Soaring towers, cobblestone walkways, and bubbling fountains inspired by a medieval Italian village mark *Borgata of Scottsdale*, a ritzy outpost of more than 50 high-fashion boutiques that carry everything from Italian leather goods to French lingerie. Curvilinear walls of sand-colored stucco, irregular shapes, and mud-form parapets mark the three-story edifice at *El Pedregal Festival Marketplace* adjacent to The Boulders in Carefree. The complex offers dining and entertainment as well as shopping in fine-art galleries and boutiques. *Biltmore Fashion Park*, located in Phoenix near the Arizona Biltmore, is a nicely landscaped complex with several fine stores, including Saks Fifth Avenue and Macy's. *Scottsdale Fashion Square* houses over 155 retailers, from Abercrombie & Fitch to Yippie-ei-O!

The ultimate golf shop can also be found in Phoenix. Diehard players for whom golf is an all-consuming passion (as well as sympathetic golf widows who don't mind fueling the fire) should pay a visit to *In Celebration of Golf*, a 12,000-square-foot "retail experience" opened in 1995 by former Marriott Golf executive Roger Maxwell. "What I am doing is trying to bring together all of the allure of the game, all of the romance, into one comprehensive retail environment which celebrates those special qualities," Maxwell said. The shop, which has more high-priced golf-themed merchandise under its roof than any other establishment in the nation, is organized into several areas, including The Antiquities of the Game (golf-related antiques, rare books); The Art of the Game (a gallery devoted exclusively to golf art); The Bag Room (customized golf bags); Ye Old Golf Shoppe (golf-themed furnishings, decorative items, gifts); The Clubmaker's Workbench (club repair service); and beautifully designed "celebrations" featuring top-of-the-line clubs, shoes, and apparel. Parked by the front door of this dream golf shop, where visitors are greeted by "caddies" outfitted in white coveralls near The First Tee (a reception area with benches, ball washers, and a "scorecard" with a layout of the store), is the golf cart used by President Dwight D. Eisenhower. Maxwell's goal—"To make every one of our customers feel as though they are members of a very exclusive private club by catering to their every need"—is achieved at this one-of-a-kind store. Note: *Ollie the Trolley*, the only motorized trolley transportation in the greater Phoenix area, services 23 resorts and 12 shopping areas on its Scottsdale-area route.

New & Noteworthy / Valley of the Sun

At the Salt River Pima–Maricopa Indian Community, west of Scottsdale, the design team of Bill Coore and Ben Crenshaw crafted the 36-hole *Talking Stick Golf Club*. (The name "Talking Stick" is derived from the Pima calendar stick used by the tribe to mark significant historic events.) The 7,133-yard *North Course*, opened in late 1997, is a low-profile test with broad fairways, no rough, and jagged, irregularly shaped bunkers. The slightly crowned greens, with their close-cropped approaches, welcome run-up shots. The North is a desert grasslands version of a Scottish links.

The 6,833-yard *South Course*, which opened in January 1998, is a stylistic contrast to the North. Crenshaw and Coore used classic American courses built in the 1920s and 1930s as their model, deploying ponds, streams, and lacy-edged bunkers to define the holes on this parkland-style layout.

Walking is permitted on both courses. Neither venue has (or will have) any homes around it. At press time, the peak-season green fee at Talking Stick was under $100.

Tucson

The physical attributes of this Old West/New Southwest destination are compelling: Majestic 9,000-foot peaks in five mountain ranges ring the "Old Pueblo" and glow reddish-orange at sunset; saguaros up to 50 feet high dominate the desert; and rare is the day that isn't sunny. Also, Tucson's selection of Mexican restaurants is so good, Mexicans themselves come here to eat. As for the golf, it's good and getting better. The two "Top 100" courses in Tucson are backed by an excellent supporting cast, with promising newcomers cropping up on the outskirts of town.

Chiseled into the foothills of the towering Santa Catalina Mountains on the northeast side of Tucson, **The Raven Golf Club at Sabino Springs** (#76) occupies one of the most stunning sites ever made available for a desert course. In addition to sharp inclines and dizzying drops, the site's concentration of saguaros is as dense as at Coronado National Forest, its neighbor. Off the fairway, you cannot hold your hands out to either side without being pricked.

Before ground was broken, the 410-acre property was surveyed in detail to produce an extensive desert preservation plan. Acting as good stewards of the land, the developers hired a biologist to walk in front of the bulldozer during construction to rescue (or shoo away) desert critters. Horticulturists, meanwhile, salvaged thousands of mighty saguaros and lesser cacti that were later transplanted. Nine natural springs and their riparian habitats were fenced off for protection during course construction. Considered one of the largest and most successful environmental preservation programs ever undertaken, the Raven stands as a prototype for future desert golf course projects.

According to designer Robert Trent Jones, Jr., the untamed site's steep hills, mesquite-lined arroyos, and craggy rock outcrops provided the basis for "a real dramatic test of golf that's a joy to play no matter what your handicap is." Better lower than higher, however: Strenuous uphill holes, forced carries over no-man's-land, and sloping, well-bunkered greens demand a full repertoire of shotmaking skills. Home course of the University of Arizona's men's and women's golf teams, the Raven also calls for an advanced degree in course management. Yes, playability is greatly enhanced from the forward markers at 6,440, 5,851, and 4,752 yards, though no advantage is too great at the 11th, an epic journey of 625 yards from the tips that calls for a pair of forced carries over thorny swaths of raw desert. It's the best par six in Tucson. The par-three 12th features *nine* tee pods, six of which bring into play a spring-fed pond built by the Hohokam Indians over 1,000 years ago. The pond nourishes an old mesquite tree with balls of mistletoe hung like Christmas decorations in its bare branches. The 18th tee, perched 200 feet above a fairway indented by a lake and flanked by bunkers, is a grand finale with 100-mile views looking south into Mexico. Like the course itself, the Raven's clubhouse, patterned after a Spanish Colonial–style hacienda, was built to harmonize with the desert environment.

"We spent a lot of effort making sure this golf course would be fun for average players," Jones explained. "We made the landing areas generous, and we made sure that the carries over desert areas are reasonable from the forward tees." From the Raven tees at 6,916 yards (144 slope, 73.2 course rating), this brawny par-71 layout is, according to longtime University of Arizona golf coach Rick LaRose, "a terrific recruiting tool." Few prospective team members seeking the fullest education imaginable can resist it.

The Raven Golf Club at Sabino Springs, Tucson, Arizona, third hole

The Raven Golf Club at Sabino Springs, 12th hole

Most first-time players on the **Mountain Course** (#44) at **The Lodge at Ventana Canyon** get so distracted by the sight of a foraging javelina or the play of light on the mountains that they lose their concentration and post some big numbers. Yet rare is the golfer who enters the boutique-style golf shop afterward to register a complaint. Most first-timers sense immediately that the Mountain's E.Q. (Excitement Quotient), based on the number of tantalizing shots to be played, far exceeds the norm.

Opened in 1984, the Mountain Course was one of the first eco-sensitive layouts etched into Tucson's high Sonoran Desert. Tom Fazio, a traditionalist who at the time rarely worked west of the Mississippi, made good on the developer's mandate to build a course that blends in with the landscape. His creation is an artistic feat, an environmental triumph, and a civil engineering project rolled into one. There is room enough to play the game, but several of the Mountain's holes are seminal examples of the target-style, be-straight-or-be-gone school of design. Certainly, no wildlife corridors were sacrificed to give golfers more elbow room—Ventana Canyon is a certified member of the Audubon Cooperative Sanctuary program.

A remarkably well-balanced design, with a different look at every hole and great variations in the length of the par threes and fives, the Mountain is routed over and around canyons and dry washes in the Santa Catalina foothills at 3,100 feet above sea level. After a pair of par fours designed to get players off to a reasonable start, Fazio lifts the curtain on a one-shotter that can take its place alongside the eighth at Royal Troon (the "Postage Stamp") and the tiny downhill seventh at Pebble Beach as one of the finest (and most treacherous) short par threes in the game. The task on the Mountain's infamous third is clearly stated: From the back tee, a pitch of little more than 100 yards must be played over a deep ravine to a green wedged into the rock. The backdrop is a pleated blanket of soaring mountain flanks dotted with saguaros. The shot is strictly a hit-or-miss affair—no recovery is possible at the "Hole in the Wall," as it's called, if a shot comes up short or is yanked to the left.

Because the third green is the last on the course to lose its frost on cool mornings, and usually the hottest at midday owing to heat radiation from surrounding rock faces, it consistently failed to nurture a healthy

The Lodge at Ventana Canyon, Tucson, Arizona, Mountain Course, third hole

For golfers, Tucson's top digs are found at *The Lodge at Ventana Canyon*, an intimate 49-suite retreat located a stone's throw from the first tee of the Mountain Course. Treated to a $5-million makeover in 1996, when distressed pine, fieldstone, and slate were used to enrich the formerly drab interior, the Lodge, taken over by Grand Bay Hotels & Resorts in 1998, is in line for another facelift, with a Golden Door spa scheduled to open in 2000. Suites are spacious and comfortable, with full kitchens, sizable living areas, and private balcony or patio. Lodge guests receive preferred tee times and discounted green fees at both the Mountain and Canyon courses.

For a full-service resort experience, there's *Loews Ventana Canyon Resort*, which updated its 398 rooms in 1998 and which enables guests to play the Mountain and Canyon courses on alternate days.

The Lodge at Ventana Canyon

The Write-In

It was bound to happen. A worthy contender for "Top 100" honors was inadvertently left off the roster of venues sent to raters. Panelists were encouraged to write in a course we did not include and assign it a grade if they felt it belonged among the elite. The top write-in was *The Golf Club at Vistoso*, a superlative test of golf located in the Oro Valley on the northwest side of Tucson. Routed by Tom Weiskopf on gently rolling terrain backdropped by stony peaks in the Tortalitas and Santa Catalinas, this expansive 6,905-yard course, opened in 1995, has generous landing areas crisscrossed by dry washes, with tall saguaros like exclamation points in the center of several fairways. The par-three third, called Tillinghast, is Winged Foot with cactus: An undulating saucer of a green is undercut by deep bunkers. The 14th is a driveable par four called Risky (for good reason), while the par fives, where shots must be leapfrogged from one landing area to the next to avoid the arroyos, call for careful planning in return for par. With greens and tees placed close together, Vistoso is a walker's delight.

stand of grass. In 1996, a sophisticated heating and cooling system was installed beneath the surface of the green to keep the temperature constant. Even under perfect conditions, however, birdies are rare at what may be, yard for yard, the most expensive hole ever built in America. The estimated cost to build a stage set for the scariest wedge shot you'll ever hit? Well over half a million dollars.

The par-five fourth tee, its elevated tee every bit as scenic as the third, parallels the ridge line of the Santa Catalinas. It clearly indicates that accuracy off the tee is essential to survive (much less score) the Mountain. Both sides of the fairway are bunkered, with a long, skinny trap on the left offset by a row of church pews up the right. These bunkers eventually give way to a lake that runs all the way to the green. Holes like the fourth (not to mention the brutal sixth, a 249-yard par three) earn the Mountain, at 6,926 yards from the black tees, its 146 slope and 74.2 course rating (par is 72). Staggered sets of forward tees shorten the forced carries and improve the angles for higher handicappers, but the Mountain yields little to indifferent play. This is a player's course, not a frolicsome resort course.

As proof, the back nine of the Mountain unleashes one stirring hole after another. Among the stronger par fours is the 15th, which proceeds uphill to an elevated, undulating green guarded by a formidable mound to the left. The backdrop is a large basaltic mound, studded with boulders, that resembles a breaching whale. The 17th, an uphill 403-yard par four with a split fairway, offers players a choice of routes to the slick, two-tiered green. Neither of them is easy, though the left side provides a slightly shorter approach. A tee shot that flies dead straight will bury into the ridge.

Like all great finishing holes, the Mountain's par-five 18th is a summation of all that has gone before. From the black tees at 589 yards, players

DINING

For fine dining, Tucson's top choices include the *Ventana Room* at Loews Ventana Canyon Resort, an elegant, softly lit room with fine views of the twinkling Tucson skyline. Mesquite-grilled game (notably buffalo tenderloin) is a house speciality. A chef's tasting menu paired with wines is available. One of Tucson's most cherished restaurants is *Janos,* now located in the Westin La Paloma, which specializes in cutting-edge Southwestern cuisine with a French twist.

Pizzas cooked in a wood-burning oven and eclectic Southwestern dishes are the top choices at *Café Terra Cotta,* which offers a good selection of California wines as well as gourmet takeout. *Bocatta* is a trendy bistro specializing in northern Italian cuisine. Its branch, *Pronto,* serves quick, moderately priced dishes.

Some of the best Mexican food in the nation is served in the family-owned restaurants of South Tucson. They include: *El Dorado Bar & Restaurant, Mi Nidito, Micha's,* and *Xochimilco.* As a Tucson rule of thumb, Mexican food gets blander and more expensive the farther north one goes. (*El Charro,* the oldest Mexican restaurant in America continuously operated by the same family, is an exception.)

Hearthstone dining room, The Lodge at Ventana Canyon

Also recommended is *Li'l Abner's Steakhouse,* its mesquite-grilled steaks, ribs, and chicken served indoors and out. Western bands entertain on weekends. *El Corral* serves a world-class prime rib in a territorial ranch house marked by wood-beam ceilings, flagstone floors, and fireplaces.

Gentle Ben's Brewing Company, a microbrewery located near the University of Arizona campus, is a favorite bar-and-patio watering hole of city residents. *Club Congress,* at the Hotel Congress, heats up on weekends. Tucson's top country-and-western nightclubs include *Maverick, Stampede,* and *Cactus Moon.*

The best 19th hole in Tucson? It's the *Flying V Bar & Grill* down the road from Loews Ventana Canyon Resort, its expanded outdoor seating area cantilevered over a lake opposite the waterfall-backed 18th hole of the Canyon Course. In addition to a specialty drink menu that includes 28 tequilas and 12 draft beers, the restaurant features an all-day tapas menu as well as dishes with genuine Southwestern/Latin American flair. Grilled and chilled shrimp with jicama and avocado is a local favorite.

are perched in the sky high above the fairway, with a spectacular view of the golf course, the resort community, and the Tucson skyline. The hole is a counterpuncher, with strategically placed traps, tall saguaros, and dense vegetation lining both sides of the fairway. The bunkers in particular are clearly intended to foil those who try to overpower the hole. Three accurate, well-planned shots will find a deep green interlaced with subtle rolls. Appearances to the contrary, the putts here and on every other green on the course break away from the mountains and toward Tucson. The Mountain's greens, resurfaced in heat-tolerant bentgrass in 1997, are superb. The only strike against? Ambitious real estate development at Ventana Canyon has hemmed in a few holes with housing.

SHOPPING

Fourth Avenue Merchants Association is a historic shopping district with dozens of specialty stores. *Old Town Artisans* in El Presidio Historic District, *Bahti Indian Arts* in St. Philip's Plaza, and *Kaibab Shops* on North Campbell Avenue all specialize in handcrafted Southwestern artifacts. *B & B Cactus Farm* carries hundreds of Tucson-grown cactus varieties, from miniature to specimen. Shipping is available. Got kids? *Mrs. Tiggy-Winkle's* is the most eclectic toy store in town. Farther afield is *Nogales,* a colorful Mexican city 65 miles south of Tucson. Haggling is suggested to obtain the best price.

More Golf/Tucson

The *Canyon Course*, Tom Fazio's second layout at *Ventana Canyon*, is nearly the equal of the Mountain Course. The front nine is set into Esperero Canyon, while the stronger back nine has great views of the Santa Catalinas. The Canyon's short par-five 18th, guarded by water, is a gambler's delight.

La Paloma Country Club, an extremely testing and visually striking 27-hole spread built by Jack Nicklaus in the mid-1980s to satisfy his own lofty standards of "challenging" play, has half the grass and twice the trouble of a normal course, with numerous forced carries over dry washes and tall saguaros required. Some of the sharper edges around the greens of the

SIDETRIPS

West of Tucson, the *Arizona–Sonora Desert Museum* is a nature center, zoo, museum, and botanical garden with 200 species of live desert dwellers, many of them contained in naturalistic open-air habitats. The walk-in hummingbird exhibit is extraspecial, as are the cageless enclosures for the desert cats. Not far from the museum is *Old Tucson Studios*, where more than 200 Western movies have been filmed since the 1930s, and where staged gunfights can be viewed near old stage sets from TV shows like *High Chaparral*.

Elsewhere, *Mission San Xavier del Bac*, founded by Jesuits in 1692, is one of the nation's finest examples of Spanish mission architecture. Aviators tend to gravitate to the *Pima Air & Space Museum*, which houses more than 180 vintage aircraft. The *Center for Creative Photography* is a world-class museum with photos by Ansel Adams, Edward Weston, Walker Evans, and others. Another must-see is the *DeGrazia Gallery in the Sun*, known for an eclectic collection of Southwestern art displayed in a group of low-slung adobe houses.

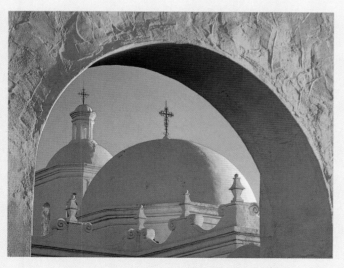

Mission San Xavier del Bac, Tucson, Arizona

LODGING

In addition to Loews Ventana Canyon Resort, Tucson's top full-service getaway is the *Westin La Paloma*, its Mission Revival–style guest buildings painted a shade of dusty rose that glows at sunset. In addition to the only swim-up bar in town, the Westin boasts the longest resort water slide in the state.

Tucson is sprinkled with mid-priced and budget accommodations. The *Doubletree Hotel* is conveniently located across the street from Randolph Park. The *Windmill Inn* at St. Philip's Plaza, near to resort courses on the north side of town, has well-priced suites that can accommodate four adults. Like bed-and-breakfasts? Try *Mariposa Inn*, a 1933 mud adobe home, where the room rate includes a gourmet breakfast.

Budget-priced accommodations can be found at the landmark *Hotel Congress*, an Art Deco hotel built in 1919 and located in the city's downtown arts district.

Canyon, Ridge, and Hill nines were softened in the mid-1990s to enhance playability, but La Paloma remains the toughest track in town from the tips.

Starr Pass, one of the region's more established daily-fee courses, is a fine target-style layout chiseled by Bob Cupp into the cactus-studded desert west of town. This former site of a PGA Tour event is very penal to offline shots. Not appropriate for spray hitters or rusty snowbirds.

Seeking a traditional test? The *Omni Tucson National Resort* is a 27-hole spread that annually hosts the Tucson Chrysler Classic on its Orange and Gold nines. Built in 1962, when the prevailing notion was to tame the desert with turfgrass, the course offers lush, wide-open fairways and well-bunkered targets.

Randolph Park, Tucson's top municipal facility, has two venues. The *North Course* is a flat, tree-lined layout with wide fairways that dates to 1930 and was touched up by Pete Dye in 1980. The 6,902-yard layout has hosted PGA, Senior PGA, and LPGA Tour events. Randolph Park's second course, *Dell Urich* (formerly the South Course), was overhauled in the mid-1990s. Formerly as flat as a tortilla, this 6,633-yard, par-70 layout is now gently rolling and even hilly in places, with hundreds of pines and eucalyptus trees lining the fairways. At press time, a round on either course was under $30 for nonresidents.

New & Noteworthy/Tucson

Thirty minutes northwest of Tucson, in Marana, is an outstanding newcomer. *Heritage Highlands Golf Club*, a 6,904-yard Arthur Hills design opened in 1997, stretches across the foothills of the Tortalita Mountains, with a good variety of holes routed over and along raw desert, rocky outcrops, and seasonal washes.

Oklahoma

The year was 1974, and Mike Holder had just taken over as coach of the Oklahoma State University golf team in Stillwater. He dreamed of building a home course for his superlative squad, which for years has ranked among the best in the nation. He had his eye on a parcel of land five miles west of Stillwater that didn't look at all like the rest of Oklahoma. No oil rigs rising from red clay dirt here—the site was heavily wooded, with a 135-foot elevation change. In 1983, Holder contacted Tom Fazio, who drew up a routing plan on a handshake agreement to build a golf course one day—if Holder could raise the money.

"Unfortunately, I started trying to raise money to build the course around the time the bottom dropped out of the oil market," Holder explained. The waiting game went on for another eight years, until

Karsten Solheim, maker of Ping clubs, emerged as a major benefactor. Fazio, to his credit, returned to keep his end of the bargain, extracting a traditional layout from the rugged terrain that manages to entertain handicap players from the white tees while giving OSU team members fits from the waybacks. There is no hint of artificiality in the design. The shoestring budget forced Fazio to limit earthmoving, which may have been a blessing in disguise. The first 15 holes are each encased within their own wooded compartments—players don't catch sight of another hole until they reach the 16th green.

Karsten Creek Golf Club (#65) opened in 1994, roughly 20 years after Holder first conceived it. The coach's patience has been amply rewarded. The layout's front nine, carved from a thick forest of gnarly

Karsten Creek Golf Club, Stillwater, Oklahoma, fourth hole

blackjack oaks and hickories, occupies hilly terrain, while the back nine flattens out, its final three holes grouped around Lake Louise, a man-made 110-acre lake named for Solheim's wife. Fairway corridors are wide, but players departing the cleared area are guaranteed to lose a ball in the underbrush. Find the fairway, and you'll be rewarded with a perfect lie: The ball sits up nicely on the zoysia-grass fairways. Greens, surfaced in bentgrass, are subtly contoured and very fast. Many have been left open in front to encourage bump-and-run shots, a sound option when the prevailing southwest breeze stirs, which it does often in Oklahoma.

Among the feature holes is the par-three 11th, which plays straight up the throat of a sunken creek bed to a large, terraced green; and the rigorous 17th, a par four stretching to 464 yards with water guarding the entire left side. It's one of the tougher holes on a layout that carries a course rating of 74.8 and a slope of 142 from the championship tees at 7,095 yards (par is 72).

A daily-fee course, Karsten Creek lies between Oklahoma City and Tulsa, an hour's drive from either. Walking is encouraged. Caddies are available. Take one: Karsten Creek is a helluva hike, even for fit collegians.

More Golf/Oklahoma

There's another college course worth checking out. It's called the *Jimmie Austin University of Oklahoma Golf Course*, and, like Karsten Creek, a story goes with it.

The school's original golf course, laid out by legendary designer Perry Maxwell and his son, Press, in 1951, had degenerated into a dust bowl by the early 1990s, prompting illustrious alumni (including oilman Jimmie Austin and PGA Tour pro Andrew Magee) to raise enough money to revive the baked-out course. Designer Bob Cupp was tapped to bring forth a cohesive layout from the site.

"When I walked the course for the first time," Cupp said, "I knew I was looking at a spectacular property." His goal was to preserve some of the "Maxwell feel"—notably the rippled fairways and caped bunkers around the greens—while giving the varsity something to chew on from the tips. (Fearless collegians get plenty of fight from the Boomer tees at 7,197 yards.)

Enough vestiges of the past were left intact to create a modern classic, thanks to a $4.5 million makeover completed in 1995. At press time, the $33 weekday green fee to play this superb course was a genuine bargain. Like most college facilities, walkers are welcome at Jimmie Austin, which is located in Norman on the outskirts of Oklahoma City.

All three Lone Star courses voted to the "Top 100" list are located in the fabled Texas Hill Country, a crescent of deep-carved, layered limestone covering 25,000 square miles in the state's southern tier. Geographically, the Hill Country is a shocker to those who arrive in Texas expecting dusty prairies, cattle herds, and oil drilling rigs. Limestone escarpments, spring-fed lakes, and fast-flowing rivers that sluice through sheer-walled canyons mark the land.

Blessed with over 300 sunny days a year, San Antonio and Austin, each a Hill Country outpost, are at their best in the spring, when bluebonnets and other native wildflowers blanket the hillsides. Summer can be hot as blazes, but fall, when the live oaks and cedars turn shades of scarlet and orange, brings delightfully cool weather.

San Antonio

Billed as one of the "final masterpieces" by the now-separated design duo of Tom Weiskopf and Jay Morrish, San Antonio's **La Cantera Golf Club** (#58) has, for a golfer, all the storied glory of The Alamo—without the long odds against. Carved from heaving terrain and a limestone quarry beside the Six Flags Fiesta Texas theme park, La Cantera ("quarry stone" in Spanish) is a Hill Country stunner that calls for a full arsenal of shot-making skills in return for victory.

The opening salvo is delivered by a king-size 666-yard par five, which plunges 125 feet downhill, its fairway signposted by a giant amoeba of a bunker, but the front nine's signature hole is the seventh, one of two (potentially) driveable par fours in the routing. The seventh's topmost tee, perched on a limestone bluff, drops 80 feet into the depths of the old rock

LODGING

The *Westin La Cantera Resort*, opening in the summer of 1999, crowns a hilltop overlooking the course, its low-rise casitas and citadel towers drawing inspiration from the varied architectural styles of early Texas. Spanish Mission and Mediterranean design influences blend with fortified structural elements to capture a style christened "Texas Colonial" by hotel designers. Exposed rock outcroppings and large limestone boulders are integrated into the design of the hotel, which has 500 rooms and more than 50 suites and casitas.

Inside, heavy wood furniture, blue-gray slate floors, metal sconces, woven fabrics, and rugs of deep red, gold, green, and black capture the look of an old Spanish Mission. Large modern outdoor swimming pools include one with a 14-foot waterfall.

quarry, its roughhewn, parchment-yellow walls flanking the right side of the hole on the far side of an irrigation pond. The green is backdropped by the wooden superstructure of The Rattler, the park's roller coaster. When the wind is right, you can hear the screams and smell the corn dogs. The designers gave a serpentine edge to a greenside bunker at the seventh but resorted to few gimmicks elsewhere, charting one strategic gem after another on classic Hill Country terrain shaded by burly oaks. Holes are artfully woven around swift-running streams, limestone outcrops, and three distinct hilltops that serve up 60-mile views of Alamo City.

The par-four 12th at La Cantera was recognized as one of the best two-shotters in Texas shortly after the layout opened in 1994. Heavy brush to the right and a row of church pew bunkers below a low rock wall on the left narrow the fairway at the 12th, while the approach shot must carry a forked stream and a gurgling waterfall. The target is a tiny, well-trapped green perched above the water.

Because Weiskopf and Morrish believe players should have a reasonable chance to make a birdie or two if pitfalls are avoided between tee and green, most of La Cantera's putting surfaces offer subtle slopes. There are, however, exceptions. The enormous green at the short par-four 16th is heavily contoured, with a deep trough dividing the dance floor into two distinct areas. Rolling the ball from one to the other rivals anything at Fiesta Texas for amusement—especially if the person putting happens to be your opponent!

Current home of the Westin Texas Open, La Cantera's five sets of tees offer plenty of thrills for PGA Tour stars, better-than-average players (country-and-western crooner George Strait is a regular), and visiting duffers. One of the nation's best-developed daily-fee layouts, La Cantera employed a grizzled local sculptor, Bob McArthur, as its Director of Art, giving him carte blanche (and three years) to carve the layout's hole markers, tee markers, and directional signs from limestone rocks and boulders with diamond-tipped saws. Their sunburst patterns are truly distinctive. Carts are equipped with club scrubbers, ball washers, watercoolers, and a flip-up notebook with color photos and playing tips for each hole. Also,

nearly 350 subsurface containers were installed to house bunker rakes. Befitting a PGA Tour stop, the 15-acre, double-sided practice facility is excellent. Springtime, when the wildflowers bloom, is the best time of year to cross swords with this memorable, entertaining layout.

More Golf/San Antonio

Hill Country Golf Club, an Arthur Hills–designed layout on the doorstep of the Hyatt Regency resort, occupies a former cattle ranch and flood plain crisscrossed by dry, stony creeks. A traditional layout, the 6,913-yard course has an interesting mix of holes routed among towering oaks and prickly pear cactus. The big double green at the ninth and 18th holes is fronted by a rock-rimmed lake.

Pecan Valley, revived in the mid-1990s, was the site of the 50th PGA Championship, where 48-year-old Julius Boros edged Arnold Palmer by

La Cantera Golf Club, San Antonio, Texas, seventh hole

one stroke for the title. Designed in 1963 by Press Maxwell, Pecan Valley is one of the state's finest parkland-style layouts. Massive pecans and live oaks line the fairways and protect the corners of the doglegs, with six holes skirting Salado Creek.

Jurassic Park without the dinosaurs? Check out *The Quarry*, a Keith Foster design stretched across the floor of an abandoned quarry near the airport. The 6,740-yard, par-71 layout's back nine, enclosed by 130-foot-high vertical rock walls, features several enticing risk-reward holes.

SilverHorn, a low-profile test routed across gently rolling terrain bisected by dry creek beds and dotted with live oaks, was laid out by Randy Heckenkemper, who worked with PGA Tour pros Scott Verplank and Willie Wood on the project.

San Antonio's premier muni is *Cedar Creek*, its $30 weekday green fee the best deal in town. Holes occupy valleys in the rugged Hill Country northwest of town, with 100-foot drops from tee to fairway. The ledged, multitiered greens are very challenging.

New & Noteworthy/San Antonio

The Bandit, a Keith Foster–designed (and named) course in New Braunfels, northeast of the city, is a superb layout crisscrossed by a tributary of the Guadalupe River, with 100-foot elevation changes, dramatic Hill Country views, and water on 14 holes.

Thirty minutes north of downtown is *Canyon Springs*, a grand-scale design by Tom Walker (a former Gary Player design associate) marked by broad fairways that lead to big, undulating greens. The premium here is on accurate approaches and steady putting.

DINING

Downtown San Antonio is the best urban 19th hole in the nation, especially if Tex-Mex cuisine, strolling mariachi bands, and a river shaded by leafy trees and plied by slow-moving water taxis is your speed. Dozens of lively open-air restaurants and cafés line *River Walk* (Paseo del Rio), which traces loops of the San Antonio River 20 feet below street level. Try hearty Tex-Mex specialties and giant margaritas upstairs overlooking the river at *Rio Rio Cantina*. *Boudro's*, a lively Texas bistro in an old limestone building with a riverfront patio, features creative Southwestern cuisine: smoked shrimp enchiladas, pecan grilled fish fillet with tequila orange butter, etc.

For inexpensive, authentic Mexican cuisine, head for *El Mirador* (Sopa Azteca—Soup of the Gods—is famous); or *La Fogata*, where northern Mexican specialties are grilled over charcoal. *Mi Tierra Café and Bakery*, open 24 hours, has solid Mexican fare, traditional mariachi music, unusual baked goods.

The River Walk

NIGHTLIFE

There's a lot of live entertainment along the River Walk, from reggae at *Acapulco Sam's* to classic Dixieland at *Jim Cullum's Landing* (at the Hyatt). If sing-alongs are your thing, drop by *Durty Nelly's Pub*. For laughs, try *Rivercenter Comedy Club*, which attracts nationally known comedians. The historic *Menger Hotel* has the Roosevelt Bar, where Teddy allegedly recruited his "Rough Riders." It's a nice quiet place for a cocktail.

Shopping

La Villita ("little town"), the city's original settlement, is today a charming district with 26 adobe shops where working artisans turn out one-of-a-kind items. Glazed pottery is a good buy. *El Mercado* is a Mexican-style market with over 40 shops featuring handicrafts, clothing, silver jewelry, and piñatas. Shopping for a Stetson? Try *Paris Hatters*. In Alamo Heights, 10 minutes from downtown, is the *Lucchese Boot Company*, maker of very fine Western boots and other leather accessories.

Austin

Fifty miles west of Austin, in sleepy Marble Falls, is the **Horseshoe Bay Resort,** a sprawling 4,000-acre spread on the south shore of Lake LBJ. In 1970, Texas developer Norman Hurd decided to build a country club community to his own singular standards. A self-described landscape artist with an affection for large rocks, Hurd spends most of his time "harvesting" boulders with which to embellish the grounds at Horseshoe Bay. Though not a golfer himself, he had the vision to hire Robert Trent Jones to build three courses at his Hill Country property. *Slick Rock*, the first to open (1973), is a pleasant member's-style spread with a $1 million waterfall gracing its 14th fairway. The third course, *Applerock* (1986), was routed roller-coaster style on heaving terrain high above Lake LBJ.

The middle course, **Ram Rock** (#79), is a fearsome layout, arguably the single toughest design Trent Jones has ever conceived. And to think Hurd and company softened it slightly to enhance its playability (and boost its appeal to disgruntled members) shortly after it debuted in 1981!

From full stretch at 6,926 yards (par 71), it has consistently been voted the toughest course in Texas by those who should know—the pros who have played it and survived to tell the tale. Jones deployed his full arsenal of penal hazards and risk-reward scenarios (with the accent on risk) at Ram Rock. Fairways bottleneck in the driving zones. Deep bunkers protect the inside corners of the doglegs. The bentgrass greens, many of them crowned and elevated above fairway level, appear flat but contain very subtle breaks along their ridges. Water comes into play at 10 holes.

Nightlife

Austin, the self-proclaimed "live music capital of the world," hangs its hat on Sixth Street, a raucous nightclub district chock-ablock with clubs, comedy shops, and theaters. Follow your ears—there's everything from Mississippi Delta blues to hard-edged garage bands. Looking for something jazzier, more refined? Head for lower Colorado Street in the city's revived "warehouse district." Lots of martini bars, smart cafés, Latin dance clubs.

Dry creek beds are a factor at six others. Barbed wire marks the out-of-bounds at several holes. Locals who depart the fairway in search of a stray shot *always* carry a club with them. Rattlesnakes, copperheads, and coral snakes live here.

Scare tactics by Trent Jones? Not at all. A stroll down the second hole, a par four listed at 488 yards from the blue tees, is scary without the snakes. A drive of 260 yards is required to reach the corner of the dogleg from the tips, leaving a second shot of nearly 230 yards to a large, slick green tightly guarded by a trio of imposing bunkers. This is not only the number-one handicap hole at Ram Rock, it's probably the toughest two-shotter in Texas. On a windy day—a steady southerly breeze is the norm in these parts—the second is really a par five.

Horseshoe Bay, Marble Falls, Texas, Ram Rock Course, fourth hole

Horseshoe Bay, Ram Rock Course, 17th hole

DINING

At the resort, dining options include the Appleheader Grill at the Cap Rock Golf Shop, where breakfast and tasty post-round fare is served. At the Yacht Club, cocktails are available at the Anchor Lounge, while dinner is served at the Fairwind, Harbor Light, or Keelway; or at the formal Captain's Table (Friday through Sunday).

After a series of semimanageable holes, at least from the regular tees at 6,378 yards, players are confronted by the ninth, one of the most nerve-racking par fives on Jones's long résumé. A firebreather from the tips at 540 yards, this daunting hole boomerangs from right to left. About 150 yards from the green, a spring-fed creek appears on the left. Fifty yards farther along, another creek appears on the right as the fairway narrows. A turtleback mound in front of the green deflects indifferent shots to water on either side. Few holes in golf can push a player's fear buttons like this one. Bravo, Mr. Jones.

The scenic back nine is more of the same. A boulder-strewn stream flanks the left side and crosses in front of the green at both the 10th and 11th holes, each an uncompromising par four. The 18th, also a par four, seems short on the card at 378 yards from the blue tees, but plays straight

WHITEWATER ADVENTURE PARK

No, not river rafting. In 1995, Horseshoe Bay unveiled a 17-acre complex that contains, among other things, ten tennis courts (four dome-covered), Oriental gardens, a fitness trail, a piano bar, a yogurt cabana, a flamingo habitat, an exotic duck and African crane exhibit, 25 fountains, and a 100-foot-long waterfall over which 30 tons of water per minute cascade into landscaped waterways and rock-rimmed ponds. The "recreational" portion of Whitewater is an 18-hole putting course lighted for night play. Your typical putt-putt layout it is not. The two-acre, 1,712-yard design is a scaled-down version of a regular course, with rough, fairways, and greens complemented by sand traps, stone outcrops, and waterscapes. Every shot is played with a putter. No mulligans allowed, even if one of the ducks happens to quack on your backstroke.

Horseshoe Bay Resort, Whitewater Adventure Park

Whitewater Adventure Park

LODGING

You must be a resort guest to play the Horseshoe Bay courses. Accommodations range from one-bedroom units at the *Inn of Horseshoe Bay* to three-bedroom condos, townhouses, and private homes overlooking the marina, golf courses, or Lake LBJ.

SIDETRIPS

In Austin, tour the *State Capitol Building* (built in 1888 of Texas pink granite), browse the *L.B.J. Presidential Library and Museum*, stroll the beautiful *University of Texas* campus, or ascend all 106 steps of Mt. Bonnell for a top-of-the-world view of the city. Barton Springs, a spring-fed pool, is a popular swimming hole within *Zilker Park*. Across the street are the *Austin Nature and Science Center* (great for kids) and *Zilker Botanical Gardens* (a 26-acre horticultural wonderland). Going batty? The world's largest urban bat colony—about 1.5 million Mexican free-tailed bats—hangs out beneath the Congress Avenue bridge from April to October.

uphill to a green flanked left and right by deep pits of sand.

If you think you've arrived as a golfer, Ram Rock is the place to measure exactly how far you've come.

The drawing card of the **Barton Creek Resort & Country Club,** tucked away in the Hill Country 30 minutes west of Austin, is the fantastic **Fazio Course** (#38). It debuted in 1986 and hosted the Liberty Mutual Legends of Golf, a Senior PGA Tour event, from 1990–94. The Fazio course not only showcases the designer's trademark playability from multiple sets of forward tees, but has three or four of the most beautiful and thrilling holes in the Southwest. And while prominently ranked on the national "Top 100" list, it is Texans who have embraced this wonder as their own, they who crow the loudest about its attributes. In a vast state

Barton Creek Resort & Country Club, Austin, Texas, Fazio Course, ninth hole

not easily given to consensus, it is probably the best-liked and most popular course in the territory.

Routed around limestone outcrops, gurgling brooks, live oaks, and fragrant cedars, Fazio took exceptional care with the 6,956-yard layout. The site was a difficult one, requiring the judicious use of dynamite to make way for several holes. Slabs of limestone were used to buttress the tee boxes, some of which are perched 100 feet or more above fairway level.

LODGING

Accommodations at Barton Creek are found in three large buildings designed (somewhat incongruously) to resemble alpine chalets. The interior public spaces and European-style guest rooms, however, are sumptuous. Note that upwards of 80 percent of the resort's business is generated by business and conference groups.

Refined over the years—a few tees enlarged, the greens converted from bentgrass to Tifdwarf bermuda in 1995—the Fazio Course showcases the beauty of the Hill Country like no other.

Among the feature holes, and there are many, is the ninth, a mid-length par three that calls for an accurate iron shot to a green propped atop a limestone shelf and protected to the left by a waterfall. Want to play the hole splash-free? Do what the members do: Carom your tee shot off a slope to the right and bounce your ball onto the rock-ribbed green.

The par-four 10th, which drops a dizzying 110 feet from tee to fairway, serves up a dazzling view of the Hill Country. Enjoy the hang time of your drive as it floats through the air, but make it straight: The fairway is flanked by a lake to the left and a nasty bunker to the right. After the fun of the drive, the real work begins: The second shot must be played uphill to a small, split-level green.

The finish on the Fazio Course is both memorable and challenging. The 420-yard 16th, a treacherouus two-shotter that usually plays into the prevailing wind, has it all. After hitting a dead-straight drive that avoids trouble left and right, players must rifle an unerring approach over a creek and its stepped waterfalls to one of the smallest greens on the course.

Pushed shots end up in the creek, which curls around the putting surface to the right.

The 17th is a long, straightforward par three, but then there's the 18th, a tremendous, one-of-a-kind par five that offers players the chance to make an eagle, a triple bogey, or anything in between.

"I am a believer that there is nothing new in golf. Everything has been done in the past," commented Fazio a few years after his namesake course opened. "But as far as I know, there is no other hole with a cave as a hazard." Indeed not. After clearing a rocky slope with dynamite to create a landing area for the 18th during course construction, a limestone cave was discovered. Fazio left the cave more as a curiosity than a hazard, installing a sand trap—a "spelunker bunker"—near its entrance to prevent wayward shots from going too deep into the cave.

A solid drive leaves golfers three options at the 546-yard finale: a lay-up short of the cave; a lay-up to a plateau above the cave but still short of the green; or a bold shot played straight uphill to a ledgetop green fronted by a rippling creek that flows into a waterfall, with sand pits and grassy hollows embracing the sides and back portions of the green. It's a glorious accomplishment to reach this green in two, but the penalty for a miss is severe. Win or lose, the 18th is unforgettable.

Access to this Texas treasure is limited. A surcharge is attached to the golf package to play it. Tee times are made available to resort guests on Tuesdays and Thursdays. Only six tee times are allocated to nonmembers on the other days of the week, and they are filled long in advance. Plan your trip accordingly to play this sensational layout.

More Golf / Austin

The *Crenshaw & Coore Course* at *Barton Creek*, a traditional design with generous playing areas wedded to the Hill Country's natural contours, features large, undulating greens. Short-game skills are tested to the maximum on this 6,678-yard, par-71 spread. Thirty minutes from the main resort complex is the *Lakeside Course*, a superb layout by Arnold Palmer–Ed Seay that features smooth, fast greens and panoramic views of Lake Travis from its hilltop fairways.

Circle C Golf Club, a popular Jay Morrish–designed daily-fee course opened in 1992 on the outskirts of Austin, offers a links-style front nine and a tree-lined back nine.

Barton Creek Resort & Country Club, Fazio Course, ninth hole

Barton Creek Resort & Country Club, Fazio Course, 18th hole

On a budget? *Riverside Golf Course*, an old-timer where native sons Ben Crenshaw and Tom Kite learned the game, was $15 weekdays, $20 weekends at press time. It's the best bang for the buck in town.

New & Noteworthy/Austin

More than 10 years after his phenomenal first act, Tom Fazio was invited by Barton Creek to return for an encore. The designer's agreement to return was based on the quality of the site, and a very fine one was chosen two miles from the main resort complex. The newcomer, referred to by the golf staff as *Fazio II* at press time, was scheduled to open in summer, 1999. Built on heaving, rock-studded terrain with water pumped to 14 of the holes, the fledgling layout stretches to nearly 7,300 yards and plays every yard of it. (The original Fazio Course, because of the large number of downhill holes, plays shorter than the listed yardage.) When it matures, Fazio II will be king of the Hill Country.

DINING

At Barton Creek, there's the Terrace for breakfast, lunch, or dinner in the Tejas Room, and more formal dining available in the Palm Court. After the round, the Crenshaw Grille serves a great hamburger (and an excellent Thai salad), while Jim Bob's is the place to shoot a relaxing game of pool at day's end.

Austin and environs abound in eclectic restaurants. Overlooking Lake Austin is *Hudson's on the Bend*, which features inspired Southwestern dishes, with the accent on grilled wild game (including ostrich). *Fonda San Miguel* and *Amaya's Taco Village* (two locations) are among the better Mexican restaurants in town, although East Austin has many authentic, family-owned spots worth finding. Looking for cutting-edge cuisine? *Zoot* and *Castle Hill Café* are two of Austin's trendier dining outposts.

New Mexico

The "Land of Enchantment," as New Mexico is known, is the driest state in the nation. Its golf courses are priced well below those in other Sun Belt states, so if you're seeking value, New Mexico is the place to go.

In Albuquerque, convenient to the airport, the **University of New Mexico, Championship Course** (#54), offers one of the finest college-affiliated venues in the nation. Designed by Robert "Red" Lawrence and opened in 1966, the rugged 7,248-yard layout, host to PGA Tour and LPGA Tour events as well as NCAA championships, has long been considered the most complete test of golf in the state. Known locally as the UNM South Course, this hilly, windswept links, with its fine views of the Albuquerque skyline and the West Mesa's volcanic cliffs, will seek out any weakness in your game and exploit it.

For starters, while the fairways are expansive, level lies are rare. Depart the fairway and you're in serious trouble: Cacti, rocks, and dense ground-hugging vegetation compose "the rough." Perhaps the signal feature of the school's most highly prized asset are the giant, elevated, multitiered greens, nearly all of them defended by deep bunkers. Reading putts on these slick, hogbacked surfaces is no easy task. Putts generally break away from the mountains and toward the Rio Grande, but factoring the correct amount of "speed" and "borrow" takes practice and patience.

The opening holes enable players to get their feet beneath them on this mile-high spread, but the middle holes were designed to winnow pretenders from champions. The sixth and seventh are both long, testing par fours, while the eighth, a par three stretching to an ungodly 248 yards, calls for a long carry from an elevated tee to a pulpit green. There's water to the right, out-of-bounds on the left, and a necklace of deep bunkers spaced around the green. It is simply one of the strongest one-shotters in the Southwest. The par-five ninth, the layout's number one handicap hole, is a left-to-right dogleg that stretches to 604 yards. It climbs uphill off the tee before swinging downhill to an enormous green, with five gaping pits of sand protecting the putting surface.

The layout's strong middle stretch continues at the 10th, a killer par

four listed at 457 yards from the tips. The fairway here rises to a turtle-backed landing area before bending sharply to the right and plunging to yet another large, liberally contoured green staked out by bunkers. The 11th, a long par three in excess of 200 yards from the back tees, calls for a forced carry over a lake to reach the well-defended green. Depending upon the wind, which can howl in the spring, this hole can play like a lion or a lamb.

Not all the holes test length and accuracy—the 15th and 17th holes are short, lay-up par fours that call for careful placement off the tee—but overall this stunning high-desert test is serious business.

In addition to a large practice facility, the complex features three regulation-length practice holes. (The fee is $3.15 to play them.) The university's nine-hole North Course is also available, its tree-lined fairways a marked departure from the vast and arid South Course.

More Golf/Albuquerque

A short drive south of town is *Isleta Eagle*, an excellent 27-hole spread laid out on Isleta Indian pueblo land. Site of the New Mexico Open in 1997–98, the facility's Mesa and Lakes nines stretch to over 7,500 yards.

Twenty miles north of Albuquerque and adjacent to the Coronado State Monument and Park (where the Spanish explorer Coronado and his gold-seeking conquistadors spent time in 1540) is *Santa Ana*, a challenging 27-holer designed by Ken Killian in 1991. Also north of town is *Paradise Hills*, like UNM South a Robert "Red" Lawrence design. This flat, high-desert layout is marked by well-bunkered greens and sharp doglegs.

Among the munis in town, most currently promoting green fees well under $20, there's *Ladera*, a solid 7,107-yard layout with gorgeous views of the Sandia Mountains; *Arroyo del Oso* (Spanish for Bear Creek), a walker-friendly facility; and *Los Altos*, a shorter test with good pedigree and smooth greens. Each of the three courses also has a sporty nine-holer on site.

University of New Mexico, Albuquerque, Championship Course, 10th hole

SIDETRIPS

Follow famous Route 66 to the *Old Town* of Albuquerque, the core of the city's original Spanish colonial settlement. Want to see forever? Ride the nearly three-mile-long *Sandia Peak Aerial Tramway*, which climbs to a station near 10,678-foot Sandia Crest. The view of the city, Rio Grande valley, and distant mountains is awesome. On the western outskirts of town, *Petroglyph National Monument* features thousands of ancient drawings inscribed in volcanic rocks and cliffs.

An hour's drive north of Albuquerque is *Santa Fe*. Home to one of the world's largest art markets, Santa Fe nestles on a plateau at the foot of the towering Sangre de Cristo Mountains, its low adobe homes, Spanish Colonial churches, and strong Native American influence making it one of the Southwest's must-see cities. There are enough authentic New Mexican restaurants (try dishes "Christmas style"—with both red and green chiles) and technicolor sunsets to win over the most sophisticated traveler.

Street vendors in Old Town

Piñon Hills Golf Course, Farmington, New Mexico, fourth hole

Piñon Hills Golf Course, sixth hole

A short drive east of Farmington in Bloomfield is *Chaco Culture National Historical Park*, an important center of Anasazi culture between the 10th and 12th centuries, with nearly a dozen major ruins, hundreds of smaller settlements and kivas, and an elaborate network of paths and stairs carved from sandstone. The park's largest and most impressive colony is Pueblo Bonito.

Best Bang for the Buck in America

Okay, it'll take you a full tank of gas to get there, and the locals may seem less impressed than they once were by your favorable opinion of their home course, but **Piñon Hills Golf Course** (#18), the best muni in America, is well worth a major detour. The fee to play the pride and joy of Farmington, N.M., doesn't just represent good value. It's a gift from the

Piñon Hills Golf Course, 14th hole

golf gods, given the exceptional quality of the course. Currently, the green fee at Piñon (pronounced pin-yon) Hills is $12.50 on weekdays, $15 on weekends.

Located in the northwest corner of the state near the Four Corners, where Colorado, Utah, Arizona, and New Mexico meet, this hidden gem is nearly 200 miles from either Albuquerque or Santa Fe. The most convenient gateway to the course is Durango, Colorado, about an hour's drive away. Having made the effort to find the course, what's the payoff? A brilliant, well-varied track sculpted from a high-desert plateau in the Upper Sonoran zone at nearly 6,000 feet above sea level. Native Americans, specifically the Navajos, hold the land in this area to be sacred. The scenery around the course is astounding: Dusty plains creased by dry washes and canyons rise to red-rock mesas and sheer sandstone cliffs.

The man entrusted with sketching Farmington's golf course was Ken Dye (no relation to Pete), a Houston-based architect who shares a design firm with Baxter Spann. Piñon Hills was one of his first solo commissions. Routed on land donated by San Juan College, the 7,249-yard layout, opened in 1989, at first functioned as a best-kept secret for area residents. Then word got out. Piñon Hills is now a connoisseur's collectible.

Challenge-wise, the whole is greater than the sum of its parts. Every hole on the course is memorable, and each offers a different view of the ever-changing landscape. Most first-timers are struck by the fine and varied par threes, often the grace notes of a memorable course. The third is a long one-shotter, 235 yards from the tips, that vaults an unimproved desert area and leads to a deep, triple-tiered green with a big sand trap front left and an equally penal grassy hollow front right. The sixth, while not long at 157 yards, nevertheless calls for a nerveless shot over a sandstone canyon. Overshoot the green, and your ball will run down the back of a hill behind the green and scoot into the desert. The 13th, stretching to 196 yards, plays from a lofty tee that serves up one of the best views of the course looking south to Farmington. In what sounds like a Piñon Hills litany, the tee shot must avoid both sand and grass bunkers that snuggle up to the green. But the most remarkable par three is the 15th, which has *nine* different tee locations (228 to 145 yards), the rear markers sited atop a sandstone cliff. The target is a well-trapped, triple-tiered green with a dry wash snaking up the left side. Exotic rock formations stake out rolling mounds at the back of the green. This is Piñon Hills's postcard hole.

As on Baltusrol's famed Lower Course, the final two holes at Piñon Hills are both long, testing par fives. Each is unreachable in two by mortals, and each is fraught with danger, with forced carries over arroyos on the 597-yard 18th. "We tried to fit the holes to the land," Dye explains, noting that very little dirt was moved to make way for the final routing on this "value-oriented" design. Dye credits town fathers for guiding the project to fruition and for keeping green fee costs well below the national average.

As he has done on his other designs, Dye constructed giant, undulating greens at Piñon Hills. Indeed, a few of the multitiered surfaces are up to 40 yards deep. These well-groomed greens (all course proceeds are directly applied to maintenance) enable short-game wizards to have their day, although green speed is kept medium-fast, not linoleum-slick. At a medium rate of speed, the generous contours on the greens are manageable, not laughable.

While the golf shop is modest, the practice facility is very presentable. There's a full-length driving range, two practice putting greens, a chipping green, and a practice bunker. The clubhouse grill serves a mouth-watering green chile cheeseburger, but overall this unpretentious muni is free of frills. Piñon Hills is content to be what it is: One of the finest golf courses in the Southwest, available at a rate completely out of proportion to its quality. If only there was a muni like this in every municipality!

LODGING

A *Holiday Inn*, *Best Western*, and *Ramada Inn* in Farmington are 10 minutes from the golf course.

Cedar, piñon, and juniper trees cloak the hills. Tall peaks in Colorado's La Plata Mountains pierce the sky to the north. Red foxes and other desert creatures routinely cross the fairways. On a clear day, which is just about every day in Farmington, the fragrance of the trees and the solitude of the setting combine to make Piñon Hills something more than a great muni with a time-warp green fee.

Nevada

Casino kingpin Gary Primm is a man of vision. On former United States government land along the Nevada-California border 40 miles south of Las Vegas, Primm set about creating a full-service destination in the early 1980s. Remote as it was, he built it, and people came. Today, Primadonna Casino Resorts boasts three resort hotels totaling 2,700 rooms, a major shopping complex, 11 restaurants, a small ocean of swimming pools, one of the nation's tallest and fastest roller coasters, and, last but not least, over 150,000 square feet of casino "gaming space." But Primm didn't stop there. Recognizing the importance of golf as a recreational amenity, he brought in Tom Fazio to create a pair of courses at **Primm Valley Golf Club.** The **Lakes Course** (#43), opened in 1997, vaulted onto the "Top 100" list a scant 15 months after its debut, a remarkable achievement given the competition. (The Desert Course made its debut in 1998.)

Money was no object in the creation of the Lakes. After packs of wild burros roaming the site were chased away, Fazio was given free rein on the bleak, pancake-flat desert floor. If he had an unlimited budget, he exceeded it—Fazio spent upwards of $34 million to create this emerald green oasis in the Mojave Desert, bulldozing more than 2 million cubic yards of dirt to create "movement" where none had existed.

To put the project in perspective, here is what Brian Hurlburt, editor of *Vegas Golfer*, had to say about Primm's prima donna: "Enough dirt was moved during construction of the Lakes Course to build an 80-mile, four-lane highway, enough sod was laid to grass 72 regulation football fields, 6,000 trees were planted, and over 200 miles of irrigation pipe was placed beneath the fairways."

In classic Fazio fashion, the course is both user-friendly and exceptionally attractive. Four tee boxes ranging from 6,945 to 5,019 yards enable players at all skill levels to enjoy their round on this par-71 design. And if the fairways seem a little wider than they need to be, it's wise to remember that this corner of the state can get very windy, especially in spring.

The Lakes is essentially a second-shot golf course. There is room galore to drive the ball, with containment mounding designed to kick stray shots back into play, but approaches must be fairly accurate to score. As for the greens, they are uniformly large and undulating, probably the

Primm Valley Golf Club, Primm, Nevada, Lakes Course, 12th hole

biggest and most intricately contoured Fazio has ever created. Like the fairways, the greens are embraced by mounds designed to serve as backstops for hard-running shots. Overall, the Lakes Course provides a fair amount of challenge with plenty of safe choices and bail-out areas, though the course record (66) indicates no one has shot the grass off the place, despite its seemingly benign look.

Ringed by distant, furrowed mountains, notably arid peaks in the McCullough Range to the east, the Lakes plays true to its name at the short par-five second, called Reflections. After rifling a drive (from the back tees) through an allée of piñon and aleppo pines, players proceed to a landing area that angles sharply to the left around a sizable lake, with a deep, sinuous bunker stretching for 50 yards between the fairway and water. (Tons of white silica sand fill the layout's beautifully sculptured bunkers.) Big hitters can go for the green in two, but for most, this is a wee bit early in the round to be contemplating heroics. Looking back from the green, the lake reflects Primm Valley's desolate setting all the way back to the tee.

As on all Fazio courses, the short par fours on the Lakes are exceptional. The best of the bunch is the 347-yard 10th, "Temptation," which dares big hitters to take a shortcut to the left by crossing a pond with their tee shots to reach the well-defended green. The carry is 260 yards from the tips. The hole can be played normally by aiming your tee shot to the right—and then flying your approach shot over the phalanx of bunkers in front of the green.

The prettiest hole on the Lakes? Most nods go to the par-three 12th, "Granite Falls," which features a gorgeous little waterfall to the right of the green below a saving bunker. But like any beauty contest, a case could also be made for the 15th, which doglegs uphill to a plateau green backdropped by the clubhouse, with the gurgling waters of Carolee Creek in play up the left side.

Is the Lakes Course the finest public-access venue in Nevada? It is and it isn't. In actual point of fact, Primm Valley Golf Club is situated five miles across the California border in San Bernardino County. But for all intents and purposes (including the 702 area code), this is a Nevada facility. Besides, what California developer would spend $34 million to build an 18-hole golf course?

In addition to a superb, bowl-shaped practice facility, Primm Valley is

Primm Valley Golf Club, Lakes Course, 15th hole

also home to the CompuSport Academy of Golf, a high-tech golf school that combines "the science of biomechanics with computer animation, video technology, and the skills of PGA professionals," according to the academy's literature.

More Golf/Primm

While the Lakes Course is a golf course in the desert (but not a desert golf course, given its oasislike lushness), the newer Tom Fazio–designed *Desert Course* at Primm Valley Golf Club, with half the water treatments of the original and with native vegetation framing its holes, is a more typical desert layout. It's also more of a "player's" course: Fairways are narrower, greens are smaller, bunkers are deeper, and the par threes and fives are longer on the Desert Course, which stretches to a formidable 7,131 yards (par 72). The choice is yours: Be transported to a fantasy realm of waterfalls and tall pines on the Lakes, or play a round on a cactus-studded newcomer that embraces the Mojave Desert. Or flip a coin. Heads or tails, you can't lose.

Las Vegas: Burgeoning Golf Mecca

As of 1998, Las Vegas was by far the nation's fastest-growing city, listed more hotel rooms (110,000 units) than any other domestic destination (as well as 14 of the world's 16 largest properties), boasted the world's fourth-largest pyramid, and claimed the nation's ninth-busiest airport. Every night, this neon Gomorrah throws the switch on the most electric skyline

LODGING

Primm Valley's Lakes and Desert courses are primarily intended for guests of the Primadonna Casino Resorts (including the country club–style *Primm Valley Resort and Casino* as well as *Whiskey Pete's* and *Buffalo Bill's*), although nonguests can gain access to the courses on a space-available basis.

Diners at the Gallery Café

Whiskey Pete's at night

Buffalo Bill's

Hoover Dam and Colorado River, Nevada

The Luxor Hotel at night, Las Vegas

on earth. What to do for an encore? Build golf courses! Here's a rundown of Glitter City's newer public-access venues, most of which have sprung up in the pale brown desert on the outskirts of the sprawling metropolis.

Reflection Bay Golf Club. Part of the $4-*billion* Lake Las Vegas Resort development in Henderson, 17 miles east of the city, this Jack Nicklaus–designed layout, opened in 1998, is the first of three resort courses planned for the Mediterranean-themed village. As in most modern designs, multiple tees were created to accommodate all levels of play. Five holes skirt 1.5 miles of shoreline, with greenside waterfalls and rocky arroyos also in play. From the back tees at 7,261 yards, better players are confronted with forced carries over creeks, canyons, and corners of the lake, though holidayers can have a ball from the forward tees.

The Royal Links. In Vegas, where the phantasmagorical is commonplace, developer Bill Walters has upped the ante for future daily-fee courses. Walters gave designer Perry Dye (Pete's eldest son) carte blanche on a 169-acre site at the foot of Sunrise Mountain 15 minutes east of the Strip. Nearly $30 million later (not including money spent to send Dye and his shapers to Britain for "research"), The Royal Links opened to the skirling notes of bagpipes in 1998. Dye moved 1.4 million cubic yards of dirt and installed 127 stacked-sod wall bunkers to create holes inspired by classic

New York Casino

links courses. The Road Hole from the Old Course at St. Andrews and the Postage Stamp from Royal Troon are represented, but so too are great holes from lesser-known British Open venues. Caddies are available.

Rio Secco Golf Club. Rio Secco (pronounced seko, Portuguese for "dry"), is an epic layout set among rolling foothills in the Black Mountain Range southeast of town, with holes distributed among canyons, plateaus, and arroyos. Designed by Rees Jones in 1997, this 7,250-yard layout stairsteps from one stunning land feature to the next, the Vegas skyline in view from the topmost holes. Subtle mounding and sizable greens lend the course a traditional look despite the skull-and-bones setting. Even before Jones knew Butch Harmon (Tiger Woods's swing coach) was opening the Harmon School of Golf at Rio Secco, he built a pair of par fives (the 631-yard ninth and double-dogleg 592-yard 14th) intended to be three-shot holes. Tiger, of course, has already reached both in two with irons. Rio Secco is reserved for guests of the nearby Rio Suite Hotel & Casino.

Shopping

The first phase of Primm Valley's million-square-foot shopping mall, called the *Fashion Outlet of Las Vegas*, was unveiled at the resort in 1998. Featuring upscale shops from many of the world's finest apparel companies, the mall re-creates several famous city street scenes. Also included is a huge food court, a virtual reality arcade, and a water thrill ride—as if experiencing credit card meltdown wasn't exciting enough.

Las Vegas Paiute Resort. Twenty miles north of the Strip, the Paiute Indians have developed two courses, *Nu-Wav Kaiv* (Snow Mountain) and *Tav-Ai Kaiv* (Sun Mountain), at a proposed 72-hole golf complex on a reservation given to the tribe by Congress in 1983. Pete Dye and code-signer Brian Curley softened Dye's trademark take-no-prisoners style in the creation of Nu-Wav Kaiv, a 7,158-yard layout opened in 1995. Vaguely reminiscent of a Palm Springs layout, the holes are bounded by the blocky spires of 11,918-foot Mt. Charleston and by eroded peaks in the Sheep Range. Unlike Dye's murderous courses elsewhere, Nu-Wav Kaiv is eminently playable: Fairways are broad, green approaches are open, and the white tortoise tees, at 6,035 yards, take most of the terror (watery graves, rattler habitats) out of play.

Shoehorned into 160 acres, the newer Tav-Ai Kaiv Course is a compact layout with more pronounced mounding alongside the fairways and greens. Players also must contend with more bunkers and waste areas on this 7,112-yard desert links, but very few golfers play from the waybacks. It's a much more enjoyable test for bogey shooters from the regular tees at 6,074 yards. Like its predecessor, Tav-Ai Kaiv has very swift greens.

Desert Pines Golf Club. Located five minutes from the Fremont Street Experience, a downtown sound-and-light show played out on a canopy above a four-block-long mall, this $20-million facility by Perry Dye is unlike any other in southern Nevada. Previously a hardscrabble city park, the 100-acre site was smeared with a thick layer of topsoil, which Dye sculpted to create lakes and fairways. Next, thousands of mature desert pines were planted on site. Out-of-play areas were covered with over 45,000 bales of thatched pine needles, hand-cut stones were used to frame the shorelines, and seasonal flower beds were created to accent the tee boxes and multitiered waterfalls.

Opened in 1996, the 6,810-yard layout possesses sound shot values. A signature hole? The 14th, called Do or Dye, is a short, "driveable" par four with consequences for misguided tee shots.

Adjoining this parkland-style layout is the Desert Pines Golf Center, a practice facility with a double-tiered range lit for evening practice, 58 climate-controlled tee stations, and five target greens that emulate famous par-three 17th holes (including Pebble Beach, Harbour Town, and the TPC at Sawgrass). To save your back from constant bending, balls are automatically delivered and re-teed after each shot is struck.

Tournament Players Club at The Canyons. Thirty minutes northwest of the Strip is this beguiling desert links, its tees, greens, and landing pods (it's a stretch to call them fairways) seemingly airlifted into the wilderness. Designed by Bobby Weed, with Ray Floyd serving as player-consultant, this TPC course, opened in 1996, has spectacular views of the Vegas valley and nearby red-rock country. To speed play (and keep egos intact), the desert and ever-present canyons are played as a lateral hazard. Among the layout's more hair-raising holes is the 14th, called Gorge-ous, a short par four where players must hit a blind tee shot to a bilevel fairway, followed by an unerring approach to a green perched on the far side of a cliff. The layout's bentgrass greens are liberally contoured and well-defended.

Shadow Creek Golf Club: The Holy Grail for High Rollers

This once ultraexclusive enclave in North Las Vegas, built by Tom Fazio and casino mogul Steve Wynn for an estimated $54 million (the most ever spent to build an 18-hole course), is currently open to players willing to shell out $1,000 for the privilege. The fee includes a tee time for one, caddie, cart, a suite for two at a Mirage resort property, and limo transportation to and from the club. Everything money can buy is here: mature trees, purling streams, undulating fairways, Augusta-like conditions. Even the driving range is perfect. According to *GOLF Magazine* editor Tom Doak, "Until I saw it [Shadow Creek], I never believed that money and genius alone were enough to create a course that would rival the greatest spectacles of Nature. Now, I do."

EDITOR'S NOTE: Shadow Creek was not included on the "Top 100" ballot sent to raters. Cost-wise, the line was drawn at Pebble Beach.

Shadow Creek Golf Club, Shadow Creek, Nevada, second hole

Lake Tahoe

Straddling the state line between California and Nevada is Lake Tahoe, a bluer-then-blue alpine lake. Embraced by mountains, this 22-mile-long, 12-mile-wide freshwater sea three hours east of San Francisco is one of the choicest playgrounds in the west. Lake Tahoe is perhaps best known for its downhill skiing, but there's a good grouping of golf courses around the lake, with several concentrated on the northwest (California) lakeshore near Tahoe City; several more are located in South Lake Tahoe on the southeast (Nevada) side. Situated in Stateline, Nevada, 60 miles below Reno, is the undisputed king of the lake, the layout by which all others in the High Sierras are judged: **Edgewood Tahoe Golf Course** (#69).

This standout course, designed by George Fazio on a former cattle ranch in 1968, is a broncobuster stretching to 7,491 yards that has everything an accomplished golfer could hope to see on the doorstep of the Sierra Nevada: tree-lined fairways backdropped by snow-frosted mountains, slick multitiered greens ringed by cloverleaf bunkers, and water in play at 12 holes. It also has a championship pedigree. Edgewood Tahoe hosted the 1980 U.S. Public Links Championship as well as the 1985 U.S. Senior Open, captured by Miller Barber with a 3-under-par score of 285. (He was the only player in the field to finish under par.) Since 1989, the Celebrity Golf Championship has been held at Edgewood Tahoe, giving fans a chance to see everyone from quarterback John Elway to superstar Michael Jordan attempting to upstage their fellow athletes with a low score on this rigorous track.

Stretched across a lakeshore meadow at nearly 6,300 feet above sea

DINING

The *Edgewood Restaurant* at the Edgewood Tahoe Golf Course, its sunset dining area a stone's throw from the lake, offers wild game dishes and stuffed prawns along with great views.

Three miles from the course is *Riva's*, a popular spot for cocktails, appetizers, and fine dining on the lake.

In Stateline is the historic *Sage Room Steak House,* a holdover from the Wagon Wheel Saloon that gave birth to Harvey's Resort. The steaks (and atmosphere) are great. Note: Many Tahoe-area restaurants offer two-for-one dinners in the shoulder season months.

level, Edgewood Tahoe was specifically designed by Fazio to separate the men from the boys. George Fazio's nephew, Tom, takes a more balanced approach to the business, and in fact, one of his lead designers, Andy Banfield, has on several occasions revised (but not softened) the course.

With water on the first three holes, there's trouble from the get-go at Edgewood Tahoe. In 1998, the first green was moved 30 yards to the left to bring a pond into play on the approach. At the second, a cart path was replaced by a creek and the green was recontoured to enliven the challenge significantly. The par-five third hole, the longest on the course at 602 yards, needed no tweaking: After crossing a stream with their tee shots, players must navigate a path around menacing bunkers and fly their third shots to a crowned, well-trapped green.

The finish at Edgewood Tahoe is one of most scenic and arresting in the West. The 558-yard 16th is a magnificent par five that plays from a raised tee to a fairway marked by a tall ponderosa pine in its center. This exclamation point, which defies players to hit the dreaded straight ball, is flanked by nasty bunkers to the left and right. Farther up the fairway, cross bunkers 100 yards short of the green punish misplayed approach shots. The green itself, perched on the shores of Lake Tahoe, is 15 paces wide and over 50 yards deep. Par here can seem like a minor miracle. The 17th is an unforgettable par three that plays across a corner of the lake's sandy beach, while the 574-yard 18th hole, its fair-

Edgewood Tahoe Golf Course, Stateline, Nevada, 16th hole

Clubhouse at Edgewood Tahoe Golf Course

SIDETRIPS

Boat tours aboard trimarans and paddlewheelers departing from South Lake Tahoe (California) are very relaxing. So are trips aboard the 50-passenger Heavenly Tram at *Heavenly Ski Resort* near Stateline that runs part way up the mountain to 8,200 feet. The 72-mile-long road that rings the lake leads to numerous state parks, national forests, and protected wilderness areas. Lake Tahoe has 36 public beaches, but be forewarned: The water warms to only 68 degrees in midsummer.

Paddlewheelers on Lake Tahoe

Edgewood Tahoe Golf Course, 17th hole

way bent slightly to the right, proceeds to a green with a pond to the left and the lake itself to the right. In the years the Celebrity Golf Championship was played here, the nation's finest pro athletes did everything they could to stay dry and keep smiling on this treacherous hole.

At press time, Edgewood Tahoe's green fee of $150 ($175 for reservations made 15–90 days in advance) was the area's highest. Despite the cost, tee times are hard to come by from June through September. With good reason. Edgewood Tahoe admits only 180 players per day. There are 12-minute tee times in the morning, which allows for generous spacing on the course. After the last group goes off at 3 P.M., the greens are hand-mown and the fairways cut with triplex mowers. Caddies are available for those who wish to walk. This is a boutique golf course that turns away 19 golfers for every one lucky enough to play it!

More Golf / Lake Tahoe

Twenty minutes outside Stateline is *Genoa Lakes,* an appealing 7,263-yard layout routed in the Sierra Nevada foothills by John Harbottle and Peter Jacobsen. Forced carries, blind shots, and topsy-turvy greens keep things interesting. *Lake Tahoe Golf Course,* an established public track in South Lake Tahoe (California), occupies a flat valley floor, with the Truckee River and five ponds providing plenty of challenge.

At the north end of the lake in Nevada is *Incline Village,* its vintage Robert Trent Jones layout marked by pine-lined fairways, thick rough, and undulating greens. The panoramic lake views are magical. There's also a 3,513-yard, par-58 executive course by Jones that serves as a nice sideshow to the championship spread.

LODGING

In Stateline, the most popular choices for visiting players (golfers and gamblers) are the town's many casino-hotel properties. The top choices are *Caesar's Tahoe, Harrah's Casino/Hotel Lake Tahoe,* and *Harvey's Resort Hotel/Casino.* Each features top-name entertainment and Vegas-style shows. Private-home rentals on the lake are also available.

New & Noteworthy / Lake Tahoe

Nestled beneath the High Sierras in Genoa, 30 minutes from Stateline, is *Sierra Nevada Golf Ranch,* a Johnny Miller–John Harbottle design routed on a historic cattle ranch. Opened in 1998, the 7,358-yard, par-72 layout, anchored by a Western-theme clubhouse, has sharp elevation changes, water hazards created by a spring-fed creek, and over 110 bunkers cut into the rugged desert landscape.

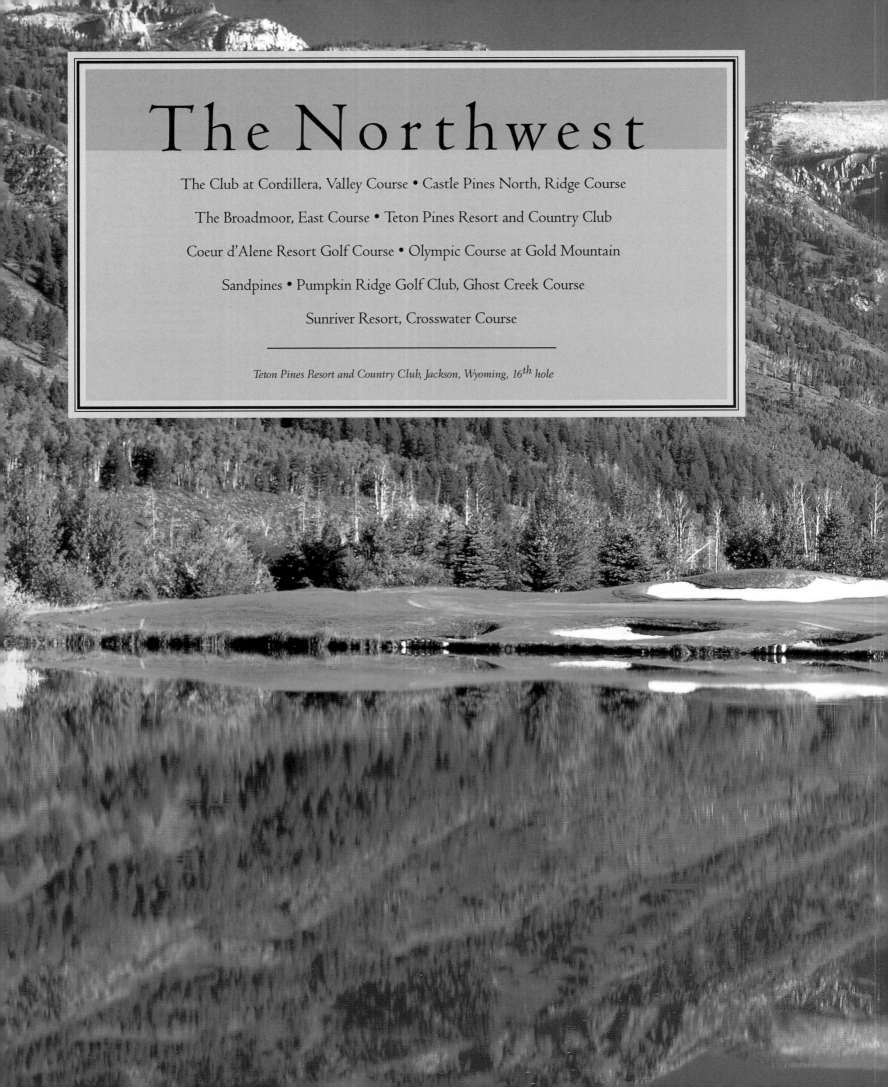

The Northwest

The Club at Cordillera, Valley Course • Castle Pines North, Ridge Course

The Broadmoor, East Course • Teton Pines Resort and Country Club

Coeur d'Alene Resort Golf Course • Olympic Course at Gold Mountain

Sandpines • Pumpkin Ridge Golf Club, Ghost Creek Course

Sunriver Resort, Crosswater Course

Teton Pines Resort and Country Club, Jackson, Wyoming, 16th hole

Colorado

Vail

"We came here to ski, but we live here because of the summers" is the mantra of well-to-do burghers who live in Colorado's stunningly beautiful Vail Valley, where everyone seems to have a bronzy tan, a flat belly, and, if they play golf, a healthy ego. Why? Because at an average elevation of 7,500 feet, balls fly up to 20 percent farther here than at sea level. A 250-yard drive in the lowlands will carry another 40 yards or more in Vail's rarefied air, making the legendary ski area a prime draw for big hitters and wannabe boomers alike. Ringed by massive 13,000-foot peaks in the Gore Mountain Range, Vail's cool, humidity-free summers are ideal for golf and other outdoor activities.

Thirty minutes west of Vail, in the shadows of the majestic Sawatch Range, Tom Fazio has fashioned the perfect place for savvy shotmakers to tee it high and let it fly. Routed on south-facing slopes at 7,200 feet, the **Valley Course** (#100) at **The Club at Cordillera** enjoys a "banana belt" climate, with extended play available from April to November. Fazio's

DINING

At the Lodge, *Restaurant Picasso,* a candlelit room with original Picasso lithographs on its hand-troweled stucco walls, is presided over by a French chef who uses no flour and very little cream or butter in his preparation of "definitely French, but lighter" dishes. Other dining options at Cordillera include *The Timber Hearth Grille* at the Mountain Course clubhouse; and *Chaparral,* located at the Valley Course clubhouse. Resort guests can also enjoy picknicking in style: Groups are escorted by a hiking instructor through fields of wildflowers to a secluded picnic area. Smoked salmon and chilled herb pasta salad are among the favored entrees. Near Vail, *Beano's Cabin* on Beaver Creek Mountain offers a superlative dining experience in a log cabin accessible by horseback or horse-drawn wagon.

The Club at Cordillera, Edwards, Colorado, Valley Course, seventh hole

trademark playability is firmly in place, especially from the forward tees, but the Valley is no fragile lily. Unusual for a Fazio-designed golf course, cross hazards—chasms, creeks, eroded canyons—must be negotiated, while wayward approach shots tend to bounce off fescue-covered hillsides into deep, scalloped bunkers.

Artfully woven through a high-desert setting, its concave bluegrass fairways framed by mountain sagebrush, lanceleaf cottonwoods, and 400-year-old junipers, the 7,005-yard, par-71 Valley Course was designed to showcase the untamed beauty of the West. But there was more at stake here than mere beauty. A master at sculpting holes into existing terrain, Fazio is equally adept at creating con-

The Club at Cordillera, Valley Course, eighth hole

tours that blend with existing landforms. On a rugged site with a 260-foot elevation change, the architect and his design team did everything they could to minimize the vertigo-inducing effect of topsy-turvy slopes.

Among the feature holes on the Valley, which debuted in 1997, is the short par-four seventh, a prospector's delight where the drive must cross a

deep ravine to find a fairway that parallels a buff-colored arroyo. Make an about-face on the green, and towering New York Mountain looms into view. The 10th, one of the prettiest par threes in the Rockies, calls for a short downhill pitch over a scrub-filled gulch to a postage stamp green backdropped by forested foothills rising to snow-frosted peaks. At the option-laden 16th, a petite par four of 334 yards from the tips, both the landing area and green are perched on knobs. Golfers must summon equal measures of precision (on the drive) and courage (on the approach) to earn a par here. Pentti Tofferi, the club's Finnish-born head pro, is fond of the 17th, a testing par four that plunges downhill into the prevailing breeze off the tee before climbing to a hilltop green protected by deep bunkers and a sheer drop-off to the left. It's the most hair-raising hole on the course. The 445-yard par-four 18th, its green perched above a deep wash, is a classic risk-reward finale.

Play on the Valley Course is limited to club members (Cordillera is a residential development) and resort guests.

More Golf / Vail

The Club at Cordillera (Mountain Course), a massive 7,444-yard layout designed by native son Hale Irwin and Dick Phelps in 1994, spans wet meadows, fir-covered ridges, and aspen groves at an elevation of 8,250 feet. One of the toughest tracks in the Rockies when it opened, the layout

OFF-COURSE ATTRACTIONS

Hiking, mountain biking, tennis, world-class fly fishing, sporting clays, horseback trekking, cattle drives, hot air ballooning, and white-water rafting are available. Chairlifts at Vail and Beaver Creek carry seasoned hikers and mountain bikers to over 6,000 acres of prime terrain. *Vail Nature Center,* a restored homestead, offers lighthearted hikes as well as more ambitious treks to the top of regional peaks. Want to smell the flowers? *Betty Ford Alpine Gardens* near Vail Village offers free interpretive walking tours of North America's highest public alpine gardens. Culture? The *Bravo! Colorado Vail Valley Music Festival* presents chamber music, orchestra, and jazz concerts in beautiful mountain venues at Vail and Beaver Creek.

Cowboys in Vail

was touched up in 1997 to enhance its playability (trees cleared, landing areas widened). Despite the extra yardage gained at this altitude, the Mountain is still a monster.

Like Cordillera's Valley Course, the *Sonnenalp Golf Club* enjoys an extended season due to its southerly exposure and lower elevation. This sagebrush-lined links in Edwards was designed by Bob Cupp and Jay Morrish. Formerly known as Singletree, the 7,059-yard layout traverses alpine meadows dotted with wildflowers; timber fences, native grasses, and rushing streams frame the holes. Sonnenalp's front nine occupies a valley floor, while the back nine climbs into mountain foothills. The greens are lightning fast.

An ultra-scenic, out-and-back design by Robert Trent Jones, Jr., *Beaver Creek Golf Course* is dotted with fanciful mansions and bounded by White River National Forest. It's a high-altitude (8,500 feet) finesse course that rewards control, not power. The first three holes (a steep downhill par three bookended by a pair of narrow, treacherous par fives) are known as "Death Valley." It's best to play them with irons. The 6,752-yard, par-70 layout widens thereafter.

SPA

The lower level of the Lodge is given over to *The Spa at Cordillera,* a full-service spa and exercise facility dedicated to "holistic fitness" (relaxation, toning, rejuvenation). In addition to a 25-meter lap pool and a full range of exercise equipment, there are saunas, steam rooms, and customized indoor and outdoor wellness and treatment programs. Spa services range from body wraps to aromatheraphy facials.

Shopping

In addition to a wide variety of outdoor cafés, brew pubs, and restaurants specializing in wild game, Vail, patterned after a Tyrolean village, has dozens of interesting shops, boutiques, and art galleries. Smaller establishments offer one-of-a-kind items. *Gotthelf's Gallery* carries a fine collection of American and Italian glass. *Slifer Designs* has eclectic picture frames, bath accessories, and home furnishings. *The Golden Bear* boasts the "signature of Vail" trademark, a golden bear set in rings and bracelets or worn on necklaces and earrings. *Skandia of Vail* features classic and contemporary Scandinavian imports. *The Squash Blossom* carries Southwestern jewelry. Also, ski shops have good off-season bargains on winter clothing and skiwear.

Vail Golf Course, the oldest course in town (1968), is a flat, friendly, walkable muni situated at the foot of the spectacular Gore Range and crisscrossed by Gore Creek.

Fun & Games

The Short Course at The Club at Cordillera, a 10-hole par-three course opened in 1997, was designed by putting whiz Dave Pelz to give beginners a confidence boost while challenging experts to sharpen their short-game skills. The one-shotters range from 65 to 205 yards, with multiple tee boxes on every hole. No matter what your level of play, the Short Course is lots of fun.

He may have been a hothead as a player, but Tom Weiskopf is one cool customer when it comes to golf course design. Witness the **Ridge Course** at **Castle Pines North** (#52) outside Denver, yet another of tempestuous Tom's fluent, well-proportioned layouts.

The holes on the Ridge, each classically styled, present players with roomy fairways, sculpted bunkers, and large, rolling greens. Carved from a thick forest of gambel oaks and towering ponderosa pines in the foothills of the Front Range, the Ridge also traces open terrain where sightlines stretch south to 14,110-foot Pike's Peak as well as to Devil's Head and Mt. Evans in the west. The shot values are a match for the scenery on this well-groomed daily-fee layout, which many Denver metro golfers believe is superior to nearby Castle Pines, the exclusive Jack Nicklaus–designed club that hosts the Sprint International, a PGA Tour event.

Arranged in two loops, the par-71, 7,013-yard layout, unveiled in 1997, gets off to a fairly gentle start before confronting players with a two-tier green ringed by multifingered bunkers at the par-three fourth, called

SIDETRIPS

Denver, the state capital and gateway to the Rockies, has emerged as a good destination for visitors seeking a mix of recreation, cultural activities, and shopping. The *16th Street Mall,* a shady mile-long pedestrian precinct, has outdoor cafés, fine shops, restored buildings, and a free shuttle bus. *Larimer Square,* with its restored Civil War–era buildings, has many fine specialty shops. The city's newest example of urban renewal is Lower Downtown (*LoDo*), which offers eclectic cafés, art galleries, nightclubs, and several brew pubs. For a delightful workout while exploring Denver, the *Cherry Creek Trail* is good for strolling, biking, and in-line skating.

Castle Pines North, Castle Rock, Colorado, Ridge Course, 17ᵗʰ hole

Castle Pines North, Ridge Course, 18th hole

"Kalahari." There's also a (potentially) driveable par four, the 307-yard sixth, where bold players who wish to air out their drives must avoid large bunkers that bottleneck the landing area and additional bunkers beside the canted green. The Redan-style seventh, a long par three known as "Calamity Jane," is an updated classic. The long, narrow green, pitched diagonally from left to right, can be safely approached from the left side,

LODGING

Three miles south of the Ridge at Castle Pines North are a number of budget-priced accommodations. Heading north to Denver, there are full-service resorts (including *Inverness Hotel & Golf Club*) as well as an array of downtown hotels.

where the close-mown approach area will generally feed the ball onto the green. Want to play directly to the pin? Your tee shot, all of 223 yards from the black tees, must carry a phalanx of deep bunkers cut below the green and land very, very softly to avoid trickling into a rear bunker.

The back nine of the Ridge is a different kettle of fish. While the outgoing nine is mildly rolling (except for the ninth, which plunges from the high point of the course at 6,650 feet down a ski slope-like fairway to the green), the incoming nine reminds players that the Ridge is a mountain track with a 300-foot elevation change. Among the more distinctive holes on this giddy roller-coaster ride through rock outcrops and evergreens is the fiendish 15th, a petite par four (only 338 yards from the tips) with a 40-foot-high ponderosa pine in the center of the fairway. It's a hole designed to humble the crusher and reward the strategist. It is also Weiskopf's favorite hole on the Ridge.

According to Mark Kizzire, the facility's director of golf, "We did a customer satisfaction survey during our first 90 days of operation and asked golfers to name their favorite hole. Incredibly, all 18 holes on the course were mentioned more than once." Were any mentioned more than the others? "Yes, the 17th and 18th holes."

The signal feature at the par-three 17th is a prominent stone tower that rises from a hill behind the rolling, humpbacked green. The par-four 18th, its back tees sited atop this stone protrusion, is a sweeping right-to-left dogleg carved from towering pines. A lone bunker off the right side of the fairway was strategically placed by Weiskopf to snare timid or unwary golfers who play too safe or misdirect their drives.

To preserve wildlife corridors, gaps on the course were left intact to make way for migrating elk herds, not to mention the wild turkeys that like to strut the grounds. As in the desert, turfgrass was used stringently to conserve water and retain the Wild West look. Still, there's plenty of room to play golf at The Ridge—if you select the correct set of tees and don't get hypnotized by the distant peaks.

Rounding out the Castle Pines North experience is a 16,000-square-foot clubhouse designed to simulate an upcountry mountain lodge. The clubhouse grill is dominated by a massive stone fireplace, while the lounge is accented by rough-hewn beams and a hammered-iron bar. There are also handsome locker rooms for men and women as well as a spacious wraparound patio from which to view the beautiful Front Range.

Bar at the Castle Pines North clubhouse

More Golf/Denver Area

Fifteen miles northwest of Denver is *Legacy Ridge,* a municipal facility designed by Arthur Hills in 1995 for the city of Westminster. Built on a former wheat farm, this mile-high 7,251-yard, par-72 layout proceeds through wetlands, fields of wildflowers, and giant cottonwoods lining an old farmer's canal. Greens are large, undulating, and very swift. At presstime, the green fee topped out at $32.

A short drive north of the city is *Riverdale,* a 36-hole public complex. The sporty, walker-friendly *Knolls Course* is fun to play, while the more rigorous *Dunes Course,* a Pete and Perry Dye collaboration opened in 1985, is a well-conditioned, links-style design that is all anyone could want on a windy day from the tips at 7,030 yards. Riverdale's green fee rates (under $30) represent excellent value.

New & Noteworthy/Denver Area

The city of Westminster will open a second golf course, *The Heritage at Westmoor,* in summer 1999, not far from Legacy Ridge. The open, windswept, treeless course, highlighted by a 180-foot elevation change and a meandering creek, was designed by Michael Hurdzan–Dana Fry and adjoins a business park.

Castle Pines North, Ridge Course, sixth and seventh holes

Colorado Springs

Fifty-five miles south of Denver in Colorado Springs is **The Broadmoor,** the swank pale pink palace in the foothills of the Rockies. The resort's **East Course** (#67), the headliner of the three layouts available to hotel guests, is a relatively wide-open Donald Ross creation dating to 1918 that is revered for its giant, lightning-fast greens. Revised by Robert Trent Jones in 1950 (purists will identify the Ross-designed holes on the East as one through three and 13 through 18), the current composite course, which knits together nicely, is a historic spread where Jack Nicklaus captured his first national championship (the 1959 U.S. Amateur), and where Annika Sorenstam claimed victory in the 1995 U.S. Women's Open. It's no surprise the USGA likes The Broadmoor's legendary layout. Take away the soaring flanks of Cheyenne Mountain backdropping its holes, and the East Course could pass for any of Ross's creations in the Northeast.

The fairways are unusually broad and inviting. As on all Ross courses, there's a big premium on pitching, chipping, and putting on the East, which stretches to 7,091 yards (par 72) but plays shorter because of the altitude. Fairways are lightly bunkered, but greens are well defended by sand and occasionally by water. Appearances to the contrary, all putts break away from the mountains. As for speed, suffice it to say they're among the slickest greens west of the Mississippi. And even seemingly flat putts have lots of break.

If the heart of the East is its long par fours—the seventh, 10th, 15th, and 18th holes are all sturdy two-shotters—then its soul resides within a tall granite tower high atop Cheyenne Mountain. It was built by Spencer

DINING

The Broadmoor's 11 restaurants and lounges feature everything from *Julie's,* a whimsical sidewalk café and soda fountain where waitresses dress in 1950s attire, to the Edwardian rooftop splendor of the *Penrose Room,* where abiding by the dress code (coat and tie required) is well worth the trouble for the privilege of enjoying fine continental cuisine, live dinner music and dancing, and stellar views of Colorado Springs and Cheyenne Mountain. Also, the show-stopping Sunday brunch at the *Lake Terrace Dining Room,* highlighted by finnan haddie, Belgian waffles, and "Bananas Foster," is worth adjusting your itinerary to experience.

Penrose, the resort's founder, to honor the memory of Will Rogers, the popular humorist. Throughout the day, the tower's ringing chimes can be heard across the course. It's hard to get too upset over a three-putt green when this music plays.

The Broadmoor, Colorado Springs, Colorado, East Course, 15th hole

The Broadmoor, East Course, 18th hole

SIDETRIPS/THE BROADMOOR

On the resort's grounds is the *Carriage House Museum,* which displays a fine collection of vintage cars and old stagecoaches. Adjacent to the resort is the *Cheyenne Mountain Zoo,* home to more than 800 animals, many of them endangered species. The high-spired Cadet's Chapel and superb planetarium are the top attractions at the *Air Force Academy* in Colorado Springs.

On the outskirts of the city is the *Garden of the Gods,* a 1,350-acre nature reserve laced with trails that lead to wierdly shaped, fiery-red sandstone formations as well as ancient cypresses and picnic areas.

Convenient to the resort in Manitou Springs is *Pikes Peak Cog Railway* ($23 roundtrip at press time), which travels high above the trees to the peak's 14,110-foot summit. On a clear day, Denver can be seen to the north, New Mexico to the south.

The Broadmoor, East Course, fourth hole

SPA

The Spa at The Broadmoor, the resort's 38,000-square-foot feel-good facility, provides what it calls "the essential elements of renewal." Designed to mirror the architecture of the resort's palatial hotel, the spa, opened in 1995, houses men's and women's locker rooms, a fitness center, golf pro shop, grill, and cocktail lounge. Wet treatments (specialized showers, aromatherapy, steam, sauna, whirlpool, and plunge pools), dry treatments (massage, reflexology, and facial treatments), as well as Broadmoor spa and beauty products made with Rocky Mountain ingredients are available.

The Spa at The Broadmoor

LODGING

The Broadmoor has 700 rooms and suites contained in several complexes. Updated rooms in the original Broadmoor Main, many with fine views of the small lake at the resort's center and the mountains beyond, are the most charming. Larger accommodations are found in the South and West towers. Priceless antiques, including Oriental art dating back to the Ming and Ching dynasties, furnish the public rooms of the original hotel, as do Della Robbia tilework and original Toulouse-Lautrec lithographs. Despite the resort's palatial grandeur, the cheerful staff helps to create a casual, unpretentious atmosphere.

Ushered into the modern era by a $100-million makeover in the mid-1990s, the "grande dame of the Rockies" boasts a long list of creature comforts rivaled by few resorts in the world. The 3,000-acre property has its own florist, pharmacy, movie theater, three swimming pools, riding stables, sporting clays, 12 tennis courts (the resort's tennis director is Dennis Ralston), an arcade with 28 specialty shops . . . the list goes on.

19th Hole

One of The Broadmoor's merriest and most convivial spots for post-round eating and imbibing is *The Golden Bee,* an authentic 19th-century English pub transported to Colorado Springs from London. The pub is accented by etched glass panels, a pressed-metal ceiling, African mahogany figures, "gingerbread" carving, and old English prints on the walls. Open for lunch and dinner, the Bee serves classic pub fare: Devonshire cheddar cheese soup, steak-and-potato pie, English trifle. Yards (and half-yards) of ale are also available. In the evenings, a ragtime pianist leads a lively sing-along (songbooks provided).

The Golden Bee

More Golf/The Broadmoor

In addition to the East, there's the scenic, sterner *West Course* designed by Robert Trent Jones. A $3 million irrigation system added to both the East and West courses in 1997 has greatly enhanced their condition, and both are served by an exquisite clubhouse occupying a former casino (circa 1891) that was remodeled in the mid-1990s. The resort's *Mountain Course,* located a few minutes away from the main complex, is a target-style Arnold Palmer–Ed Seay design marked by narrow fairways lined with scrub oaks and crossed by deep ravines.

Wyoming

Nowhere do the mountains rise more abruptly off the plain than in Grand Teton National Park, a fact not lost on early French-Canadian trappers, who gave the Grand Tetons in northwest Wyoming their name. (It's French slang for big breasts.) However, there's nothing soft and bosomy about the jagged, sawtooth spires that rise up around Jackson Hole, a renowned ski resort that in summer attracts attracts fly fishermen, mountain bikers, river runners—and golfers seeking a truly majestic stage for the game.

If the mountains are in a class of their own, so too is **Teton Pines Resort and Country Club** (#81), a spellbinding layout routed on a former cattle ranch by Arnold Palmer and Ed Seay in 1987. A half-dozen peaks over 12,000 feet high are reflected in the layout's 40 acres of streams, lakes, and ponds, quite a sight for a flatlander. But this drop-dead beautiful spread is more than a 7,412-yard postcard that elicits oohs and aahs from tender-footed golfers. With water in play at 16 of the 18 holes, this is no place to get swept away by mountain magic. Teton Pines, which functions primarily as a private club within a 360-acre residential community, is a first-class test of golf with everything a discerning golfer could want: manicured bentgrass greens, a fine practice facility, a stable of knowledgeable caddies. (Despite the 6,200-foot elevation, Teton Pines is quite flat and very walkable.)

Routed opposite the winding loops of the Snake River and walled in by snow-frosted peaks, the layout, described by Palmer as "one of the finest I've planned or played," is chockablock with great holes. The seventh, a gargantuan par five stretching to 634 yards, has an array of bunkers lurking down the right side and a huge lake fronting the shallow, bunkerless

DINING

Within the Teton Pines clubhouse is the *Grille at the Pines,* a casual, Western-theme room with fabulous views and excellent seafood presentations. In the town of Jackson is the *Snake River Grill,* where game dishes (including elk) and custom pizzas are the entrees of choice. For Tyrolean cuisine, *Steigler's,* located at the Jackson Hole Racquet Club, is the place to go. Within Teton National Park a half-hour north of Jackson is *Jenny Lake Lodge,* where the Sunday evening buffet dinner is highly recommended.

Teton Pines Resort and Country Club, Jackson, Wyoming, eighth hole

LODGING

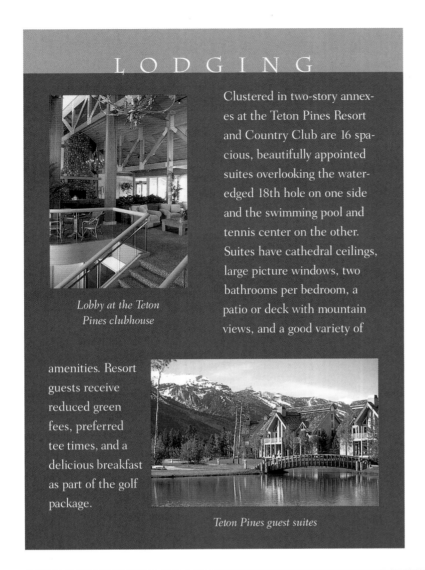

Lobby at the Teton Pines clubhouse

Clustered in two-story annexes at the Teton Pines Resort and Country Club are 16 spacious, beautifully appointed suites overlooking the water-edged 18th hole on one side and the swimming pool and tennis center on the other. Suites have cathedral ceilings, large picture windows, two bathrooms per bedroom, a patio or deck with mountain views, and a good variety of amenities. Resort guests receive reduced green fees, preferred tee times, and a delicious breakfast as part of the golf package.

Teton Pines guest suites

green. It is rated the toughest hole at Teton Pines. An almost equally severe test is posed by the long par-four 15th: Here, thick rough and a giant bunker to the right narrows the fairway as it bends gently to the left, while the green is set beyond a pond favored by white pelicans and trumpeter swans. Forced carries over water are required at three of the four one-shotters (holes 8, 12, and 16). A wooden bridge leads to the green at each watery par three.

There's a hidden extra at Teton Pines: Because this corner of Wyoming is located at the extreme western edge of the Mountain Time zone, it stays light until 10 p.m. during the summer months. The soaring flanks of the mountains take on an ethereal glow at sunset, a fact not lost on players who secure afternoon tee times in order to see moose, elk, deer, coyotes, and other creatures that wander by after hours.

More Golf/Jackson Hole

Jackson Hole Golf & Tennis Club, a stellar 7,168-yard layout reworked by Robert Trent Jones Sr. and Jr. in 1967, is bisected by the Gros Ventre River and is marked by tall cottonwoods, elevated greens, great par fives, and water in play at 11 holes. Outstanding views of the Tetons are available from every hole on this well-groomed public course, which has hosted the U.S. Public Links Championship (Men's in 1988, Women's in 1993).

SIDETRIPS

There's world-class fly fishing for cutthroat, rainbow, and brown trout in the Snake River, which runs the entire length of the 50-mile-long Jackson Hole valley. For excellent instruction and guide service, contact the *Jack Dennis Outdoor Shop* at Teton Pines. River rafting on the Snake is popular, as is canoeing and windsurfing on the valley's lakes.

In addition to over 200 miles of hiking trails, ultrascenic roads offer

American elk at Yellowstone National Park

splendid views of the highest peaks within Grand Teton National Park: *Rockefeller Parkway* traces the east side of Jackson Lake and the Snake River; *Signal Mountain Road* serves up a top-of-the-world view of the mountains.

Two hours north of Jackson is *Yellowstone National Park,* which covers 2.2 million acres. The park's Grand Loop Road leads to most of the major attractions, including Yellowstone's icon, the Old Faithful geyser.

Sunset at Oxbow Bend, Grand Teton National Park

Idaho

Your own private Idaho? Look no further than Coeur d'Alene in north Idaho, 35 miles east of Spokane, Washington. In addition to giant aromatic cedars and thickets of wild huckleberries, there is no greater concentration of lakes in a Western state than the heavily forested panhandle of Idaho. Lake Coeur d'Alene, cited by National Geographic in 1993 as "one of the five most beautiful lakes in the world," is home to a thriving population of bald eagles and ospreys. It's also home to the Coeur d'Alene Resort, a full-service getaway with a golf course that showcases its watery setting like no other layout in the nation.

For starters, the golf routine at **Coeur d'Alene Resort Golf Course** (#55) is totally unique. Players hop aboard one of two custom-designed mahogany speedboats (Eagle and Double Eagle) to be whisked across the lake to the resort's immaculately groomed course. After warming up at the lakeside practice tee, where floating balls are hit to floating targets, uniformed forecaddies armed with hand-held laser guns that are used to measure distances to the pin direct players to the first tee. Ample amounts of local knowledge and encouragement are provided during the round. A pleasurable outing is virtually assured by the extra-friendly staff.

There are many fine holes on this 6,309-yard, par-71 course layout created by Scott Miller, a former Jack Nicklaus design associate. The layout, covered in a smooth carpet of bentgrass from tee to green, is a multitheme spread with several holes carved from a thickly wooded ridge, others cut from classic parkland-style terrain, a few with Fernan Creek in play (resort

SIDETRIPS

Strollers can make a two-mile loop around the Tubbs Hill nature trail adjacent to the resort. Just outside Coeur d'Alene is Silverwood Amusement Park, which features daily live entertainment and over 24 rides.

Forty miles south of town are the garnet-rich grounds of Emerald Creek. Visitors can secure a permit and dig for star garnets from May through September. The deep purple gems are found only here and in India.

Driving east on I-90 from the resort is the Silver Valley, the largest silver-mining region in the world. For a step back in time, check out Wallace—the entire town is listed on the National Register of Historic Places. Just outside Kellogg, another old silver mining town, sightseers can ride the world's longest single-stage gondola 3,400 vertical feet to the top of Silver Mountain, where hiking and mountain biking are available.

owners transformed the silt-laden stream into a thriving trout habitat), and three holes set along the shores of the lake.

But there is one hole at Coeur d'Alene that transcends mere signature hole status, a one-of-a-kind one-shotter that is every bit as famous (at least among golfers) as the state's potatoes. This is the par-three 14th, which sports the world's first and only floating, moveable green. The 15,000-square-foot green, resting on 104 blocks of Expanded Polystyrene (EPS) encased in concrete and covered by a liner and topsoil, is heavy-duty: It's 10 feet deep (five feet are below the water) and weighs nearly five million pounds (that's 2,500 tons). A computerized cable system enables the timber-faced target to be anchored in the lake anywhere from 100 to 175 yards from the tee. To keep the challenge fresh, the green is repositioned daily.

In addition to the putting surface, the island also contains a pair of sand traps, beds of red geraniums, and five small trees. A ferry shuttles golfers from tee to green. The ferryboat's skipper tends the pin, rakes the bunkers, records the scores, and will even snap your picture for posterity. Golfers who birdie, par, or bogey the hole receive a gold-leaf Certificate of Achievement. Make an ace? The resort staff literally rolls out a

Coeur d'Alene Resort Golf Course, Coeur d' Alene, Idaho, 11th hole

Coeur d' Alene Resort clubhouse, 14th hole

Cruising boat and floating green at Coeur d' Alene

Floating green at Coeur d' Alene

red carpet and presents an engraved trophy to those who score a hole-in-one at the 14th. The tee shot, by the way, is none too intimidating even at full stretch, because the target area is twice the size of a normal island green. Take the pro shop's advice: Use a new ball on the 14th tee to instill confidence.

The floating island green at the 14th tends to steal the limelight from one that is a marvelous test of golf, generously landscaped and meticulously manicured. To avoid interference with play, course maintenance is performed at night by a roving band of perfectionists who drive mowers equipped with specially designed lights. Ball washers and trash receptacles are attached to the golf carts so that they don't clutter the landscape.

LODGING

The Coeur d'Alene Resort offers 337 lakeside rooms and condos, including 173 oversize minisuites in the 18-story Lake Tower that are among the most thoughtfully conceived hotel accommodations ever devised. Twenty-five rooms have fireplaces and most have balconies with fabulous views of the lake.

The resort's 3,300-foot floating boardwalk—the world's longest—provides access to waterfront restaurants as well as a marina where scenic cruises aboard the Mish-an-Nock and other vessels can be arranged. (The boats swing by the floating green at the 14th.) Sailboats, canoes, and fishing charters are also available. The *Coeur d'Alene Plaza*, accessed via a glass skybridge, offers 50 shops, cafés, and lounges. There's also a full service spa at the resort.

DINING

Beverly's, located atop the resort's Lake Tower, would be a multistarred gourmet mecca in any major city. There's a well-varied Northwest menu with wines to match, and the lake and mountain views from the dining room are spectacular.

If you liked the floating green at Coeur d'Alene's 14th, check out *Cedars Floating Restaurant*, a shipshape dining room. For the juiciest burgers in north Idaho, head for *Hudson's Hamburgers*, which has been serving this distinctly American specialty since 1907.

Beverly's Restaurant

If flawless conditions rank high on your list, Coeur d'Alene is a must-play. The golf course gives the impression of a groomed, spotless lakeside park.

There are longer, more challenging courses on the "Top 100" list than the Coeur d'Alene Resort Golf Course. There are even a few that can match its exceptional scenery. But none deliver as much pure golfing pleasure as this one.

More Golf/Coeur d'Alene

There are two public courses of note near the resort. The *Highlands Golf & Country Club* in Post Falls is a pleasant 6,369-yard spread with plenty of water in play. Fifteen miles north of Coeur d'Alene is *Twin Lakes Village Golf Course,* a mature 6,277-yard layout with a strong back nine.

Washington

The Northwest's best new muni? It's the **Olympic Course** at **Gold Mountain** (#82) on the Kitsap Peninsula, which is located in Bremerton, an hour's drive around Puget Sound from Seattle. Because the city's original layout, renamed the Cascade Course, was forced to turn away over 40,000 players a year—demand for golf has outstripped supply in this corner of the country—the city decided to build a second course of championship caliber on prime watershed property free of housing.

Tacoma native John Harbottle, who understudied Pete Dye early in his career and who considers the Olympic Course his finest solo effort, adapted old-style architecture to the undulating terrain to provide strategic interest. As in olden days, skilled shotmaking and wily thinking are required in return for par. The subtly contoured greens are set at various angles, forcing players chasing birdies to hit draws and fades to reach the pin. Several greens on the Olympic Course are set up for airborne approaches; others invite a running shot. Also, the routing constantly changes direction, bringing the prevailing westerlies into play at different angles. From the championship markers at 7,003 yards, better players need brains and brawn to succeed. Average players can have a great time from the white tees at 6,003 yards.

Harbottle worked hard to create risk-reward scenarios, massaging the site's hills and valleys to yield a course with a fascinating array of holes. For example, no two par fours are remotely alike. Ironically, one of the best holes, the second, was originally intended to be a par four but was converted during construction. Now a short uphill par five stretching to 521 yards, the second confronts players with a huge cross bunker that bites off half the fairway 90 yards short of the raised green. This bunker can deceive players into thinking the green is closer than it really is.

Olympic Course at Gold Mountain, Bremerton, Washington, second hole

Olympic Course at Gold Mountain, seventh hole

Many Seattle-area golfers believe the collection of par threes at the Olympic Course is second only to the par threes at Pebble Beach. A case could be made. Each of the one-shotters varies in length and heads to a different point of the compass, bringing the wind into play at a different angle. Slopes and swales, water and sand defend these greens. A signature par three? The 188-yard seventh plunges downhill across water to a wide, shallow green indented in front by a pot bunker and backdropped to the left by tall evergreens.

The Olympic Course reaches a crescendo at the 621-yard 18th, a monstrous three-shotter that doglegs from left to right, its generous landing area protected to the right by a sea of broom and by what Harbottle calls a "grass dungeon" on the left. The final shot is played downhill to a narrow green framed by water, fescues, bunkers, and firs dotting the amphitheater-like bowl behind the green. The setting is custom-made for the viewing of a championship.

When the Olympic Course at Gold Mountain opened in 1996, Larry Gilhuly, western director of the USGA, commented that the "City of Bremerton has one of the best municipal golf courses . . . that we have viewed in the past decade of visits to golf courses in the western U.S." High praise for a course that listed a $31 weekday green fee at press time.

More Golf/Bremerton Area

The Olympic Course has grabbed the spotlight at Gold Mountain, but the facility's original *Cascade Course* is an appealing parkland-style test

In Port Orchard, there's *Tweten's Lighthouse,* a waterside steak-and-fish house. Salmon and halibut are the entrees of choice. The *Yacht Club Broiler* in nearby Silverdale can also be recommended.

marked by speedy, saucer-shaped greens.

A few miles east of the Gold Mountain complex in Port Orchard is *McCormick Woods,* a beautifully conditioned course marked by big greens and no adjoining holes. The 7,040-yard layout occupies a former Christmas tree farm. Wildlife ranges from bald eagles to black bear.

North of Port Orchard, across the Hood Canal on the Olympic Peninsula, is *Port Ludlow,* its original 18 (the Tide and Timber nines) comprising one of the most delightful resort layouts in the Northwest, with rolling fairways routed through old-growth cedars and giant rhododendrons. Regrettably, the newer Trail nine is too severe for most players.

New & Noteworthy/Seattle Area

The region's brightest newcomer is *Trophy Lake* in Port Orchard, a John Fought–designed course with a "fishing club" theme scheduled to open in summer 1999. Unlike many of the Northwest's narrow, tree-lined courses, Trophy Lake will feature roomy fairways and over 100 flashed-face bunkers.

LODGING

Silverdale on the Bay Resort Hotel, located 15 minutes from the Gold Mountain Golf Complex, offers pleasant accommodations. Scheduled to open in late 1999 is a full-service resort and conference center at *McCormick Woods* in nearby Port Orchard. There's also a well-run *Holiday Inn* in Port Orchard.

The area's most anticipated new development is *The Golf Club at Newcastle,* a 36-hole complex set on the flanks of West Cougar Mountain, nearly 1,000 feet above Seattle. Newcastle's two Bob Cupp–designed courses offer stellar views of Puget Sound, Lake Washington, the Olympic and Cascade Mountains, and the downtown skyline. *Coal Creek* (the club rests on a former coal mine) opened in spring 1999. *China Creek* is scheduled to open in 2000.

Olympic Course at Gold Mountain, ninth hole

Oregon

The scorecard at **Sandpines** (#72) in Florence is subtitled "Golf on the Oregon Dunes," certainly a tantalizing prospect. Sand dunes are every designer's favorite medium. Sand is easy to sculpt and provides an excellent base for turfgrass. But the sand dunes available for golf are rare. According to designer Rees Jones: "You get an opportunity to design a property like Sandpines only a few times in a lifetime. Just driving up the road and seeing the native grasses and dunes hit me immediately. I felt like I could design a course like they might have had 400 years ago."

Situated near the mouth of the Siuslaw River a few miles south of the Sea Lion Caves and 60 miles west of Eugene, the sprawling 6,954-yard links, which debuted in 1993, exhibits great variety. Seven holes on the front nine wander through a pine forest; the remainder play over and through rolling, bearded dunes. The larger sand hills create an amphitheater effect, much like the famous links courses routed at the base of towering dunes in England (Royal Birkdale), Ireland (Ballybunion), and Scotland (Cruden Bay). Water insinuates itself at six holes (including 16, 17, and 18, each of which wraps around an irrigation pond), but the tone of play is set by onshore coastal winds that pick up steam as the day progresses.

Mindful that not everyone can tee off before noon to avoid the brisk ocean breezes that routinely sweep the links, Jones designed holes with generous landing areas mounded on both sides. These minimize the penalty for slightly errant shots. He also installed relatively flat, open-faced greens. The sand base of the acreage (up to 120 feet in places) ensures excellent drainage in the wettest of conditions.

Among the better holes at Sandpines, built as a centerpiece for a future residential community, is the sixth, a strong 426-yard par four that swings uphill to the right to a perched green defended by sand and grass bunkers. The ninth, a long, straightaway par four protected to the left and right by pine trees, calls for an unerring approach to an oblong green guarded by bunkers left, right, and behind—but not in front. The par-five

18th at Sandpines, only 501 yards from the tips, is an excellent risk-reward hole with water in play up the entire left side. The fairway bottlenecks and swings sharply to the left, away from an imposing dune, as it nears the large, gently rolling green. Players attempting to reach the green in two must flirt with disaster to get home, although it can be done when the hole plays downwind. It's a pleasant three-shot hole for those who can blaze a path up the right side, away from the water.

More Golf/Florence

It's not long at 6,018 yards (par 71), but *Ocean Dunes Golf Links* in Florence, carved from giant sand dunes anchored by rhododendrons, Scotch broom, and shore pines, is an intimate, quirky spread with lots of character. Locals are happy to point the way on blind shots. It's a fun walking course.

Sandpines, Florence, Oregon, 16th, 17th, and 18th holes

Bandon Dunes: The Best Natural Golf Course of the 1990s?

A few years ago, a theory was expounded that all the premier sites available for golf in the United States had been taken. That theory was put to rest with the opening in May 1999, of *Bandon Dunes,* an ambitious 2,000-acre development on the southern Oregon coast, 100 miles north of the California state line. Perched on headlands 100 feet above the crashing Pacific, the first of three proposed courses will likely be chronicled as one of the great public-access success stories of the 1990s.

Chicago-based Mike Keiser, an avid golfer who made his fortune in recycled greeting cards, entrusted the design of the first course at Bandon Dunes to an unknown 29-year-old Scot, David McLay Kidd, who is listed as lead designer for Gleneagles Golf Developments, a Scottish firm. While Kidd had only a few solo design credits on his résumé (and none in the U.S.), what he did have is an intimate knowledge of exactly what comprises an authentic links. That knowledge, along with his brogue, landed him the most enviable commission imaginable.

The land, probably the finest made available for a golf course in America since Alister Mackenzie (another Scot) was shown the site for the Cypress Point Club on the Monterey Peninsula, is a sea of tumbling dunes anchored by sturdy gorse and other seaside vegetation. Some of these wind-tossed dunes are 40 feet high. Interspersed among them are knoblike hummocks, wind-twisted pines, and scalloped craters. Far below is a tawny beach strewn with driftwood. Migrating gray whales occasionally spout offshore.

Bandon Dunes, sixth hole

Bald eagles and ospreys sail overhead. Looking south from the cliffside holes is the town of Bandon, its sea stacks and monoliths rising like chess pieces from the roiling sea. Punctuating a broad sweep of coast 15 miles north is the Cape Arago Lighthouse. The breeze on the links is generally steady but not overwhelming. And while the Oregon coast is notoriously foggy, the sun seems to shine most of the time at Bandon Dunes. Seven holes on the links parallel the coast; all 18 have a view of the Pacific.

Handed a ¾-mile stretch of headlands high above the sea, Kidd set about "finding" the course in the field, identifying holes as he went along. Moving very little sand or soil, Kidd and his band of shapers accentuated existing features and softened a few of the site's bigger rolls to shoehorn the holes into the terrain. "Basic Scottish cultural practices" were used in the construction of the course. No soil amendments, for example, were made to the enormous greens, which were built atop clean beach sand. The layout's chief merits are its naturalness and individuality: Not only are no two holes alike, no hole conspicuously resembles any from a famous links abroad.

A clubhouse with 21 guest rooms is scheduled to open concurrent with the golf course. In addition, four 12-room cottages are expected to open by fall 1999, with accommodations for 123 golfers on site. According to general manager Josh Lesnik, Bandon Dunes is designed for walkers only (caddies are available), with just a few carts available for disabled players.

LODGING

In Florence, *Driftwood Shores Resort & Conference Center* is a popular, midpriced property fronting a 10-mile stretch of uninterrupted beach. Each room has a private balcony with a view of the Pacific. Golf packages are available.

Portland

Oregonians like to say that the Golden Age of golf course architecture was officially revived at **Pumpkin Ridge Golf Club**, a 36-hole complex located 20 miles west of Portland. On a well-treed site with generous elevation changes are a pair of exceptional courses that turn back the clock to the 1920s: Witch Hollow, a private club that hosted the match-play portion of the U.S. Amateur in 1996 (captured by Tiger Woods) as well as the 1997 U.S. Women's Open; and **Ghost Creek** (#13), its public-access sister. Both courses were designed by Bob Cupp, a former senior designer for Jack Nicklaus, with input from Portland native John Fought, a U.S. Amateur champion who played the PGA Tour in the early 1980s. Both

Pumpkin Ridge Golf Club, Cornelius, Oregon, Ghost Creek Course, tenth hole

courses are enchanting, but if truth be told, the public may have gotten the better half of the bargain at Pumpkin Ridge.

With no jagged edges, conspicuous mounds, or topsy-turvy greens, Ghost Creek was one of the first courses of the 1990s to signal a return to classic, traditional designs. Tees are of the old-fashioned rectangular variety. Each seemingly spacious fairway has a prime landing area. Subtly contoured greens range in size from tiny to enormous, depending upon the type of shot they're designed to receive. It's all very well thought out, and it looks as if it's been there for 80 years. It's that classic. And that well conditioned. The bentgrass tees, greens, and fairways are manicured to perfection. (Not for nothing are many of the nation's top grass seed and turfgrass farms located in the Portland area.)

Routed on rolling, fertile farmland where the Willamette Valley meets the foothills of the Tualatin Mountains, Ghost Creek rambles through a mixed stand of Douglas firs, maples, and oaks, with water or sand in play at nearly every turn. The routing is intimate, and most of the holes are closely grouped, yet there is no feeling that the holes are crowded together. (The three Portland businessmen behind Pumpkin Ridge originally wanted an 18-hole course on the 350-acre site. Cupp convinced them that a 36-hole spread could be artfully woven through the meadows, wetlands, and forest.)

The prettiest holes at Ghost Creek are the five par threes, four of which play downhill, though the risk-reward par fives are exceptional. Other adjectives apply to the 469-yard ninth (water on the left) and 454-yard 18th (water on the right). You may linger, but you won't last at Ghost Creek with only one shot pattern. Skillful shotmakers find their reward here because, according to Cupp, "the more chances you take and the closer you flirt with danger off the tee, the better your angle of approach to the green." Only a complete golfer in total command of his game can erase the fine line between bold and prudent play at Ghost Creek.

By popular consensus, Ghost Creek's par-36 front nine (3,640 yards from the championship tees) is ranked the toughest stretch of golf at Pumpkin Ridge. For good reason. The majority of the par fours are long and fraught with danger, while the single par four under 400 yards from the tips, the 371-yard sixth, has all the charm of a boa constrictor. Here Ghost Creek, a man-made rill pumped to the top of the course from an irrigation lake, snakes down the right side of the hole, with out of bounds far to the right. The fairway, protected to the left by wetlands and a series of bunkers, angles gently left to a skewed green, where a nooselike effect is created by the creek and a deep bunker inset with a grass island. The hole is short, but the consequences are dire for a misplayed approach shot. The ninth, one of the most demanding two-shotters in the state, calls for a long, accurate drive that avoids Ghost Creek to the right and out of bounds to the left. The approach, played to a green that hugs a small lake, must be perfect if you're planning to make par, although there is room to bail out to the right. In the summer months, the prevailing northwest breeze is in a player's face at the ninth, further enhancing the challenge.

Pumpkin Ridge Golf Club, Ghost Creek Course, 16th hole

Pumpkin Ridge Golf Club, Ghost Creek Course, 17th hole

The par-35 back nine, while shorter, is every bit as beguiling as the front, with meandering Ghost Creek providing numerous risk-reward scenarios, notably at the 17th, a potentially driveable par four where the creek trickles across the fairway 90 yards short of the green. Most players lay up short of the brook to set up a short-iron shot to a bi-level green flanked by sand to the left and a rock-rimmed pool of water to the right.

Walking is encouraged at Ghost Creek. Indeed, 90 percent of the players walk the layout. And because golf carts must stay on the paths at all times of year (Pumpkin Ridge gets less rain than Portland, but it's still more moist than dry), walking is the only way to experience this eminently fair but very testing layout. In 1998, Pumpkin Ridge introduced a caddie program (available on a seasonal basis) that affords golfers the ultimate pleasure: Striding the fairways of a classic championship spread in the company of a knowledgeable looper.

LODGING

A short drive from Pumpkin Ridge is the *Marriott Residence Inn* in Hillsboro, which offers comfortable, spacious accommodations. It's where competitors and USGA officials stay when a championship comes to town.

SIDETRIPS

Among Portland's must-sees is *Washington Park,* a gorgeous spot in the city's west hills renowned for its *International Rose Test Garden* (established in 1914, it has more than 400 varieties of blooms); and the 6.5-acre *Japanese Garden* (teahouse, pavilion), reputed to be the most authentic of its kind outside Japan.

Also worth a visit is the *Portland Saturday Market* in the *Old Town District* (March through December), a lively food, arts, and crafts fair featuring 300 merchants and live entertainment.

More Golf/Portland & Environs

The city's top municipal venue is the *Great Blue Course* at *Heron Lakes,* site of the U.S. Amateur Public Links Championship in 2000. Designed by Robert Trent Jones, Jr., this well-conditioned layout, with its numerous water hazards, plentiful bunkers, and speedy greens is not for the faint of heart. A second layout at Heron Lakes, the *Greenback Course,* is more user-friendly.

Portland is the self-proclaimed microbrewery capital of America, with dozens of boutique breweries and affiliated pubs sprinkled throughout the city and its environs. Convenient to Pumpkin Ridge and The Reserve is *McMenamins Cornelius Pass Roadhouse Pub & Brewery,* which occupies a three-story farmhouse dating to 1866. Excellent pub fare (burgers, jambalaya) as well as 17 to 20 beers and ales are available, most of them brewed on premises and all served on draft. The three most popular brews are Hammerhead (a hoppy pale ale), Ruby (light and fruity raspberry-flavored ale), and Terminator (a stout so rich "you could float a horseshoe in it," according to management). The atmosphere is fun and festive.

Portland's most classic test is *Eastmoreland,* a rolling, wooded course laid out in 1921 by H. Chandler Egan (who had a hand in the design of Pebble Beach). The 6,529-yard layout, updated in 1995, skirts Crystal Springs Lake, the city's Rhododendron Test Garden, and Johnson Creek.

The *Reserve Vineyards & Golf Club,* a 36-hole complex 20 miles west of the city, has a chateau-style clubhouse where private label wines can be sampled—and a pair of courses that stand in marked contrast to each other. The *Fought Course,* a John Fought design opened in 1997, emulates a traditional parkland-style look, with more than 130 bunkers sprinkling the site. The *Cupp Course,* laid out by Bob Cupp and debuted in 1998, is marked by complex landforms, spill-off greens, and only 20 bunkers. At press time, The Reserve rotated its two courses every 15 days between members and the public.

In Aurora, 20 miles south of Portland, is *Langdon Farms,* a former seed and sod operation where the wooden superstructure of an old barn serves as the front gate. A sign overhead reads, "Public Only." The course, by John Fought, is a links-style test marked by crowned greens and a large berm built to shield players from traffic noise on I-5, a major highway. A big red barn serves as the clubhouse.

Bend

It is not known where Tiger Woods celebrated his U.S. Amateur victory at Pumpkin Ridge in 1996, but he might have considered a busman's outing on **Crosswater** (#15) at **Sunriver Resort**, 15 miles south of Bend and about a three-hour drive from Portland. Even Tiger, king of the bombers, could have let out the shaft from the tips on this behemoth, a Bob Cupp–John Fought design that stretches to an ungodly 7,683 yards from the gold tees, its course rating (76.7) and slope (150) among the highest in the Northwest. Opened in 1995, Crosswater is not only a 21st-century golf course, it's environmentally sensitive, too. Which means you can jump into a revitalized trout stream after you've torn out your hair trying to figure how to hopscotch your ball safely from one landing area to the next.

Located on the eastern flank of the Cascade Range and framed by distant volcanic peaks, including the snow-frosted cone of 9,060-foot-high Mount Bachelor, Crosswater, inspired by Scotland's grand heathland courses, occupies a high desert plateau. The majority of the holes are traced or crossed by the oxbow loops of the Deschutes and Little Deschutes rivers. In addition to a smattering of ponderosa and lodge pole pines, this sprawling layout is framed by alpine meadows and wetlands. The color and texture of plant life in these preserved areas changes with the seasons: lavender irises in June, purple lupines in July, khaki fescues in August, golden willows in the fall.

"The site for Crosswater is one of the most magnificent I have ever seen," said Cupp, noting that the original plan called for 36 holes on the 600-acre site before the current owners, Lowe Enterprises, decided to build a championship-caliber 18 with a low-density development at its perimeter. A semiprivate club, Crosswater is open to Sunriver Resort guests.

Forward tees give average players a fighting chance, but Crosswater challenges expert golfers to a heated scuffle at nearly every hole. Even from the white tees at 6,185 yards, several forced carries over river branches and soggy meadows are called for. From the back tees (7,273

Sunriver Resort, Sunriver, Oregon, Crosswater Course, ninth hole

Sunriver Resort, Crosswater Course, 12th hole

yards from the silver markers, 6,811 yards from the blues—no one plays the golds), no fewer than 16 carries over water are required from both tee and fairway. Fussy low-handicappers will be pleased, however, by the layout's superb playing conditions: Crosswater was the first course in central Oregon to sport bentgrass fairways. Also, cleverly routed boardwalk-style wood pilings and beamed bridges span ponds and wetlands, bringing golfers close to the elk and otters, eagles and osprey that live here. (Crosswater is enrolled in the Audubon International Cooperative Sanctuary program.)

Crosswater gets off to a reasonable start, but the game is on at the fourth, a relatively short par four that bends to the left around an open meadow near the Little Deschutes River. The ideal drive flirts with a series of bunkers dotting the left rough. The perched green is surrounded on three sides by wetlands. It gets better. The fifth, a lengthy par four, is the kind of hole that would give U.S. Open contestants the willies. The tee shot must soar over a bend in the river, while the lengthy approach must carry a horseshoe of wetlands and sit quickly on a diagonal green

divided by a long ridge. It is followed by the toughest hole on the course, a double-dogleg par five with a two-tiered fairway that demands a pair of forced carries over water and marshland. Fraught with danger, it stretches to more than 600 yards from the gold and silver tees. By the time players reach the enormous 17,000-square-foot dance floor on the par-four ninth, they may be in need of oxygen and a massage.

Crosswater's back nine is more of the same. Flowing river, verdant wetlands, looming peaks. And tons of challenge. At the par-five 12th, listed at 687 yards from the tips (it's 572 yards from the white tees!), a 22-acre lake engulfs the entire left side of the hole, with Mount Bachelor peaking above the pines at the far end of the hole. Clever fairway bunkering and a grouping of lakeside pines imperil the second shot, while water and sand defend the minuscule green. Because the hole generally plays into the prevailing wind, six is a good score for most on the 12th.

Like all great courses, Crosswater's 18th, a sturdy par four, brilliantly summarizes all that has gone before. After steering clear of the lone bunker up the right side of the fairway, players must reach deep one last

237

Sunriver Resort, Crosswater Course, 18th hole

time to produce a full-blooded approach shot that carries over the Little Deschutes and comes to rest on a long, angled green backdropped by tall pines. Elation? Weariness? It depends on how you play. It's no surprise that Crosswater has become a cult course for advanced players seeking to plumb the depths (so to speak) of their ability.

After the round, players can repair to a handsome clubhouse overlooking the ninth and 18th greens. Patterned after the region's classic timber lodges (stone base, cedar siding, peeled pine logs, slate roof), the low-rise clubhouse fits its riverside setting beautifully. Inside, distressed hardwood floors lead from a boutique-size golf shop to The Grille, which serves superb Northwest cuisine, notably game dishes cooked on a wood-burning grill. Outside, airy terraces and porches are set with rocking chairs. Relaxation, it seems, is what most golfers yearn for after repeated river crossings on Crosswater.

More Golf/Bend

In the blink of an eye, more than 20 public-access layouts have sprung up in and around Bend, gateway to central Oregon. Courses range from high-desert links at 4,500 feet, their fairways framed by lava rock outcrops, twisted junipers, and peppery sagebrush, to parkland-style layouts

DINING

In the Cascadian-style Sunriver Lodge is the window-walled *Meadows* restaurant (try seared razor clams and eggs for breakfast, pan-seared salmon with rosemary pinot gris beurre blanc for dinner). For casual dining, the *Owl's Nest Pub,* with a huge hand-split ponderosa pine serving as the bar, has light fare, regional wines by the glass, and top Pacific Northwest microbrews on tap. There's also live entertainment on selected evenings.

Bend's oldest restaurant, the *Pine Tavern,* has 200-year-old ponderosa pines growing in the middle of the dining room. The steaks are choice. Other top choices include *Rosette,* a superb dining room featuring Northwest cuisine with an Oriental twist. Also noteworthy is the *Broken Top Club,* a private golf community where the mountain views from the tables of the club's restaurant are a match for the meals.

Central Oregon's microbreweries are among the nation's best. If you're serious about the suds, drop by the *Deschutes Brewery* in Bend, which offers superb handcrafted ales (try the Bachelor Bitter) and casual dining.

Sunriver Lodge

Accommodations at Sunriver Resort include 211 guest rooms, suites, and chalets in the Lodge Village complex, most of which feature golf course or mountain views, cathedral ceilings, stone fireplaces, decks, and rustic chairs made from tree boughs. The resort also has a rental pool of over 200 private homes and condos.

Sunriver Lodge

stretched across broad meadows or shaded by mighty ponderosa pines. Sunshine is abundant in this semiarid zone—10,000-foot peaks in the Cascades screen the rain. Crosswater commands a premium green fee, but most of the region's venues are priced well below the national average. Walkers are welcome at all courses. The season runs from May to October.

Sunriver Resort (Woodlands). Designed by Robert Trent Jones, Jr., this mature layout occupies an arid plain framed by lava rock, seven lakes, tall pines, and sagebrush, with nice views of Mount Bachelor. Slicers beware—most of the water is on the right side of the course. The par-four 18th, a hairpin dogleg with a lake in its bend and water beside the green, is a doozy.

Sunriver Resort (Meadows). The resort's original course, previously a dull, flat affair that played along meadows and through pine groves, was completely reworked by John Fought. Reopened in spring 1999, the course now has generously rolling fairways, a clever bunkering scheme, enhanced water features, and receptive, gently undulating greens.

Black Butte Ranch (Big Meadow). This gorgeous layout, built by Robert Muir Graves, is set in a glacier-carved valley with stirring views of the Cascades. The parkland-style front nine is routed around marshes, ponds, and pines; the hillier back nine plays to a towering rocky crag known as Black Butte.

Widgi Creek. Formerly Pine Meadows Country Club, Widgi Creek is now a well-maintained, semiprivate course set in beautiful woodlands on the road to Mount Bachelor. Designed by Robert Muir Graves, the 6,879-yard layout has several ponds, giant pines, and a deep ravine to keep things interesting. The smooth, multilevel greens are among the region's best.

OFF-COURSE ACTIVITIES

When it comes to high-quality recreation, Bend outshines them all. Tackle white-water rapids in the upper *Deschutes River,* windsurf in *Elk Lake,* fish for landlocked salmon in backcountry lakes (fly fishermen can angle for trout in the world-class *Metolius River),* ride a bike (or a horse) along a scenic riverside path, or take a canoe, raft, or kayak down a gentle stretch of the Deschutes River. For a few weeks in May, it's possible to go downhill or cross-country skiing in the morning at Mount Bachelor—and play golf in the afternoon! Fans of extinct volcanoes can visit *Lava Lands Visitor Center* (interpretive displays, slide presentations). Sightseers can drive to the top of *Lava Butte* for a fabulous view of the Cascades. Live animal presentations at the *High Desert Museum* feature river otter, porcupine, and birds of prey. For a fascinating all-day expedition, *Crater Lake National Park,* the deep blue remnant of an ancient volcano that exploded thousands of years ago, is located 100 miles south of Bend.

Crater Lake

California

Pebble Beach Golf Links • Spyglass Hill Golf Course • The Links at Spanish Bay

Pasatiempo Golf Club • La Purisima Golf Course • Pelican Hill Golf Club, Ocean South Course

Pelican Hill Golf Club, Ocean North Course • Four Seasons Resort Aviara Golf Club

Torrey Pines, South Course • PGA West, TPC Stadium Course

La Quinta Resort & Club, Mountain Course

Four Seasons Resort Aviara Golf Club, Carlsbad, tenth hole

California

California, a vast and diverse land, has 11 courses on the "Top 100" roster, more than any other state. Also, with deference to the many wonderful golf getaways sprinkled around the nation, it must be said straightaway: The Monterey Peninsula, specifically the troika of Pebble Beach, Spyglass Hill, and Spanish Bay, comprise the most alluring and coveted golf destination in America. The golf courses are as varied as they are legendary. Pebble Beach offers vast open spaces, clifftop thrills, and the game's best finish. Spyglass Hill is a cutthroat carved from iceplant and pines, while the facsimile dunes at Spanish Bay resemble those created eons ago by an ancient sea. It is every golfer's dream to go, at least once.

Moving south from Monterey, several "Top 100" courses are found on or near the Pacific coast, ranging from the fabulous 36-hole spread at Pelican Hill in Newport Coast to Torrey Pines outside San Diego, the state's top-rated municipal facility. In the Mojave Desert, 100 miles east from Los Angeles, is greater Palm Springs, an expanding golf mecca walled in by steep, stony mountains. Here visitors, 40 percent of whom play golf, are rewarded by 320 days of sunshine, boulevards named for celebrities, and two of Pete Dye's dandiest creations—the murderous TPC Stadium Course at PGA West and the stylish Mountain Course at La Quinta.

Monterey Bay area

Monterey Peninsula/Crown Jewel of American Golf

Pebble. You don't even need the Beach. Just Pebble. Because every golfer in America knows this links on a first-name basis.

There are two types of golfers in the world. Those who've been to Pebble and can't wait to return; and those who haven't and desperately want to go. Because, despite the outrageous cost to play (at press time, $305 for outside players), **Pebble Beach Golf Links** (#1) is, unquestionably, the nation's single finest golf experience. You don't think all those movie stars and corporate chieftains would endure the chill and fog and rain at the AT&T Pebble Beach National Pro-Am every winter to play any old public-access course, do you? When a sampling of *GOLF Magazine's* readers were asked a fantasy question— "Where would you go if you won a free trip to any golf resort in America?"—their overwhelming first choice was the burnished jewel of the Monterey Peninsula, itself the nation's most exalted chunk of wave-battered rock.

You say three bills is too much to pay for a single round of golf? The golf shop staff will gladly point out that a round at Pebble costs no more than a pair of the best seats at the opera or a box seat at a World Series game. We're talking a once-in-a-lifetime tour of the Creator's backyard that is beyond the ken of television, photographs, even written descriptions. In the early 1990s, ad copy for the fabled links ran as follows: "Obtain World Peace . . . Achieve Total Consciousness . . . Win a Pulitzer Prize . . . Pilot the Space Shuttle . . . Play Pebble Beach . . . Fortunately, some of life's aspirations are more attainable than others." Yes, the price is hefty. But then, a round of golf at Pebble is an epic event staged on the noblest firmament imaginable.

Amazingly, the Pebble Beach Company has not been content to rest on the mighty laurels of its highly prized links. The Mona Lisa has even been given a new dimple. There were a few cries of dissent at first, but when a parcel of land beyond the fourth green became available in 1997, the Pebble Beach Company paid $8.9 million for the property in order to secure the ideal site for a new par-three fifth hole to be perched on bluffs above Stillwater Cove. The previous fifth hole, a quirky, uphill affair, was the only one in a stretch from the fourth to the 10th that did not skirt the headlands or seashore. The reason? At the time Samuel F. B. Morse (the peninsula's farsighted developer) built the course, a private landowner demanded a king's ransom of $20,000 for the clifftop property. The year was 1916. Morse decided against purchasing the land and zigzagged the links away from the coast.

Jack Nicklaus, who has yet to amend his long-ago statement: "If I had only one more round of golf to play, I would choose to play at Pebble Beach," was the logical candidate to design a new hole for the old links.

Pebble Beach Golf Links, Pebble Beach, seventh hole

Pebble Beach Golf Links, ninth hole

was a rather dismal detour on a links of this magnitude—is remarkable. If Pebble had a weak link, it's been fixed. Fittingly, the log cabin that belonged to the holdout owner has been moved to the 10th hole to serve as a halfway house. "Mimi's Bar & Grill," it's called.

In addition to the new hole, a $5-million coastal restoration project designed to combat erosion caused by the relentless pounding of the sea at the ninth and 10th greens as well as the 17th and 18th holes was completed in 1999. "We took this vital action," said Paul Spengler, vice president of golf operations, "to preserve one of golf's most fabled courses from the natural forces of wind, surf, and rain. Ironically, it is the very breathtaking beauty of its positioning above the Pacific that has endangered its architectural integrity." The entire length of Pebble's heroic 18th, which runs along the water's edge a mere eight feet above the high tide mark, is now protected by a concrete sea wall capped with sandstone-colored blocks and buttressed by artificial rock indistinguishable from the real thing.

His 187-yard concoction (151 yards from the white tees), unveiled in late 1998, plays slightly downhill to a small, skewed green embraced by bunkers, with the shimmering waters of Stillwater Cove below to the right. The drama and continuity provided by this new hole—the old fifth The wall also swings behind cliffs near the 17th green. A new, enlarged tee box at 18, built atop a concrete bulkhead, changes the sightline of the hole slightly by placing players closer to the water. There's now added temptation for big hitters to bite off more of the ocean with their drives.

LODGING

The Lodge at Pebble Beach, which made its debut as the Del Monte Lodge in 1919, is a traditionalist's dream. Its 161 refurbished guest rooms and suites, most with working fireplaces (oak logs stacked daily), handsome dressing areas, and oversize baths, have garden, golf course, or ocean views. Casa Palmero Resort, a new lodging option with 24 luxurious cottages, as well as The Spa at Pebble Beach, scheduled to open in late 1999. The staff at The Lodge aims to please, and a service charge of $18.50 per room night relieves guests of the need to tip in any area of the hotel except the food and beverage outlets. (This gratuity policy is also in effect at The Inn at Spanish Bay, a sister property.) In addition to

the fabled links, to which guests receive preferred tee times and slightly discounted green fees ($275 at press time), The Lodge offers its own high-tech golf academy; the Beach & Tennis Club (12 courts, heated outdoor pool with sun deck, a patio with ravishing views of Stillwater Cove); and the nearby Equestrain Center (riders have access to 34 miles of paths within Del Monte Forest). Cycling is also popular. There's also an arcade of fine shops spaced around the practice putting green, including Pebble Beach Markets, purveyors of all the ingredients anyone could want for a gourmet picnic. But then, the experience of playing America's greatest links may be feast enough.

The Lodge at Pebble Beach from the 18th hole

DINING

Stillwater Bar & Grill, formerly the Cypress Room, is a lively restaurant with beautiful views of Pebble's 18th green and the ocean. Stillwater's offers an outstanding variety of imaginatively prepared seafood dishes as well as a raw bar. The wine selection, including reasonably priced bottles from several Monterey County wineries, is excellent. For more formal fare (and a lighter approach to French cuisine), there's Club XIX, which offers à la carte dining as well as prix fixe four-course meals. Outdoor dining is available on a wind-shielded brick patio warmed by fire-

Stillwater Bar & Grill

places. The Tap Room, every golfer's favorite 19th hole, is patterned after an English pub and features an eclectic collection of golf-related memorabilia along with the peninsula's best artichoke soup (and spiciest Bloody Mary). The Gallery, overlooking the first tee of the links, serves a hearty breakfast.

The Tap Room

Other changes for the better: Excess earth from the construction of an underground parking garage built on the left side of the par-five second hole was used to create a berm that effectively hides the access road that runs along the right side of the fairway. All 87 bunkers on the course have been excavated, equipped with new drainage, and filled with fresh sand. All tee surfaces, green collars, and approaches on the links have been sodded with a uniform stand of ryegrass. Whispered complaints about inferior conditions are no longer heard on this sparkling compound. Today, Pebble is a polished, purring Rolls-Royce circa 1919.

An icon among courses, the links was laid out by amateur champions Jack Neville and Douglas Grant. "It was all there in plain sight," Neville later said. "The big idea was to get in as many holes as possible along the bay. It took a little imagination, but not much. Nature had intended that it be nothing else." On this magnificent site, originally platted for a housing development (golfers everywhere are in Morse's debt, for it was he who pulled up the stakes), the two amateurs devised an elongated figure-8 routing that takes full advantage of the sweeping headlands. The

designers also built tiny greens, surrounding them with bunkers, troughs, mounds, and rough. No championship course in America has smaller, more elusive targets. The grand scale of the links tends to obscure these

Pebble Beach Golf Links, 17th hole

Pebble Beach Golf Links, 17th hole

Pebble Beach Golf Links, 18th hole

firm, canted, speedy little surfaces. Even from the collar, decent chips and pitches tend to trickle out of tap-in range. Out of long grass, forget it. Needless to say, putting these greens can be maddeningly difficult.

Pebble's highlight reel begins at the sixth, a 516-yard par five that surmounts a headland 60 feet above Stillwater Cove before veering right to an exposed green sited at land's end. The seventh, according to golf writer Cal Brown, "is a mischievous piece of work that can be attributed to either genius or blind luck, both of which are needed to play the hole." Measuring just over 100 yards, the hole drops from the elevated tee to a kidney-shaped green that commands its own rocky point and is staked out by six bunkers. The hole is a poem and a painting: Glistening light, smashing waves, briny spray. Wind, too. The shot can be anything from a short pitch to a punched four-iron, depending on the breeze. "You don't pick the club on seven," comments Glen Waggoner in *The Traveling Golfer.* "The wind does."

The eighth kicks off a stretch of holes that people cross oceans and continents to play. Previewing the course before the 1992 U.S. Open,

architect Tom Doak called the sequence from seven through 10 the "Cliffs of Doom." The ominous name stuck, although the mere sight of these holes, the finest in the sport, fills most pilgrims with joy and elation. From a sea-level tee, players at the eighth are asked to hit a blind drive up the face of a hill. The hole then swings to the right around a precipice, the linoleum-slick green beckoning on the far side of a rocky gorge. The surging sea and a sandy beach stand between golfer and target. Nicklaus has called it "the most dramatic second shot in golf." Legions agree.

The ninth, Pebble's longest par four at 464 yards, is truly world class. The broad, promenading fairway, gently listing to starboard, is easy enough to hit, but the long approach shot is usually played from a downhill, sidehill lie to a sunken green defended in front by a deep hollow and to the left by a cavernous bunker. Oblivion awaits to the right.

The par-four 10th, which prolongs the clifftop drama and brings players to the far end of the course, was lengthened by 20 yards in 1998 and now poses a firmer challenge. Because indentations in the jagged coast eat into the fairway, and because the 65-yard-long bunker guarding the left side of the landing area is quite penal, the drive at the 10th is daunting. "It's the scariest tee shot on the course," says Johnny Miller. While shorter than the ninth, the 10th fairway is more sharply inclined to the ocean, and its tiny green is perched closer to the bluffs than any other hole on the course.

The links turns inland at the 11th, but the view of the ocean looking back from the rising fairway—and from many of the interior holes—is mesmerizing. Before returning to the sea at the finish, Pebble makes an important stop at the par-five 14th, the number-one handicap hole. Yes, it's the toughest hole on the course, this without the threat of cliffs or sea. The drive is played to a very wide fairway that eventually sweeps past a picket row of OB stakes up the right and leads to an elevated, two-tier green tucked behind an imposing wall of sand. An enormous swale and an overhanging tree guard the green to the right. A true three-shotter, this hole calls for two cannon shots followed by the highest-flying, softest-landing approach shot you can hit.

The par-three 17th, one of the most feared one-shotters in the game, returns players to the brink of the Pacific. Looking left, players can spy the sixth fairway ascending a sheer bluff on the far side of Stillwater Cove. But attention should be directed to the target, a skewed hourglass-shaped green set on a narrow promontory, a pair of curvilinear bunkers in front and deep grass everywhere else. The wiry rough had no effect on Tom Watson, who pulled his tee shot to the left of the 17th green in the final round of the 1982 U.S. Open—and miraculously chipped in for a birdie to edge Jack Nicklaus for the championship.

Pebble's par-five 18th, one of the most famous holes in the world, provides a grand journey home. On top of the nature show—leopard seals basking on the rocks, sea otters frolicking in the kelp beds, ocean waves thudding on shore—the crescent-shaped 18th offers not one but two heroic options. Go-for-broke gamblers can cut off as much of Carmel Bay as they dare with their drives. They can also elect to cross the seawall on the second shot in an attempt to reach the narrow entrance to the green in two. Among amateurs, two players in a million might succeed. The safer route is up the right side, a pair of trees in the fairway providing the target. A giant pine and menacing bunkers defend the green to the right, so the approach must be delicately played to a putting surface that appears flat but is subtly sloped from back to front. In any conditions, fair or stormy, five is a fine score.

Assessed clinically, Pebble Beach has six good holes, six great holes, and six average (except for the setting) holes. Like a classical symphony, Pebble has harmony and balance, with a pleasing blend of notes at both ends of the register. Thrilling stretches, like holes six through 10 and the powerful finish at 17 and 18, are offset by more ordinary holes carved from tall Monterey pines. These holes, on both nines, are nevertheless charged with expectancy at what is to follow, because Pebble is the perfect ebb-and-flow links. Drama is sustained

throughout the round. More than at any other course on the planet, the whole is greater than the sum of its parts at Pebble Beach.

Of course, the sensory experience of playing the links is so overpowering—the play of light on the wave-tossed sea, gunsmoke mist fastened to the Big Sur coast—it's a wonder golfers can concentrate on the task at hand. (When the wind blows, they can't.) No worries. A high score at Pebble is better than a low score anywhere else.

A final note. Arrange for a caddy. There's simply no way to appreciate this magnificent layout from the vantage point of the curbed cart paths.

Of all the storied layouts on the Monterey Peninsula, only one is a fearless stalwart with a swashbuckler's heart. **Spyglass Hill Golf Course** (#5) was best described by the late sportswriter Jim Murray, who wrote, "If it were human, Spyglass Hill would have a knife in its teeth, a patch on its eye, a ring in its ear, tobacco in its beard. It is a privateer plundering the golfing main, an amphibious creature, half ocean, half forest. It's a 200-acre unplayable lie." The evolution of this ornery pirate of a golf course is worth reporting.

In the early 1960s, the Northern California Golf Association tapped Robert Trent Jones to build a straightforward course that would weave through seaside dunes before disappearing into a thick forest of pines. Not only is the routing he produced unique, the holes are named for characters and landmarks in Robert Louis Stevenson's *Treasure Island*. (Stevenson, who lived for a time in a house overlooking the sea and wrote many of his stories and novels here, famously described the Monterey Peninsula as "the most beautiful meeting of land and water that nature has produced.")

Spyglass Hill is hands-down the toughest track in northern California from the tips. The layout stretches to 6,855 yards, course rating 75.3, slope 148, but demanding uphill holes and heavy sea air make Spyglass play much longer than the listed yardage. From the white markers at 6,347 yards, Spyglass, sloped at 141, is a millstone around the neck of the

Spyglass Hill Golf Course, Pebble Beach, third hole

Spyglass Hill Golf Course, fourth hole

average duffer seeking to match his handicap. Ladies get a break from the red tees at 5,618 yards, where par is 74. From a pure shot value point of view—the shots a good golfer must play in return for par, and the price he pays if these shots are poor—this Trent Jones masterpiece is technically the best test of golf on the Monterey Peninsula. Of the more than 500 courses he has designed worldwide, Jones himself includes Spyglass Hill in his Favorite Five, along with Ballybunion (New), Firestone South, Mauna Kea, and Sotogrande in Spain.

With no "breather" holes, Spyglass Hill is without a single weakness. Captivating on a bright and sunny day, Spyglass is sinister in fog and can play monstrously difficult in wind. The opener, the best first hole on the peninsula, is a gigantic downhill par five of 600 yards that promenades players directly to the dunes, its islandlike green encased in a sea of sand. Play ensues for the next four holes among sandy wastelands and broken dunes cloaked in ice plant, a succulent with stems like rubber tentacles. These holes, among the most charming Jones ever built, represent target golf at its very best. The setting is exquisite. Sea lions bark from Seal Rock, bathers wave from Fanshell Beach, a salty mist thrown up by rumbling waves fills the air. If the entire layout shared this treeless dunescape, no course in America could match it.

In his book *Golf by Design*, Robert Trent Jones, Jr. had this to say about the fourth, "Blind Pew," his favorite hole at Spyglass Hill: "My father's work is known for long 'runway' tees, fairways that extend from tee to green framed by large bunkers, and expansive, contoured, elevated greens. A stimulating mix of these features awaits the golfer at Spyglass Hill's

inland forest holes. However, the measure of a truly fine architect rests with his ability to sometimes go against his own tendencies in favor of creating a special hole. In my father's case, the fourth is the antithesis of his basic design principles. It sits like a crown jewel in the midst of brilliant white sand dunes next to the glittering cobalt sea. The tee shot from any of the small individual tees on this short par four offers numerous options. The driver is often replaced by a 3-wood or long iron because proper placement of the ball on the correct side of the fairway (usually the right) is rewarded with a preferred angle to this well-guarded punch-bowl green nestled deeply among the forbidding sand dunes."

If this green is a punch-bowl, it only holds a few drops. Only a high-flying shot with plenty of backspin can hold this long, impossibly narrow green, which is not only blind, but slopes away from the line of play.

Bird Rock, a landmark perch for shoreline birds off 17-Mile Drive, is the distant target at the fifth, a par three set back from the shore that plays to a paddle-shaped green guarded in front by a trio of bunkers. Spyglass then departs the sea at the sixth for a roller-coaster journey through towering Monterey pines and cypress trees within Del Monte Forest. The seaside thrills are over. Now, solid ball-striking and steady putting must be produced at every turn to yield results.

Jones's philosophy of a "hard par, easy bogey" is in full effect at Spyglass Hill. Resistance to scoring is provided by narrow, tree-lined fairways crossed by ravines; large, crowned greens ranked among the slickest on the peninsula; uphill holes that belie the yardage on the scorecard; and ponds guarding the greens on three of the par fives and two of the par

Spyglass Hill Golf Course, 15th hole

threes. No wonder pros competing in the annual AT&T Pebble Beach National Pro-Am don't consider a lead safe until they've survived an outing on Spyglass Hill.

The foundation of this sterling layout is its stupendous collection of par fours. The 395-yard eighth, "Signal Hill," marches up a tree-lined ribbon of fairway that falls away to the right. The kidney-shaped green, perched high above the rising fairway, is defended in front by a fortresslike bunker. There are longer holes on the course, but none is rated tougher than the eighth.

If you've paused for refreshments at the turn, your main concern at the downhill par-four 10th, "Captain Flint," is not the group of trees in the center of the fairway at the turn of the dogleg. It's the watchful crows who know if you've purchased a sandwich. Leave your cart unattended for a moment on the 10th fairway, and these clever birds will eat your lunch. Reason enough to carry your own bag or, better yet, arrange for a caddy through the golf shop.

Among the brawnier par fours on the back nine is the 440-yard 13th, "Tom Morgan," a cutthroat if ever there was one. Because this tree-lined hole, which bends slightly to the left, ascends steadily but unspectacularly from tee to green, players can be fooled into thinking the hourglass-shaped green is closer than it really is. Extra club is needed to reach it, assuming yet another long, straight drive has been rifled down the center of the fairway. Few courses anywhere place stronger demands on the tee shot than Spyglass Hill. Crooked drives tend to dart into brush-filled gullies or thick woods from which there is no recovery.

The finest par five at Spyglass, "Long John Silver," is also its greediest—this is a pirate who can really rob you of strokes. The double-dogleg, 560-yard 14th asks for a well-placed drive to a landing area pinched by big trees. The second shot must be laid up short of an oblong, rock-rimmed pond that fronts a wide, shallow green. Par here is a fantastic score. Locals will tell visitors to bear down and concentrate—even if they hear the sound of laughing pirates in the trees behind the green. The kindliest hole on the course—if in fact any hole at Spyglass can qualify—is the dainty 130-yard 15th, "Jim Hawkins." Then again, a fluffed tee shot pushed to the right of the boomerang-shaped green set below tee level ends up in the drink. A shot pulled long and left buries into bunkers cut into the side of a hill.

The 16th, "Black Dog," is perhaps the most scurrilous hole at Spyglass Hill. Consistently ranked among the toughest holes on the PGA Tour, this 465-yard par four crosses a ravine from a hilltop tee to a bunkerless fairway that doglegs to the right around a large pine. The tiny, canted green, set well below the landing area and defended front left by yawning bunkers, is very difficult to reach in regulation. This is true even from the white tees at 434 yards. The Black Dog's bite is worse than its bark.

How to combat this superlative, unyielding test of golf, probably the single finest course ever built by Robert Trent Jones? For starters, a drainage upgrade completed in 1996 solved the layout's habitual nemesis, soggy fairways. (Unlike the sandy soils elsewhere on the peninsula, the clay subsurface at Spyglass Hill is not porous.) Plan to visit from May through October, when the fairways are firm and shots roll far. Also, be

DINING

Roy's restaurant at The Inn and Links at Spanish Bay

The opening in 1995 of *Roy's,* its tantalizing "Euro-Asian" fare (Szechuan-spiced baby back ribs, blackened ahi with soy-mustard sauce) the tastiest food available on the peninsula, established The Inn at Spanish Bay as a genuine culinary hotspot. With its spectacular ocean views, Roy's is also one of the prettiest resort dining rooms in the nation.

The *Bay Club,* a more formal room, offers refined continental cuisine, a superb selection of California wines, and soft classical music. The airy *Clubhouse Bar & Grill,* overlooking the first tee of the Links, is the perfect choice for a casual lunch (grilled seafood, excellent salads) before or after the round, while appetizers and complimentary hors d'oeuvres are available in *Traps,* a fireplace lounge and bar that stocks a fine selection of single malt Scotch whiskeys.

observant: Several greens are visible from adjoining holes and can be checked for pin position. And remember to align yourself correctly on tees that point away from prime target areas, a favorite Trent Jones ploy.

Jones, commenting on his vintage designs from the 1960s, wrote: "I do feel that the introduction of the heroic concept, skillfully mixed with the strategic and, occasionally, the penal, set new standards for the modern golf course." He could have been describing the multiple personalities of the Monterey Peninsula's most treacherous resident, Spyglass Hill.

Nestled between Del Monte Forest and the ocean shore five miles up the road from Pebble Beach is **The Links at Spanish Bay** (#45), one of the few seaside links available for resort play in America. Robert Trent Jones, Jr., who collaborated on the design of the course with five-time British Open champion Tom Watson and former USGA president Frank "Sandy" Tatum, had this to say when the layout opened in 1987. "There are two distinct games played under the same heading: golf. Most Americans are familiar with the parkland game played through the air to soft manicured

The Links at Spanish Bay, Pebble Beach, seventh hole

LODGING

The Inn at Spanish Bay, its ivory stucco buildings sheltered by tall Monterey pines near 17-Mile Drive, is one of the most deluxe and best-liked hotels in the nation. Nearly half of the 270 spacious rooms in the swank yet understated Inn have ocean views, and all feature gas-operated fireplaces, posh marble bathrooms, and spacious balconies. Guests have access to the Spanish Bay Club, which features an indoor gym with state-of-the-art fitness equipment and personalized instruction.

The Inn at Spanish Bay

The Links at Spanish Bay, 14th *hole*

emerald lawns. This style is 50 years old. The other game has been played since the inception of the idea to hit a small ball cross country to a distant hole in the ground. It is called Links Golf, named after the old Scottish word for a sandy wasteland, usually near the sea. This game is played under the wind along the firm and true hard surfaces provided by the tawny colored fescue grasses cut tight, originally by the sheep. This game is 500 years old."

Decades in the making, Spanish Bay is situated in a "reclamation area." As part of its agreement with Monterey County, the Pebble Beach Company reconstructed 100 acres of dunes up to 24 feet in height on the site of an old sand quarry. (Nearly 600,000 cubic yards of sand was brought to the site on a two-mile-long conveyor belt.) These dunes were then hydroseeded with common grasses to stabilize the soil and planted with a variety of native species, including golden beach poppies, pink sand verbena, and yellow bush lupine. Dune sedge and red fescue were added to provide a buffer between the dunes and the fairways, and two riparian areas were enhanced to attract waterfowl. To create a semblance of the original tree line, native Monterey pines were brought closer to the coast. With the canvas stretched, the designers were free to weave rolling fairways through the humps and dunes, pockmark these fairways with dozens of pot bunkers, and hire a kilted bagpiper to skirl his notes at twilight on the stone terrace of the Inn. When a salty mist wafts across the layout in late afternoon, an hour or so from "the interval between night and day when time stops and examines itself," according to Monterey storyteller John Steinbeck, even the dourest of Scotsmen would have trouble guessing the origin of this rumpled links.

The first hole, an unusually wide par five that proceeds directly to the sea and into the prevailing wind, sets the tone for the round. Players will note immediately that poorly struck shots balloon in the wind or are pushed off line, usually into trouble. Canted fairways, which create sidehill lies and force players to assume awkward stances, are a key feature. Mishit shots, the kind most players produce from a hanging lie, usually end up in matted dunes, the coastal marsh, or one of the diabolical traps that intrude upon the line of play. The bunkers at Spanish Bay, a few of them directional but most of them deep pots or gathering bathtubs, demand penance. Glory shots cannot be played from their depths. The old adage holds true at Spanish Bay: "When in doubt, wedge it out."

The links kicks into gear at the par-four third, a sharp right-to-left dogleg that swings around a nest of bunkers in the elbow of the dogleg. Jones, a master at conjuring risk/reward scenarios, dares better players to drive these bunkers to set up a short approach shot to a slightly concave green. As in Britain, tactics are important, especially if the breeze is fresh, which it usually is on this treeless sweep of sandy linksland.

The par-four seventh kicks off what locals call the "Terrible Triangle." Seemingly benign at 418 yards, this potential round-wrecker heads downhill toward the ragged arc of Spanish Bay. A marsh edges the left side of the fairway and noses into the landing area roughly 280 yards from the blue tees, 225 yards from the white markers. Like the governor on an engine, Jones believes the lay-up shot is an equalizer that eliminates mindless blasting and calls for proper club selection. The 163-yard eighth, which

SIDETRIPS

Carmel, a chic seaside village dedicated to the good life located due south of Pebble Beach, is a wonderful place to stroll. One-of-a-kind shops, trendy cafés (many with outdoor seating), and dozens of art galleries are tucked away on narrow, shaded lanes.

Farther south is *Point Lobos State Reserve,* a wildlife refuge and tree-clad headland with picnic areas, hiking trails, and wooden staircases built down to secluded beaches. In the winter months, migrating gray whales spout and dive offshore at Point Lobos.

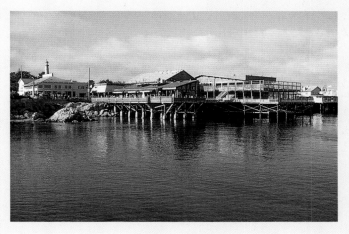

Fisherman's Wharf

On the site of a former sardine cannery in Monterey is the *Monterey Bay Aquarium,* a world-class facility with superb exhibits. The three-story Kelp Forest exhibit and million-gallon Outer Bay galleries (including the enormous jellyfish display) are perennial favorites.

Fisherman's Wharf and *Cannery Row,* both of which figured prominently in several of John Steinbeck's novels, today contain dozens of factory outlets, informal cafés, and touristy souvenir shops.

plays from an elevated tee near 17-Mile Drive, requires a forced carry over a bog to an elongated, gull wing–shaped green. The par-four ninth heads away from the shore, with a linear white dune festooned with twisted pines flanking the right side of the fairway. The deep green, contoured to reject approach shots hit left and right of center, is nerve-racking.

Holes 10, 11, and 12 disappear into a forest of tall Monterey pines behind the resort's low-rise hotel complex, while the tiny par-three 13th, a pastiche of the "Postage Stamp" hole at Royal Troon in Scotland, plays across a creek to a wee green set on a precipice that falls away sharply to the right. The links marches back to the sea at the 571-yard 14th, a tremendous hole with a broad fairway full of hillocks that tumbles to the brink of the Pacific. In a quartering wind, dunes to the left, willow marsh on the right, a smattering of steep-walled kettle bunkers, and an elongated trench in the center of the fairway 100 yards from the green all conspire to bring down the best of players.

The Links at Spanish Bay, 17th hole

The course flexes its muscles from here on in, for the remaining holes play along linksland exposed to brisk winds off Spanish Bay. After negotiating the hogback green at the par-three 16th, players must rise to the occasion at the 414-yard 17th, the toughest two-shotter on the homeward nine. Here a wild dunescape stares golfers in the face from the tee. After a well-placed drive, the approach must carry a tufted ridge and hold a perched green that falls away on all sides to bunkers and beach grass. Par is a tall order, especially into the prevailing wind.

A few words of advice to first-timers. Unless you're a low single-digit handicapper, bypass the blue tees (6,820 yards, course rating 74.9, slope 146) in favor of the white markers, which may seem short at 6,078 yards, but the slope rating of 134 tells the story. The red tees, at 5,309 yards, are manageable by most women.

Spanish Bay was designed to be walked. Your appreciation of its squawking gulls, ocean combers, and subtle vegetation will be greatly enhanced by strolling the links.

A final note: The stiff, bristly fescue grasses native to British seaside courses that were first planted on Spanish Bay's tees, fairways, and greens

did not thrive. The boldy contoured greens, consisting of poa annua and bentgrass, are similar in texture to the greens at Pebble Beach. These greens putt a trifle slower than greased lightning. The fairways, mostly rye and bluegrass, are softer than the coarse fescues, but the turfgrass, cropped close to encourage low, running shots, emulates an authentic links in the drier seasons—April through October. This is the time of year to savor a Scottish golf experience on the Monterey Peninsula.

More Golf/Monterey Peninsula

In addition to the Big Three—Pebble Beach, Spyglass Hill, and Spanish Bay—the Pebble Beach Company offers play on the 5,526-yard *Del Monte* layout, the oldest course west of the Mississippi (1897); and an amusing nine-hole, par-three course across the street from Pebble Beach named for an early Scottish pro, *Peter Hay.*

Poppy Hills, one of three courses played in the AT&T Pebble Beach National Pro-Am, is a tight, hilly course authored by Robert Trent Jones,

Jr. The 6,861-yard layout has a beautiful setting within Del Monte Forest, several fascinating (some say controversial) holes—but no ocean views.

Pacific Grove, a municipal links designed by Jack Neville and often called the "poor man's Pebble Beach," has a rather pedestrian front nine redeemed by a links-style back nine with superb greens set in seaside dunes. At press time, the green fee topped out at $30.

Laguna Seca, a 6,157-yard, par-71 layout by Robert Trent Jones seven miles inland from Monterey, is a hilly, scenic shotmaker's track.

Fort Ord, a decommissioned Army base north of the peninsula, offers two revived courses, the long, narrow Bayonet and shorter, sportier Black-horse, both with distant views of Monterey Bay.

Moving inland from Carmel, there's *Rancho Cañada,* a pleasant 36-hole facility, and *Carmel Valley Ranch,* a 6,515-yard, par-70 layout updated by Pete Dye in 1995 that features tricky multilevel greens and radical elevation changes on the back nine.

At the top of Monterey Bay, less than an hour's drive north from the peninsula's more famous courses, is **Pasatiempo Golf Club** (#17) in Santa Cruz, the only course on the "Top 100" roster laid out by the legendary Scottish designer Dr. Alister Mackenzie, who is best known for his work at Cypress Point and Augusta National. When Mackenzie's working

Pasatiempo Golf Club, Santa Cruz, first hole

17-Mile Drive

One of California's great attractions, this privately maintained, two-lane road provides a glorious showcase of the Pacific coastline as well as its native plants and wildlife. Among the more spectacular stopping points on the celebrated drive, which weaves through the 5,000-acre Del Monte Forest, is the famed Lone Cypress clinging to its rocky perch; Fanshell Beach, where harbor seals return each spring to bear their pups; and Seal and Bird rocks, where herds of sea lions and flocks of birds can be observed on the self-guided nature walk. The nominal fee to enter 17-Mile Drive is waived for resort guests.

Bird Rock on the 17-Mile Drive

days were done, he retired to a modest home alongside the sixth fairway: Pasatiempo ("passing the time" in Spanish) was one of his favorite places in golf. The course, opened in 1929, not only embodies his design principles, it has always welcomed outside play.

Routed on sloping terrain three miles from the ocean, Pasatiempo's tree-lined fairways serve up magnificent views of coastal mountains and Monterey Bay. Don't be deceived by the scorecard: This semiprivate club plays much, much longer than its listed yardage from the blue tees (6,483 yards par 71); the tip-off is the course rating (72.9) and slope (138). The layout is chockablock with fascinating holes, several of them among the finest Mackenzie ever devised.

The prospect from the elevated first tee is daunting, but this short par five has more bark than bite. First-timers, however, do not know this. With an array of traps pinching a narrow fairway already hemmed in by enormous cypress and eucalyptus trees, there appears to be no safe place to land the opening drive of the day. Nothing could be further from the truth. The first fairway is more than accommodating, though were he alive today, Mackenzie would arm himself with a chain saw and embark upon an aggressive tree-pruning program at Pasatiempo. (In fact, several overhanging trees were removed on the first hole in 1998.) Mackenzie, who mastered the art of camouflage while serving as a field surgeon during the Boer War, applied what he knew about concealment and optical illusion to golf course design. The first hole looks hard, but in fact is rated the easiest on the course. In his book, *Golf Architecture,* Mackenzie writes: "It is an important thing in golf to make holes look much more difficult than they really are. People get more pleasure doing a hole which looks almost

Pasatiempo Golf Club, 16th hole

impossible, and yet is not so difficult as it appears." Pasatiempo's first hole fills the bill.

The par-three third hole, 217 yards from the tips, is rated the second-toughest hole on the course. It's really a par 3½. The tee shot is played uphill to a heavily contoured green embraced by deep bunkers. Macken-zie's bunkers are brilliant, both in their aesthetic flair and clever position-ing, and remain the envy of modern-age designers. Most players would be well advised to hit their driver—certainly nothing less than a 3-wood—to avoid sand and find the green on the third.

Pasatiempo's back nine showcases one thrilling hole after another, the fairways spliced with deep, wooded ravines. The greens, in particular, are among the most wickedly contoured in the West. (Clearly, Mackenzie wanted a player in possession of a canny short game to have a chance to defeat the long-ball artist.) The 10th, a grand-scale par four at 444 yards, calls for a long forced carry over a barranca followed by a downhill approach shot to a sloping green. This shot calls for careful judgment and perfect execution. The par-four 11th, a slight dogleg to the left, belies the yardage at 394 yards. The listing fairway climbs uphill and asks players to vault a ravine (usually from a sidehill lie) and hit a tiny green canted from back to front and tightly guarded by trees and sand. The 12th, a par four of 376 yards, proceeds downhill to a wide landing area, but the second shot calls for unerring accuracy. Hooked approach shots topple into a ravine, never to be recovered.

ATTRACTIONS

No visit to Santa Cruz would be complete without a visit to the town's antique boardwalk and a ride or two on its 1911 *Merry-Go-Round* and famed *Giant Dipper* wooden roller coaster. Both amusements are National Historic Landmarks. Or make a tour of *Neptune's Kingdom*, which features a miniature golf course with robotics and fiber-optics special effects. Something closer to nature? *Natural Bridges State Park* is known for its butterfly colony and tidepools.

The best hole at Pasatiempo and arguably the finest two-shotter on the good doctor's resume is the 16th, a down-and-up par four rated the number one handicap hole. After a blind, downhill tee shot, the approach is played over a wide, ball-swallowing ravine to a slick triple-tier green underslung by a gaping pit of sand. This splendid conception demands two fine long shots and two well-gauged putts in return for par. "It is the successful negotiation of difficulties, or apparent ones, which give rise to pleasurable excitement and makes a hole interesting," Mackenzie wrote. He added that memorable holes are "usually those in which a great advantage can be gained in successfully accomplishing heroic carries over hazards of an impressive appearance." The barranca at the 16th certainly qualifies as an impressive hazard, though what the architect described in his writings as the "long handicap man" can lay up short of the chasm and hit his third shot to the green. This option fulfills Mackenzie's notion of a versatile golf hole. "An ideal hole," he wrote, "should provide an infinite variety of shots according to the varying positions of the tee, the situation of the flag, the direction and strength of the wind, etc." By any measure, Pasatiempo's 16th is an ideal hole. And by any measure, Mackenzie was among the first of the Golden Era designers to embrace golf architecture as a new art closely allied to that of the sculptor, albeit one with scientific underpinnings.

With characteristic iconoclasm, Mackenzie concludes Pasatiempo with a go-for-broke par three, here a 173-yarder that plays across a deeply incised ravine to a sizable putting surface replete with subtle undulations. It's a grand stage on which to conclude a match, and adventurous match-play golf is what Mackenzie had in mind when he built Pasatiempo. Because greens and tees are close together, this hilly, rugged course can be walked by fit players. Caddies can be arranged through the golf shop.

Host to the 1986 U.S. Women's Amateur Championship and annual site of the Western Intercollegiate Invitational (Tiger Woods competed here while attending Stanford), Pasatiempo is revered by shotmakers. Every hole on the course has a different character, yet all 18 mesh together. The grandeur of the layout's heaving terrain and perilous hazards coupled with the exquisite surroundings—towering trees, shaded glens, ocean views—combine to provide a majestic setting for the game. Even local surfers set their boards aside on occasion to sample its delights.

Happily, architect Tom Doak, an ardent fan of Mackenzie's work, has been retained by the club to devise a master plan for the restoration of the course.

LODGING

The *Inn at Pasatiempo,* located a 3-wood shot from the first tee, offers comfortable accommodations in 54 rooms. Suites have canopied beds, jacuzzis, and a sitting room with fireplace.

DINING

In addition to Peachwood's at the Inn at Pasatiempo, there's the *Hollins House,* former home of 1920s amateur star and entrepreneur Marion Hollins, who hired Alister Mackenzie to design Pasatiempo. The dining room, which overlooks the golf course and the sea, serves superb continental cuisine.

In Santa Cruz itself, there's *India Joze,* featuring exotically spiced Southeast Asian cuisine. *Stagnaro Brothers,* one of many casual family-style restaurants on the Municipal Wharf, specializes in a wide array of seafood.

Hollins House

More Golf / Santa Cruz area

Delaveaga Golf Club, a Santa Cruz muni, is not long at 6,010 yards, but narrow fairways and adjoining ravines can spell trouble for stray hitters. Eight miles south of Santa Cruz is *Aptos Seascape,* a short, tight, hilly course circa 1926, lined with mature pines and flanked by 80-foot-deep barrancas. Three lengthy par threes measuring well over 200 yards provide plenty of challenge.

In an oak-studded valley surrounded by haystack-shaped hills about an hour's drive east of Santa Cruz is *San Juan Oaks,* a Fred Couples–Gene Bates design in Hollister. The layout's front nine flows past five man-made lakes interconnected by meandering creeks. The back nine climbs 200 feet above the valley floor to the brink of San Juan Canyon. This well-varied test, marked by exceptionally smooth greens, is anchored by a California Mission–style clubhouse inspired by the nearby Mission San Juan Bautista, a low, colonnaded structure founded in 1797. San Juan Oaks is virtually fog-free and open year round.

Central Coast area

Some remotely located golf courses, lacking glamour or a nationwide reputation, don't get the respect they deserve. Such a facility is **La Purisima Golf Course** (#60) in Lompoc, a sleepy flower seed capital on the Central Coast an hour's drive north of Santa Barbara, itself two hours north of Los Angeles. Named after the local mission, La Purisima stands for purity, as in the Immaculate Conception. But when a westerly sea breeze funnels through the rolling brown hills of the Lompoc Valley—which it does like clockwork every afternoon—La Purisima turns into a wind tunnel that results in the immediate destruction of most golfers' games. This is especially true from the tips, where the 7,105-yard, par-72 layout carries a course rating of 74.9 and a slope of 143, among the highest in the state. When the first stage of the 72-hole PGA Tour Qualifying School was held at La Purisima in 1998, an eight-over score of 296 made the cut. Thankfully, there are multiple sets of forward tees listed at 6,657, 6,200, and 5,763 yards that cater to all levels.

Designed in 1986 by Robert Muir Graves, an Oregon-based designer with a background in landscape architecture, La Purisima is a pure, unfettered test of golf free of housing and other reminders of civilization.

SIDETRIPS/WINE TOUR

Napa and Sonoma enjoy a lofty reputation for producing great wines, but the Santa Ynez Valley vintners are catching up. Byron, Gainey, Firestone, Sanford, and Zaca Mesa are among the top local wineries that welcome visitors. Maps are available at area hotels.

At the Sanford Winery

La Purisima Golf Course, Lompoc, fourth hole

The only building on site is the landmark bell tower and Spanish Mission–style golf shop and restaurant. Which means that golfers are free to concentrate on the task at hand.

The opening holes trace the valley floor, with ponds and streams in play on five holes, notably on the outside curve of the dogleg at the par-five first, the inside corner of the dogleg at the par-four second, and again at the third, a short par three where the wide but shallow green, benched in a hill, is fronted by water and sand. The fifth, the number one handicap hole, begins the rugged ascent to higher ground, while the tee at the sixth, a grand par five of 566 yards, claims the high point of the course. The fairway here sweeps downhill along the bias of a slope, dips low, then

D I N I N G

The top choice in Lompoc is *The Jetty,* where the accent is on fresh-caught local fish. In nearby Buellton, *A. J. Spurs* and *The Hitching Post* are casual steakhouses popular with golfers. The barbecue at both is excellent. Solvang has dozens of aroma-filled bakeries serving Danish pastries and other specialties. For dinner, the *Royal Skandia Restaurant,* its three cottage-style dining rooms decorated with quaint Scandinavian furnishings, offers traditional American fare as well as a Danish smorgasbord. Atmospheric inside and out, *The Danish Inn* serves the best smorgasbord and Danish *morbrod* (pork medallions sautéed with red wine, shallots, and mushrooms) in Solvang.

The Danish Inn at Solvang

proceeds uphill to a plateau green canted from back to front and defended fore and aft by Graves's signature bunkers. These bunkers are elongated, sinuous pits defined by steep curving walls. They do not offer easy escape. At the seventh, a dramatic downhill par four of 427 yards, Graves cut a series of church pew bunkers into a hill along the left side of the fairway at the 150-yard mark to snare wayward drives. The front nine ends nobly at the 227-yard ninth, which plays from a chute of towering eucalyptus trees over a sandy barranca to a narrow, well-protected green.

Visitors never fail to comment on the 12th, a monstrous par five of 609 yards where a smattering of oaks plays a key strategic role, but it's the finish at La Purisima that gets everyone's attention. In fact, the last five holes are known as "Amen Corner West." The verdant 14th is a short par four with a slim, bunkerless fairway laid into a valley. Like most of the greens on the course, the target here is rather small, a little tilted, and extremely fast. The 15th, a Z-shaped par five where the drive must be essayed through an alley of oaks and where subsequent shots must be leapfrogged from one safe landing area to the next, is followed by the 436-yard 16th, which appears claustrophobic from the tee but opens up in the playing area and plays to a green nestled in dense scrub oak. The 17th is a downhill par three that plays over a water-filled barranca to a minuscule green ringed by bunkers, while the par-four 18th, which doglegs to the left around a giant cloverleaf of sand, provides a solid finish to a fair but exacting test.

There are no ocean views at La Purisima. The golf shop will never pass for a Rodeo Drive designer boutique. Yet dollar-for-dollar (at press time, the weekday green fee was $50), walker-friendly La Purisima may well be the best public-access course in California, a tribute to Graves's subtle artistry and the site's natural attributes.

More Golf/Central Coast

Santa Barbara's top public-access course is *Rancho San Marcos*, a spectacular layout by Robert Trent Jones, Jr., nestled in the Santa Ynez Mountains on the site of a historic ranch. The front nine, spread across the

La Purisima Golf Course, 12th hole

New & Noteworthy / Central Coast

valley floor, rambles past a restored riparian habitat and thousands of centuries-old live oaks. The back nine ascends a plateau that transports players into a magical realm, with stunning vistas of sky-blue Lake Cachuma, distant furrowed peaks rising to 7,000 feet, and striated bluffs where bald eagles nest. Opened in 1998, the layout has undulating, open-entry greens that are among the best Jones Jr. has done.

Another option is *Glen Annie*, a Robert Muir Graves–designed layout located in Goleta's coastal foothills. Opened in 1997, the sporty 6,420-yard, par-71 course offers sharp elevation changes, fine views of the Pacific, and environmentally sensitive areas called "frog crossings."

In Goleta, 10 miles north of Santa Barbara, is *Sandpiper*, a popular public course slated to be transformed by Johnny Miller into one of the nation's most compelling seaside resort layouts. Stretched along nearly a mile of 100-foot-high oceanfront bluffs that drop to a deserted beach, the sparsely treed, links-style layout, backdropped by the Santa Ynez Mountains, is scheduled to open in July 2000 and will feature seven holes on the sea. A 400-room hotel is to be located at the north end of the course. Sandpiper, previously characterized as "Pebble Beach with better weather," now has a layout and clubhouse that can be compared to the kingpin of the California coast.

Orange County area

There aren't many developers with the patience (or deep pockets) to battle the California Coastal Commission for 30 years seeking approval to build a seaside golf course. Fewer still have the power of persuasion to lure Tom Fazio west of the Mississippi. But the developers of **Pelican Hill Golf Club** prevailed, and Fazio made the most of a spectacular stretch of rugged coastal canyons near the surfing mecca of Newport Beach, about an hour's drive south of Los Angeles.

The first course to open at this estimable 36-hole complex was the Ocean Course, later renamed the **Ocean South Course** (#50). Shortly after its debut in 1991, it was hailed as southern California's answer to Pebble Beach. Golf-wise, it asks more questions than it answers, as a top course should, but it's the scenery that shines through. All 18 holes have a view of the Pacific; four are routed on bluffs high above the tawny beach. At least one, the par-three 12th, has emerged as a modern classic. This hole, "Pelican's Nest," ranges from 134 to 212 yards and nestles among dramatic rock outcroppings with a large waste area fronting a long, thin green. A front or back pin placement can spell a four-club difference here. A brisk sea wind can further complicate club selection, for the 12th is one of four holes in the routing located west of Pacific Coast Highway 1 and therefore on the brink of the sea. Rather than monopolize the precious coastal yardage with a long hole, Fazio followed the 12th with another par three. The petite 13th, all of 121 yards from the tips (88 yards from the red tees), is called Double Trouble, with reason. Two tiny greens, each backdropped by Newport Harbor, are divided by an imposing waste bunker, with the coastline's rocky bluffs in view down the left side. Multiple sets of tees create interesting angles of attack on a hole rated the easiest on the course. And on a calm day, the tee shot is short and relatively

Pelican Hill Golf Club, Newport Coast, Ocean South Course, 16th hole

simple. But with the wind blowing, the greens at the 13th shrink to half their size, and the waste bunker looms large. According to Andy Banfield, Fazio's associate designer at Pelican Hill: "Building a golf course is more an art than a science, and these two holes are pure art."

The uphill par-five 14th, "Turning Home," plays much longer than its 541 yards. The drive must avoid out-of-bounds to the left, bunkers to the right, and trees, mostly pine and eucalyptus, on both sides of the fairway. A prudent lay-up leaves a third shot to an elevated, two-tier green. After passing under the highway, players emerge at the par-four 15th, which plays from an elevated tee to an uphill fairway and asks for an unerring approach that steers clear of bunkers and a deep canyon to the right and a stand of eucalyptus trees to the left of the large, bi-level green. Golf-wise, it's one of Pelican Hill's finest and most thrilling scenarios. The Ocean Course South concludes brilliantly at the par-four 18th, called "Double Cross." The tees, benched into the hillside of a canyon, look across a gorge to an island fairway, with players invited to bite off as much of the abyss as they dare. The second shot—the double cross—is back across the canyon and down to a green set below the clubhouse.

Fazio's first effort at Pelican Hill is not only challenging (it's a par 70 stretching to 6,647 yards, with five sets of tees offering plenty of options), it's also high tech. A computerized system takes readings from two weather stations on the course before irrigating the fairways with reclaimed water. During course construction, fairways were sodded with a drought-tolerant hybrid bermudagrass, while the 5,000 trees and 40,000 shrubs planted alongside the fairways were selected for their ability to thrive in low-water conditions. Finally, fiberglass-reinforced concrete was used to re-create natural rock outcrops and give golfers the illusion they're playing closer to the edge of hillsides than they actually are. These measures give eloquent answer to many of the questions that were posed by environmentalists over the years leading up to course construction.

DINING

At the *Four Seasons Newport Beach,* the elegant *Pavilion,* set beside a bower of palms and flowers, presents innovative Mediterranean cuisine with a California influence. The more casual *Gardens Café and Lounge* has excellent salads and pasta dishes. Many players never get past, *The Grill at Pelican Hill,* which is operated by the Four Seasons and offers mesmerizing ocean views along with stylish fare. Something more laid-back? Go where the golf staff goes—to *The Place* in nearby Corona del Mar, a hole-in-the-wall sports bar that serves good burgers. Themed dining? *The Five Crowns* in Corona del Mar is a faithful replica of Ye Old Bell, reputedly England's oldest inn. Waitresses and barmaids wear Elizabethan dress. The roast beef with Yorkshire pudding is recommended. A wide range of British ales is available.

Pelican Hill Golf Club, Ocean North Course, 14ᵗʰ hole

Tom Fazio returned to build a second course at Pelican Hill, this one sprawled across a plateau creased by ravines 300 feet above the glistening Pacific. And while thousands of trees and shrubs were imported to landscape the original layout, indigenous vegetation was used to flesh out the brawnier **Ocean North Course** (#46), formerly known as the Links Course. This magnificent spread stretches to 6,856 yards from the tips (par 71) and plays at least three strokes harder than its predecessor. A championship-caliber design with an ocean view at every hole (Catalina Island can be spotted far offshore on a clear day), the open, windswept North is marked by small, undulating greens and, from the tips, several forced carries over deep canyons from which there is no recovery. Even a slightly offline approach can drift into an abyss, though Fazio's trademark playability (at least from the multiple sets of forward tees) is in evidence throughout.

Pelican Hill Golf Club, Ocean South Course, 18ᵗʰ hole

Pelican Hill Golf Club, Ocean North Course, 17th hole

Sharp elevation changes and linkslike terrain that promotes creative shotmaking characterize the Ocean Course North, which is generally preferred by low handicappers to the South. The par-three second, patterned after the famed "Postage Stamp" hole at Royal Troon in Scotland, is the first of several forced carries on the course. The key here is alignment: Fazio, perhaps tired of holding a golfer's hand every step of the way, provided no directional aid with his free-form tee boxes. Players must take their own aim and fly the canyon with their tee shots. The fourth, a 413-yard called "Cliff Hanger," is a textbook risk-reward design: The drive must favor the right side while avoiding the canyon, as the safer left side obstructs the view to the green and tends to lengthen the hole. Shots pushed to the right of the green end up in a sandy trench or topple down the side of a cliff. Another strategic gem, but far more difficult, is the long par-four seventh, where a looming central bunker directs play to the right, the longer but flatter route; or to the left, which is harder to hit but offers a superior angle of attack to the cliffside green.

The North's back nine is marked by shorter, trickier holes—with a few notable exceptions. The green at the short par-four 11th, "Go For Broke," can be driven in a following wind, though the crowned putting surface and its surrounds are severely undulating. The tables are turned at the 15th, an uphill par four of 446 yards that plays a little shorter owing to the prevailing ocean breeze but is no picnic. The tee shot, played over a lake, must avoid a deep fairway bunker down the left side. A generous opening into the skewed green welcomes a low-running approach shot.

The layout's signature hole, and perhaps the single finest conception at Pelican Hill, is the grand par-five 17th, called "Gut Check." Fazio emptied

his bag of tricks on this bold and beautiful hole. The drive, played from an elevated tee, must avoid a large lake and a giant inkblot bunker up the right side of the fairway, while a long uphill carry across the corner of a gorge peppered with coastal scrub is required on the second shot. From the gold tees at 543 yards, only a long-hitting pro would dream of going for the green in two. A lone toyon tree and the ocean horizon beyond the shelflike green create an optical illusion for the approach, but stay left—regardless of the distance remaining or the club chosen, the putting surface falls away to a deep bunker on the right. Over the green is oblivion.

The slight divergence in design style on the Ocean Course North was inevitable. According to Fazio: "The South was so well received that we created our own competition. It's been a big challenge for us to match its quality," he said at the time the North opened in 1993. Match it he has: Pelican Hill, with its lofty $210 weekend green fee at press time, offers the finest 36 holes of public-access golf in southern California. The facility's Spanish Mission–style clubhouse, golf shop, and practice center are a match for two of Fazio's most inspired creations.

More Golf/Orange County area

Located in Irvine is *Oak Creek,* a Tom Fazio–designed course situated beside an office complex near a major highway. The user-friendly layout, walled in by a berm that protects it from the hue and cry of commerce and transportation, also boasts a first-class practice facility. *Strawberry Farms,* a daily-fee course in Irvine, was developed by former major league baseball player Doug DeCinces and laid out by Jim Lipe, a senior designer for Jack Nicklaus. In Dana Point, 15 miles south of Pelican Hill, is *Monarch Beach Golf Links,* a Robert Trent Jones, Jr.–designed layout with fine ocean views. The course, routed through canyons and arroyos, has two holes set near the sea, with onshore winds stiffening the challenge. Walkers are welcome.

SIDETRIPS

Among the highlights of coastal Orange County is *Huntington Beach,* the surfing capital of the continental U.S. You can watch the action from 1,800-foot-long Huntington Pier—or check out the *Museum of Surfing* in the pavilion across the street. In Newport Beach, often described as "Beverly Hills by the sea," the charming byways of Newport Harbor can be explored. Across the marina is the Balboa Peninsula, known for the Victorian-era *Balboa Pavilion,* which today houses cafés and shops, and is a departure point for whale-watching cruises. A quiet walk on a beautiful, uncrowded beach? *Corona del Mar,* less than a mile from Pelican Hill, is the place.

San Diego area

Located in Carlsbad, 30 miles north of San Diego, is the Batiquitos Lagoon, a 2½-mile stretch of inland water ranked among the finest private wildlife preserves in North America. The restored waterway, home to 130 bird species, is the centerpiece of an upscale residential community anchored by **Four Seasons Resort Aviara Golf Club** (#70), which rolls and tumbles across coastal hills adjoining the lagoon.

Designed by Arnold Palmer and Ed Seay, the golf course took nearly a decade to complete, owing to the city of Carlsbad's ecological concerns—and the developer's preservationist leanings. A model facility, Aviara uses reclaimed water for 95 percent of its irrigation needs. More than 22,000 eucalyptus trees (many more than 50 years old) were preserved during course construction, and landscaping materials were selected based on their ability to survive in drought conditions. Native wildflowers and thickets of chaparral that can survive on 10 inches of rain per year

LODGING

Set on a plateau overlooking the lagoon, the ocean, and the golf course, the 331-room *Four Seasons Resort Aviara,* opened in 1997, is an exceptionally posh hotel. Rooms, occupying low-rise Spanish colonial-style buildings, are generously sized and feature spacious marble bathrooms. Ground-level rooms have private, landscaped terraces. Upper rooms have large balconies. Golf packages are available, as are a tennis center, swimming pools, and a full-service Spa & Fitness Center.

Four Seasons Resort Aviara Golf Club, Carlsbad, third hole

(Carlsbad's annual average) creep to the edge of the fairways. Balancing the arid setting are Aviara's oases of water: Seven lakes cover 10 of the layout's 180 acres, with cascading waterfalls and gurgling streams framing several of the greens. When it opened in 1991, Aviara established itself as one of the most tastefully landscaped and visually appealing layouts in southern California.

Committed to preserving the site's existing natural features, Palmer and Seay sculpted an outstanding layout that traces the natural topography of three valleys. There's a good variety of holes on this compelling 7,007-yard layout, and excellent playability as well. Aviara provides a suitable test for 10-handicappers from the back tees at 6,591 yards and a firm but fair test for higher handicappers from the middle tees at 6,054 yards. In lieu of the typically red ladies' tees, Aviara's forward markers, measuring 5,007 yards, are painted a welcoming shade of yellow. They're ideal for ladies, seniors, and novices.

Sloping terrain, sharp elevation changes, prevailing ocean breezes, and large, undulating greens dictate the challenge at Aviara. Among the feature holes on the front nine is the third, a petite par three (only 149 yards from the Palmer tees) set in a verdant valley. With a pair of streams flowing left and right into a pond fronting the green, the demand for accuracy is critical, especially when the wind swirls. Indian coral trees and other exotic specimens were used to landscape this exquisite hole.

DINING

The top restaurant at the Four Seasons is *Vivace* (Italian for lively), its floor-to-ceiling windows framing views of the Pacific and its menu featuring innovative regional Italian cuisine. Afternoon tea overlooking the hotel's *Palm Courtyard* is served in the lobby lounge, while a splendid seafood buffet is showcased on Friday evenings in the sophisticated *California Bistro*.

Aerial view of the Four Seasons Resort

SWING FIX

Aviara Golf Academy, founded in 1991 by Kip Puterbaugh and greatly expanded since, offers three- and four-day programs that feature a low student-to-pro ratio, in-depth video analysis of a pupil's swing on and off the course, and the opportunity to play Aviara daily (green fees and carts are included in the tuition). Puterbaugh, one of *GOLF Magazine's* "Top 100 Teachers," likens building a golf swing to building a house. "If the house has a poor foundation, it falls down," he says. "The same applies to one's golf game. It's been said that learning is a journey, not a destination. Golf is not something one masters, but only gets better at. Expectation levels may change, but there's always a higher level." The spacious practice facility, overlooking the Batiquitos Lagoon, is certainly an inspiring place to refine your swing.

Lecture at the Aviara Golf Academy

The downhill par-five eighth is cast in the heroic mold, daring players chasing birdies to try for the green in two. It can be done, but with water guarding the green and sand traps tucked up to the left and right of the putting surface, it's a risky gamble. Especially from a downhill lie.

Aviara's longer back nine raises the ante. The 14th is a breathtaking downhill par three of 201 yards where players hit from an elevated tee over a cascading water feature to a very wide green. A giant filigreed bunker snares players who overclub or draw their shots too far to the left. Tall eucalyptus trees screen players from the wind, but an airborne golf ball enjoys no such advantage.

The par-four 18th hole at Aviara, a left-to-right dogleg, is one of the toughest finishing holes in the San Diego area from the tips at 443 yards. Palmer's advice is to direct the tee shot toward the fairway bunkers and away from the lake that protects the right side of the hole. According to Arnie: "The shot to the green is visually exciting with the rock and waterscape highlighting the approach." Which is Arnie's way of saying you better hit a low, boring long-iron shot that pierces the wind and avoids water

Four Seasons Resort Aviara Golf Club, 18th hole

SIDETRIPS

Five minutes from the Four Seasons Resort Aviara is *Carlsbad,* a seaside village known for its long stretches of uncrowded beaches. Want to see how high-tech golf equipment is made? *Callaway* and *Taylor-Made,* among other top manufacturers, are located in Carlsbad (a.k.a. "Titanium Alley"). Each offers a factory tour.

to the right as well as an expanse of sand behind the green. Much like Arnie himself would in his prime.

After the round, players can repair to an exceptionally attractive, early California–style clubhouse featuring luxurious men's and women's locker facilities, a handsome golf shop, and the Argyle, an appealing restaurant (delectable salads, designer pizzas) with shaded outdoor seating overlooking the 18th green and Batiquitos Lagoon.

In the tony enclave of La Jolla, on the outskirts of San Diego, is **Torrey Pines**, a 36-hole municipal complex that is one of the busiest (upwards of 220,000 rounds annually) and best public facilities in the nation. There's a big brother and little brother in residence at this civic treasure, which has

hosted a PGA Tour event since 1968. Both courses are routed on bold, sloping headlands indented by deep ravines and punctuated by rare Torrey pines rooted in crumbling sandstone, their trunks twisted by the wind. The North Course offers a charming, manageable test from the middle tees at 6,326 yards but, golfers being golfers, most out-of-towners desire to play the TV tournament course at Torrey Pines. This is the long, demanding **South Course** (#93), a genuine championship spread that, on a breezy day, rivals its illustrious neighbor up the coast, Pebble Beach, in difficulty. Sneaky quick greens, nettlesome kikuyu rough, and dizzying drop-offs into plunging ravines provide a test for the best, as witness the quality and depth of its winner's circle over the years. Jack Nicklaus, Tom Weiskopf, Tom Watson, Johnny Miller, Phil Mickelson, Davis Love III, Mark O'Meara, and Tiger Woods are among the many great champions who have been crowned at Torrey Pines.

Not only must the elements be overcome to succeed at this heavily patronized layout, but so too must something else beyond the ken of the average handicap player—distance! The likes of Tiger Woods and John Daly may not flinch from the blue tees at 7,055 yards, but even from the so-called "regular" tees at 6,705 yards, the South Course, laid out by William F. "Billy" Bell, Jr., in 1957, presents way too much real estate for the average duffer to cover. (The red tees, at 6,457 yards, are equally daunting for ladies.) Purists, by the way, should plan to visit Torrey Pines

In Del Mar, near Torrey Pines, the restaurant of choice is *Jake's Del Mar,* a very popular spot on the beach serving excellent California continental cuisine. Also recommended is *Cilantros,* where the hybrid Mexican-Southwestern menu (barbecued pork tenderloin with tequila-chili relish) and frozen margaritas are appealing. The top choice in La Jolla is *George's at the Cove,* a multilevel dining spot with inspiring ocean views, excellent seafood, and rich desserts. Arrive hungry—portions are very generous. Outdoor dining terraces are available upstairs.

shortly before or after the PGA Tour's Buick Invitational in February to be assured of groomed fairways and smooth greens. With its perfect year-round conditions for golf—this land of perpetual spring has an annual average temperature of 71 degrees and a delightful Pacific breeze at most times of year—the wear and tear on this cherished muni is considerable.

At first glance, the South Course may look wide open, but it doesn't play wide open owing to its sticky rough and ever-present winds. Club selection is all-important, though a cannon may be required to reach some of the layout's longer par fours, starting with the first, a straightaway two-shotter stretching to 453 yards. The green, like most, is girdled left and right by sand. Traditionally, all putts at Torrey Pines break toward the ocean, but there are lots of "secret" breaks on the greens known only to seasoned locals. Expect a few surprises the first time around.

The third, a short par three that drops sharply to a well-trapped green backdropped by the sea, is a knockout, but the standout holes on the front nine are the fourth, which parallels the ocean for the entire length

of its 453 yards, and the seventh, a left-to-right dogleg of 454 yards that plays to a skewed, well-bunkered green. Both holes consistently rank among the toughest holes on the PGA Tour. Both play as par fives for mere mortals.

The South's back nine is more of the same. The 12th, at 456 yards, is yet another gargantuan par four, this one spread across a broad fairway that moves uphill into the prevailing ocean breeze to an elevated green straddled by bunkers. Just another par five for the average Joe. Golfers who play it smart and manage to avoid the gully prefacing the green can make time at the 13th, a 535-yard par five that plays away from the sea to a wide but shallow green. The 18th, a par-five of only 499 yards, provides a genuine birdie opportunity, though cleverly placed fairway traps and a greenside pond can sink a player's chances in a heartbeat.

While the clubhouse and practice facilities at Torrey Pines are modest by PGA Tour standards, there's a reason why the world's best players return each winter to play this West Coast mainstay. Most relish the opportunity to stride heaving fairways overlooking the sea and be tested by the elements on a true Everyman's course.

The two properties most convenient to the golf complex are *The Lodge at Torrey Pines,* which has 74 rooms with balconies overlooking the courses; and the *Hilton La Jolla Torrey Pines,* a low-rise, 400-room property set within a modern corporate park a few hundred yards from the South Course.

Because of the tremendous demand at Torrey Pines, visitors are advised to purchase the Golf Playing Package, which includes a guaranteed tee time, green fee with cart, and the guidance of a golf pro who accompanies each group for the first three holes and who gives players a brief history of the course and tips on how to play it. At press time, the package was $95 Monday through Friday, $110 Friday through Sunday and holidays. Reservations can be made a few weeks in advance.

More Golf/San Diego area

San Diego has over 40 public-access courses in a variety of oceanfront, mountain, and desert settings.

The sporty *North Course* at *Torrey Pines,* which is played by the pros during the first two rounds of the Buick Invitational, is four to six shots easier than the longer South Course and has great coastline views.

Riverwalk, located on the site of the former Stardust Golf Course in Mission Valley 15 minutes from downtown, reopened in 1998 as a 27-holer marked by undulating fairways, several lakes, and numerous waterfalls.

Torrey Pines, La Jolla, South Course, 12th hole

Torrey Pines, South Course, 14th hole

La Costa Resort & Spa, across the street from Aviara in Carlsbad, has two courses, North and South, a composite of which hosts the WGC–Andersen Consulting Match Play event inaugurated in 1999. Holes 15–18 on the South, "Golf's Longest Mile," form the backbone of the layout. La Costa's courses are open to hotel guests only.

Carlton Oaks, east of San Diego in Santee, is a prodigious 7,088-yard layout with deep pot bunkers, multitier greens, lots of railroad ties, and water in play at nearly every hole.

New & Noteworthy/San Diego

The Meadows Del Mar Golf Club, Tom Fazio's first design project in the San Diego area, opened in 1999. The upscale, daily-fee layout, cornerstone of a 134-home golf community, offers an expansive clubhouse, golf shop, and practice facility.

ATTRACTIONS

La Jolla has quaint shops, trendy boutiques, museums, galleries, and oceanfront restaurants set high on a bluff overlooking the ocean. *La Jolla Playhouse,* at the University of California at San Diego, attracts Hollywood and Broadway talent to its productions.

Torrey Pines State Park, located on rugged bluffs near the town of Del Mar (known for its thoroughbred racing in summer), offers a superb wilderness environment laced with hiking trails. Seeking serious thrills? Hang gliders, paragliders, and sailplanes can be launched from *Torrey Pines Gliderport* 320 feet above the beach.

The jewel in the crown of 1,074-acre Balboa Park is the *San Diego Zoo,* where the hippo pool and tiger habitat are just two of many attractions found within the world's foremost zoological garden. Nature in the wild? The annual migration of gray whales can be observed from *Cabrillo National Monument* on Point Loma in the winter months.

Nightlife? The historic 16-block *Gaslamp Quarter,* San Diego's "Bourbon Street by the Pacific," is the place to go.

A display at the San Diego Zoo

Palm Springs area

Pete Dye has singlehandedly caused golfers more misery than any other architect, but for sheer agony nothing can touch the **TPC Stadium Course** (#24) at **PGA West** in La Quinta. Other Stadium courses have been softened over the years, but this excruciatingly difficult layout remains a chamber of horrors for the average player. It is no accident. It is by design.

In the mid 1980s, Dye's instructions from developers Ernie Vossler and Joe Walser were simple: "Build us the hardest golf course in the world." On pancake-flat scrubland 20 miles east of Palm Springs, Dye outdid himself by bulldozing more than two million cubic yards of dirt into a sea of heaving mounds. He dressed up his grassy guillotine with 5,000 railroad ties, 250,000 gorse-like cassia shrubs, and eight lakes trimmed with rough-cut boulders, many of them dyed blood red. Enormous waste bunkers up to 200 yards in length were installed to frame the dimpled fairways. The targets are topsy-turvy greens guarded by crater-like bunkers, some seemingly dug halfway to China. From the back tees, there are no bailout areas and no holes where you can't make at least a double bogey as the result of a slight miscue. This isn't a golf course. It's a bermudagrass Colosseum with 18 hungry lions poised to devour out-of-towners.

Dye, who strongly believes that technological advances in equipment have given skilled golfers an unfair advantage in the chess game waged between designer and player, more than fulfilled the developer's mandate with this merciless links. Since the day it opened in 1986, the Stadium has been a lance capable of puncturing the thickest armor. Including titanium armor. Dye specifically designed the course to seek out, identify, and exploit the slightest flaw or weakness in a player's game. Especially

PGA West, La Quinta, TPC Stadium Course, 17th hole

the mental side of the game. The guts and concentration required to stave off calamity on a course where every single hole is a disaster waiting to happen is enough to shake anyone's confidence. And that includes members of the PGA Tour, who absolutely refused to play the Stadium a second time after their humiliating debut in the 1987 Bob Hope Chrysler Classic. (Some of the scores submitted by the world's best golfers were high enough to make a 10-handicapper blush.) Sooner or later, the Stadium Course overmatches nearly every golfer who tackles it, yet the parking lot at PGA West is full in high season. (At press time, an outside prebooked green fee at this masochist's delight was $260, certainly not an inexpensive way to have one's golfing soul laid to waste.)

How to get around this torture track with dignity intact? Choose to drive with the club you hit the straightest. Dye puts a premium on accuracy. Bring a trusty sand iron to escape the cavernous bunkers; and a 60-degree wedge for the lob shots you'll need to hit over the steep mounds that surround

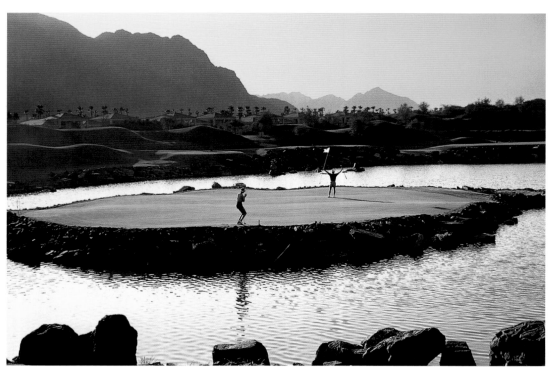

PGA West, TPC Stadium Course, 17th hole

the greens. Big hitters should intuit immediately that trying to overpower the course is fruitless and should throttle back to keep the ball in play. Modest, straight shots are preferable to long, crooked ones on the Stadium Course.

Shortly after the course opened, one wag stated that a player needed to bring a camel, a canoe, a priest, and a tourniquet to survive a round on the Stadium. The advice still holds. Add a bulletproof ego and a bottle of gripe water if you plan to keep score. Bring a camera if you're out for a lark: Despite the unsightly rows of condos located beside many of the fairways, the Stadium, backdropped by the soaring flanks of the Santa Rosa Mountains, has its own brand of beauty.

The full measure of the course is gauged from the championship tees at 6,739 yards. (The tournament tees, stretching to 7,266 yards, are often not marked. Even participants in the Skins Game held on the Stadium from 1986–1991 did not play every hole from all the way back.)

From the regular men's tees at 6,166 yards, average players are faced with partial or forced carries of 150–175 yards over shrubs, sand, or water at more than half the holes. Also, Dye directs a golfer's attention to the multitudinous hazards, not to safe landing zones. On the plus side, fairways only appear smaller and less welcoming than they really are. The trick is to play your game, despite the subliminal messages of doom sent by this stalker of a course.

Oddly, women love the Stadium Course at PGA West, and they account for roughly 15 percent of the rounds played there. From the ladies' tees at 5,092 yards—placed with care by Alice Dye, Pete's better half—there are only a handful of forced carries of any appreciable length.

Individual holes? The late Speaker of the House Tip O'Neill once spent the better part of an afternoon attempting to extract his ball from the 19-foot-deep pit that eats into the left side of the 16th green. (Locals refer to this trap as the San Andreas Fault. Tip thought it was Pete's Fault.) The par-three 17th, "Alcatraz," reduces the game to its barest elements. Either you hit the rock-rimmed island green (bravo); splash into the water; or knock it in the hole for an ace, as Lee Trevino did in the 1987 Skins Game. The par-four 18th, with water in play up the entire left side, is a tried-and-true format replicated elsewhere by Dye, notably on the Stadium Course at Sawgrass. But because of the angles, the 18th on the Stadium at PGA West is more ruthless than any other on his résumé. Perversely, it's also a welcome sight to players humiliated by four and a half hours of punishment under the desert sun.

It goes without saying that most golfers would fare better on one of the more open and less penal courses in the area. But try telling that to the diehard enthusiast who's traveled halfway across the country to test his skills on the course that sent the pros packing.

KSL Recreation, the leisure branch of a high-powered Wall Street firm that acquired **La Quinta Resort & Club** in 1993, surprised everyone by turning the private **Mountain Course** (#35), the prettiest and most playable of the many Pete Dye courses in the neighborhood, into a resort facility. Reopened in 1994 after a major overhaul, this 6,758-yard layout, backed up against the base of the Santa Rosa Mountains, offers a superlative test of golf along with breathtaking vistas and occasional sightings of roadrunners and coyotes.

The Mountain, which debuted in 1980, is the best-liked and most-admired public-access course in greater Palm Springs. Site of many major events, including the 1985 World Cup and the 1989 Senior Skins Game, the layout both demands and rewards accuracy—minus the dire consequences meted out for timid efforts on the nearby Stadium Course at PGA West. The Mountain is a classic target-style course, arguably the best Dye has ever built. Grassy swales, sandy waste areas, and deep pot bunkers define the line of play. Everything fair, nothing over the top, penalties handed out in proportion to the mistake made. Sharp elevation changes, slim landing pods, and generously contoured greens, many of them small, ledged targets perched above fairway level, do a credible job of defending par without breaking a player's back. Still, the Mountain is steep: The course rating is 74.1 (par 72) and the slope is 140 from the tips,

PGA West, TPC Stadium Course, 16th hole

The *Palm Springs Aerial Tramway,* the largest vertical cable rise in America, climbs to the 8,516-foot mountain station in Mount San Jacinto State Park in 14 minutes. New circular tramway cars introduced in 1999 give riders a 360-degree view of their ascent through five life zones, from the Sonoran Desert to the alpine wilderness. Bring a sweater—the temperature in the park is 40 degrees cooler on average than the desert floor.

The Living Desert, a 1,200-acre interpretive desert center with a zoo (mountain lions, golden eagles, coyotes), has nature trails that traverse a variety of desert gardens. *Indian Canyons,* a favorite oasis of the Agua Caliente Band of Cahuilla Indians centuries ago, is a fine place to view waterfalls, hot springs, fan palms, and ancient cliff dwellings. An hour's drive from Palm Springs is *Joshua Tree National Park,* a wildlife sanctuary dotted with wind-sculpted rocks and oddly shaped Joshua trees, their branches raised like arms to the sky.

Culture? There's the *McCallum Theatre for the Performing Arts, Annenberg Theater* in the Palm Springs Desert Museum, or the *Valley Players Guild* in downtown Palm Springs. Something extra special? The Fabulous Palm Springs Follies is a razzle-dazzle, vaudeville-style revue starring retired (but still talented) showgirls, dancers, and singers. The show is staged at the historic *Plaza Theatre* in downtown Palm Springs.

Shopping? *El Paseo* is the Rodeo Drive of Palm Springs. Inexpensive gifts? Cactus planters and delicious Medjool dates are widely available.

Palm Springs Aerial Tramway

very high numbers for a course that measures under 6,800 yards. In sum, nowhere in the California desert do beauty and challenge combine as they do on La Quinta's Mountain Course.

Among the more intriguing holes is the second, a long, testing par three squeezed by water to the left and sand to the right. The fourth, a short par five, doglegs to the left around the mountains and dares big hitters to try for the green in two. A very risky proposition: The deep two-tiered green is well guarded by grass bunkers. At the ninth, a sturdy par four stretching to 443 yards, players are offered a choice of landing areas. The fairway to the left is easier to reach, but driving to the right of a central pot bunker to a plateau fairway leaves a better shot into the green. A hooked drive finds water, a sliced tee ball finds sand. The slightly downhill approach shot is played to a deep, elevated green guarded left and right by bunkers. From start to finish, the ninth is a superior par four.

The 14th, one of the more scenic holes on the Mountain, is a 389-yard par four where players must carry their drives over the raw desert to an elevated landing area that is semiblind from the tee. A deep ravine swallows drives pushed to the right; an errant pull to the left ends up in the desert. The second shot is played to a perched, two-tier green canted from back to front and protected by a ravine to the right and bunkers on the left. Four is a great score here.

The par-three 16th is the Mountain's acknowledged signature hole. From tees

La Quinta Resort & Club, La Quinta, Mountain Course, second hole

La Quinta Resort & Club, Mountain Course, 14ᵗʰ hole

Swing Fix

PGA West boasts two name-brand golf academies: the *Jim McLean Golf School* and the *Dave Pelz Short Game School.* "Three days at the school can change a golfer's game forever," said Pelz, who is known as 'Professor Putt' on the pro tour circuits. "Through our course, golfers of all levels learn to improve their distance wedges, pitching, chipping, sand shots, and putting, which is often the most neglected and misunderstood part of the game." The Jim McLean program is more oriented to the full swing.

SPA

With dozens of feel-good retreats, Palm Springs, long revered as a healing ground by the Cahuilla Indians, is the nation's spa capital. Among the area's newest facilities is the 23,000-square-foot *Spa La Quinta,* opened in 1998 adjacent to the resort's 30-court tennis center. Signature treatments include the PGA West Golf Massage, which concentrates on hands, arms, lower back, and shoulders, and Celestial Shower, a traditional Swiss shower in a private open-air setting. Golf & Spa packages are available.

cut into the side of a mountain—have a whack from the tips at 168 yards, it's worth the thrills—the shot is played straight downhill to a long, narrow green embraced by rocks and brush. It's a waterless version of Dye's dreaded "Alcatraz" hole on the Stadium Course.

The 17th, at 446 yards the longest hole on the course, asks for a solid drive that avoids a huge waste bunker up the left side. The approach shot is a postcard, with the slightly elevated green pushed up against the stony mountain base. The short par-five 18th, which turns sharply to the left, is reachable in two if you can carry an imposing pot bunker off the tee and hit a laserlike approach to a slender green peppered with hidden pits of sand.

A tip for success on this shotmaker's track: The mountain backdrop can wreak havoc with depth perception. Targets on the Mountain Course tend to be farther away than they appear. Club yourself accordingly. And enjoy a course Dye built to challenge club members, not make them despair and take up tennis.

La Quinta Resort & Club, Mountain Course, 16th hole

LODGING

A former hideaway for Hollywood's "Golden Era" movie stars, *La Quinta Resort & Club,* founded in 1926, is where Frank Capra penned most of his award-winning film scripts and where Irving Berlin was inspired to write "White Christmas." These many years later, the venerable property has evolved into a 72-hole desert heavyweight that nevertheless manages to retain its old California charm. The resort's 640 updated rooms and suites are housed in quaint Spanish Colonial–style casitas spread across 45 acres of manicured lawns and well-tended gardens, with 25 swimming pools and numerous hot tubs framed by tall palms and citrus groves. La Quinta's hub is the Plaza, where saltillo pathways, tile fountains, and watercourses flanked by multicolored flowerbeds lead to specialty shops and cafés. The concierge can arrange horseback riding, bicycle tours, desert jeep tours, and hot air ballooning.

Casitas at La Quinta Resort & Club

DINING

La Quinta's dining experiences are nearly as varied as its golf courses. *Montañas* offers an excellent seafood-oriented Mediterranean menu in a handsome room evocative of old California. Superb regional Mexican cuisine and champion margaritas are served in the lively, colorful *Adobe Grill*. Morgans, a 1920s-style American bistro decorated in brass, glass, and dark polished wood, is open for breakfast, lunch, and dinner, with patio dining available. Afternoon tea is served in the *Santa Rosa Lobby Lounge*, which has huge open fireplaces and exposed-beamed ceilings. *Mulligans* is a sports bar with a big-screen TV—and locally brewed Mulligan's beer.

The Adobe Grill at La Quinta Resort and Club

With nearly 700 restaurants, greater Palm Springs does not lack for dining options. *Robi,* located in an old Spanish villa in the city of La Quinta, offers a three-course, six-hour dining experience where patrons are free to observe chefs preparing steak, veal, and tilapia meuniere. Also convenient to the resort is *Cunard's,* an elegant spot featuring stylish Continental cuisine with wines to match. The *Dining Room* at the nearby Ritz-Carlton Rancho Mirage offers one of the finest formal dining experiences in southern California. *Le Vallauris* in Palm Springs, a 1927 landmark, delivers consistently excellent French cuisine—and a very French ambience.

Something more casual? *Palomino Euro Bistro* in Palm Desert specializes in spit-roasted entrees amd thin-crust pizza. Also in Palm Desert is *Jillians,* where the seafood pasta dishes are recommended; and *Tommy Bahamas,* a trendy tropics-themed restaurant serving contemporary American cuisine. For superb Southwestern fare (Yucatan fish, taco salads), make a beeline for the *Blue Coyote Grill* (two locations).

More Golf / Palm Springs

There are close to 100 courses in greater Palm Springs, qualifying this desert oasis as a genuine golf mecca. A few highlights:

At La Quinta Resort & Club, there's the *Dunes Course,* a target-style layout by Pete Dye with a risk-reward scenario at nearly every hole. The spectacular par-four 17th, a dogleg left with water in play on the drive and approach, is one of the nation's toughest two-shotters.

The *Jack Nicklaus Tournament Course* at PGA West, a solid 7,126-yard test, is highlighted by stark mounding, sharp-edged waste bunkers—and a huge double green shared by the ninth and 18th holes.

Desert Dunes, inspired by Scottish links courses, is a Robert Trent Jones, Jr., creation in Desert Hot Springs marked by rolling fairways framed by mesquite and tamarisk trees that lead to heavily contoured greens well defended by bunkers. The 6,876-yard layout, subject to afternoon winds, is free of housing.

Mission Hills North, a Gary Player–designed course at the Westin Resort in Rancho Mirage, is a dramatic layout set off by extensive waterscaping, drought-resistant trees, and gold-tinted "fines" (pulverized stone). There's water in play at 14 holes, but forward tees reduce the challenge.

Something less serious? Tommy Jacobs Bel Air Greens features an 18-hole miniature golf course and a nine-hole executive walking course with a night-lit driving range.

New & Noteworthy / Palm Springs

Desert Willow, a 36-hole municipally owned complex in Palm Desert, has a unique claim to fame: Its *Firecliff Course,* opened in 1997, is the only golf course ever featured on the cover of *Smithsonian Magazine,* thanks to its environmentally sensitive design. The team of Michael Hurdzan and Dana Fry, with input from PGA Tour pro John Cook, used desert landscapes and indigenous plants in the design of this brilliant 7,056-yard course. Reclaimed water is used to irrigate the fairways. A second layout, the more user-friendly *Mountain View Course,* opened at Desert Willow in 1998. Both venues share spectacular views of the Santa Rosa Mountains. There's also a David Leadbetter Golf Academy at the club.

The *Greg Norman Course* at PGA West, expected to open by December 1999, will give the sprawling complex six layouts (three public-access, three private). Further in the future, a keenly anticipated Tom Fazio–designed course at the Ritz-Carlton Rancho Mirage is expected to open in mid-2000.

Hawaii

Mauna Kea Beach Golf Course • Mauna Lani Resort, North Course

Princeville Resort, Prince Course • Kauai Lagoons, Kiele Course • The Challenge at Manele

Koolau Golf Course • Kapalua Resort, Plantation Course

Kauai Lagoons, Lihue, Kauai, Kiele Course, fifth hole

Hawaii

Mark Twain's oft-quoted ode to what were then the Sandwich Islands—"the loveliest fleet of islands that lies anchored in any ocean"—turns out to be true. A tiny archipelago of mountaintops that bubbled up from lava vents in the North Pacific floor, Hawaii offers the nation's most paradisal settings for the game. Whenever *GOLF Magazine* has asked subscribers where they would most like to take a dream golf vacation, Hawaii is always numero uno. An understandable quorum. The weather is mild year round. The people, Polynesian to the core, invented the aloha spirit. And the golf courses—seven "Top 100" courses sprinkled across five islands, some carved from lava flows, others dropped into jungles—are simply off the charts for aesthetics. If you're the type of golfer who can set aside the scorecard pencil for a moment or two, this Eden of Oceania is for you. Worth crossing an ocean to play? One whiff of an exotic blossom after a rain shower, one glimpse of a double rainbow arching across the mountains, one trip in a helicopter over a bubbling volcano is answer enough.

Big Island

It was 1960, the year after Hawaii attained statehood, and Laurance Rockefeller, at the invitation of Governor William F. Quinn, was cruising the leeward side of the Big Island. Quinn hoped that Rockefeller, a visionary developer, would be inspired to build a resort along the lines of Caneel Bay and Dorado Beach, a pair of Caribbean retreats that had found favor with sophisticated travelers. Rockefeller had expressed no interest in building a resort in Hawaii, but thirty-five miles north of Kailua-Kona, he caught sight of a perfect crescent of palm-fringed sand below an ochre plain of lava. He changed his mind.

LODGING

Optional TVs are now available in the once-austere guest rooms of the open-air *Mauna Kea Beach Hotel*. Equipped with new marble bathrooms, the hotel's 310 rooms have large lanais, rattan and willow furnishings, and other subtle enhancements. Rockefeller's 1,600-piece collection of Asian and Pacific artifacts is tastefully displayed about the public areas.

The Mauna Kea Resort's sister property, the newer *Hapuna Beach Prince Hotel*, is a low-profile, 350-room property nestled on bluffs with a sweeping view of the Kohala Coast from its see-through lobby.

Guest room at the Mauna Kea Beach Hotel

Setting aside the region's remoteness and aridity, Rockefeller decided that this was the place to build a special getaway where discerning travelers could get in touch with nature and escape the pressures of modern life. And though its ownership and management has changed often over the years, the open-air public spaces of the Mauna Kea Beach Hotel, reopened in 1995 after a major refurbishment, remain filled with Rockefeller's fabulous collection of Asian and Pacific artifacts.

The developer's challenge to Robert Trent Jones to inscribe a golf course on the desiccated remains of a 5,000-year-old lava flow resulted in a spectacular layout with ocean views from every green. Visible as well are Mauna Kea (white mountain), a 13,796-foot peak named for its wintertime cap of snow; and Mauna Loa, earth's largest active volcano. The **Mauna Kea Beach Golf Course** (#22), opened in 1965, forced Jones to devise new methods of construction. He adapted earth-moving equipment to pulverize the ancient lava

Mauna Kea Beach Hotel, Kohala Coast, Big Island

Mauna Kea Beach Golf Course, third hole

into red dust, improvised a watering system so that grass seedlings could sprout in the manufactured soil and laid out a course that, significantly upgraded in 1998, endures as one of his masterpieces.

More than an engineering marvel, Jones followed Rockefeller's dictate that Nature reign supreme at Mauna Kea. "I built the course to fit the land," Jones wrote in his book, *Golf's Magnificent Challenge,* adding that he was excited when he first walked the desolate, undulating terrain because "there were elevations for the tees, nice pockets for the greens, everything you would want for a great course. When you have the land, you can add the beauty." The coconut palm, Chinese banyan, wili-wili, plumeria, monkeypod, and rainbow shower trees he planted alongside the fairways are now fully mature, and soften the corners of the course beautifully.

Hillier than neighboring Kohala Coast layouts carved from flatter, more recent volcanic flows, Mauna Kea is a counterpuncher of a course that climbs from sea level to 300 feet. Some holes bend to the right, others to the left. Several holes drop sharply from their skybox tees to sinuous

Mauna Kea Beach Golf Course, 11ᵗʰ hole

fairways far below. Others climb to perched greens that surmount lava hills. Fairways are generously wide, but the corners of the doglegs and all the greens are well protected by flashed-face, cloverleaf bunkers, a shape pioneered and perfected by Jones in the 1960s.

Mauna Kea's signature hole, one of the great seaside par threes in the world, is the third, where golfers tee from a lava promontory and attempt to carry their do-or-die shots across a wide expanse of pounding surf to a sprawling, kidney-shaped green girdled by seven traps. The green, 60 yards deep, has three distinct levels. If you're on one and the pin is on the other, brace yourself for a minimum of three putts. With the trade winds blowing, which they do all winter long, any tee shot that lands on terra firma is acceptable.

The heroic third is a photographer's dream, but the par-three 11th, which plunges 247 yards from a hilltop tee shaded by coconut palms to a domed green perched above the sea that tapers away to deep bunkers and the exposed roots of banyan trees, presents an even stiffer challenge. Especially when the breeze ripples the flag.

The 11th kicks off a stretch of very testing holes. Indeed, the incoming nine is three to four strokes tougher than the outgoing holes. The par-four 14th, for example, is a grand conception that sweeps to the left on tumbling ground to the bleak prospect of a shallow, heavily bunkered green set atop a hill. Hard par, easy bogey? Not from a sidehill lie, not when a sea breeze is astir. The 17th, a gigantic par five stretching to 555 yards, presents a very wide landing area that doglegs to the left and leads to yet another well-trapped green. At the home hole, a thrilling par four that plays from an elevated tee, players must beware a stand of trees and a nest of bunkers on the drive, which should be aimed toward the hotel. The

ever-present breeze will usually swing the ball back to the center of the fairway, setting up a short approach to a subtly contoured green.

While many of the more radical undulations on the greens were toned in the mid 1970s, they still pose quite a challenge to the uninitiated. Perhaps the most significant improvement to the course was made in 1983, when 22 championship and alternative tees were added to create more flexibility for players at all ability levels. PGA Tour hopefuls can tackle the black tees at 7,114 yards, while the blue (6,737 yards), orange (6,365 yards), and white (5,277 yards) markers offer sound options for everyone else. Because of guest demand, walking is permitted at certain times, a delightful alternative for fitness-conscious players. New fairway grasses and the replacement of native coral sand in the bunkers with whiter, less granular sand have also enhanced the experience at Mauna Kea. Hotel residents receive preferred tee times and reduced rates, though nonresort guests can play the Big Island's big kahuna on a space-available basis.

DINING

Breakfast in the *Pavilion* at the Mauna Kea Beach Hotel features fresh tropical fruits, macadamia nut waffles, banana pancakes, Kona coffee, and other island specialties. The sandwiches and pupus (appetizers) served at the 19th Hole are excellent. *Batik*, a gorgeous two-level room with open-air dining specializing in Euro-Asian cuisine, is the hotel's finest restaurant. A jazz duo performs in the Batik Lounge nightly. There's also a traditional sunset luau on the shores of Kauna'oa Bay on Tuesdays, and a twice-weekly clambake at the *Hau Tree/Gazebo Bar* on the beach.

Among the dining choices at the *Hapuna Beach Prince* are *Hakone* (authentic Japanese cuisine and the island's best sushi bar); *Coast Grille* (local seafood, oyster bar); and *Arnie's* (all-American fare in the Hapuna Golf Clubhouse).

More Golf/Mauna Kea

The resort's second venue, *Hapuna Golf Course,* was chiseled into volcanic foothills 700 feet above the blue Pacific by Arnold Palmer and Ed Seay in 1992. Treeless and windswept, this target-style desert links presents a formidable test of accuracy. Most of the holes demand a forced carry of 50 to 150 yards to reach narrow landing pods framed by native plants and trees. The bowl-shaped greens are receptive, but the rough is punishing. Fantastic views of the Big Island's scalloped coastline from the higher holes is fair compensation.

Here's a surprise. The voting panel's choice at the 36-hole **Mauna Lani Resort** a few lava flows away from Mauna Kea is not the South Course, a spectacular spread carved from licorice-black a'a lava that plays nip and tuck with the sea. Long-time site of the Senior Skins Game, the South, an aesthetic delight, is the course most visitors to Mauna Lani want to play. But from a pure golf standpoint, the resort's **North Course** (#75) offers a superior test, its rolling fairways carved from an older bed of reddish-brown pahoehoe lava that supports a grove of gnarled kiawe trees. A 230-acre archaeological district forms the northern boundary of the layout, while feral goats occasionally wander across the savannalike spread.

If you've always wanted to go after the big one, here's your chance: The Big Island's Kona Coast is world-renowned for giant Pacific blue marlin. A neophyte's chance of landing a trophy gamefish is about the same as winning money in Las Vegas, though expert captains can slant the odds in your favor. Check with your hotel concierge on how and where to book a deep-sea charter.

Both courses at Mauna Lani were named for Francis H. I'i Brown, a sportsman of royal Hawaiian lineage who counted Babe Ruth, Bing Crosby, and the Prince of Wales among his friends. The two golf courses at Mauna Lani ("mountain reaching heaven") occupy Brown's 3,200-acre estate at Kalahuipua'a, which encompasses prehistoric fishponds, lava tube dwellings, and petroglyph fields.

To meet rising guest demand, the resort hired the Hawaiian design firm of Nelson-Wright-Haworth in 1991 to create a second venue. The designers wisely opted to split the original 18. Nine new holes (four through 12) were melded to the original back nine to create the North,

Mauna Lani Resort, Big Island, North Course, 17th hole

279

Mauna Lani's most popular restaurant is the *CanoeHouse*, where the terrace doors open to spotlit waves and where musicians play and sing the songs of old Hawaii. Regional Hawaiian cuisine with Pacific Basin influences is featured: Pesto-seared scallops with roasted taro and guava sauce is a typical entree. For casual dining, the refurbished *Ocean Grill*, shaded by a milo tree, serves three meals daily (designer pizzas at lunch, grilled prawns available all day). *Knickers*, a mahogany-paneled bar and lounge opposite the golf shop, serves a first-rate lunch. The *Bay Terrace*, serving breakfast in a gardenlike setting, has a lavish Sunday brunch and a popular seafood buffet on Friday and Saturday evenings. Mauna Lani's *Honu Bar*, named for the Hawaiian green sea turtle, serves up light supper, live music, gourmet desserts, and fine wines and cordials in a sleek lounge with a beautiful fresco of the Big Island's mountains over the bar.

a superlative test of golf that calls for well-placed tee shots aimed to one side of the fairway or the other to set up the correct angle of attack to the green.

The 6,993-yard course, always in top shape, gets down to business at the par-four third, where the tee shot from the blue markers is made through a tree-lined chute, with a pair of tall kiawe trees serving as goal posts 115 yards from the large, circular green. At the par-four fourth, the drive, played from a perched tee, must carry a wide gully designated as an archaeological preserve, while the approach shot must avoid a pair of amorphous traps guarding the elevated green. The fifth, a mid-length par three aimed straight into the trade winds, calls for an unerring tee shot to a green flanked on three sides by a lagoon. A small waterfall backdrops the hole and feeds a stream that flows along the right side of the green. The ninth, rated the toughest hole on the course, is a lengthy par four (455 yards from the tips) with a wide fairway that invites a big drive. The downhill approach is played to a narrow green guarded by a lava-rimmed tidal pond and lots of sand. Heliotrope trees, a salt-and-pepper rock beach, and the turquoise-blue sea backdrop the hole.

The back nine works its way south to the petite par-three 17th, one of the jewels of Hawaiian golf. Only 91 yards from the white tees, the hole calls for a well-judged pitch to a green set within an amphitheaterlike bowl of lava. Even from the elevated tees, the hole, encased in spiky rock, is sheltered from the wind. A monolithic slab of lava rises from a shallow bunker in front of the green, partially obscuring the putting surface. This rock can do serious damage to a low hook. The home hole, a sturdy par

four, plays directly to the sea. On a clear day, which is just about every day on the Kohala Coast, the target line is 10,023-foot Mt. Haleakala on Maui.

After the round, drop by Mauna Lani's golf shop, a cross between a Fifth Avenue designer boutique and a fine London haberdashery. Choose from Egyptian cotton shirts embroidered with the resort logo of a leaping marlin, slim chocolate brown leather golf bags made in Italy, and interesting golf mementos wrought in silver.

More Golf/Mauna Lani

Mauna Lani's *South Course*, one of America's most pleasureable resort spreads, was designed to be enjoyed by the average duffer, not just the champion. Fairways are broad, green contours are mild, and forced carries are rare. The exception is the par-three 15th, where golfers tee from a lava platform and play across a surging inlet of the Pacific to an enormous green staked out by tall coconut palms and cloverleaf traps.

SIDETRIP/HAWAII VOLCANOES NATIONAL PARK

Want a face-to-face meeting with Pele, the volcano goddess? Pay a visit to *Hawaii Volcanoes National Park*, where Kilauea, the world's most active volcano, can be viewed from the Crater Rim Road or from branch routes like the Devastation Trail. In addition to hissing steam and sulphur from vents deep within Halemaunmau Crater, Pele's home, the 344-square-mile park doubles as a nature reserve of black sand beaches, fern jungles, rain forests, and wooded glades full of wild orchids and butterflies.

Seeking a truly unique golf experience? *Volcano Golf and Country Club*, situated at 4,280 feet above sea level near the rim of Kilauea Crater, offers cool air, spectacular views, and a sporty 6,250-yard test routed among colorful ohia trees.

Kilauea Volcano

DINING/LUAU

The Friday night luau at Kona Village Resort, the Big Island's oldest continuously running Aha'aina (feast), is also one of its best and most authentic. The menu includes Kalua Pig roasted in an imu (underground oven), lomi salmon, steamed taro, and other traditional foods. A Polynesian revue, featuring the hula (dances) of Hawaii, follows the meal.

Preparing pig for a luau at the Kona Village Resort

More Golf/Big Island

Farther south on the Kohala Coast are the *Waikoloa Beach Resort,* which offers the *Beach Course,* a sporty, Robert Trent Jones, Jr.–designed layout that swings near the sea, and the *Kings' Golf Club,* a windswept Tom Weiskopf–Jay Morrish creation routed among lava outcrops and blue lagoons.

Also nearby is *Hualalai Golf Club,* a Jack Nicklaus–designed course that debuted in 1996 and is limited to guests of the on-site *Four Seasons Resort.* Home of a Senior PGA Tour event, the well-groomed course begins in a lush kipuka (oasis), flows across forgivingly wide fairways carved from black lava, and finishes along the sea. Hualalai also swings near the historic *King's Trail,* once the seaside pedestrian highway for an indigenous population.

LODGING

At *Mauna Lani Bay Hotel and Bungalows,* treated to a $10 million "refreshment" in 1997, renovations in the chevron-shaped, 350-room seaside hotel included the upgrading of entryways and bathrooms using light-colored Jerusalem stone and European fixtures in the bathrooms. Tall palms, tropical greenery, waterfalls, streams, and pools stocked with koi (prized multicolored carp) grace the hotel's dazzling open-air atrium. In 1998, the hotel became the first in the state to be powered by commercial-scale solar electric energy.

Mauna Lani's five secluded bungalows, each with its own butler, spa, and private swimming pool, are the summit of luxury. For what they cost, they should be: At press time, the nightly tariff at the Bird of Paradise bungalow was $4,400. Another option is the *Orchid at Mauna Lani* (formerly a Ritz-Carlton) nestled on 32 acres of seaside property near the North Course.

Kauai

On the site of an 11,000-acre plantation at the northern tip of Kauai is **Princeville Resort**, the Garden Isle's first major golf retreat. Seeking to establish his own identity after years of working in his father's shadow, Robert Trent Jones, Jr., laid out the 27-hole Makai Course in 1971. It is a lovely test of golf. But Jones the Younger, restless in his quest to build a course that breathes as much fire as Pele, the volcano goddess, returned several years later to design his masterpiece, three holes at a time, to comply with environmental restrictions. "No golf course on earth offers more beautiful vistas from more challenging terrain," Jones deigned to say when his work was done.

Alternately the most mesmerizing and backbreaking layout in the Pacific, the **Prince Course** (#19) lacks nothing for grandeur and spectacle. The heaving fairways, spread across rolling tableland nestled between the blue Pacific and pleated volcanic palisades streaming with waterfalls, are crossed or bordered by gorges, streams, and gullies choked with mango, guava, and lauhala ("tourist pineapple") trees. Jones calls these verdant creases in the earth "the edges of doom."

Here's the tale of the tape on the Prince: 7,309 yards from the tips, course rating 75.6 (par 72), slope 144. Crash-and-burn holes, no two of

SIDETRIPS

A catamaran cruise along the famed Na Pali coast west of Princeville is a great way to see one of Hawaii's—and the world's—most spectacular shorelines. City slickers can join paniolos (Hawaiian cowboys) at *Princeville Ranch* on a full-fledged cattle drive, or take a horseback ride on a high plain overlooking the Hanalei Valley and its patchwork of taro plantations. *Hanalei River* kayak and snorkeling tours are also available. So is superlative hiking above massive seacliffs along the North Coast. Something tamer? Take a stroll through the picturesque town of Hanalei.

Na Pali Coast

Princeville Resort, Kauai, Prince Course, 12ᵗʰ hole

Princeville Resort, Prince Course, 16th hole

DINING

In addition to a Friday night seafood buffet and superb Sunday brunch in *Café Hanalei*, formal

Brunch at the Café Hanalei

La Cascata restaurant

dining at Princeville is available at *La Cascata*, designed to resemble a southern Italian coastal villa (terra-cotta floors, trompe l'oeil paintings). There's also a beach luau on Thursday nights. The sleek clubhouse at the Prince Course serves breakfast and lunch. Before or after dinner, cocktails are served on the outdoor terrace adjoining the hotel lobby's living room, where the technicolor sunsets are worth writing home about. Want to rub elbows with the locals? Check out *Tahiti Nui* in Hanalei, a North Shore mainstay offering pupu platters (appetizers), mai tais, and live music.

which parallel each other, sprawl across 390 acres of triple-bogey country. The risk-reward scenarios on this behemoth aren't merely memorable— they are riveting. On a breezy day from the tips, the Prince has all the charm of a sumo wrestler suffering from indigestion. Jones, who maintains a residence in nearby Hanalei, lavished more than the usual care and attention on the Prince. He borrowed design motifs from the world's top courses to go the limit here. The bunkering is kept to a minimum, and the greens (once you get to them) are puttable, but this bruising layout, unveiled in 1990, remains a big-time track for skilled, confident golfers. Beginners should book a day trip to Hanalei rather than book a tee time on the Prince. Middle handicappers who can cope with daunting forced carries can survive the ordeal from the resort tees at 6,005 yards. But only if they're brave. Because there's no way to play the Prince cautiously or conservatively. Only bold, accurate strokes find their reward here. Single-digit campaigners will enjoy the white tees at 6,521 yards but will have all they can handle from blues at 6,960 yards.

The golf course, named in honor of the 19th-century "Prince of Hawaii," Prince Albert Edward Kauikeaouli Leiopapa A Kamehameha (a scratch player, no doubt), signals its intentions at the very first hole, a wicked S-shaped par four calling for a well-placed drive that avoids Anini Stream to the left. This tropical burn makes an oxbow loop around the green and also cuts in front of the putting surface, dunking approach shots that come up short.

As for homage holes, the sixth, a breathtaking par four stretching to 428 yards, careens downhill through a valley past a minefield of bunkers, the ocean's foaming surf in view beyond the green. The old-fashioned cross bunker 40 yards short of the sixth green was inspired by a similar sand pit on the 11th hole at Pine Valley. The seventh is a do-or-die par three with nine sets of tees that captures some of the seaside magic of the legendary 16th at Cypress Point.

The back nine is a showcase for Jones's design wizardry. The 10th, nicknamed "Burma Road," is a fishhook-shaped par five that dares better players to cross a heavily vegetated gorge to reach the wide, shallow green in two shots. At the par-four 12th, "Eagle's Nest," the drop to the slender, jungle-lined fairway is nearly 100 feet. A stream flows around three sides of a bunkerless green encased in a mossy amphitheater of fern-covered rock. The stakes are raised even higher at the 13th, a sharp left-to-right dogleg that ranks as one of the most intriguing par fours Jones has ever built. The drive must be laid up short of a stream that crosses the fairway about 195 yards from the white tees. The second shot must find an oval green flanked by a pair of traps to the left, with flowing water nearly skimming the right side of the putting surface. From a tunnel built by coolie labor in the mid 1800s, a ribbon of water now falls into Anini Stream behind the green. It's the niftiest bit of stagecraft on a course full of intrigue.

Assuming players have survived the first 17 holes, the 18th is sure to produce a bogey or worse. This laborious par four, 455 yards from the Prince tees, treks uphill into the prevailing breeze to a large, well-

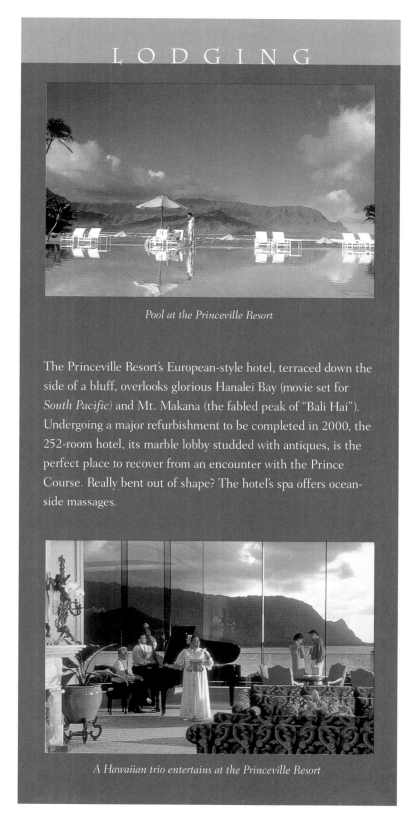

Pool at the Princeville Resort

The Princeville Resort's European-style hotel, terraced down the side of a bluff, overlooks glorious Hanalei Bay (movie set for *South Pacific*) and Mt. Makana (the fabled peak of "Bali Hai"). Undergoing a major refurbishment to be completed in 2000, the 252-room hotel, its marble lobby studded with antiques, is the perfect place to recover from an encounter with the Prince Course. Really bent out of shape? The hotel's spa offers ocean-side massages.

A Hawaiian trio entertains at the Princeville Resort

bunkered green. "Hope you don't need a par to break 80," chortles the yardage book. A touch of local humor, to be sure. Like others before it, the ruthless 18th tends to overreach for dramatic effect, but there is no denying that the musclebound Prince is a regal spread. Just don't expect to snatch his crown without a tussle.

Kauai Lagoons, Kauai, Kiele Course, fifth hole

More Golf / Princeville

Princeville Resort's 27-hole *Makai Course,* offering three well-groomed nines, promises a pleasurable outing. The Ocean nine, highlighted by two hair-raising par threes, is exceptional. At the third, a short iron is played from a tee cut into a hill to a jungle-fronted green 100 feet below. At the 142-yard eighth, a giant thumbprint in the coastline separates tee and green, the ocean boiling in a rock-bound chasm far below.

LODGING

Set above a quarter-mile stretch of beautiful Kalapaki Beach, an azure cove at the foot of Nawiliwili Bay, the *Kauai Marriott* spent liberally to create a lush tropical setting and distance itself from the site's former tenant, a glitzy European-themed mega-resort destroyed by Hurricane Iniki in 1994. The hotel's 356 rooms are small but comfortable. Most have lanais with ocean views. Incidentally, if the lush, rugged scenery across the bay from the resort looks familiar, there's a reason—dozens of movies (including *Jurassic Park*) have been filmed in the vicinity.

DINING

The *Kauai Marriott's* restaurants, Kukui's, Kalapaki Grill, and Duke's Canoe Club & Barefoot Bar, are refreshingly casual. The collection of rare photos, paddles, Hawaiian outriggers, and original surfboards at Duke's Canoe Club, named for Duke Kahanamoku, the father of Hawaiian surfing, is engrossing. Whalers Brewpub, overlooking the Kiele's oceanfront 13th hole, offers seven fresh specialty beers as well as good burgers and stir-fry entrees. The Terrace Restaurant adjacent to the spa offers a well-varied menu at breakfast and lunch. Off property, *A Pacific Café* in nearby Kapaa is a stylish "destination restaurant" worth finding for its cutting edge Pacific Rim cuisine.

Named for the sweet fragrance of the gardenia, the **Kiele Course** (#64) at **Kauai Lagoons** in Lihue, a 7,070-yard knockout by Jack Nicklaus that skirts a rain forest on the front nine and tightropes sea cliffs on the back nine, is the layout that pushed Kauai to the head of the class as a golf destination.

At the head of the Wailua River, where the war canoes of Kaumualii, the King of Kauai, once assembled, is the *Fern Grotto*, a hauntingly beautiful cave luxuriant with tropical greenery. Tour boats are available at the Wailua Marina. Also in the vicinity is *Smith's Tropical Paradise*, a 23-acre botanical garden; and *Kamokila*, a replica of an ancient Hawaiian village on the Wailua River.

The resort's Kalapaki Kids Club, featuring safari boat rides, beach activities, lei making, and hula lessons, is one of the best in the islands. Like to splash around? The property's 26,000-square foot, rosette-shaped swimming pool, highlighted by five gazebo-covered marble jacuzzis, four waterfalls, and an island of royal palms, is Hawaii's largest. There's also a spa at the resort.

Opened in 1988, the Kiele starts with a wide-open par four and a short, downwind par five before tightening the noose at the third, a long par four where the drive must avoid a central bunker and the second shot must be played uphill over sand to a shallow, kidney-shaped green. No easy task from the tips at 436 yards into the prevailing trade winds. The fourth, a two-shotter stretching to 470 yards, is even tougher. A bold drive over a corner of an imposing bunker leaves an approach shot to a bowl-shaped green that slopes away from players. The inland holes on the front reach a climax at the par-three fifth, the Eagle. (Each hole on the Kiele is named for an animal, and each tee is graced by an impressive marble statue of it.) The tee shot here is played over the canopy of a rain forest to the largest green on the course. (The target only appears small from the vantage point of the tee.) Arm yourself with extra club and take dead aim at one of the exposed rocks in the volcanic ridge backdropping this exquisite hole. At the sixth, a short par five, players are invited to bite off as much of the gorge's verdant fronds as they dare. Aggressive players who hew close to the enormous fairway bunker that swings along the right side of the fairway can set themselves up for a shot at the sizable green.

The Kiele's incoming nine is worth crossing an ocean to play. Indeed, it is the dramatic seaside portion of the 262-acre layout that prompted Nicklaus to famously quip when the course opened, "On a scale of one to 10, I'd rate the Kiele a 13."

The excitement begins at the 12th, a long downhill par four that plunges through a bunker-lined valley directly to the brink of the sea, its bilevel green (like many on the course) set on a diagonal to the fairway. A deep, menacing bunker snares approach shots pulled to the left.

The par-three 13th, among the most picturesque holes in Hawaii, brings golfers to a clifftop perch, the waves lashing the rocks far below. From here a well-struck tee shot must carry the ocean's foaming inlet to find a pedestal green framed by swaying palms and shored up by dense vegetation. Fifty feet below the green is a black sand beach dotted with golf balls. The safest play is to the right, where the close-mown hillside will direct shots to the putting surface.

A mild-mannered par four called the Peacock cuts inland, but then the Kiele doubles back to the sea at the 15th, a downwind par five stretching to 529 yards that gives big hitters a legitimate shot at birdie. The canted fairway, guarded to the right by a nest of bunkers, leads to a shallow, undulating green undercut by deep traps and set on bluffs above a waterspout, a craterlike hole in the lava-rock shoreline that spumes water with each incoming wave.

The petite par-four 16th, the Turtle, is one of the trickiest short par

Kauai Lagoons, Kiele Course, 12th hole

Kauai Lagoons, Kiele Course, 13th hole

More Golf/Kauai Lagoons

The *Lagoons Course*, laid out by Nicklaus on agricultural land removed from the sea but well within view of Lihue Airport's runways, is a nearly treeless, links-style track where large waste bunkers and small, undulating greens provide the challenge. It's no cakewalk from the gold tees at 6,960 yards, especially on a breezy day, though wider fairways, softer slopes, and fewer forced carries add up to a pleasant test from the forward markers. The Kiele and Lagoons courses share one of Hawaii's largest practice facilities.

More Golf/Kauai's Best Bargain

While a round of golf at a top Hawaiian resort averages well over $100 with cart, *Wailua Golf Course*, a municipal facility north of Lihue, lists a green fee in the $25–$35 range. Three-time site of the USGA Amateur Public Links Championship, the 6,981-yard links wanders across rolling terrain near the ocean, its fairways framed by ironwood trees and coconut palms.

fours Nicklaus has ever built. Also one of the prettiest. Only 279 yards from the white tees, this downhill, downwind charmer calls for a blind drive to the crest of a hill. The approach shot, usually played with a nine-iron or pitching wedge from a perched lie, is played to a triangular green that commands a lava promontory near a lighthouse. Tidepools left, ocean right. Aim straight for the pin, and you run the risk of darting across the marble-slick green into a gathering trap 12 feet below the putting surface. Far wiser to line up your approach with the base of the hill on the right—and allow the ball to carom off the slope.

Pointed directly into the prevailing breeze, the Kiele's par-four 18th is a potential round-wrecker. A lagoon not only defines the entire right side of the hole, it swings across the fairway near the green. A solid drive gives players the option of trying for a small peninsula green ringed by bunkers and backdropped by palms. Fraught with peril, the 18th was originally to be called the Happy Buddha. Nicklaus insisted on another mascot: the Bear.

Kauai Lagoons, Kiele Course, 16th hole

Lanai

Lanai may be the third smallest of Hawaii's eight major islands, but **The Challenge at Manele** (#37) has put the former "Pineapple Island" on the aloha radar screen for golfers. A Jack Nicklaus–designed showstopper opened in 1993, the Challenge is a target-style desert links creased by ravines and cut along the bias of a volcanic slope rising to 500 feet above sea level. All 18 holes claim an expansive view of the turquoise-blue sea. The arid terrain, marked by lava rock formations, kiawe groves, and wild ilima trees (which produce a beautiful flower woven into leis), provides a sharp contrast to the layout's manicured turf and glorious vistas.

After years of building extremely difficult courses only he and a handful of others could play, Jack came of age as a designer in the early 1990s. At the time he built the Challenge at Manele, his courses were evolving into more user-friendly facilities, with wider fairways and generous bailout areas for players of lesser attainment. The quote on Jack's voluminous design résumé says it all: "Nothing can replace the feeling of walking up the 18th at Augusta with a chance to win, but for me, the next best thing

Challenge at Manele, Lanai, 12th hole

Challenge at Manele, 11th hole

Challenge at Manele, 17th hole

Many visitors have typecast the outgoing nine on the Challenge as a mere warmup for the high drama of the incoming holes, several of which tightrope 150-foot-high red lava cliffs. But the front nine holes are uniformly excellent. At the par-three third, the tee shot must carry twisted kiawe trees rooted in lava rocks and find a giant, horseshoe-shaped green split by a deep pit of sand. The daunting par-four fifth, which climbs to the apex of the course and offers incredible views of Maui and the island of Kahoolawe, calls for a blind drive over a saddle followed by an approach shot that drops 60 feet to a well-bunkered green. Even from these heights, the loud CRACK! of a humpback whale slapping its tail on the water can be heard during the winter months.

The Challenge at Manele's back nine is a revelation. It is by turns the most scenic and thrilling stretch of golf Nicklaus has ever created. The par-four 10th, a right-to-left dogleg flanked by archaeological preserves (including a blue rock quarry

is taking what I've learned in golf and designing courses that will be used by generations of golfers."

From the Nicklaus tees at 7,039 yards, the Challenge is a world-class test for the best, but four sets of forward markers—the red tees measure 5,024 yards—give everyone a fighting chance, especially since most of the holes play downhill to greens shaped like a catcher's mitt, their edges tipped to the middle to corral incoming shots. Better players, too, are presented with more shot options and risk-reward scenarios on the Challenge than were previously available on Jack's my-way-or-the-highway torture tracks. Strategy is important at Manele. So is the ability to block out the mesmerizing scenery (if only for a moment) to concentrate on the task at hand—especially when the wind socks on the flagsticks are taut.

mined for tools by prehistoric islanders), calls for a pinpoint drive aimed at a pair of colorful Indian coral trees. Manele's signature hole, the 12th, calls

Challenge at Manele, 18th hole and clubhouse

for a lusty trans-Pacific tee shot—202 yards from the tips—that must soar from a sea-blackened bluff to a green that clings to a cliff. The "fairway" is a surging ocean inlet 150 feet below the tee box. Long is definitely better than short here. As knee-knockers go, this astounding one-shotter is world-class, a fact not lost on Microsoft titan Bill Gates, who got married on the 12th tee in 1994. The 13th, a short par four that parallels Huawai Bay, is a fine vantage point from which to observe breaching humpback whales in winter and schools of playful spinner dolphins all year long.

Accuracy, not wayward length, is rewarded, although big hitters can try to roll the ball onto the right side of the green with their drives. (A cavernous trap indents the left side.)

The Challenge proceeds inland before returning for a glorious seaside finale at the par-four 17th, where golfers play their drives from a steep lava cliff across a cove to a sloping, bunkerless fairway. Staggered tees give everyone a fair shot at getting across, though a Nicklausian clout of 230 yards or more is required to cross the water from the back tees. When the hole plays into the tradewinds, the 17th will drain the plaid from most knickers. Even on a calm day, it is without question Hawaii's most demanding tee shot. Having found the far shore with their drives, players face a downhill approach to a kidney-shaped, cliffside green defended by a sizable mound and a ball-gobbling bunker set directly in front of the

DINING

The Manele Bay Hotel is known throughout the islands for its fabulous Ihilani ("heavenly splendor") dining room, where the French-Mediterranean cuisine features entrees that combine local game and produce with imported ingredients. This is a genuine gourmet outpost that attracts a steady stream of foodies from Honolulu 60 miles away. The hotel's less formal Hulopo'e Court, with its fine ocean views, is also excellent. Don't wish to leave your sumptuous room? *Gourmet Magazine* recognized Manele Bay's room service as the nation's best in 1998.

At *The Lodge at Koele,* Manele Bay's upcountry sister property styled after a colonial-era plantation house and located 20 minutes away in Lanai's highlands, there's the Formal Dining Room, its rustic, flavorsome New American cuisine and exceptional service every bit the equal of Ihilani. Like Ihilani, most of the entrees start at $40. There's also The Terrace, a more informal restaurant overlooking the resort's gardens.

The Ihilani dining room at the Manele Bay Hotel

The opulent *Manele Bay Hotel,* its low-rise annexes grouped around themed courtyard gardens, is set on red lava bluffs above the white sandy beach of Hulopo'e Bay. In addition to 250 beautifully furnished guest rooms, each with luxurious bath and all with private balconies or terraces, the hotel has comfortable sitting areas graced by Asian artifacts, Oriental antiques, and chinoiserie murals. There's also a quiet library for reading, writing, and contemplation. For outdoor peace, the courtyards are filled with tranquil pools and aromatic flowers. Spa services are available.

Japanese courtyard at the Manele Bay Hotel

putting surface. From start to finish, the 17th is one of the finest holes in the Pacific.

The sturdy par-four 18th returns to the spectacular clubhouse, which features a 180-degree view of the sea as well as a poached ginger chicken Hawaiian-style salad with green papaya and vine-ripened tomatoes that generally compensates for any cliffside disasters players might have experienced along the way. Want to refine your technique for a second assault on the Challenge? The resort's practice range, built on a plateau high above the ocean, may be the most inspiring place in America to groove your swing.

More Golf/Lanai

The immodestly titled *The Experience at Koele* course can be found at Manele Bay's sister property. The Experience, a Ted Robinson–Greg Norman creation, is routed on a plateau 2,000 feet above sea level, with Everest-like views of offshore islands from elevated tees on the opening holes. At the signature par-four eighth, the tee shot drops a dizzying 250 feet to a wooded gorge, delivering players to flatter terrain enlivened with water features.

Oahu

Koolau Golf Course (#78), carved from a rain forest on the windward side of the 2,000-foot Koolau Range 15 miles outside Honolulu, is King Kong in a grass skirt. Never mind that the USGA's maximum allowable slope rating is 155. Koolau turns the dial well past the stopping point.

Set within the crater of an ancient volcano, with a 2,000-foot vertical ridge walling in one side of the course, Koolau (pronounced Ko-oh-lau) is marked by sharp elevation changes, jungle-choked ravines, and three distinct climate zones, not to mention spectacular views of streaming waterfalls and the blue Pacific. Beauty and beast rolled into one, Koolau is a place unto itself. The challenge from the tips is akin to flying to the moon in a helicopter.

This Frankenstein of a layout was brought to life by Dick Nugent, a Chicago-based designer commissioned by Japanese clients to produce something that would give avid players a good reason to fly all the way from Tokyo for a round of golf. Sold at auction to an American firm for less than 15 percent of its $82 million construction cost when the bottom dropped out of the Asian market in 1998, Koolau is hemmed in by lush vegetation and requires numerous long forced carries over bottomless jungle. Ammunition quota? Bring double as many balls as you have strokes in your handicap. The local joke is that the course record is 69. Balls, not strokes. There's nowhere to run, nowhere to hide at Koolau, which packs the punch of 18 erupting volcanos from the gold tees at 7,310 yards (par 72, 76.4 course rating, 162 slope). The forward tees are no bargain. The slope ratings from the layout's blue and white tees are an appalling 158 and 154, respectively. For women brave enough to battle this beast, the slope is 143 from the red tees. Frequent rain showers, by the way, make Koolau play longer than the listed distance. In sum, this uncaged monster is the most brutal course in America. Why bother? Because the golf course occupies one of the most extravagantly beautiful places in a state known for its garden spots. Just remember to bring a soft eraser and a bulletproof ego.

Shortly after it opened in 1992, the par-72 course was rated by Dean Knuth, the USGA's senior director of handicapping, who said he was "somewhat dubious" about the layout's original slope of 152 before he played it. One tour of Koolau convinced Knuth the rating was too conservative. "Basically there are no bail-outs . . . you have numerous forced carries over jungle, where a ball can neither be found nor played." Comments head pro Paris Ernst: "If you lose fewer balls than your handicap, you've broken par." Par, he said, is "about 90" for the average player.

There isn't a giveaway hole in the routing, but special attention must be paid to the par-four 18th, a left-to-right dogleg that calls for forced carries over tree-filled gorges on the drive and approach. From the gold tees at 476 yards, even a Tour pro would shiver to play this hole. Knuth said, "The 18th at Koolau would be a tough hole even if you played it as a par six."

Koolau's enormous greens are surfaced in bentgrass, the only course on Oahu that can support this cool weather varietal. There are 80 sand traps on the layout, many of them gigantic waste bunkers built to save stray shots from plunging into the deep gulches that interlace the holes.

Koolau can be walked, although most players choose to ride after sighting a wild boar foraging in the "rough."

After the devastation that most rounds devolve into, players can compose themselves in the facility's luxurious clubhouse, which features a two-story waterfall and floor-to-ceiling windows with views of Kaneohe Bay.

Koolau Golf Course, Oahu, 12th hole

Maui

Terraced among silvery-blue pineapple fields above a flawless beach in glamorous west Maui, **Kapalua** is the only resort in the nation that manages to combine an essentially rural character with world-class sophistication. Fittingly, Kapalua is also the world's first resort to be certified as an Audubon Heritage Cooperative Sanctuary. Its logo is a monarch butterfly with a pineapple for an abdomen, symbolizing the metamorphosis of a pineapple plantation into a resort synonymous with tropical splendor—and great golf.

The signature track at this 54-hole complex is the **Plantation Course** (#26), a brilliant design by Bill Coore and Ben Crenshaw that rambles over dramatic terrain creased by heavily jungled ravines and swept by brisk trade winds. This is golf on the grandest scale imaginable, the promenading fairways, huge greens, and bold bunkers a match for the sprawling, verdant site.

Routed on steeply sloping land facing Pailolo Channel and the island of Molokai, the Plantation offers spectacular views of the cobalt-blue Pacific from every hole. "What we've tried to do is fit the holes to the terrain," Crenshaw said when the course opened in 1991. Tried, and succeeded.

Stretching to a mighty 7,263 yards from the back tees (par 73), the Plantation, home of the Mercedes Championships, the PGA Tour's season-opening tournament of champions, blends beautifully into its surroundings. It also features holes that mirror the environment. For example, fairway bunkers on the left side of the downhill first hole, a long par four, replicate the waves splashing against the peninsula in the distance. On the 11th, the back nine's lone par three, the green mirrors the sea cliffs a mile down the slope. From the tee of the 14th, a beguiling short par four, the small plateau green appears as flat as the tabletop mountain beyond.

"It's about golf, but it's also about art, texture, lines, composition, and angles," says Coore. "A golf hole has to look comfortable in its surroundings, as if it has belonged there for generations." By Coore's definition, the Plantation makes the grade. Tall native grasses frame the fairways, with a few stands of Norfolk pines scattered around the perimeter. No water comes into play, but there's an abundance of luxuriant growth sprouting from the gorges. Good golfers tend to keep their eyes on the horizon.

Crenshaw, renowned for his putting prowess, helped to author enormous greens every bit as contoured and racy as those at Augusta National. The antithesis of a target-style course, the Plantation offers oodles of options along with its grand ocean vistas. Golfers must take the pitch and roll of the terrain (and the speed and direction of the wind) into account when planning shots. Greens are open in front; barely airborne bump-and-run approach shots are not only encouraged, they're necessary to control the ball in the wind.

Says Davis Love III, an ardent fan of the Plantation: "You can throw away the yardage book. It's all about feel and playing the slope and the trade winds." It's also about hitting blind tee shots over hilltop markers (at the par-four fourth and 10th holes), or aiming 50 feet to the right or left of a pin to gain

Kapalua Bay Hotel & Villas, Plantation Course, Maui, 11th hole

The 194-room *Kapalua Bay Hotel & Villas,* an open-air structure camouflaged by vegetation and terraced down to a lava rock peninsula, reopened in 1997 after a $15 million makeover. The hotel, now managed by the prestigious Halekulani group, has spruced-up rooms and refurbished public spaces. Top-of-the-line accommodations can also be found at the splendid *Ritz-Carlton Kapalua,* a low-rise structure built into a hillside among century-old Cook pines and sited high above Honokahua Bay. Lighter colors and woods in the guest rooms and public areas lend the hotel a less formal and more tropical look than can be found in a typical Ritz-Carlton. Accommodations are also available in one- and two-bedroom villas, many of them spaced around the golf courses.

access to it, and also putting (not chipping) the ball from off the greens for best results, as is done in Scotland. Imagination and creativity are required to score this strategic gem.

But Crenshaw wasn't interested in signing his name to a course only he could play. Unlike most championship venues, the average player

ACTIVITIES

Fronting Honolua Bay, the beach at Kapalua (Kapalua means "arms embracing the sea" in ancient Hawaiian, referring to the site's lava peninsula coastline) has been ranked the best beach in America by the University of Maryland's Coastal Research Lab. Guests receive complimentary rentals for up to two hours of snorkel sets, boogie boards, and air mattresses, while children can explore tidepools or build sand castles in Kamp Kapalua. A picnic snorkel sail aboard the resort's catamaran is available, as are sunset sails. Entertainment? Weekly "slack key guitar" and traditional hula shows are staged at the Kapalua Shops, a collection of over 20 distinctive retail outlets.

Pineapple plantation tours give visitors a historical perspective of the 23,000-acre property, where pineapple is still harvested. In addition, the Kapalua Nature Society, established by the resort in 1995, offers two exclusive hikes into the majestic West Maui Mountains. The Maunalei Arboretum and Puu Kaeo Nature Walk, with mauka (mountain) and makai (ocean) views of Honolua Valley, highlights nearly a century of pineapple, coffee, and ranching activities. The 1.75-mile hike (roundtrip) takes four to five hours. The longer, more arduous Manienie Ridge Hike follows a ridgeline trail offering stellar views of Honokohau Valley and a pair of verdant gulches.

armed with a wind-cheater (a ball hit low) can find his way around the Plantation from the regular tees without undue difficulty. At least until the 18th, a gargantuan 663-yard par five around which the rest of the course was formulated. This downhill, downwind hole is reachable (by the likes of Love and a handful of others) given the assisting winds and favorable slope. A gentle right-to-left dogleg with a dense thicket of vegetation set below fairway level along the entire left side, the hole's vast panoramas make distance judgment difficult. Elongated bunkers protect the left side of the fairway from 100 yards in, though the right side is banked and will funnel a well-played approach shot to a large, receptive green. Few courses in Hawaii or anywhere else end as grandly as the Plantation.

Like the course itself, the Plantation's clubhouse fits its surroundings hand-in-glove. The exterior of the building is constructed from graystone mined from a nearby quarry, as are rock walls around the course. From this vantage point, the fairways look a little wider, the gorges a little narrower on Maui's most exhilarating golf course.

Kapalua Bay Hotel & Villas, Plantation Course, 15th hole

More Golf/Kapalua

Kapalua's *Bay Course,* site of the U.S. Women's Amateur Public Links Championship in 1998, is a sporty, open layout with a pair of thrilling oceanside holes where breaching humpback whales are a common distraction. Designed in 1975 by Arnold Palmer and Frank Duane, the 6,600-yard Bay Course is a near-perfect resort spread. The *Village Course,* laid out by Arnold Palmer and Ed Seay in 1980, climbs 800 feet into the West Maui Mountains. The fifth and sixth holes skirt a lake atop a ridge that plummets hundreds of feet into a lush green valley. The top-of-the-world views of Molokai, Lanai, and the limitless Pacific from these holes are stupendous.

The Audubon Cooperative Sanctuary Program for Golf Courses

Properly managed, golf courses play a significant role in enhancing and protecting wildlife habitat and natural resources. Which is why numerous Top 100 Courses, seeking to preserve the game's natural heritage, have sought certification by the Audubon Cooperative Sanctuary Program for Golf Courses, a division of Audubon International, a not-for-profit environmental organization that specializes in sustainable resource management. Certification is designed to recognize and support golf courses that have worked to ensure a high degree of environmental quality for both people and wildlife. Certification also demonstrates a course's leadership, commitment, and high standards of environmental management.

In order to become certified, a golf course must implement projects in six environmental quality areas and document their efforts. They are: Environmental Planning; Wildlife & Habitat Management; Integrated Pest Management; Water Conservation; Water Quality Management; and Outreach & Education.

Eleven of the Top 100 Courses have been named Certified Audubon Cooperative Sanctuaries:

Tournament Players Club at Sawgrass, Stadium Course, #7
Pumpkin Ridge Golf Club, Ghost Creek Course, #13
Kapalua Bay Hotel & Villas, Plantation Course, #26
Barton Creek Resort & Country Club, Fazio Course, #38
The Greenbrier (Greenbrier Course, #41; Old White Course, #97)
The Links at Spanish Bay, #45
Castle Pines North, Ridge Course, #52
La Cantera Golf Club, #58
Cantigny Golf & Tennis (Woodside–Lakeside), #66
Fowler's Mill Golf Course (Lake–River), #77

In addition, 44 Top 100 Courses are registered members of the Audubon Cooperative Sanctuary Program and await certification:

Pinehurst Resort & Country Club (No. 2 Course, #2; No. 7 Course, #56)
Bethpage State Park, Black Course, #4
Spyglass Hill Golf Course, #5
Troon North Golf Club (Monument Course, #6; Pinnacle Course, #30)
Harbour Town Golf Links, #9
Kiawah Island Golf & Tennis Resort, Ocean Course, #10
World Woods Golf Club (Pine Barrens, #11; Rolling Oaks, #33)
Sunriver Resort, Crosswater Course, #15
Pasatiempo Golf Club, #17

Piñon Hills Golf Course, #18
Princeville Resort, Prince Course, #19
Sugarloaf Golf Club, #20
Bay Hill Club, #21
PGA West, TPC Stadium Course, #24
Linville Golf Club, #25
Reynolds Plantation, Great Waters Course, #28
Pine Needles Lodge & Golf Club, #31
Barton Creek Resort & Country Club, Fazio Course, #38
Pelican Hill Golf Club (Ocean North Course, #46; Ocean South Course, #50)
Grayhawk Golf Club, Raptor Course, #49
Grand National (Links Course, #51; Lake Course, #59)
The Boulders (South Course, #53; North Course, #91)
Coeur d' Alene Resort Golf Course, #55
Golden Horseshoe Golf Club, Gold Course, #57
Taconic Golf Club, #61
Dancing Rabbit Golf Club, #63
The Broadmoor, East Course, #67
The Wilds Golf Club, #68
Grand Cypress Resort, New Course, #73
High Pointe Golf Club, #74
The Raven Golf Club at Sabino Springs, #76
The Koolau Golf Course, #78
Teton Pines Resort and Country Club, #81
New Seabury Country Club, Blue Course, #83
Kemper Lakes Golf Course, #84
Caledonia Golf & Fish Club, #85
Augustine Golf Club, #94
Eagle Ridge Inn & Resort, The General, #95

Finally, Pinehurst No. 8, the Centennial Course, ranked #48 on the Top 100 Courses roster, is the first course in North Carolina to become an Audubon International Signature Sanctuary (Bronze Level). The Fazio design team worked with Audubon International during the design and development phases to maximize wildlife habitat and minimize potential impact on the environment. The No. 8 Course was also among the first facilities in the U.S. to become involved in the United States Fish and Wildlife Service's "Safe Harbor Program," which is aimed at protecting endangered species by establishing an agreement with private landowners. In this case, the Red-cockaded Woodpecker, endemic to pine forests of the southeastern United States, is the federally endangered species.

Directory to the Top 100 Courses

1 Pebble Beach Golf Links, 17-Mile Drive, Pebble Beach, CA 93953; (800) 654-9300.

2 Pinehurst Resort & Country Club (No. 2 Course), Carolina Vista Street, Pinehurst, NC 28374; (800) 795-4653.

3 Blackwolf Run Golf Club (River Course), 1111 W. Riverside Dr., Kohler, WI 53044; (800) 344-2838.

4 Bethpage State Park (Black Course), Farmingdale, NY 11735; (516) 249-0707.

5 Spyglass Hill Golf Course, Stevenson Drive and Spyglass Hill, Pebble Beach, CA 93953; (800) 654-9300.

6 Troon North Golf Club (Monument Course), 10320 E. Dynamite Blvd., Scottsdale, AZ 85255; (602) 585-5300.

7 Tournament Players Club at Sawgrass (Stadium Course), 110 TPC Blvd., Ponte Vedra Beach, FL 32082; (904) 273-3235.

8 Bay Harbor Golf Club, 5800 Coastal Ridge, Bay Harbor, MI 49770; (616) 439-4028.

9 Harbour Town Golf Links, 11 Lighthouse La., Hilton Head Island, SC 29928; (843) 842-8484.

10 Kiawah Island Golf & Tennis Resort (Ocean Course), 1000 Ocean Course Dr., Kiawah Island, SC (843) 768-2121.

11 World Woods Golf Club (Pine Barrens Course), 17590 Ponce de Leon Blvd., Brooksville, FL 34614; (352) 796-5500.

12 The Homestead (Cascades Course), P.O. Box 2000, Hot Springs, VA 24445; (800) 838-1766.

13 Pumpkin Ridge Golf Club (Ghost Creek Course), 12930 Old Pumpkin Ridge Rd., Cornelius, OR 97113; (503) 647-9977.

14 Stonehouse Golf Club, 9540 Old Stage Rd., Toano, VA 23168; (800) 552-2660.

15 Sunriver Resort (Crosswater Course), P.O. Box 4818, Sunriver, OR 97707; (800) 962-1769.

16 Cog Hill Golf & Country Club (No. 4 Course), 12294 Archer Ave., Lemont, IL 60439; (630) 257-5872.

17 Pasatiempo Golf Club, 18 Clubhouse Rd., Santa Cruz, CA 95060; (831) 459-9155.

18 Piñon Hills Golf Course, 2101 Sunrise Pkwy., Farmington, NM 87402; (505) 326-6066.

19 Princeville Resort (Prince Course), 3900 Kuhio Hwy., Princeville, HI 96722; (800) 826-4400.

20 Sugarloaf Golf Club, R.R. No. 1, P.O. Box 5000, Carrabassett Valley, ME 04947; (800) 843-5623.

21 Bay Hill Club, 9000 Bay Hill Blvd., Orlando, FL 32819; (407) 876-2429.

22 Mauna Kea Beach Golf Course, 62-100 Mauna Kea Beach Dr., Kamuela, HI 96743; (808) 880-3480.

23 Royal New Kent, 3001 Bailey Rd., Providence Forge, VA 23140; (800) 552-2660.

24 PGA West (TPC Stadium Course), 56-150 PGA Blvd., La Quinta, CA 92253; (760) 564-7170.

25 Linville Golf Club, Linville Avenue, Linville, NC 28646; (828) 733-4363.

26 Kapalua Resort (Plantation Course), 300 Kapalua Dr., Kapalua, HI 96761 (808) 669-8877.

27 White Columns Golf Club, 300 White Columns Dr., Alpharetta, GA 30201; (770) 343-9025.

28 Reynolds Plantation (Great Waters Course), 100 Linger Longer Rd., Greensboro, GA 30642; (706) 485-0235.

29 Doral Golf Resort & Spa (Blue Course), 4400 N.W. 87th Ave., Miami, FL 33178; (800) 713-6725.

30 Troon North Golf Club (Pinnacle Course), 10320 E. Dynamite Blvd., Scottsdale, AZ 85255; (602) 585-5300.

31 Pine Needles Lodge & Golf Club, 1005 Midland Rd., Southern Pines, NC 28387; (800) 747-7272.

32 Wild Dunes Resort (Links Course), 5757 Palm Blvd., Isle of Palms, SC 29451; (800) 845-8880.

33 World Woods Golf Club (Rolling Oaks Course), 17590 Ponce de Leon Blvd., Brooksville, FL 34614; (352) 796-5500.

34 Blackwolf Run Golf Club (Meadow Valleys Course), 1111 W. Riverside Dr., Kohler, WI 53044; (800) 344-2838.

35 La Quinta Resort & Club (Mountain Course), 50-200 Vista Bonita, La Quinta, CA 92253; (800) 742-9378.

36 The Dunes Golf & Beach Club, 9000 N. Ocean Blvd., Myrtle Beach, SC 29572; (843) 449-5236.

37 The Challenge at Manele, P.O. Box L, Lanai, HI 96763; (808) 565-2222.

38 Barton Creek Resort & Country Club (Fazio Course), 8212 Barton Club Dr., Austin, TX 78735; (800) 336-6158.

39 Tidewater Golf Club & Plantation, 4901 Little River Neck Rd., North Myrtle Beach, SC 29582; (800) 446-5363.

40 Cambrian Ridge, 101 Sunbelt Pkwy., Greenville, AL 36037; (334) 382-9787.

41 The Greenbrier (Greenbrier Course), 300 W. Main St., White Sulphur Springs, WV 24986; (800) 624-6070.

42 Lakewood Shores Resort (Gailes Course), 7751 Cedar Lake Rd., Oscoda, MI 48750; (800) 882-2493.

43 Primm Valley Golf Club (Lakes Course), P.O. Box 19129, Primm, NV 89019; (800) 386-7867.

44 The Lodge at Ventana Canyon (Mountain Course), 6200 N. Clubhouse La., Tucson, AZ 85715; (800) 828-5701.

45 The Links at Spanish Bay, 2700 17-Mile Dr., Pebble Beach, CA 93953; (800) 654-9300.

46 Pelican Hill Golf Club (Ocean North Course), 22651 Pelican Hill Rd., Newport Coast, CA 92657; (949) 759-5190.

47 Grayhawk Golf Club (Talon Course), 19600 N. Pima Rd., Scottsdale, AZ 85255; (602) 502-1800.

48 Pinehurst Resort & Country Club (No. 8 Course), Murdocksville Road, Pinehurst, NC 28374; (800) 795-4653.

49 Grayhawk Golf Club (Raptor Course), 19600 N. Pima Rd., Scottsdale, AZ 85255; (602) 502-1800.

50 Pelican Hill Golf Club (Ocean South Course), 22651 Pelican Hill Rd., Newport Coast, CA 92657; (949) 759-5190.

51 Grand National (Links Course), 3000 Sunbelt Pkwy., Opelika, AL 36801; (800) 949-4444.

52 Castle Pines North (Ridge Course), 1414 Castle Pines Pkwy., Castle Rock, CO 80104; (303) 688-0100.

53 The Boulders (South Course), 34631 N. Tom Darlington Dr., Carefree, AZ 85377; (602) 488-9028.

54 University of New Mexico (Championship Course), 3601 University Blvd. S.E., Albuquerque, NM 87131; (505) 277-4546.

55 Coeur d'Alene Resort Golf Course, 900 Floating Green Dr., Coeur d'Alene, ID 83814; (800) 688-5253.

56 Pinehurst Resort & Country Club (No. 7 Course), U.S. 15-501, Pinehurst, NC 28374; (800) 795-4653.

57 Golden Horseshoe Golf Club (Gold Course), 401 S. England St., Williamsburg, VA 23185; (800) 447-8679.

58 La Cantera Golf Club, 16641 La Cantera Pkwy., San Antonio, TX 78256; (800) 446-5387.

59 Grand National (Lake Course), 3000 Sunbelt Pkwy., Opelika, AL 36801; (800) 949-4444.

60 La Purisima Golf Course, 3455 State Hwy. 246, Lompoc, CA 93436; (805) 735-8395.

61 Taconic Golf Club, Meacham Street, Williamstown, MA 01267; (413) 458-3997.

62 The Westin Innisbrook Resort (Copperhead Course), P.O. Box 1088, Tarpon Springs, FL 34688; (727) 942-2000.

63 Dancing Rabbit Golf Club, 1 Choctaw Trail, Philadelphia, MS 39350; (888) 372-2248.

64 Kauai Lagoons (Kiele Course), 3351 Hoolaulea Way, Lihue, HI 96766; (800) 634-6400.

65 Karsten Creek Golf Club, Rte. 5, P.O. Box 159, Stillwater, OK 74074; (405) 743-1658.

66 Cantigny Golf & Tennis, 1 South 151 Winfield Rd., Wheaton, IL 60187 (630) 668-3323.

67 The Broadmoor (East Course), 1 Pourtales Rd., Colorado Springs, CO 80906; (800) 634-7711.

68 The Wilds Golf Club, 14819 Wilds Pkwy. N.W., Prior Lake, MN 55372; (612) 445-4455.

69 Edgewood Tahoe Golf Course, U.S. Hwy. 50 and Lake Parkway, Stateline, NV 89449; (702) 588-3566.

70 Four Seasons Resort Aviara Golf Club, 7447 Batiquitos Dr., Carlsbad, CA 92009; (760) 603-6900.

71 Emerald Dunes Golf Course, 2100 Emerald Dunes Dr., West Palm Beach, FL 33411; (561) 687-1700.

72 Sandpines, 1201 35th St., Florence, OR 97439; (541) 997-1940.

73 Grand Cypress Resort (New Course), 1 N. Jacaranda, Orlando, FL 32836; (800) 835-7377.

74 High Pointe Golf Club, 5555 Arnold Rd., Williamsburg, MI 49690; (800) 753-7888.

75 Mauna Lani Resort (North Course), 68-1310 Mauna Lani Dr., Kohala Coast, HI 96743; (808) 885-6655.

76 The Raven Golf Club at Sabino Springs, 9777 E. Sabino Greens Dr., Tucson, AZ 85749; (520) 749-3636.

77 Fowler's Mill Golf Course, 13095 Rockhaven Rd., Chesterland, OH 44026; (440) 729-7569.

78 The Koolau Golf Course, 45-550 Kionaole, Kaneohe, HI 96744; (808) 236-4653.

79 Horseshoe Bay Resort (Ram Rock Course), P.O. Box 7766, Horseshoe Bay, TX 78657; (830) 598-6561.

80 Treetops Sylvan Resort (Tom Fazio Premier Course), 3962 Wilkinson Rd., Gaylord, MI 49735; (888) 873-3867.

81 Teton Pines Resort and Country Club, 3450 Clubhouse Dr., Jackson, WY 83001; (800) 238-2223.

82 Olympic Course at Gold Mountain, 7263 W. Belfair Valley Rd., Bremerton, WA 98312; (800) 249-2363.

83 New Seabury Country Club (Blue Course), P.O. Box 549, Mashpee, MA 02649; (508) 477-9110

84 Kemper Lakes Golf Course, Old McHenry Road, Long Grove, IL 60049; (847) 320-3450.

85 Caledonia Golf & Fish Club, 369 Caledonia Dr., Pawleys Island, SC 29585; (800) 483-6800.

86 The Pines at Grand View Lodge, South 134 Nokomis, Nisswa, MN 56468; (218) 963-0001.

87 The Cloister/Sea Island Golf Club, 100 Retreat Ave., St. Simons Island, GA; (800) 732-4752.

88 Legend Trail Golf Club, 9462 Legendary Trail, Scottsdale, AZ 85262; (602) 488-7434.

89 Treetops Sylvan Resort (Rick Smith Signature Course), 3962 Wilkinson Rd., Gaylord, MI 49735; (888) 873-3867.

90 Boyne Highlands (The Heather Course), 600 Highland Dr., Harbor Springs, MI (800) 462-6963.

91 The Boulders (North Course), 34631 N. Tom Darlington Dr., Carefree, AZ 85377; (602) 488-9028.

92 Pinehurst Plantation Golf Club, Midland Road, Pinehurst, NC 28374; (800) 633-2685.

93 Torrey Pines (South Course), 11480 N. Torrey Pines Rd., La Jolla, CA 92037; (800) 985-4653.

94 Augustine Golf Club, 76 Monument Dr., Stafford, VA 22554; (540) 720-7374.

95 Eagle Ridge Inn & Resort (The General), P.O. Box 777, Galena, IL 61036; (800) 892-2269.

96 Nemacolin Woodlands Resort (Mystic Rock Golf Course), P.O. Box 188, Rte. 40, Farmington, PA 15437; (800) 422-2736.

97 The Greenbrier (Old White Course), 300 W. Main St., White Sulphur Springs, WV; (800) 624-6070.

98 Sawgrass Country Club, 10034 Golf Club Dr., Ponte Vedra Beach, FL 32082; (800) 457-4653.

99 University of Wisconsin, University Ridge Course, 7120 County Trunk PD, Verona, WI 53593; (800) 897-4343.

100 The Club at Cordillera (Valley Course), P.O. Box 1110, Edwards, CO 81632; (800) 877-3529.

Index

Editor: Margaret L. Kaplan
Designer: Robert McKee
Photo Editor: John K. Crowley
Library of Congress Cataloging-in-Publication Data

McCallen, Brian.
Golf Magazine's top 100 courses you can play / by Brian McCallen.
p.   cm.
ISBN 0-8109-4134-1
1. Golf courses–United States.   I. Golf magazine (New York, N.Y.: 1991)
II. Title.   III. Title: Golf magazine's top one hundred courses you can play.
GV981.M32   1999
796.352 ' 025 ' 73–dc21   99-21273

Printed and bound in Japan

Harry N. Abrams, Inc.
100 Fifth Avenue
New York, N.Y. 10011
www.abramsbooks.com

Photograph Credits